YOUNG RUSSIA

YOUNG RUSSIA

The Genesis of
Russian Radicalism
in the 1860s

Abbott Gleason

The University of Chicago Press
Chicago and London

ACKNOWLEDGMENTS

Campbell Thomson & McLaughlin Ltd.: From *Roots of Revolution* by Franco Venturi

Edward H. Carr: From *The Romantic Exiles* by Edward H. Carr.

Samuel Dolgoff: From *Bakunin on Anarchy*, edited by Samuel Dolgoff.

Alfred A. Knopf, Inc.: From *My Past and Thoughts: The Memoirs of Alexander Herzen*, translated by Constance Garnett, revised by Humphrey Higgens. Copyright © 1968 by Chatto & Windus Ltd. Reprinted by permission of Alfred A. Knopf, Inc.

Open Court Publishing Company: From *Natalie Herzen: Daughter of a Revolutionary*, edited by Michael Confino, translated by Hilary Sternberg and Lydia Bott. Introduction by the editor, Michael Confino. Published by Open Court Publishing Company. © 1974 by Michael Confino.

This edition is reprinted by arrangement with Viking Penguin Inc.

The University of Chicago Press, Chicago 60637
The University of Chicago Press, Ltd., London

Library of Congress Cataloging in Publication Data

Gleason, Abbott.
  Young Russia.

  Reprint. Originally published: New York: Viking Press, 1980.
  Includes bibliographical references and index.
    1. Radicalism—Soviet Union—History—19th century.
2. Soviet Union—Politics and government—1855–1881.
3. Social movements—Soviet Union—History—19th century.
4. Socialism—Soviet Union—History—19th century.
I. Title.
[HN530.Z9R33 1983]   947.08′1   82-23875
ISBN 0-226-29961-9 (pbk.)

For Sarah

Contents

Introduction

As will quickly become evident, the origins of this book lie in my experience of the American politics of recent years, both national and university. As I lived through the decade between 1964 and 1974 and at the same time tried to teach American students about nineteenth-century Russian radicalism, I became more and more confused by and dissatisfied with the secondary literature that I was reading myself and giving to my students. Taking full account of the enormous differences between Russian and American historical development, I couldn't but feel that there were strong historical parallels between Russia in the late 1850s and 1860s (when the revolutionary movement began) and my own historical time. Were we going to have an American radical Populism? The beginnings of an American revolutionary movement? For a time it seemed possible. In any case, a sense of the relatedness of the historical periods had been forced upon me, and I now looked at that stretch of Russian history very differently from the way I had approached it as a student in the 1950s —when "revolution" was sinister, out-of-date, romantic: something seen through the wrong end of a telescope. In the late 1960s, I wanted to bring my contemporary experience to bear on the Russian radicalism I was teaching and studying, but I wanted to avoid the pitfalls of easy and anachronistic analogy. This enterprise seemed to me a great challenge. Even before I was conscious of what I was working on, a book on "the radicalization of Russian society" (as I now thought of it) began to take shape in my mind. I wanted to write about how socialism ceased to be something that intellectuals talked about in salons and became a social movement.

No treatment of the period 1855–70 satisfied me. As far as most Soviet historical literature was concerned, I was bothered by what I took to be a vulgar Marxist stress on the relationship between the economic substructure of society and its intellectual and cultural developments. That is to say, as I watched the radicalization of American society—in particular of American youth —and then its deradicalization, I became aware of how unrelated to major structural economic developments the entire process was. No doubt the affluence, the security, the loneliness of American liberal capitalism was in some way the "bottom line," but that capitalism did not have to encounter major structural "contradictions" for there to be major political and cultural disorder. I therefore began to wonder about the relations between economic development and cultural crisis in my period; I became suspicious of the stress laid by Soviet historians (without much evidence) on the "breakdown" of feudalism—reflected, above all, in the Emancipation of the serfs—and the ceremonial entry of capitalism onto the historical stage as an "explanation" of what is generally referred to as the "revolutionary situation" of 1859–61.

Again, Soviet and some other Marxist historians tend to regard the ideas of prominent radicals like Alexander Herzen and Nikolai Chernyshevsky as in the last analysis a "reflection" of the historical situation of the Russian peasantry and its alleged attempt to liberate itself from serfdom and exploitation more generally.[1] As I watched the American Left struggle to develop a coherent view of itself and of the outside world, I was struck by how closed the process was in a way, how unrelated to what American working people believed they wanted. This radicalization seemed to be an affair of the intelligentsia itself, to use the term in the broadest possible way. The views of Tom Hayden did not strike me as a "reflection" of the views of any segment of the white working class; nor did Eldridge Cleaver's *Soul on Ice* strike me as a "reflection" of the historical situation of black people, although the fit here might be a little closer. And here again I focused these impressions on the radicalization of Russian intellectuals a century before.

I had many similar thoughts about American youth culture and the student movement in the late 1960s. How powerful it was, what messianic feelings it engendered, and yet how insubstantial it was! I began to think about the relationship of a vanguard minority to broader strata of opinion in a new way. I became conscious of the importance of radical iconography, style, and vocabulary, and of the confused yet hopeful way that people invest their inchoate aspirations in a set of "ideas" and in a movement. Nikolai Dobroliubov certainly cannot be described by any such imprecise cliché as "the Bob Dylan of his time," but in class I was often tempted to do so.

Perhaps most of all, I felt that the secondary literature at my disposal could not give my students the sense of historical relatedness to the period that I was discovering and wanted to convey to them. Novels like Turgenev's *Fathers and Children* helped, of course. But the real sense of the period that I wanted for them was to be had only by immersion in the memoir literature of the period, most of which was inaccessible to my students because most of it was untranslated. Even so distinguished and politically engaged a monument of historical scholarship as Franco Venturi's *Roots of Revolution* often seemed remote, even dry, to my students, and this despite its powerful and detailed rendering of the heroism of many of the radicals about whom he wrote. At times, even I felt that Venturi, in his zeal not to diminish his subjects, accepted their own vision of themselves and their struggle more than was warranted. Somehow he also imposed on them a kind of uniform heroism that sometimes had the effect of creating a socialist pantheon and populating it with marble busts. To make what appears to be a rather harsh criticism is in no way to deny the fact that I and all my contemporaries are deeply in debt to Venturi's book. With enormous erudition and skill he has mapped the terrain of Populism, and all scholars of my generation will be guided and influenced by his work.

Partially in reaction to the difficulties of teaching Venturi's book to my students, I have tried to give a more experiential dimension to my account of Russian radicals, to give my version of what things felt like. I fully recognize the subjectivity of such an attempt. What it *really* felt like to be radicalized in the University of St. Petersburg in the late 1850s is out of the reach of the historian. My version is grounded in what is at best a tantalizingly similar situation that took place—or continues to take place—a hundred years later in a very different culture.

To some readers, this book may seem in various ways reactionary—because it stresses the relatedness of radical and reactionary ideas, because I psychologize about ideas and why people hold them (rather than judging those ideas in some straightforward way on their merits as I perceive them), and because there is so much emphasis on the politics of style and fashion. I am in fact concerned that my own experience of student politics in the United States may have induced in me a certain pessimism and cynicism that will show up in this book in the form of "seeing through" the libertarian aspirations of Russian radicals. The Russian radicalism of that time *did* have a greatness and a heroism about it. Franco Venturi may have given it an element of hagiographic uniformity; Soviet historians constantly stress that heroism but feel constrained to remind the reader very often that the Populists did not "understand" the dialectic, the historical mission of the proletariat, and so on.

I am under no such constraints; indeed, outside the Soviet Union even Marxists seem no longer to believe that the proletariat, whatever that term may mean at present, has any historical mission. People choose their own missions, for one reason or another; the Russian intelligentsia, with enormous passion and persistence, chose for its mission the liberation of Russia.

Central to that mission, we can now see, was a revolt against that state power which played so disproportionate a role in Russian development. Both the Slavophiles and the Populists, and the whole circle of those who were touched by their ideas, saw the real values of Russia and Russian creativity not in the state or the forces that had disciplined and unified the country from above, but in society, in "the people." Still, the countervailing tradition was very powerful: in Russia you get things done from the top, by force. And within that radicalism whose wellsprings were so anarchist, there quickly developed more statist, centralist, power-centered currents. And gradually the statist tradition reasserted itself; the power of centralism became manifest. Populism and anarchism, Russians came to understand, were utopian. My book is also about a stage in *that* development.

Finally, I live in a time and in a place in which it is impossible not to regard the Russian Revolution as having failed in very basic ways. The private feelings of Soviet historians are no doubt various and complicated, but their published work must contribute to the celebration of that Revolution. Almost all Western European and American observers agree, however, that whatever the successes of Soviet power, the Russian Revolution has not realized the hopes of the nineteenth-century Left (including those centering on the problem of alienation) and do not seem likely to do so any time soon. With every year that passes, it becomes more difficult to regard the state that issued from the Revolution as even ambiguously "progressive," as that term used to be employed. This perspective, and the inevitable ironies that accompany it, are built into this book. Our unwelcome knowledge forces on us certain ironic attitudes toward the generous utopianism of Russian intellectuals then. There are other perspectives for students of these events, and there will be more; perhaps if they are unencumbered with "Western" liberal irony, they will better succeed in rendering the nobility and courage of the Populists.

It seems to me better to be explicit about my viewpoint. I want to derive what insights I can from it and explore it as far as I can. But the ambiguities of my attitude have certainly not diminished my admiration for the nineteenth-century Russian intelligentsia. Those Russian intellectuals remain, for me, about the most remarkable, many-sided, and congenial people whom I have heard or read about. Their story is still, for me, an inspirational story.

In conclusion, I should like to thank the American Philosophical Society, the Howard Foundation, the Russian Research Center of Harvard University, and Brown University for lending various kinds of support, tangible and nontangible, to my work. Miriam Berlin, James Billington, Daniel Field, Sarah Gleason, Norman Naimark, James Patterson, Richard Stites, and Glenn Whitmore gave me the benefit of detailed criticism. Mary Chaffin did some research for me and read several of my chapters with a critical eye. Conversations with Duncan Kennedy and Sande Cohen helped make me conscious of my perspective and its limitations. Elisabeth Sifton, of The Viking Press, encouraged me to realize the project of this book.

YOUNG RUSSIA

1

Russian Society on the Eve of Emancipation

History generally, and the history of revolutions in
particular, is always richer in content, more varied
and more many-sided, more lively and "subtle" than
the best parties and the most class-conscious van-
guards of the most advanced classes imagine.
—Vladimir Il'ich Lenin, *Left Communism*

Alexander Herzen wrote in 1851 that the history of Russia since
the reforms of Peter the Great was by and large "the history of
the Russian government and the Russian nobility."[1] Although
rhetorically phrased, Herzen's words contain a good deal of
truth: "history" was still being made, in mid-nineteenth-century
Russia, by a tiny group of people. All aspects of culture and
politics were conditioned by the enormous gap between the two
cultures of Russia: that of *obshchestvo,* or "society," and that of
the *narod,* the people or peasantry.

What does the term *obshchestvo* mean?[2] How it was used may
tell us something about the social realities of Russia in the 1850s.
Although the term always had strong aristocratic connotations, it
does not refer to old Muscovite society but, in its origins, to the
service gentry that was created by the reforms of Peter the
Great. One aspect of its meaning was close to what the French
meant by *le monde* or the English by "society" in the sense of
"high society." But virtually until 1917, *obshchestvo* had another

meaning—or, more properly, another sense or emphasis—for which there was no analogue in nineteenth-century France or England. The term was often employed to indicate those active in the life of the nation: men of affairs, artists, thinkers, and even rebels—provided they were not *peasant* rebels like Emel'ian Pugachëv, whose massive revolt shook the empire in the early 1770s. Thus, in a sense, there was a meritocratic element in *obshchestvo* membership, which reminds one that Peter the Great attempted, albeit not very successfully, to ensure that membership in the gentry was open to commoners of great ability. More central to the significance of *obshchestvo* is the fact that until very nearly the end of Imperial Russia a small social elite was simply assumed to be the source of all high culture, the agent of the government, the representative of the nation. The people whom one might "meet" or "receive" were the only people who did important things. Such an equation had existed in most European societies, but only in Russia did it survive unchallenged into the second half of the nineteenth century. And only in eighteenth- and early-nineteenth-century Russia was the culture of society assumed to be non-native, that is, "Western."

After 1860, a less class-bound term, *obshchestvennost'*, began to be used to describe the active, civic, culture-bearing element of the population. *Obshchestvennost'* coexisted with *obshchestvo* and gradually replaced it, a change that reflected the steady fragmentation of the Russian elite, the fading of aristocratic values, the increasing disjunction between birth and talent. Crucial to this process was the rise of the liberal professions and the economic decline of the Russian gentry after the Emancipation of the serfs in 1861. Alexander Herzen was born in 1812 and died in 1870; radicals of his generation were all members of *obshchestvo;* this generalization cannot be made of the oppositional figures of the next generation.

The world of Russian radicalism into the 1870s was small and closed, and for the historian who has become acclimatized to it, reading a book on French or English radicalism can be something of a shock. Russian radicals, throughout most of the nineteenth century, were largely isolated from the 90-odd percent of the country that they felt to be their natural constituency: the peasantry.* But in Christopher Hill's *The World Turned Upside Down,* for example, the picture of seventeenth-century England that emerges is of a genuine social pyramid, with various layers and strata shading into each other—at any rate, until very near the top. Even in the seventeenth century, English radicalism might become a "popular movement" (for a time, at least) in a way that Russian radicalism did not achieve for well over two hundred years. England was not anything that might be called an "open society" in the modern sense of the term, but the amount and variety of contact and interaction between diverse social elements is—to the student of Russia—extraordinary. In Russia, serfdom and manorial agriculture provided the only real context for relations between the peasantry and *obshchestvo.*

Why this enormous gap (abyss, with its slightly melodramatic connotations, is probably the right word) between the peasants —the *narod*—and the small world of *obshchestvo?* (There were merchants, of course, and a few other odd intermediate groups, but none was either numerically or sociologically significant.) Part of the answer lies in Russia's enormous size, her poverty, and the endless series of foreign wars that attended her unification. Economic "modernization" or development did not come from below, but was sponsored by the crown, in particular during and after the reign of Peter the Great in the first quarter of the eighteenth century. Agriculture and industry developed not on the basis of free labor but through increased socioeconomic exploitation of the peasantry, through serfdom. Russian military advance and economic development increased rather than diminished this abyss between the monarchy and gentry on the one hand, and the *narod* on the other. At the same time, it took on a profound cultural dimension as well. In the course of the eighteenth century, the upper echelons of Russian society be-

*Russia's total population in 1858 was roughly seventy-four million. Jerome Blum estimates that rather more than fifty million people were either serfs or "state peasants." See *Lord and Peasant in Russia from the Ninth to the Nineteenth Centuries* (Princeton, 1961), pp. 476–77. According to the Soviet economist Pëtr Lyashchenko, the Russian population was 94.3 percent rural in 1858 and 5.7 percent urban. All but a smattering of the rural population were peasants of some kind. See *A History of the National Economy in Russia* (New York, 1949), p. 273.

came thoroughly Europeanized—in many cases coming to feel
most at home in a European language (French), of which the
narod could know nothing. To many peasants, their masters
were not only their bosses but quite literally foreigners.

This division of Russia into *obshchestvo* and *narod* powerfully
shaped the whole of Russian life and culture in the imperial
period, and after 1860 it quickly became the major problem for
activist Russian radicals. Even those who were problematical
members of *obshchestvo* from the point of view of the social elite
were, because of their Western culture, indubitably members
from the point of view of the *narod*, and they were forced to
operate almost wholly within its boundaries. Until the very end
of the century, the greatest single problem that confronted Russian radicals was escaping from the charmed circle of *obshchestvo* and finding support in the *narod*.

In seeking to understand the Russian village and its history,
Russian radicals turned to songs, tales, legends, and proverbs—
which helps to explain their apparently disproportionate interest
in ethnography. They studied the songs and tales of the peasantry in search of the imagery of spirituality (if they were Slavophiles) or revolt (if they were of a *narodnik* turn of mind). And
later generations of historians have turned to those same texts to
try to understand the consciousness of the peasantry—how they
thought of the Tsar, for example, or how they experienced the
reforms of Peter the Great.

Neither in England nor in France were the laboring classes so
culturally remote or sharply demarcated from their social superiors. Nineteenth-century English radicals came from diverse social backgrounds; members of the English laboring classes were
frequently found in reforming movements and radical politics.
But only a tiny handful of nineteenth-century Russian radicals
was from the *narod*. The most that can be said is that individual
peasants or workers—and precious few of the latter until the
1890s—or small groups, on occasion, showed a certain interest in
radical ideas, particularly if they could be rooted in an actual
situation of unusual popular misery and given a traditional-Chris-

tian resonance. But large-scale participation of peasants and workers in radical action did not come about until the turn of the century.

Much of the failure of Russian radicals to communicate their moral outrage, their sense of social justice, and their radical programs to the Russian peasant is explicable in these historical-cultural terms. The two segments of Russian society lived by different notions of law, property, and sovereignty. They sought the assistance of different saints (though much of *obshchestvo* had given up saints by this time), and they organized their lives according to different calendars. Their joys and pleasures, except for the most basic ones, were very different. Above all, they understood each other very poorly, and largely in terms of stereotypes that had proved of limited usefulness to one side or the other.

Until the century's end—by which time Russian society was rapidly diversifying—Russian peasants and the urban lower classes were unable to distinguish between their gentry or bureaucratic tormentors (whose predatory practices formed a major part of their lives) and the idealistic young people, from the same social and cultural background, who came to them bearing socialist utopias. Time and again, the advances of the "repentant noblemen"* were rebuffed. In Moscow and other large cities, the lower classes (egged on by the police) repeatedly broke up student demonstrations, easily persuaded that the students were demonstrating in favor of the restoration of serfdom or "against the Tsar." When thousands of students and other educated Russians "went to the people" in the summer of 1874, their complicated message (which mingled compassion, guilt, repudiation of privilege, and revolutionary propaganda) induced incomprehension and incredulity in the villagers, who frequently ended by summoning the constable. Perhaps only in some of the few urban workers' circles organized by radicals

*A term frequently employed in the 1870s to designate guilty members of *obshchestvo*, who were possessed by the idea that their material well-being and personal culture had been achieved at the expense of the *narod*. See James H. Billington, *Mikhailovsky and Russian Populism* (Oxford, 1958), pp. 91–92, for the origins of the term.

during the 1870s did the mutual incomprehension begin to lessen. And these circles were soon broken up by the police.

Central to the mutual incomprehension of the *narod* and the radical representatives of *obshchestvo* is the vexed question of peasant monarchism. It has generally been maintained by historians (and there is ample evidence to support them) that in traditional, monarchical societies the peasantry has tended to be a "conservative" element, and that when such a society begins the complex and tortuous "modernization" process, the peasantry is likely to remain loyal to the personification of the monarchy, if not to the old regime as a whole. The discontent and hostility that peasants feel toward the existing order of things are likely to be directed against targets less exalted and nearer at hand: the local nobility, the bureaucracy, or some emergent group of bourgeois notables. Still, Charles Tilly and other scholars have shown how dangerously imprecise sweeping generalizations in this area may be.[3] The peasant response to violent conflict and to either revolutionary or counterrevolutionary propaganda is conditioned by many other factors: religious loyalties, conflict among local elites, concrete economic conditions—the whole web of regional and local conditions.

At first glance, Russia in the nineteenth century seems to provide a clear-cut, even dramatic confirmation of this general hypothesis about peasant conservatism and monarchism. The Russian peasant was unusually isolated from the rest of Russian society, and almost all of *obshchestvo*, with relief or regret, accepted the proposition that the peasants were loyal to their "Little Father." This is not to say that the government was not in a constant state of nerves about the solidity of peasant monarchism or that elements on the extreme Left were not almost pathetically hopeful that these peasant illusions could be done away with. Indeed, one of the crucial foundations of Russian Populism was that the peasantry's belief in the Tsar could be destroyed, whether quickly and easily, or by education and propaganda over time. The renowned anarchist Mikhail Bakuhin, who had no sense of peasant monarchism, was perhaps the most sanguine of

Russian radicals, believing that the peasantry was a "powder keg" under the old regime to which one needed only apply a match. But such notions almost never stood the test of actual contact with the inhabitants of Russian villages.

Examples abound of peasant veneration for the Tsar.* After the Emancipation of the serfs in 1861, the belief was widespread that the Tsar had granted the peasants a "true liberty" (which meant, among other things, a thoroughgoing repartition of gentry and even state land) but that the gentry and bureaucracy had conspired to distort his message beyond recognition. This widely held belief resulted in numerous bizarre episodes: Russian peasants from northern villages left for the Crimea, for example, in the belief that the Tsar had escaped from his aristocratic captors and was seated there on a golden throne, giving "true liberty" to all those who came to him.

The notion of the "good Tsar," usually contrasted with the evil retainers surrounding him, had a very deep and broad resonance in Russian folklore. Popular legends of this type clustered in particular around Ivan the Terrible and Peter the Great. At first glance, this appears surprising. To any student of sixteenth-century Russia, the very idea that the peasantry should remember Ivan the Terrible kindly seems nonsensical. The endless wars of his reign, the financial exactions, the dislocations caused by his division of the realm and resettlement policies—all these gave rise to massive peasant flight, then and later, and would seem to ensure popular execration. And considering the social costs (to use a euphemistic modern term) of Peter the Great's "Westernization," the wars of *his* reign, the heavy taxation, and his brutal interference in the traditional life of Russian society, one might expect the popular memory of him, too, to be heavily negative.

But the reverse is, in fact, true. Judging by the stories that were still being told in the nineteenth century, both Ivan and Peter were regarded as having been "simple" men—"big men." They were strict, on occasion brutal, but they were just, and *above all*

*The title of Emperor, in official use since the time of Peter the Great, points to the modern, abstract notion of the state, wholly accepted by *obshchestvo*. But the peasantry lived in a patriarchal world, headed by a Tsar, not an Emperor. *Obshchestvo* and *narod* even had different rulers!

they were generally represented as hostile to the "boyars," meaning aristocrats in general, and friendly to the *narod*. Ivan, according to one historical tale, had been born an ordinary peasant and been made Tsar by God. Only around the cities of Novgorod and Pskov, which had felt the particular weight of Ivan's displeasure, were the stories hostile. Elsewhere in central Russia the picture of Ivan the Terrible as a "just Tsar" seems to have remained much what an English doctor found it to be two hundred years earlier:

Juan [Ivan] in a disguise sought a lodging in a village nigh the city, none would let him in but a poor man whose wife was then in Travel, and deliver'd whilst he was there; away he went before day, and told the man he would bring him some Godfathers next day; accordingly he and many of his nobility came and gave the poor Fellow a good largess, and burned all the houses in the Village but his, exhorting them to charity, and telling them, because they refused to admit Strangers into their houses, they should be forced to seek their Fortunes, and try how good it was to lie out of doors in the Winter.

Sometimes he would associate with thieves in a disguise, and once he advised them to rob the Exchequer; for (says he) I know the way to it; but one of the Fellows up with his Fist and struck him a hearty good blow on the Face, saying, Thou Rogue, wilt thou offer to rob his Majesty who is so good to us; let us go rob such a rich *Boyar* who has cozen'd his Majesty of vast sums. At this Juan was well pleased, and at parting chang'd caps with the fellow, and bid him meet him next morning in the Duaretz (a place in the court where the Emperour used often to pass by) and there (said he) I will bring thee to a good cup of *Aquavitae* and *Mead*. The Thief came accordingly, and being discover'd by his Majesty, was call'd up, admonished to steal no more, preferr'd in the Court, and serv'd for a discoverer of Thieves.[4]

Peter the Great was also a "just Tsar"—ironically enough, in view of his secularization of Tsar into Emperor. His folkloric image also included highly negative elements, which originated among the Old Believers, the seventeenth-century schismatics, whose early descendants often viewed him as Antichrist, but the dominant image is favorable. While Ivan was remembered as hostile to the boyars, Peter punished anyone who wouldn't work; he might reward either a peasant or a provincial governor if he got the job done. Both Ivan and Peter were in a sense "democratic," but with a difference. Peter's practicality and expertise are prominent in many of the stories told about him. One anecdote may suffice as an illustration: Peter is working anonymously in a shipyard, building the first steamboat. He proposes that the vessel be named after the worker who can cut most deeply into a log with his ax. When the finished vessel is inscribed with the name PETER THE GREAT, all the workers know who their anonymous comrade is.

The bond felt by the peasantry toward the Tsar is clear in most of these legends. He is "their" man, either by blood or as revealed in his actions, and he embodies their hopes and their aspirations for a justice they seldom actually received. The Ivan stories are closer to the classic form of the "just king" idea, as embodied in the English tradition, for example, by King Richard in the Robin Hood ballads.[5] The stories about Peter, for obvious reasons, are more concerned with labor and building. The mood is less archaic; the social scene is more variegated, populated by a range of recognizable common people who encounter Peter on his productive travels around Russia.

Despite the enormous sufferings of the Russian peasantry, the "just king" tradition still provided a kind of support for the autocracy in the nineteenth century, and it confronted Russian radicals with their most difficult tactical problem. From the government's point of view, to be sure, peasant veneration of the "Little Father Tsar" was of limited value, since peasant sympathy did not extend to the monarch's agents or policies. Peasant monarchism provided a bulwark against most revolutionary propaganda, but it did not create a constituency for government policy in the village or countryside.

A famous and fascinating example of peasant monarchism and one kind of radical response to it was provided by the so-called Chigirin Affair of 1877.[6] The background of what took place was the failure of the "movement to the people," when thousands of upper-class Russians had streamed out into the countryside; hundreds of radicals and ideologically amorphous sympathizers were eventually arrested. Amid the ensuing confusion and demoralization there was a general feeling that much tighter organization and more sophisticated tactics were essential. It was under these circumstances that several revolutionaries, of whom Ia. A. Stefanovich was the central figure, decided that they would exploit peasant monarchism in the interests of the revolution.

They chose, as the arena for their plans, the district of Chigirin, an impoverished area of the Ukraine where disputes about land allotments had been endemic among the recently emancipated state peasants,* and where the poorer peasants seemed to be struggling for the equitable principles of communal redistribution of land. There had been a good many arrests, and troops had been quartered on the villages, so the ground seemed well prepared. After some preliminary contact had been made, Stefanovich brought the peasants a "Secret Imperial Charter" and something called the "Code of the Society of 'The Secret *Druzhina.'* "† Stefanovich arranged for both documents to be printed in Kiev. The gist of his message to the peasants, substantiated and elaborated in these forged materials, was that the Tsar had been unable to prevail against the wicked nobility and that his original Emancipation decree had been distorted out of recognition. The Tsar, wrote Stefanovich, had struggled against the nobility for twenty years, but it was now clear that he could not prevail against his powerful and unscrupulous adversaries without the direct assistance of his loyal subjects. The peasants were therefore instructed to organize and arm themselves, with a view to an insurrection, in the name of the Tsar, against their gentry oppressors.

The scheme was eventually betrayed from within, and many peasants, as well as their radical organizers, were arrested. But until the betrayal it did seem clear that some modest success had been achieved; something on the order of a thousand peasants had been "organized." From a practical point of view, the tactic was not devoid of merit, considering the utter failure of the

*The state peasants were not serfs of an individual landlord but were bound to the state. On the eve of the Emancipation they were slightly more numerous than the serfs (sometimes known as "landlord's peasants"), and their economic situation was, on the whole, better.

†In medieval times, *druzhina* referred to the military retinue of a Russian prince.

"movement to the people" and the continuing disarray among the radicals. But its propriety or morality was another thing, and although Stefanovich had his defenders, no one seemed disposed to emulate him subsequently. A general belief came to prevail among Russian revolutionaries that peasant monarchism had somehow to be overcome; it could not be capitalized upon, even for the highest ends.

Recently, Daniel Field's extensive and intelligent analysis of the Chigirin Affair has called the whole idea of peasant monarchism into question. To begin with, he has shown that both the government and the peasants found "naive" peasant monarchism convenient in the aftermath of the events at Chigirin. The peasants who had been enrolled in the *druzhina* found it expedient to assert that they had been misled and their credulity exploited by an unscrupulous agitator, for otherwise they would have left themselves open to charges of conscious rebellion. The government found it expedient to believe them and therefore to make their punishment light, for otherwise it would have had to confront the notion that many peasants believed the existing order of things sufficiently unjust to warrant rebellion of a kind. Therefore, Field has concluded, it is pointless to raise the question of the *sincerity* of the peasants' convictions. That the peasants were naive monarchists was an accepted convention for discourse across the great gulf dividing *obshchestvo* from peasant Russia.

The usefulness of the "myth" of peasant monarchism is suggested by its duration. A Marxist might be inclined to argue that the Russian peasantry suffered from "false consciousness," that their true interests lay in massive revolt. But a belief in the weakness of peasantries with respect to social and political action has been a staple conclusion among students of the subject. The geographical dispersion of peasants, their technological backwardness, and their intense localism have made anything more than spontaneous and local action unusual and difficult—without the guidance of an outside elite. As Marx put it, "they are . . . incapable of enforcing their class interest in their own name, whether through a parliament or through a convention. They cannot represent themselves, they must be represented. Their representative must at the same time appear as their master." To which a later commentator adds: "the only thing to be objected to in this statement is the absoluteness of its terms, which has been refuted by later events."[7] The Russian radicals of the 1860s and 1870s could provide only the rudiments of such elite guidance, and the peasants were wise indeed not to deliver themselves into the hands of such as Stefanovich.

There was, moreover, another strain of peasant folklore that dovetailed curiously with the myth of the "just Tsar": the folklore of banditry and peasant insurrection.[8] Central here are the cycles of legends and tales that glorified the leaders of the great peasant rebellions: Stenka Razin in the seventeenth century and Pugachëv in the eighteenth. Not surprisingly, these legends were of great interest to the radical ethnographers of the 1860s and 1870s, suggesting as they did the "revolutionary potential" of the *narod*, or at least its insurrectionary capacity. But even in the Razin and Pugachëv cycles the rebel-avengers were the enemies of the boyars rather than of the Tsar. In the folklore of the *narod* there was no real opposition between the notion of the "just Tsar" and that of the peasant insurrectionary; indeed, the cossack Pugachëv represented himself as the "true Tsar," Peter III, who in fact had been murdered by his wife, Catherine the Great.

The landed elite that benefited from the labor of the *narod* was a curious, composite grouping generally known as the gentry *(dvorianstvo, dvorian'e)*.[9] Neither "nobility," as the term is employed in England or France, nor "gentry," in the English sense, is really adequate to describe the Russian *dvorianstvo*, but we shall follow customary usage and call them the gentry. In the 1850s this group numbered about 500,000 persons of both sexes.[10] Its history is extremely intricate and confusing; some knowledge of it is vital to an understanding of the main lines of Russia's history before the revolution.

The gentry was in fact not an aristocracy in the Western European sense and certainly not a class as either Marx or most contemporary sociologists would employ the term. Medieval Russia had an indigenous aristocracy, made up primarily of the families ruling in the various principalities absorbed by Muscovy, and the great lords who served them. The latter were known as boyars, a term that is often loosely used to indicate all of this aristocratic constellation. In Russia, as elsewhere in Europe, the consolidation of the modern state involved the subjugation of the old aristocracy by the crown. But in Russia the destruction of the old aristocracy was far more thoroughgoing than in the France of the ancien régime or in Prussia. What had emerged by the seventeenth century (and was consolidated by Peter the Great in the eighteenth) was a socially diverse body of men, bound by the monarchy to serve the state and receiving, in exchange, the exclusive right to own serfs. If there was a social contract in Russia prior to 1861, this was it. With characteristic brilliance, Alexander Herzen described the relationship in the following terms:

Could not the tsar say [to the gentry] "You want to be free? What's the point? Take *obrok* [quitrent] from your peasants, take their labor, take their children as servants, cut back their land, sell them, buy, resettle, beat, whip them, and if you get tired, send them to me at the police station and I will gladly whip them for you. Isn't that enough for you? You want to know honor? Our predecessors yielded you a part of our autocracy; by binding free men to you, they cut off the hem of their purple robe and threw it over the poverty of your fathers. You did not renounce it, you, too, are covered by it and live under it—so how can you and I talk of freedom? Stay bound to the tsar, so long as orthodox Christians are bound to you."[11]

In a more sober vein, Herzen observed acidly in his memoirs that

West European aristocracy is indeed so completely alien to us that all accounts of our grandees may be reduced to stories of savage luxury, of banquets in which a whole town takes part, of innumerable house-serfs, of tyrannising over the peasants and inconsiderable neighbors, together with slavish subservience before the Emperor and the Court. The Sheremetevs and the Golitsyns with all their palaces and great estates were in no way distinguished from their peasants except by wearing a German coat, reading and writing French, and enjoying wealth and the tsar's favor. They were all constantly confirming [the

Emperor] Paul's dictum, that he had no one about him but people in high positions; those, that is, to whom he spoke, and while he was speaking. All that is very good, but one ought to recognize it. . . . The habits of the Polish Pans were nasty, barbarous and now almost unintelligible; but they were of a different calibre, a different cast of personality, and there was not a shade of servility in them.[12]

What Herzen does not say is that the Polish aristocracy maintained its prerogatives against the crown with such brilliance that the Polish state disappeared for more than a century; still, his principal point is correct. In Russia the monarchy was far more successful in its struggle with the aristocracy than was the case in Western Europe, and the Russian gentry was more timid and more closely tied to it than were comparable groups in the West.

But one should not overdo the contrast. In Western Europe, too, aristocracies were subdued by the monarchy and often significantly bureaucratized. Large segments of the nobility were dependent upon salaries, and "noble" status might be the result of a royal grant, as in eighteenth-century France. Still, the French and English nobility profoundly affected their countries' histories by their struggles against the crown. In Russia, the struggle was far more one-sided, and "aristocratic" opposition after the early seventeenth century was largely indirect and literary, save in time of crisis, and it left behind little more than a cluster of nostalgias and snobberies among the more illustrious gentry families.*

Peter the Great made admission to the gentry depend on service to the state, and although the *obligation* to serve did not survive the eighteenth century, the possibility of achieving noble rank through service did. Still, formidable difficulties confronted those who aspired to noble status through a career in state service. The Russian educational system was small and primitive,

---

*During the so-called Time of Troubles (1605–13), and during the interregnum in 1730, aristocratic groups made serious efforts to limit the monarchy. Not only were they unsuccessful, but on neither occasion did an important oppositional tradition survive. The Decembrist Revolt of 1825 had a certain aristocratic component to it as well. But the mythology of the Decembrists, as it developed in the nineteenth century, provided historical precedent not for aristocratic frondeurs but for the intelligentsia radicalism that was to come.

even after the reforms at the beginning of the nineteenth century, and it was difficult to rise high enough in the service hierarchy to achieve hereditary nobility without more education than was readily available to most nongentry Russians. Nor did the simple and archaic structure of Russian society stimulate the kinds of ambition that one ordinarily finds in modern societies where careers open to talent are less hedged about with difficulties. And, finally, the pool from which new talent could be drawn was, relative to the Russian population as a whole, extremely small. Serfs and state peasants were, with the rarest exceptions, altogether excluded. So great was the gulf between the peasant village and *obshchestvo,* in fact, that movement from one to the other was virtually nonexistent, which meant that a cluster of special categories—like the sons of village priests or lower-ranking army officers and bureaucrats—were the only significant native source of upwardly mobile personnel.

As Peter the Great conceived them, gentry and bureaucracy were identical. But particularly after the abolition of the mandatory service obligation in 1762, the two groups grew apart. Many members of the gentry served the state only for a while, or not at all. At the same time, a hereditary bureaucratic caste began to develop, technically within the gentry, but less and less related to landed wealth and more and more to a tradition of bureaucratic service.

At the same time, the eighteenth century saw the gentry become more "aristocratic." Taking advantage of the indolence and political weakness of successive monarchs, they gradually weakened the tie between privilege and service that had been one of the linchpins of the Petrine system. In 1785 Catherine the Great confirmed the accumulation of gentry privileges, added some new ones, and granted the gentry corporate organization as an estate of the realm. Concurrently, members of Russia's "aristocracy" were now recognized as full owners of their estates; they were exempt from corporal punishment, as well as personal taxation; and, through the newly established provincial marshals of the nobility, they might petition the crown. Until the Decembrist Revolt helped swing the pendulum in the other direction, the gentry appeared to be moving toward the achievement of genuine aristocratic status.

One cannot equate *obshchestvo* with the gentry as a whole. Many people who were technically members of the gentry were extremely poor and ill-educated, and spent their lives struggling for economic survival in out-of-the-way parts of the empire. In 1858 there were in Russia an estimated 3,633 serf owners without any land at all. These men constituted 4 percent of all serf owners, and they owned, on the average, 3 serfs apiece. Forty percent of all serf owners in Russia owned between 1 and 20 serfs.[13] Many of these provincial *hobereaux* could not be considered part of *obshchestvo* genealogically, culturally, or in terms of any worldly accomplishment. Some of them certainly led lives that were scarcely to be distinguished from those of the more prosperous peasantry.* On the other hand, the nationalist historian Mikhail Pogodin was born a serf in 1800; his family was not manumitted by its owner until he was six years old; by his own industry and talent, Pogodin put himself through the University of Moscow and then had a successful career as a historian, editor, and journalist. Although his gentry friends were often caustic about what they regarded as the crudities of his character (and thus indirectly about his plebeian origins), Pogodin was considered a member of *obshchestvo*.

Finally, we should take note of the changing relationship between *obshchestvo* and the government. Under Catherine, Paul, and Alexander, the terms were not perceived as antithetical in any significant way. But from the early years of Nicholas's reign onward, *obshchestvo* and *pravitel'stvo* (government) became in various ways *opposed*—or at least sharply differentiated. This divergence had a great deal to do with the Decembrist Revolt of 1825, which led Nicholas to regard the gentry class as a whole with considerable suspicion, and particularly its more literate representatives. It also had something to do with the sharpening differentiation between bureaucracy and gentry, between those

---

*And of course one should not, within the gentry, make wealth alone the criterion for membership within *obshchestvo*. A very rich but ignorant and provincial boor was unlikely to be accepted.

who governed Russia and those who created Russian culture. Under Nicholas, literary culture in particular became more and more steeped in "political" values, and the government regarded it as automatically oppositional and dangerous. The divorce between *pravitel'stvo* and *obshchestvo* was more or less accomplished in the 1860s, and with the steady democratization of Russian intellectual and cultural life that followed, the term *obshchestvo* itself became increasingly anachronistic.

The term "intelligentsia" was devised in Russia in the 1860s to refer to a group once thought to be peculiarly Russian. But the term has proved highly attractive to historians, and intelligentsias have been discovered in virtually all modern societies, European and non-European alike. Once there was only the Russian intelligentsia; now Chinese, French, and Nigerian intelligentsias have turned up. Students of Russia used to delight in asking "What is the intelligentsia?" before proceeding to a discussion of Herzen and Chernyshevsky, but the same question may now be so broad and vague as to be impossible or useless. Still, there is something to be gained by asking it, as one cannot discuss the beginnings of the Russian revolutionary movement without having an idea of what is to be understood as "the intelligentsia."[14]

It is easiest to begin by indicating what it is *not*. For instance, we may reject the view that an intelligentsia—in Russia or elsewhere—is simply those elements in society with access to higher education and the skills that go with it. If one adopts this extremely broad characterization, all sense of the special radical and critical orientation of the intelligentsia is dissolved and finally lost. Nor may we relate the intelligentsia in any direct way to the means of production, as some Marxists have attempted to do.

Toward the end of his great book on the nineteenth-century Chinese liberal Yen Fu, Benjamin Schwartz distinguishes two powerful influences in nineteenth-century European social thought, particularly as it was reflected in the writings of non-Western thinkers, like his subject. The first he called "the Faust-

ian-Promethean strain," which he found to be characterized by
"the exaltation of energy and power both over non-human nature and within human society, involving the 'rationalization' (in
the Weberian sense) of man's whole socio-economic machinery."
Schwartz called his second category "the stream of social-politi-
cal idealism." The latter, "represented by such terms as freedom,
equality, democracy and socialism, has been concerned with the
nature of relations among men within the larger macroscopic
structures of political and social life and with the shaping of those
structures to promote social-ethical ends."[15]

These two categories—which, of course, are always somewhat
intermingled—define the goal of the intelligentsias that have
come into existence since the philosophes led the way in eighteenth-century France. An intelligentsia is an essentially modern
phenomenon, related to the process of secularization: its members perform at least some of the functions earlier fulfilled by
priests or other representatives of religion. Since around 1500,
first Europe and then the rest of the world have been drawn into
patterns that we vaguely think of as "modern"—involving secularization, rationalization of more and more areas of human life
(especially public life—let us call this "bureaucratization"), and
industrialization. The forms that "modernity" has taken and is
taking vary enormously,[16] and the social costs of modernization
do, too. England and the United States are countries where the
social cost of modernization has been *relatively* low; the experience has been more painful in Germany and China, while India
is still not fully launched into the process.

The modernization experience is an agonizing one; and of
course there is no ultimate reason why a nation need undergo it.
As yet, however, no society with any degree of self-consciousness
has been willing to resist the essentials of the process, whatever
national or ideological coloring the modernizing elite may give
to "their" modernity. This is apparently because power, if not
survival, seems to depend on undergoing the tremendous
upheavals attendant on drastically altering the premodern social
order. As Schwartz has pointed out, two myths lie behind what
he calls the power of "the West": the myth of Faust and the myth

of Prometheus.[17] Faust, making his pact with the Devil in order to understand the innermost secrets of nature, in order to *dominate* nature, and Prometheus, stealing fire from the gods in order to bestow it on his fellow man—these are the most important archetypes of our civilization.*

The modernization process has not, of course, proceeded without criticism from individuals and social groups affected by it. Sometimes this criticism has been mild, sometimes bitter, sometimes violent. Sometimes it has been intended to expedite the modernization process, sometimes to change its course, sometimes to stop it entirely. Much of this criticism of modernity has come from individuals and groups that may be accurately described as intelligentsia.

But an intelligentsia's drive for "wealth and power" is not always compatible with its social idealism. In general, the less wealth and power a nation has, the more "backward" and powerless it seems to be, the more sharply its intelligentsia is likely to focus on the achievement of material power. This diminishes the stream of social idealism, though rarely dams it up entirely. Thus nineteenth-century Chinese intellectuals like Yen Fu were far more concerned with the sources of Western power than were nineteenth-century Russian intellectuals.

For all its attraction toward power, the intelligentsia's critique of modern Western civilization has at bottom been a moral one and is a derivative of the intelligentsia's sacerdotal inheritance. Although there has been considerable variety in the moral and political positions taken by *intelligenty* (to use the Russian plural, meaning "members" of the intelligentsia), their criticism can in general be classified as either "counterrevolutionary"/romantic or socialist. Clearly, if one is going to criticize the growing ratio-

*As Herman Melville knew before Yen Fu. As he wrote in "The Bell-Tower": "A practical materialist, what Bannadonna had aimed at was to have been reached, not by logic, not by crucible, not by altars; but by plain vice-bench and hammer. In short, to solve nature, to steal into her, to intrigue beyond her, to procure someone else to bind her to his hand;—these, one and all, had not been his objects; but, asking no favors from any element or any being, of himself, to rival her, outstrip her, and rule her. He stooped to conquer. With him, common sense was theurgy; machinery, miracle; Prometheus, the heroic name for machinist; man, the true God." Melville, *Billy Budd, Sailor, and Other Stories* (Harmondsworth, England, 1970), Penguin edition, p. 210.

nalism, bureaucratization, and industrialization of modern times, the most natural response is either to create a model of the good society that is in jeopardy or has been lost, or to envisage a more humane and equitable form of society that might be—that ought to be—achieved in the future. It is hardly necessary to add that this kind of moral critique will be dismissed as "utopian" by the practical statesmen who have momentary charge of their nation's destiny.

The acceptance by almost everyone who writes about these problems of such terms as "counterrevolutionary," "romantic," and "socialist" suggests the dominance of a Europe-centered Marxist or liberal historical framework, carrying with it strong overtones of inevitability. The romantic, "backward-looking" critique of modernity has frequently been dismissed as merely useless and nostalgic. Perhaps—if our sense of historical possibility becomes somewhat greater, as both the liberal and Marxist ideas of progress become even more problematical—our condescending attitude toward "nostalgic" or "utopian" ideas and viewpoints will change.

Naturally there are major intellectual differences between "radical" and "reactionary" intelligentsia viewpoints, particularly with respect to attitudes toward national and cultural traditions, the proper principles of social organization, the phenomenon of rationalism itself. In general, the "Left" *intelligent* has tended to see the modernization process as issuing in a socialist revolution, which would *fulfill* rationalism rather than destroy it, and would realize all the wealth-creating possibilities of modernization while eliminating the national and social inequalities it has created. The intelligentsia of the "Right," by contrast, has tended to be programmatically hostile to the whole idea of modernization. In practice, however, Right and Left are not always easy to distinguish.

On occasion, an intelligentsia viewpoint can be related directly to the social interests of an influential social class or group. The landed aristocracies of Europe—particularly in Germany, for example—were a powerful force in the creation of a coherent structure of ideas opposed to the French Revolution and justifying the social values it threatened.[18] Still, the "social content" of the intelligentsia's ideas, or its relationship to concrete interest groups in society, is a difficult matter, and the intellectual structures created by intelligentsia critics are not always easy to relate to the practical economic interests of social groups. We shall have occasion to see how difficult it is to do so in nineteenth-century Russia.

Despite the important differences between "radical" and "reactionary" intelligentsia viewpoints, there are some striking points of correspondence. Two ideas in particular are common to both critiques. Both "radicals" and "reactionaries" believe that the individual man in modernizing or modern society is alienated from his work and from his social and intellectual surroundings. He seems to have lost a harmonious "wholeness" in his being; his intellectual, moral, and aesthetic faculties are fragmented or at war with each other. Though radicals locate the source of alienation more specifically in economic factors—property relations, work, and so on—while reactionaries usually look to the recovery of certain traditional values, often religious, as the main thing, the problem of alienation is central to almost all intelligentsia criticism of modernity, in Russia as elsewhere.

The other influential proposition is that the large, faceless, rationalized society of modernity must be replaced by some kind of "community," whose members will be related to each other "organically," where impersonality, boredom, and compulsion will be, if not eliminated, greatly decreased. In some manifestations, the ideal of community[19] strongly resembles that put forward by nineteenth-century European conservatives against what they regarded as the corrosive rationalism and individualism of their time; the elements stressed being

not the abstract and impersonal relations of contract but personality inextricably bound to the small social group; relationships of ascribed status and tradition; the functional interdependence of all parts of a society, including its prejudices and superstitions; the role of the sacred in maintaining order and integration; and, above all, the primacy of society to the individual.[20]

The kind of community exalted by the conservative intelligentsia gave each of its members an identity:

in [the community], the tasks of work, the responsibilities of the family, the worship of the gods, and the pursuit of virtue are fused. In peasant societies throughout history, men's obligation to their work, their children, their fellows, and the Divine has been seen as a part of an indissoluble whole; and in most primitive societies even today, an intimate nexus exists between family, social obligation, work, ritual, magic, and religion. . . . In such communities, the demands of the mind, the hands and the heart are fused. The peasant does not merely work his land, he cares for it. The fisherman not only exploits the sea, but stands in awe of its ferocity and prays for its calm. The hunter not only kills the animals he hunts, he also often worships them as his highest gods. And toward his broader community, toward the other members of his village and tribe, he feels kinship based not on rational awareness of common purpose and custom, but on instinctive loyalty derived from a sense of special humanity. Many primitive communities refer to themselves merely as "the people," thus distinguishing their own special humanity. . . . Within such primary communities, what men do and what they think is a part of what they feel and what they worship: cognition, action, feeling, morality and reverence are fused.[21]

The radical idea of community has been somewhat different. In general, peasant or other "primitive" communities have seemed less directly available as models, although in Russia, as we shall see, the peasant commune helped the Populists imagine the social order of the future. Radical communitarians have been more reluctant to repudiate the modern concerns for individual differentiation, liberties, and well-being that have been commonplaces of liberal ideology. Often the reconciliation of communal integration with the achievements of bourgeois individualism has seemed a particular problem to communitarians of the Left. As Alexander Herzen once put it: "How is the independence of the Englishman to be kept without the cannibalism, how is the individuality of the [Russian] peasant to be developed without the loss of the principle of the commune? Precisely in this [dilemma] lies the whole agonizing problem of our century, precisely in this consists the whole [problem] of socialism."[22] So left-wing seekers after "community," not surprisingly, have tended to found their own more or less "utopian" communes— of which there have been thousands, from Brook Farm to the still numerous communities in the United States at present.*

A crucial goal of virtually all the communitarian experiments of the last one hundred fifty years has been the ending of "alienation," the "reintegration" of the shattered and fragmented faculties of modern man. However diverse the suggested *means* for overcoming alienation may be, radicals and reactionaries paint a remarkably similar picture of the hypothetical "integrated" (or reintegrated) person. Let us allow the Slavophile Ivan Kireevsky to speak for the reactionaries:

the first condition . . . is that man should strive to gather into one indivisible whole all his separate forces, which in his ordinary condition are in a state of disunity and contradiction; that he should not consider his abstract logical capacity as the only organ for the comprehension of the truth; that he should not consider the voice of ecstatic feeling, uncoordinated with the other forces of the spirit, as an infallible guide to truth; that he should not consider the inspiration of an isolated aesthetic sense, independent of other concepts, as the true guide to the comprehension of the higher order of the universe; that he should not consider even the overmastering love of his heart, separate from the other demands of the spirit, as an infallible guide to the attainment of the supreme good; but that he should constantly seek in the depths of his soul that inner root of understanding where all the separate forces fuse into one living and whole vision of the mind.[23]

Human reintegration, for Kireevsky, depended on the achievement of a new civilization, based both on communalism and on a profound rediscovery of the principles of Orthodox Christian-

---

*An excellent picture of recent American communalism can be found in Raymond Mungo, *Total Loss Farm* (New York, 1970). Edward Shils notes that "the new 'communitarian,' 'participatory' culture . . . is really the romantic hunger for *Gemeinschaft* on a more grandiose scale." See "Dreams of Plenitude, Nightmares of Scarcity" in Seymour M. Lipset and Philip G. Altbach, eds., *Students in Revolt* (Boston, 1970), p. 18. Compare the American experience with the Russian communes established by A. N. Engel'gardt in the 1870s. See Richard Wortman, *The Crisis of Russian Populism* (Cambridge, England, 1967), pp. 47–60.

ity; the two were linked, he believed. For Karl Marx, the greatest *intelligent* of the Left, reintegration could occur only with the achievement of communism through a worldwide revolution that would abolish private property. But for Marx, as for Kireevsky, the egoism created by modern society and state was the ultimate enemy. Only under communism, according to Marx,

"does self-activity coincide with material life, which corresponds to the development of individuals into complete individuals and the casting off of all natural limitations." Marx illustrates the casting off of limitations by saying that "in communist society, where nobody has one exclusive sphere of activity but each can become accomplished in any branch he wishes, society regulates the general production and thus makes it possible for me to do one thing today and another tomorrow, to hunt in the morning, fish in the afternoon, rear cattle in the evening, criticize after dinner, just as I have a mind, without ever becoming hunter, fisherman, shepherd or critic."[24]

The focus on reintegration and community does not exhaust the content of intelligentsia thought, but simply provides a focus for their preoccupations. Members of Left intelligentsias generally supported the main thrust of Enlightenment radicalism as the key to the good society of the future, while intelligentsia groups of the Right have gravitated toward some form of the preindustrial or "native" values of their own society as the key to the future. A certain tension arises between nationalist and internationalist attitudes in an intelligentsia, particularly if their own society is suffering from the humiliations of underdevelopment. Their view of the good society transcends, at least in part, their own national culture, and yet their own wounded sense of themselves as Russians, Chinese, or Africans spurs their criticism. Kenneth Kaunda, for example, criticized what one might call the "Faustian" strand of Western modernity in the following nativist terms: "I do believe that there is a distinctively African way of looking at things, of problem-solving, and indeed of thinking. We have our own logic system, which makes sense to us, however confusing it might be to the Westerner. The Westerner has a problem-solving mind, while the African has a situation-experiencing mind."[25] When a society is developed and powerful, nationalist attitudes in its intelligentsia, like the craving for wealth and power, diminish.

In addition to its moral critique of modernity and its stress on the related themes of community and alienation, the *social isolation* of the intelligentsia has always been one of its essential characteristics. Either out of necessity or by choice, members of the intelligentsia have tended to remain apart from the established institutions of their society. Indeed, some theoreticians have gone so far as to suggest that the development of an intelligentsia is simply a function of a society's economic backwardness. A developing country, so the argument runs, inevitably produces people who are overeducated or educated inappropriately; there may be too many lawyers, for instance, in a society whose real need is for engineers. So a well-educated lawyer who is likely to be conversant with modern European culture, and in that sense "better educated" than most of his countrymen, cannot be used (or perhaps even employed at all) by his society, and for this reason is likely to become embittered and highly critical.[26] No one can really deny that this situation is conducive to the recruitment of an intelligentsia, but to use it as the paradigm of how intelligentsias originate leaves too much out of account. The situation in nineteenth-century Russia, where the intelligentsia originated, was rather different; nor does the simple combination of overeducation and economic backwardness explain the presence of a critical intelligentsia today in Europe (including the Soviet Union) and the United States. It seems preferable simply to note the strong inclination of an intelligentsia to live by moral ideas and to insist that, for whatever reason, members of an intelligentsia must stand somewhat apart from the institutions of their society.

Like many a convenient category, this notion of the intelligentsia gets rather blurred at the edges. Should Jonathan Swift be called an *intelligent?* Noam Chomsky? Chomsky is a brilliant and innovative theoretician in linguistics, and he is integrated into American society to the extent that he finds it possible to function as a professor at the Massachusetts Institute of Technology. But the primacy of moral ideals in his life and his activities as a social critic and publicist invite one to classify him as a member of the radical intelligentsia.

Finally, the social idealism of the *intelligent* is clearly not always in harmony with his aspirations toward wealth and power. Powerlessness is so important in generating the kind of criticism that intelligentsias produce that not unnaturally they often exhibit a strong ambition to achieve power, both for their society and for themselves. Indeed, in many developing societies the intelligentsia must be seen as the nucleus of a new ruling elite; their orientation toward power and away from social idealism increases as a "revolutionary situation" draws near. But in those countries (almost always economically developed) where the intelligentsia has no chance of "coming to power," the stream of social idealism tends to flow unhindered. In late Imperial Russia, the Bolsheviks were of all intelligentsia groupings the one most oriented toward the realities of seizing and exercising power; the component of social idealism was weak among them from the 1890s on. It diminished even further after 1917, when they formed a new elite; the revival of social idealism in Trotskyism was almost entirely the consequence of Trotsky's political destruction.

Just as the Bolshevik regime has generated a new intelligentsia to oppose it (*not* an intelligentsia that can be much interested in power!), it is clear that the elites of the former colonial regimes of Asia and Africa, unless they are remarkably successful in meeting the needs of their constituents, will face a new intelligentsia critique, which will be the more maximalist because of the absence of virtually all Western-style, "bourgeois" politics. Their Solzhenitsyns and Amalriks are not far down the road, although it may be that many "post revolutionary" regimes will be willing and able to employ sufficient coercion and terror to prevent an intelligentsia opposition from emerging publicly. For it seems to be the case that an intelligentsia can have a public existence only in a society where there are at least rudimentary democratic attitudes or in a society that is unable to apply sufficient force to repress it.

One cannot tell the story of nineteenth-century Russian *intelligenty* if one is not attuned to their specific *mentalité* and to the specific problems that loomed so overwhelmingly for them: human reintegration, the burden of their parasitical culture, achieved at the expense of the *narod*. If one does not take this intellectual climate into account, their lives can seem merely extravagant, in the way that supercilious Westerners sometimes refer to as "typically Russian."

We can say in the most generalized sense that the Russian intelligentsia developed out of the gentry, following its emancipation from compulsory state service in 1762.[27] Crucial to its emergence was the general process of "Westernization" that Russia had been undergoing since the seventeenth century, and particularly the fact that a minority of the Westernized gentry began to feel "cramped" in Russia, to use Martin Malia's apt term.[28] The imperial bureaucracy provided the only outlet for their developing civic idealism, and its sluggish routines were not attractive to the most able and ambitious among them. Cut off from any "practical" political activity, they lived more and more in the realm of ideas; and the ideas among which they chose to live were Western ideas, either directly critical of existing political and social conditions—such as the ideas of the French Enlightenment—or indirectly so, as with early-nineteenth-century Romanticism.

Aleksandr Radishchev, author of the famous *Journey from St. Petersburg to Moscow,* is often referred to as the first Russian *intelligent.* His only rival for the title is Nikolai Novikov, journalist, scholar, philanthropist, and Freemason. When we observe that Radishchev was arrested in 1790 (shortly after his *Journey* was published) and that Novikov was arrested in 1792, we have a sense of how to date the beginnings of the intelligentsia.

It has often been debated whether the Decembrist rebels of 1825 were part of a Russian intelligentsia, or whether one ought to refer to them by some awkward term such as "proto-*intelli-*

gent," or whether they were not *intelligenty* at all. To my way of thinking, most of the Decembrists were too deeply rooted in existing Russian society—that is, insufficiently alienated—to be so designated. But the debate is worth pursuing only for the pleasure of the thing, for intellectual exercise. It is clear that the Decembrists were *to some degree* estranged from the operations of their society, and that their criticisms had a strong moral basis, rooted in Enlightenment ideas, rather than being simply the prescriptions of concerned and practical reformers. But neither they nor Radishchev nor Novikov was conscious of belonging to some larger collectivity that served a critical function in society. Nor were they concerned with problems of "alienation" and "community," preoccupations that developed only following the massive infusion of German idealism and philosophical Romanticism into Russia between 1820 and 1848.

The reign of Nicholas I (1825–55) saw the Russian intelligentsia take on its characteristic nineteenth-century form, although the term "intelligentsia" was not actually coined until the early 1860s.[29] Nicholas's repressive thirty-year reign drove all critical or in any way oppositional thought out of the public arena and into intimate groups, or "circles." The dominant intellectual framework of the circles, particularly in the 1830s and 1840s, was provided by German idealism; French socialism and various forms of Romanticism and conservatism were also present in an intoxicating intellectual mix. Small wonder that the straightforward eighteenth-century radicalism (much of it very moderate) so characteristic of the Decembrists was replaced by far more ambitious and complex recipes for human liberation. The new extremism was due primarily to pressure from the regime, which regarded all independent speculation on these matters as inherently dangerous, an attitude that induced a kind of emotional radicalism in all those who were interested in social and political questions. Because the intelligentsia was deprived of any outlet or public forum, its ideas became more extreme and fantastic, unmoderated by the kind of practical experience characteristic of Western Europe. Secondly, both Romanticism and German idealism squarely posed the questions of individual alienation and of the replacement of social rationalism (particularly in its Manchesterian form) with some new form of human community. The socialism of the Saint-Simonians and Charles Fourier was also concerned with these issues; in fact the socialism and Romanticism of 1830 had a good deal in common. So, under considerable pressure from the state, and with the bewildering intellectual riches of nineteenth-century Europe as their major resource, a coherent set of problems and a sense of group identity emerged for the extremely small minority of *obshchestvo* that concerned themselves with the realm of ideas. Their provincial isolation from the "metropolitan" centers—Paris and Berlin—only heightened the passion with which they lived and suffered through these ideas.

Between 1840 and 1848, the least repressive period of Nicholas's reign, the discussions of the intelligentsia emerged somewhat from the salons and found at least a veiled expression in journals and magazines. It is at this point that we can perceive a division between the "radical" and "reactionary" intelligentsia positions. The "radicals" were christened "Westerners" by their opponents,* and although the designation was intended pejoratively, it was accepted as a badge of honor. The Westerners— who included Alexander Herzen, the literary critic Vissarion Belinsky, the historian Timofei Granovsky—were visionaries of the same stamp as the Left Hegelians in Germany. They saw history moving dialectically through ever higher stages to a new civilization that would reconcile individualism and community (in a national form) and bestow its blessings on those segments of the population that had hitherto remained outside of historical development altogether. Whether the final achievement of this new civilization would be a matter of evolution or revolution was a question about which individual Westerners might differ, but on the general nature of the process they were agreed. Thus, in their Hegelian scheme, the conquest of true individuality and

---

*I am oversimplifying the category here. Certain of those who were known as "Westerners" were neither Hegelian nor interested in socialism. Pëtr Chaadaev, for example, was determinedly Romantic and antimodern in his orientation. But because the focus of his traditionalism was Rome and the Mediterranean world, rather than "Old Russia," he was considered a Westerner.

community lay at the end of history and was linked with a deeper
and fuller triumph of "reason," rather than its repudiation.
Hence, the Westerners in the 1840s were not backward-looking
and had little nostalgia for earlier forms of social life, particularly
in Russia, which they regarded as only having begun to emerge
from an ahistorical slumber and stagnation at the time of Peter
the Great.[30]

Although the Slavophiles—Russia's "reactionary" *intelligenty*
—were likewise obsessed by the achievement of personal reintegration within a true communal order, their approach to the
problem was quite different. Although Ivan Kireevsky was
touched by French socialist thought and both he and Aleksei
Stepanovich Khomiakov knew their Hegel and Schelling well,
their greatest intellectual debt was to the Romantic conservatism
of the Restoration period in Germany. The Slavophiles looked to
pre-Petrine Muscovy, whose civilization and culture they substantially distorted to create a historical existence for their religious and social ideals. They regarded what they called "Old
Russia" as a network of local communities, deeply Christian and
profoundly traditional, without a Roman sense of private property and without "individualism" in the modern sense. Law and
custom were virtually identical. They claimed that the Russian
monarchy—until the destructive introduction of modern, rationalizing, "Western" ideas—had an extremely limited function: it
conducted foreign relations on behalf of the entire collectivity,
and the Tsar served as a supreme, paternal judge. The contrasting typologies of Old Russian and Western civilizations in the
Slavophile formulations are close to those of Romantic theoreticians and early sociologists, the classic expression of which is
probably to be found in Ferdinand Tönnies's contrast between
community *(Gemeinschaft)* and society *(Gesellschaft)*.[31] But in
the work of the Slavophiles, this contrast between premodern
integration and modern alienation took a national form: in Russia
the communal and religious culture had been preserved in an
undeveloped form in the way of life of the *narod,* and in the West
it had been lost altogether.

The fact that the Slavophiles grotesquely distorted early Russian history, although easy enough to demonstrate, is fundamentally beside the point. They were not historians but intelligentsia critics whose interest was really in the present and future. They, quite as much as the Westerners, were critics of the Russian autocracy, which in its violent, sporadic, and often inefficient way had been the principal vehicle for modernizing Russia, at least from the time when Peter the Great had replaced the Tsar by the Emperor. The Slavophiles' fundamental preoccupations were very close to those of the Westerners—which helps to explain the intense love-hate relationship between the two groups, as well as some reciprocal influence. But the Slavophiles had even more difficulty than the Westerners in plausibly suggesting how their ideals might be implemented. That Russia might return to such a version of its national past in shaping its contemporary life seemed even more farfetched than the notion that Russia might soon witness the triumph of historical Reason, in either evolutionary or revolutionary form.

After 1847–48, the bipolarity of the intelligentsia began to change. Belinsky died and Herzen emigrated, and very quickly the Westerner position became fragmented. The Slavophiles were only slightly more unified, and without the Westerner "enemy" to encounter in the salons of Moscow and the pages of journals, their group existence became less important. Not until the development of what came to be called Populism *(narodnichestvo)* was a significant proportion of the intelligentsia able to develop an intellectual focus for their criticisms of Russian society.

2

Slavophiles
and Populists

*Two Russias have been confronting each other in
hostile fashion since the beginning of the eighteenth
century. On one side was governmental, imperial,
gentry Russia, wealthy and armed not only with
bayonets, but with every kind of bureaucratic and
police trick. . . . On the other, the Rus' of the black
people—poor, agricultural, communal, democratic,
unarmed, taken unaware, conquered—in fact—
without a battle.*
—Alexander Herzen, *Baptized Property*

*What is called Tolstoy's "anarchism" essentially and
fundamentally expresses our Slav anti-Statism,
which, again, is really a national characteristic, in-
grained in our flesh from old times, our desire to
scatter nomadically. Up to now, we have indulged
that desire passionately, as you and everyone else
know. We Russians know it too, but we always break
away along the lines of least resistance; we see that
this is pernicious, but still we crawl further and further away; and these mournful cockroach journeyings are called "the History of Russia," the history of
a State which has been established almost incidentally, mechanically—to the surprise of the majority
of its honest-minded citizens—by the forces of the
Variags, Tartars, Baltic Germans and petty officials.*
—Maxim Gorky, *Reminiscences of Tolstoy,
Chekhov and Andreev*

Populism is the grand term that is generally used to describe the ideology of Russian radicalism that emerged in the late 1850s. But it cannot be used without some definition. In the first place, no one in the 1860s or 1870s actually used the term "Populism" in this inclusive way, a fact that should make the conscientious historian pause. Radicalism then was often referred to by the vague and elusive term "nihilism," a designation that itself needs clarification. And finally, because it was largely the affair of isolated student and intelligentsia circles, the radicalism of the 1860s took on a conspiratorial, underground, and elitist cast that has quite properly led historians to call it "Jacobinism" or "Blanquism."*

Some years ago, the American historian Richard Pipes presented a telling critique of the use of the term "Populism" *(narodnichestvo)* to designate an entire stage of the Russian revolutionary movement.[1] He showed that the term originated in the mid-1870s and described (often with pejorative intent) only one current of the Russian radicalism of the day. Originally the Populists, or *narodniki,* were simply Russian radicals who believed that the intelligentsia had no business imposing its ideals on the Russian people—or its timetable for revolutionary action, either. The original Populists believed that the intelligentsia should learn from the people, go to school with the people, immerse themselves in the people, and that the intelligentsia's role in the future transformation of Russia should be modest and limited.

Over the next twenty years, the scope of the term became ever more inclusive. Finally, in the debates of the 1890s over the future of Russian revolutionary development, the then Marxist Pëtr Struve designated as Populists *all* those radicals who denied the progressive character of capitalism, who idealized the natural economy and the spirit and institutions of the Russian peasantry. Significantly, Struve insisted on the relationship of Populism to Slavophilism and regarded Herzen and Chernyshevsky as its founding fathers.[2]

*Blanquism takes its name from the French socialist Louis Auguste Blanqui, and denotes the view that a small but determined minority can seize power and "make" the revolution.

Struve's characterization of a broad Populist position was developed in the course of a heated polemical struggle by Russian Marxism against that very position. But we should be wary of rejecting it for that reason. His general view was then taken up by the influential historian of nineteenth-century Russian radicalism V. Ia. Iakovlev (Bogucharsky), who wrote in the immediate prerevolutionary period, and it has formed the basis for virtually all discussions of the problem by Soviet historians.[3] Outside of the Soviet Union, Franco Venturi has also adopted Struve's general viewpoint in his monumental *Roots of Revolution.*

If we grant that the Struve-Venturi definition of Populism is an artificial construct, created by a polemicist and taken over by historians, how can one justify continuing such usage? I think that the primary reason for doing so is that Struve and those who followed him, however polemical their intentions, did discern that the intellectual framework within which Russian radicals operated from the 1860s into the 1880s (and in some cases beyond) had a gestalt of guiding ideas and one must recognize that framework in order to understand the intellectual unity of the period. *Narodnichestvo,* or Populism, is the most convenient designation for the aggregate of those ideas. No other term will serve as well. If one abandons the effort to provide a term that characterizes those ideas and their interrelations, some intellectual relatedness and connection will be endangered. We would then have to fall back on the confusing vocabulary employed by the historical actors themselves, and all but the most experienced reader would find himself or herself lost in a verdant jungle of socialists, Socialist Revolutionaries, Populists, rebels, countrypeople, Jacobins, and nihilists. The fact is that almost all the radicals and revolutionaries of the period, as well as more moderate and amorphous public opinion, were deeply affected by a series of linked ideas, which in turn helped create a much vaguer tissue of belief, prejudice, habit, and slogan that had a profound effect on Russian politics and culture, far beyond the 1860s and 1870s. These ideas were given their initial "radical" formulation by Alexander Herzen, but he was much indebted to the Slavophiles, so we must begin our analysis there.

Most of these cultivated, culturally Westernized landowners, whose ideas dominated the Moscow salon discussion in the 1840s, were from ancient families that had suffered eclipse following the reforms of Peter the Great and the rise to prominence of new grandees under Catherine the Great. The views with which they so shocked their Westerner rivals were complex and have been commonly misinterpreted.[4] Their nationalism, their developed hostility to rationalism, and their deep belief in Orthodoxy and its historical mission have often led historians (particularly Soviet historians) to place them on the far right of the political spectrum.* Others have seized upon their muted opposition to the reign of Nicholas I, their championship of the prerogatives of society as opposed to the state, and their general opposition to serfdom, and called them "liberals," using the concept with that ambiguity which seems unique to students of Russia.

I believe that the label that best describes the Slavophiles is the slightly cumbersome term "utopian reactionaries." They were hostile to the bureaucratized monarchy of their day, but not in the name of socialism, liberalism, or progress. Instead, they opposed to the barbarous present an idealized tableau of a patrimonial, premodern monarchy and repeatedly attacked Peter the Great, whose reforms had sealed the doom of the old aristocracy and created the modern "gentry." The aristocratic inheritance of nineteenth-century Russia was rather weak, but the Slavophiles clearly derived something of their inspiration from it. Hence their opposition to the extreme claims of the autocracy—as well as their horror of Western industrialism, liberalism, and democratic forms.

One reason there has been confusion about where the Slavophiles ought to be placed in the context of nineteenth-century politics is that historians have a reflexive tendency to use a Right-Left political axis as the organizing principle. With such a simple device, one probably does have to locate the Slavophiles on the Right, while the Populists—or at least their more mili-

---

*But not always. See the recent and interesting, if highly uneven, articles contained in the symposium "Literaturnaia kritika rannikh slavianofilov," *Voprosy literatury*, nos. 5, 7, 10, and 12 (1969).

tant representatives—take their place on the extreme Left. Now this linear gradation from "reactionary" to "radical," with intermediate shadings of "conservative," "liberal," and so on, may be roughly satisfactory when one is talking about politics in a modern society, where certain general conceptions about political life are broadly understood and politicking occurs at least partly in the open. But for nineteenth-century Russia it merely obscures the relationships between the various operative intellectual systems. The Slavophiles and those who were strongly marked by Slavophilism had varying political opinions; the political significance of Slavophilism is ambiguous. Despite its intellectual origins in Romantic and counterrevolutionary values, Slavophilism counterposed the Russian people and the Russian state in a provocative fashion that had the profoundest consequences for Russian culture in general and social thought in particular. Since the 1840s, Slavophile ideas have affected all segments of the Russian political spectrum from the extreme Right to the extreme Left. Even a cursory analysis[5] of the political and social ideas of Aleksandr Solzhenitsyn reveals that Slavophile formulations have not lost their attractive power even today—especially today, one might say, for there has been a notable revival of interest in Slavophile ideas among Soviet intellectuals in the last decade. Some of them regard Lenin and Stalin as having robbed Russians of their religious and national inheritance—the same charge that the Slavophiles had leveled against Peter the Great.

The key idea that Populism took from Slavophilism was that the Russian peasant would be the savior of modern Russian society, and perhaps of the Western world as well. In one or another of its guises, this was one of the most widespread and influential ideas entertained by educated Russians in the mid- and late nineteenth century. It repeatedly crops up in the writings of Dostoevsky, and it is equally striking in the later work of Tolstoy (from *Anna Karenina* on), though the two never could agree on the nature of the peasant—or, for that matter, on how his redemptive mission would be carried out. Generations of Russian publicists and politicians simply could not escape the idea or the emotional waves it created. It became embedded in Russian culture; it affected all the political parties that emerged in the brief constitutional period between 1905 and 1917. And, of course, it was the central idea of Populism.

Russian peasants had been living in village communities, with various forms of collective land ownership and governance, since the beginnings of recorded history, although the periodic repartition of communal land almost certainly derived from Peter the Great's fiscal policies in the early eighteenth century. But it was the Slavophiles who in the salon debates of the 1840s first saw the future of the nation in the spiritual and social life of the peasant and in his determined resistance to modernity. As P. V. Annenkov, one of the original opponents of the Slavophiles, wrote in his memoirs:

Everybody is familiar with the fact that a specifically *Russian* socialism, or what could be called popular or folk economic concepts . . . consisted of the doctrine involving the principles of the village commune [*obshchina*] and the guild [*artel'*], i.e., the doctrine of the possession and utilization in common of the means of production. In the modest and limited form which our entire history gave it, *Russian* socialism was, in fact, first advanced by the Slavophiles with the amendment, however, that it served not only as a model of economic organization for anything pertaining to agriculture and the trades but also as an example of combining the idea of Christianity with the needs of external, material existence.[6]

As Annenkov points out, the Slavophile conception of the peasantry was a religious one, tailored to the aristocratic nostalgia of those expatriates from the developing world of the nineteenth century. The Slavophiles felt that the integral Christian civilization of pre-Petrine Russia had been partially preserved—and in a largely unself-conscious way—in the Russian peasant.* He was

*Dostoevsky has been called a Populist *(narodnik)*, and at times his rhetoric could be confused with that of his radical contemporaries. "In virtually every respect we are poorer than the *narod*," he wrote on one occasion; and again, "it is we who ought to bow down before the *narod* and look to it for everything, both thoughts and forms; bow down before the truth of the *narod* and recognize it as the truth." (Quotations from Aleksandr Ivanov, "Zagadka slavianofil'skoi kritiki," *Voprosy literatury*, No. 5 [1969], p. 98.) But the reader soon realizes that the "truth" to which Dostoevsky is referring is ancient and religious—a Slavophile version of peasant truth, not a Populist one.

regarded as a communal being to whom Roman law and private property were alien, whose spiritual faculties had not been fatally damaged by Western rationalism. He still lived in a religious universe that included his social world; he was not yet touched by alienation. As one of the younger Slavophiles put it, in Russia "the people has preserved in itself the gift of self-sacrifice, the freedom of moral inspiration and the respect for tradition. In Russia, the sole shelter of toryism is the black hut of the peasant. In our administration, in our university lecture halls, blows the desiccating wind of whiggery."[7]

The Populists agreed with the Slavophiles in regarding the reintegration of the human personality and the end of alienation as dependent upon the development of peasant communalism, particularly the mir, into the dominant institutions of the Russia of the future. But there were great differences. The most obvious one pertains to the distinction between those who idealized the prerational institutions of the past and those who (to some degree, at any rate) accepted rationalism, individualism, and industrialism, and sought to create a new kind of communalism that would humanize rather than reject the achievements of the French and Industrial revolutions.

Here we must take note of the heritage of the Westerners, who contributed as much to Populism as did the Slavophiles. While for the Slavophiles the reforms of Peter the Great shattered Russia's "natural," organic culture, for the Westerners they meant the beginning of Russia's *rapprochement* with Western Europe, the vital center of Western civilization. For the more radical Westerners, hope for the future lay not in any kind of popular democratism, of a kind that the Populists later discovered, but in the ideas of European liberalism and socialism. These, along with Western philosophy, science, and industrialism, had been brought to Russia first by the state, under Peter and Catherine, and then by rebels like Radishchev and the Decembrists.

Populists vacillated between the Slavophile and the Western inheritances: they were ambivalent about Peter the Great, sensitive to the extreme cosmopolitanism of European socialism, and so on. But despite the powerful influence of more Western Populists like Chernyshevsky, the "reactionary" inheritance of Slavophilism was nearer the surface in Populism than was generally the case with pre-Marxist socialist currents in Western Europe. Sometimes, in Populist writing, industrialism itself seemed the enemy; the various Russian words for "bourgeois" bore a pejorative weight among radicals that seems greater than was usual among Western socialists. This vague but passionate hatred of the bourgeoisie and its works greatly influenced the development of Russian politics before 1917, weakening the "liberal" center at the expense of both the Left and the agrarian Right.

Speaking of the nostalgic and—it might be claimed—reactionary elements in Populist thinking, which he relates to Russia's political and economic backwardness, Alexander Gerschenkron has written that

... the populists, in dealing with the problem [of Russia's destiny], "clearly saw the advantages of Russia's being a late-comer upon the modern historical scene" and "the possibility of adopting the results of foreign experience without incurring the heavy cost of experimentation." But they did so only in order to abandon the argument by an almost imperceptible twist and to raise the paradoxical claim that the preservation of the *old*—of the field commune *(obshchina)* and the workers' cooperative *(artel')*—rather than the easy adoption of the *new* constituted the advantages of backwardness.

But Gerschenkron then cites the admirable response of Venturi to the general view that Populist communalism represented a "tragic surrender of realism to utopia":

An idea that appears to look backward in time, remolds itself on the past, seems to prefer what has been, and to eschew what will be— does really such an idea, whose function is destined to be negative, constitute a utopian retarding factor in economic and social development? Or does it not rather, at least at times, represent an act of *reculer pour mieux sauter,* that is to say, a fruitful attempt to preserve the most precious aspects of the past in order to transmit them to the future? History is not made just by looking forward but, I should say, by looking both forward and backward. Socialism is the idea of community and equality regarding material goods and of an economy based on solidarity. Is not socialism [so conceived] a legacy of the past that has been preserved by being transformed into an ideal for the future?[8]

Clearly the argument between these two distinguished historians transcends the question of the specifically reactionary aspect of Populism. It raises, in fact, the deepest questions of historical development: Is it inevitable or desirable or possible to make the steady achievement of political and economic rationality one's primary criterion for judging a modern nation? Or should we not admit that history is a maze of crooked roads and pathways, leading to destinations that constantly elude our predictive efforts? Should words like "romantic" and "nostalgic," with their implications of the speaker's certitude about historical development, be used by social "scientists" in the fashion that has become habitual to them?

The *image* of the peasant in Slavophilism and Populism is an important index of the difference between the two ideologies. For the Slavophiles, the peasant was religious not merely in the sense of being pious, but in that he still inhabited a religious and nonrational universe; the communal and the religious were inseparable. The Orthodox Church was the spiritual and transcendent manifestation of the communalism that permeated the peasant's daily round and was institutionally embodied in the village commune. But the operation of the community was not "democratic," in the sense of head-counting, majority rule, factionalism, and all of the other detestable innovations of Enlightenment thinking. The organism decided matters according to Christianity and tradition, and not by any kind of politicking. (The Slavophiles distinguished sharply between tradition and Roman law, under which category they tended to subsume a great deal of positive law, and which they regarded as an evil— in the abstract, at any rate. When it actually came to their property rights, they sometimes changed their tune.) And as aristocratic spokesmen often have, the Slavophiles tended to view the peasant as endowed with a kind of childlike sweetness, but capable, at the same time, of being corrupted as a child might be corrupted, and also—more ominously—of being prone to childlike rages and tantrums. In the benevolent social setting of the future, this peculiar moral sweetness and abhorrence of violence would give the new civilization much of its religious and moral tone.

The Populist view of the essence of the peasant was quite different. Communalism retained the central place in the tableau, but it now pointed forward to socialism. The absence of a Western sense of law and in particular a Western sense of private property was conceded to be a survival, a kind of primitivism, but a fortunate one that would enable those whom history had seemingly left behind to leap over the debris of Europe's failures into the socialist future. Here certainly was one of the "advantages of backwardness."

Many Populists were violently opposed to the Slavophile notion that the Russian peasantry was profoundly religious. Their view was well expressed by that radical Westerner of the previous generation, Vissarion Belinsky. "What a lie!" Belinsky wrote in his famous *Letter to Gogol* of 1847.

The foundation of religiosity is pietism, reverence, the fear of God. But the Russian pronounces God's name while scratching his backside. He says of the icon: "it's good for praying—and you can cover the pots with it, too."
Take a harder look and you will see that this is a profoundly atheistic people. There is a lot of superstition but not a trace of religiosity . . . mystical exaltation is not in the nature [of the Russian people]; it has too much good sense, its mind is too lucid and positive for that, and it may be in this very fact that the immensity of its historical destiny resides.[9]

Others, like S. M. Kravchinsky, a prominent Populist spokesman in the 1870s, were willing to admit that the Russian people were "religious," if by that one means merely a way of life that is dominated by ethical norms and full of ritual observance.[10] But it was the schismatics and the sectarians* who really stirred the interest of many Populists.[11] The sectarians in particular, with their denial of Orthodox ritual, their rationalism, and their belief in the earthly achievement of the New Jerusalem, seemed very near to the secular radicalism of the intelligentsia. Surely it would not be hard to lift the almost transparent veil of mysticism and irrationalism and reveal to them that their ideas were, in essence, identical with those of the intelligentsia, that their radical millenarianism was only a religiously expressed socialism. But this project, which attracted a good many socialists in the 1870s, was never realized. The Old Believers and the sectarians, whatever their religious differences with the Orthodox peasantry, and despite the persecution that the government had visited on them, belonged to the world of the Russian village and countryside. They remained finally as difficult to reach as their Orthodox brethren.

Thus there were two major Populist views of peasant religiosity: either it was a myth, zealously fostered by government and clerical interests for their own purposes, or it was a particular archaic vocabulary for expressing indigenous social and economic values. If the latter were true, the task of the intelligentsia was to help the peasant understand what he really believed, to eliminate the religious mode of expression, to raise him to self-consciousness.

And finally, while the Slavophiles regarded the peasant as childlike, submissive, and hostile to violence (the wishful thinking in this depiction is evident), the Populists wanted to see the peasant as rebellious, independent—able and willing, in the last analysis, to conquer what was rightfully his. While the Slavophiles painted an idyllic picture of traditional communal life, rich in religious ritual and inspiration, pacific and unchanging, the Populists turned to the traditions of peasant rebellion and

*The schismatics, generally known as Old Believers, separated from the Orthodox Church in the seventeenth century, having refused to accept a variety of reforms in Church ritual. The sectarians were Russian offshoots of European Protestantism, although their doctrine and practice took on a thoroughly Russian luxuriance and eccentricity.

viewed the uprisings of Stenka Razin and Pugachëv as foreshad-
owings of the peasant revolution that was soon to occur. Populists
whose fantasies and imaginings tended to the bloodthirsty, such
as Mikhail Bakunin, were enthralled by the Pugachëv rebellion:

The brigand, in Russia, is the true and only revolutionary—the revolutionary without phrasemaking and without bookish rhetoric. Popular revolution is born from the merging of the revolt of the brigand
with that of the peasant. . . . Such were the revolts of Stenka Razin
and Pugachëv . . . and even today this is still the world of the Russian
revolution.[12]

But most of the Populists, most of the time, did not envisage the
revolution in quite so elementally destructive a fashion; the notion of a new *Pugachëvshchina* was not something that many
serious and educated Russians, even radical ones, could contem-
plate without misgivings. But fascination with the folklore of
peasant revolt was an important aspect of the new image of the
Russian peasant that the Populists were creating. Both P. I. Iakushkin and I. A. Khudiakov, two of the radical folklorists of the
1860s, were deeply interested in what the *narod* had made of
these revolts in its folklore. And there is no question that the
Populists were psychologically impelled to endow the peasants
with the very activist qualities that the Slavophiles denied and,
perhaps, feared. As the Populists saw the matter, the peasant had
to provide the elemental force that would sweep away the old
order. If the peasant could not or would not do this, the first line
of radical defense was to take refuge in Blanquist and Jacobin
ideas, or in other forms of intelligentsia elitism. Beyond these
remedies lay helplessness, apathy, and despair—and the kind of
"conversion" to Slavophile nationalism and conservatism that
afflicted the movement in times when reaction seemed triumphant.[13]

The Slavophiles were opposed to and at times terrified of peasant revolution. Their notion of the coming of a new civilization
to Russia was vaguer and much less plausible than the Populists';
it depended on the conversion of a dominant part of the Russian
elite to their own values—a most unlikely proposition. And one

feels that beneath their hopeful talk they suspected it would never happen.

The strongly elitist cast to both Slavophilism and Populism emerged with particular clarity when disappointments had been suffered. The Slavophiles, indeed, scarcely tried to *reach* the people at all. So we return to the dilemma of the intelligentsia's relationship to the Russian masses. When Lenin pessimistically and somewhat contemptuously said that the working class by itself could achieve only "trade union consciousness," he was responding to much the same dilemma. The relationship between socialist intellectuals and their working-class constituency, a central problem in the history of socialism, was posed in Russia with special sharpness and even brutality. With the help of World War I and the self-destructiveness of the Russian government, Lenin found a "solution" for the problem, but it was a perilous resolution indeed for the humane and liberating core of socialism.

Another, rather vaguer idea that was commonly held by Slavophiles and Populists has generally been called the "idea of the separate path" for Russian development. Partially the product of feelings of inferiority among Russian intellectuals, this notion could easily become the vehicle for compensatory feelings of superiority. The idea that one nation should have a path of development distinct from that of others does not strike the late-twentieth-century reader as nearly so strange as it did the opponents of the Slavophiles and the Populists. But the Westerners of the 1840s, influenced to one degree or another by Hegelianism, found the idealized communalism of the Slavophiles hard to reconcile with historical progress. And the early Russian Marxists were committed to a rigid and unitary developmental scheme (which may have owed more to Engels than to Marx) that they believed all nations would experience. To Georgy Plekhanov, the first Russian theoretician of Marxism, it was absurd to think that a nation might in any way "skip" the capitalist stage of development and move directly from agrarian backwardness to socialism —and Plekhanov's early Marxist articles attacked the Populists on just this point. The bourgeoisie, he argued, had first to be able to perform its essential tasks: the achievement of a certain amount of political freedom and, above all, the creation of industrialism and material wealth. If a group of political conspirators tried to seize power and "make" the revolution before capitalism had matured and begun to decay, the result was sure to be a new kind of despotism—what Plekhanov liked to refer to as "Peruvian communism." And in certain respects the history of the Soviet Union has borne out Plekhanov's strictures.

Our own attitude toward historical regularity, toward models of historical development, is—or should be—far more cautious and chastened. Certainly we should recall Venturi's words, that history is made "by looking both forward and backward"—to which the pessimist might add that it is only with the greatest luck that we ever "make" history at all. In any case, the violation of some preordained scheme of development seems much less heretical to us than it seemed to the Hegelian and Marxist critics of the nineteenth century.

The great hope of the first generation of Russian Slavophiles was that Russia had a unique destiny among the nations of the world: to save herself and others from the disastrous path of modernity that had begun when the Roman Catholic Church cut itself off from the Orthodoxy in the late Middle Ages. Papal autocracy and Roman rationalism, according to the Slavophiles, had bred the extremes of Protestant subjectivism and the political rationalism that had created both modern rationalizing despotism and secular political democracy—as embodied, most catastrophically, in the French Revolution and Napoleon.[14] In the course of the nineteenth century, Western philosophy and social forms had increasingly revealed their bankruptcy. By the 1840s, the Slavophiles hoped, the time was rapidly approaching when Russia would reverse her disastrous emulation of this brutal and diseased Western civilization and recover her old Christian communalism, to the ultimate benefit of "the West" as well.

None of the Slavophiles could say with any precision how this transformation was to be effected. None of them, it is fair to say, could really imagine what the new civilization would be like. But despite substantial inner uncertainty, they projected a faith in

Russia's future that their Westerner opponents often derided but may unconsciously have envied. Herzen once noted acidly that Russia's principal influence upon Europe consisted in the dispatching of troops in times of radical upheaval, but he was to develop a messianism akin to that of the Slavophiles.

The Populist notion of Russia's "separate path" and unique destiny centered on the idea that the communal institutions of the peasantry were a primitive form of protosocialism and that when the peasantry finally erupted into revolution a socialist society either would emerge, more or less spontaneously, from the upheaval or could be brought about through a combination of the people's instinct and the political leadership of the intelligentsia. Now this general idea was often expressed in a primitive and sloganistic fashion in the 1860s, and later as well. But one might go into considerable detail about the many technical problems that would have to be faced. What should the state apparatus do in the postrevolutionary period? How strong should it be? What kind of aid should the state render to the popular institutions, political and economic, that the spirit of the people would bring into existence? What form would those institutions take? And a central question in the debates between those who trusted the people wholeheartedly and those who did not: How long would the state have to endure? Populists tinged with Jacobinism (in some cases more than tinged) tended to stress the importance of the revolutionary state. Those of a more anarchist cast of mind—and there was a strong anarchist tendency in Populism—feared that the revolutionary state might turn into a new kind of despotism, that it might separate itself from the people's aspirations rather than embody them. Bakunin, in his *Letters to a Frenchman*, wrote that

Throughout the world the authoritarian revolutionists have done very little to promote revolutionary activity, primarily because *they always wanted to make the Revolution by themselves, by their own authority and their own power.* This could not fail to severely constrict the scope of revolutionary action because it is impossible, even for the most energetic and enterprising authoritarian revolutionary, to understand and deal effectively with all the manifold problems generated by the Revolution. For every dictatorship, be it exercised by an individual or collectively by relatively few individuals, is necessarily very circumscribed, very shortsighted, and its limited perception cannot, therefore, penetrate the depth and encompass the whole complex range of popular life; just as it is impossible for even the most gigantic vessel to contain the depths and vastness of the ocean. . . .

What should the revolutionary authorities—and there should be as few of them as possible—do to organize and spread the Revolution? They must promote the Revolution not by issuing decrees but by stirring the masses to action. They must under no circumstances foist any artificial organization whatsoever upon the masses. On the contrary, they should foster the self-organization of the masses into autonomous bodies, federated from the bottom upward.[15]

On another occasion, Bakunin accused "doctrinaire socialists" (and although he was referring chiefly to Marxists, his accusation was directed against a much larger group) of trying to overthrow existing regimes in order to create a dictatorship of their own. Such socialists, he angrily claimed,

. . . are the enemies of contemporary governments only because they wish to replace them. They are enemies of the present governmental structure, because it excludes the possibility of their dictatorship. At the same time they are the most devoted friends of governmental power. For if the revolution destroyed this power by actually freeing the masses, it would deprive this pseudorevolutionary minority of any hope to harness the masses in order to make them the beneficiaries of their own government policy.[16]

In the 1880s and 1890s, in part because the Populists were then faced with a full-dress attack from the Russian Marxists, the debate about the possibilities inherent in peasant institutions took on a greater economic complexity and sophistication. In 1882, V. Vorontsov, a rather unrevolutionary Populist, wrote a book entitled *The Fate of Capitalism in Russia.*[17] There was scarcely a trace of Slavophile messianism in this well-argued and influential economic treatise. Rather, Vorontsov stressed that for a variety of economic reasons—chiefly her late entry into the industrialization process—Russia could not follow the capitalist path best represented by English development. The industrial products of Russian capitalism would never be able to capture their share of the world market, and the peasantry was too poor and backward to provide the necessary market, either; therefore the government should abandon its efforts to promote capitalism (which were beginning to be noticeable by this time) and devote itself to strengthening the communes and the small producers' cooperatives. Branches of industry that were of necessity very large and demanded large amounts of capital should be nationalized.

Vorontsov simply urged this point of view on the Russian government. But his program might have been expected to appeal more to moderate Populist radicals than to the men actually in charge of the Ministry of Finance; in that sense, one might say that it was a blueprint for postrevolutionary action. As Richard Pipes points out,[18] Vorontsov's scheme was "by no means utopian," and in fact was not unlike the so-called New Economic Policy (NEP) that Lenin introduced in 1921.

In the 1860s and the 1870s, however, the idea of the "separate path" was discussed in much simpler and more moral terms. One can see in it a strong dose of nationalism and wounded pride: like the early Christians, Russian radicals believed that "the last shall be first." Slavophile and Populist proponents of Russia as the creator of a new civilization had a good deal in common, despite their differences as to what that new civilization would be like.

One of the most significant aspects of the Slavophile position was that it separated the modern Russian state from Russian society and located Russian virtue in the latter. This hostility to the state was not set forth in clear, unambiguous language, even by Ivan Kireevsky, who came closest to directly expressing it. What we find instead is an attack on the despotic, rationalizing institutions of the West, coupled with a denunciation of Peter the Great for having attempted to import these institutions to Russia.

Khomiakov was a good deal more ambiguous on this point than Kireevsky. Khomiakov believed that the development of the autocracy was necessary for the creation of a strong and unified

Russia—but that necessity was tragic, in that the triumph of the autocracy meant wounding, seriously if not mortally, the communal basis of Russian society. Although he detested Peter the Great and his "Germanization" of Russia, Khomiakov was even willing, upon occasion, to approve some of Peter's state-building policies.

Kireevsky, by contrast, never spoke of Peter's achievements, and his picture of the premodern sovereign power in Russia is illuminating. The prince, to begin with, had the most limited power over the life of society: acting as a kind of supreme judge was about the extent of it. The various communities determined their own internal life in a traditional way and were directly influenced by the network of churches, monasteries, and other ecclesiastical centers that infused the social body with the spirit of Orthodoxy. The princes played a much larger role in foreign affairs, but the striking feature of Kireevsky's tableau—which is, of course, of limited historical accuracy—is that Russian society lived its own life, undisturbed by the state.[19] All this changed with the coming of Peter the Great. The modern Russian state violated sacred tradition without let or hindrance and interfered in the life of its citizens to the very limits of its ability. To Kireevsky, although for political reasons he was cautious about saying so, the principal bearer of modern rationalism in Russia was not the middle class, as in England or France, but the Romanov dynasty and its state apparatus, no matter how "conservative" they appeared or believed themselves to be.

As time passed, the antistate element in Slavophilism conflicted with Russian nationalism (which was already obvious in the first Slavophile generation, particularly in Khomiakov). Among the second-generation Slavophiles, Iury Samarin, for example, found it possible to serve the state in a variety of capacities, from emancipating the serfs to fact-finding missions in rebellious Poland. It is in Populism that we find Slavophile antistatism picked up and developed. Sometimes Populist expressions of the opposition between state and society have an uncannily Slavophile ring, even when they are most "radical." Georgy Plekhanov, writing in 1880 when he was still a Populist, described the phenomenon in the following terms:

According to us, the inner history of Russia consists only in the long tragedy-filled tales of the struggle to the death between two forms of collective life which are diametrically opposed: the *obshchina* which springs from the people and the form which is at the same time statist and individualist. This struggle becomes bloody and violent like a storm when the masses are in movement during the revolts of Razin and Pugachev. And it has never stopped for one moment, though taking on the most varying forms.[20]

Furthermore, many of the Populists believed not only that the state was deeply opposed to the interests and human development of the Russian people but that it was weak and artificial as well; it did not grow organically out of Russian soil; it corresponded to the interests of no segment of the population, not even the gentry. Franco Venturi, in describing the attitude of the People's Will revolutionaries toward the Russian state, writes that they found it "very different from Western states. How was it possible to describe it as 'a commission of the plenipotentiaries of the ruling classes'? In fact, of course, it was an independent organization, hierarchical and disciplined, 'which would hold the people in economic and political slavery even if there were no privileged class in existence.' "[21]

To almost all Marxists, such a conception of the state was absurd, impossible by definition, as it were. Marx, in 1882, had supplied a foreward to Plekhanov's Russian translation of the *Communist Manifesto,* in which he was by no means totally unsympathetic to Populist aspirations. Marx speculated that if the outbreak of a revolution in Russia touched off the proletarian revolution in the West, Russia might indeed be able to utilize the peasant commune to pass immediately to a higher stage of development.[22] And Marx and Engels were both deeply moved and impressed by the struggle of the People's Will terrorists, which finally resulted in the death of Alexander II in March 1881. But the Populist notion of a state without real class content was impossible to swallow. The state, to Marx, was an "epiphenomenon of the class struggle,"[23] which would disappear only with the transition to communism. As Engels put the matter:

The state is therefore by no means a power imposed on society from without; just as little is it "the reality of the moral idea," "the image and reality of reason," as Hegel maintains. Rather, it is a product of society at a particular stage of development; it is the admission that this society has involved itself in insoluble self-contradiction and is cleft into irreconcilable antagonisms, which it is powerless to exorcise. But in order that these antagonisms, classes with conflicting economic interests, shall not consume themselves and society in fruitless struggle, a power, apparently standing above society, has become necessary to moderate the conflict and keep it within the bounds of "order"; and this power, arisen out of society, but placing itself above it and increasingly alienating itself from it, is the state.

. . . As the state arose from the need to keep class antagonisms in check, but also arose in the thick of the fight between the classes, it is normally the state of the most powerful, economically ruling class, which . . . becomes also the politically ruling class, and so acquires new means of holding down and exploiting the oppressed class.[24]

What should we make of these structural similarities between Slavophilism and Populism? How should they be understood? The vague term "influence" is of no use here, though in some cases it might be applied in a highly specific fashion. Many young women and men in the late 1850s, and subsequently, became Populists without being at all aware of Slavophilism. And even in those cases in which individuals had been attracted to Slavophile ideas and later became Populists, we must ask *why* they made this transition, and why they made it when they did.

In discussing the relationship between Slavophilism and Populism, we must return to one of the large themes of this study: the relationship between the educated minority in Russia and the masses of the population, the peasantry. The Slavophiles, like the Populists, had a moral vision of communality, which they found missing in the Russian society of their day, which they found deeply attractive, and which they persuaded themselves would be part of a better future for Russia. Both parties found this ideal embodied in the peasantry's way of life. But both found it extremely difficult to make any contact with the source of their values. There is thus some continuity in the vision of the good society entertained by significant portions of the Russian elite over several generations; the quality of Russian life under a crude, rather inefficient bureaucratized monarchy obviously made Russians yearn in a special way for communal forms of life, as an Englishman or a Frenchman did not. And the survival of the peasant commune in Russia offered an indigenous model, the adoption of which could also minister to wounded national pride.

In confronting the question of the "rise" or beginnings of Populism, we must not fall into the trap of supposing that Slavophile modes of thinking suddenly came to a halt in the late 1850s and Populism took over. Slavophile influences persisted, in various forms, throughout the remainder of the nineteenth century and into the twentieth. The writers and critics who in the 1860s gathered around the journals *Time (Vremia)* and *Epoch*—the Dostoevsky brothers, Apollon Grigor'ev, Nikolai Strakhov—were known as *pochvenniki,* from the Russian term *pochva* (which means "soil," and as used by these writers picked up some of the nationalist connotation of the German *Boden*). Here a more conservative communal ideal persisted, along with the Slavophile hatred of "abstract reason" and the insistence on the religiosity of the Russian people. In the next generation, the philosopher Vladimir Solov'ëv based much of his philosophical speculation on Slavophile themes, and a good deal of the so-called Russian religious renaissance of the twentieth century indicates an intellectual and spiritual debt to Slavophilism. Nicolas Berdyaev in particular reveals his Slavophile roots in his advocacy of a Christian and irrationalist reintegration of the human personality.

Still, the obvious fact is that, beginning in the late 1850s, most of the Russian intelligentsia was much more receptive to an activist, socialist communalism than to the socially passive, religious kind, where human reintegration would be a mystical and private achievement. This preference can largely be explained by the reforming excitement of the new era, by the sense of human possibility and the desirability of change with which *obshchestvo* responded to the death of Nicholas I. And the prospect that emerged of the *liberation* of the peasant brought a kind of anticipatory atmosphere that was more hospitable to visions of radical social reform than to those of what amounted to religious conversion; people tended to project their communal vision boldly into the future, rather than to try to excavate it from the past.

Of course the intelligentsia was not uniformly radical in the 1860s, and not all of *obshchestvo* was thirsty for communal forms of salvation and human reintegration. The journalistic success of the renegade Westerner Mikhail Katkov, following the Polish revolt of 1863, showed that many educated Russians would become devoted readers of journals whose point of view was unabashedly patriotic and Pan-Slav.[25] And although *obshchestvo* became more Populist during the 1860s, it soon became clear that radical reform or revolution was not the simple, almost automatic affair it had seemed to many students and young radicals between 1859 and 1862. In fact, radical discouragement with "the masses" is one of the salient characteristics of the Left intelligentsia between 1863 and 1870.

After the death of Emperor Nicholas in 1855, reformist sentiment mounted rapidly in Russia; what was needed was a "progressive" ideology that could convincingly assert a socialist future. But after 1848 and the Crimean War such an ideological vision could not be too "European"; it had to take full account of Russia's impatience with the Western masters to whom she had so long been apprenticed. Above all, it had to put the Russian people, the *narod,* at the heart of things—not as the bearers of a timeless religious truth (as the Slavophiles had seen them); the *narod* now had to be young, vital, strong, and the vision had to be social.

It was Alexander Herzen who produced the intellectual synthesis and the political vocabulary for the young radicals after 1855. He was the founding father of Populism. His basic ideas, drawn from the arsenals of both Slavophiles and Westerners (and owing something to Proudhon as well), were simple and wonderfully uplifting. That they were lacking in economic sophistication and did not provide detailed blueprints for the future in no way

diminished their appeal. Once they had become the common
property of the intelligentsia, Herzen's successors, beginning
with N. G. Chernyshevsky, could rephrase and refine them and
provide various economic underpinnings for them.

Born illegitimate into a wealthy and aristocratic Moscow family,* Herzen as a young man had gravitated toward French socialism, had undergone political exile and returned to lead the
Westerner party in the Moscow salons of the 1840s.[26] Much of the
significance of his early life consists in the process by which his
basically aristocratic sense of liberty was transmuted into socialist
conviction. His mature opinions began to take shape in 1847,
when he was thirty-five years old and in effect already in European exile. He disliked what he saw of French and Italian society
on his travels: even before experiencing the Revolution of 1848
in Paris, Herzen was disposed to be "disillusioned" with Europe.
When the new French Republic called in regular army troops
against the workers of Paris in the June Days, Herzen repudiated
not only the French bourgeoisie but Paris (now a "decrepit vam-
pire," sucking the blood of her working-class victims) and the
French radical tradition that had sustained him so long. This was
his first large area of agreement with his former opponents, the
Slavophiles: that modern Europe was politically, intellectually,
and morally bankrupt. "Europe is approaching a terrible cataclysm," he wrote in his essay *The Russian People and Socialism*
(1851).

The world of the Middle Ages has come to an end. The world of
feudalism is expiring. The religious and political revolutions are pe-
tering out under the weight of their own complete impotence. They
have great achievements to their credit, but they have failed to
complete their tasks. They have stripped throne and altar of the
prestige they once enjoyed, but they have not established the era of
freedom. They have lit new desires in the hearts of men but they
have not provided ways of satisfying them. Parliamentarianism, Protestantism—these are mere prevarications, temporary measures, attempts to stave off the flood, which can arrest only for a short time

---

*The family's name was Iakovlev; the name "Herzen," meaning child "of the heart,"
indicates his illegitimate status.

the process of death and rebirth. The time for them has passed. Since 1848 it has become apparent that no amount of delving into Roman law, of barren casuistry, of thin philosophic deism, of sterile religious rationalism can hold back society from fulfilling its destiny.[27]

In this welter of violence and decay, wrote Herzen (not altogether accurately), "men's eyes turn involuntarily to the East." He then went to considerable pains to disassociate the Russian people from the Russian government, speaking rather vaguely of a Pan-Slav Federation of the future and remarking that "the historic forms of the state have never answered to the national ideal of the Slavs, an ideal which is vague, instinctive if you like, yet by the same token gives promise for the future of a truly remarkable vitality."[28]

Developing this dichotomy between the people and the state, Herzen spoke of a curious "detachment" or "apathy," with which the Russian people have historically responded to cataclysmic changes visited upon them from above or outside: the reception of Christianity, or (and here the Slavophile note is strong) how "five hundred years later, a part of Russia accepted in just the same manner a civilization that had been ordered from abroad and bore upon it a German trademark."[29] Rebutting Jules Michelet's silly charge that "the Russian is a liar and a thief," Herzen noted that

The Russian peasant who has, as you have rightly observed, a strong aversion to every form of landed property, who is improvident and indolent by temperament, has gradually and imperceptibly found himself caught up in the tentacles of the German bureaucracy and the feudal power. He has submitted to this degrading yoke with, I agree, the passivity of despair, but he has never believed either in the authority of his lord, or in the justice of the courts, or in the equity of the administration. For almost two hundred years, his whole life has been one long, dumb, passive opposition to the existing order of things: he has endured oppression, he has groaned under it: but he has never accepted anything that goes on outside the life of the rural commune.[30]

The Slavophile elements here are striking but they are undergoing changes: the separation of the real life of the people from the despotic, alien force of the state, identified as "German"; the hostility to the notion of landed property and the focus on the rural commune as the center of life. Even the description of the peasantry's indolence and improvidence is not far from the Slavophile point of view, although the Slavophiles were usually less forthright about it. But Herzen laid more stress on the pure *oppression* that had been the peasants' lot, and there is a hint of possible rebelliousness in the future. There is no mention of the religious element in pre-Petrine culture: the communalism of the peasant appears fundamentally secular. And Herzen dealt with the peasantry's attachment to the Tsar the way almost all socialist (and liberal) historians have chosen to do: the peasant regards the Tsar as a mythic "embodiment of justice," as an "avenger of evils."[31] Apart from the idealized Tsar and—Herzen admitted—the clergy to some extent, the peasant is hostile to every segment of Russian society. Through laws that he in no way understands and that have nothing to do with his own way of life— which, like the state power itself, were imposed on him from above—the bureaucracy and the nobility attempt to squeeze from the peasant every ounce of toil and as much money as they possibly can. Against this oppression the peasants employ the only weapons available—cunning and duplicity. "Outside the commune," Herzen concluded, "there are no obligations for him—there is simply violence."[32]

Herzen's analysis of the peasants' way of life in their own milieu was quite as fanciful as that of the Slavophiles—only secular and protosocialist.

"There is one fact," he wrote, "that has never been denied by anyone who has any real first-hand knowledge of the Russian people."

And that is that they very rarely cheat one another. An almost boundless good faith prevails amongst them: contracts and written agreements are quite unheard of.

Problems connected with surveying are necessarily extremely complicated on account of the perpetual subdivision of the land according to the number of people working on it. And yet the peace of the Russian countryside is never disturbed by any complaints or litigation. . . . The petty differences that arise are quickly settled either by the elders or by the commune: everyone abides by such decisions without reservation. The same thing happens in the nomadic communes of artisans (the *artel*).[33]

And, he claimed, communal bonds are even closer when the peasants are not Orthodox, but dissenters. Finally he came to the point:

The commune has preserved the Russian people from Mongol barbarism, from Imperial civilization, from the Europeanized landlords and from the German bureaucracy: the organic life of the commune has persisted despite all attempts made on it by authority, badly mauled though it has been at times. By good fortune it has survived right into the period that witnesses the rise of Socialism in Europe.

For Russia this has been a most happy Providence.[34]

The historical role of both the gentry and the autocracy, Herzen believed, was finished. The gentry had been created by Peter the Great to staff the army and bureaucracy that he brought into being. It had then been instrumental in bringing Western ideas into Russia (which Herzen, it appears, still regarded as essential). But its usefulness is over; its feebleness and rootlessness stand fully revealed. And the government, Herzen remarked mordantly, "which originally cut itself off from the people in the name of civilization, has now, a hundred years later, cut itself off from civilization in the name of absolutism."[35] For civilization, in nineteenth-century Europe, is crucially bound up with liberalism and socialism, so the "civilizing" role of the autocracy had come to an end. From the accession of Nicholas I, "the sole aim of Tsarism has been Tsarism, ruling for ruling's sake. . . . But autocracy for autocracy's sake is ultimately an impossibility: it is too pointless, too sterile."[36]

For the Slavophiles, the reign of Peter the Great was the focal point in the break with the idyllic Russian past. Peter's reign was less crucial for Herzen—it merely inaugurated the latest phase in the far older story of the oppression of the Russian people—

but one feels the memory of the arguments with the Slavophiles a few years earlier about what Peter's reign had meant. In the 1840s Herzen had defended Peter; now he regarded him with more mixed feelings as the consolidator of the latest and most ruthless phase of the oppression of the Russian people, the creator of the gentry and modern bureaucracy. Peter the Westernizer and civilizer was not mentioned.

The Slavophiles had no real prescription for the autocracy and the gentry. They clearly felt that the Emperor should in some way, by some social alchemy, transform himself into the "pious Tsar" of old. He should curb, if not eliminate, the bureaucracy; he should allow the body of the Russian people to infuse in him the old Orthodox, communal spirit. He should again become a benevolent patriarch, instead of a semirationalist importer of secular Western ideas. But this was scarcely a program. The Slavophiles were oddly silent, too, about their own estate, the gentry. Many of their attitudes were aristocratic, but there was no place for the gentry as a group in their murky vision of Russia's renewal, except the assumption that people like themselves would have to take the lead in creating the new Christian and communal Russia. It is plausible that had the Slavophiles been able to function in a more political fashion, they would have provided a distinctly agrarian kind of leadership; their opposition to the crown might have become more outspokenly aristocratic and at the same time more mundane. But with the concrete defense of interests so difficult a matter, their elitism retained its distinctly historical quality: more redolent of the older aristocratic groups that had been ground under the heel of Muscovite absolutism than of the real social existence of the gentry in their own time.

Herzen's prescriptions were neater and simpler. Both the autocracy and the gentry had made the rather malign (though undeniably significant) contribution to Russia's history that they had to make. It was time for them to leave the stage.

Herzen found the Russian government in the time of Nicholas bankrupt—and so was Europe after 1848. Europe, he thought, had "stated the problem" of the opposition between the individual and society but had not solved it. And Europe,

now on the point of taking the first step forward in a social revolution, is confronted by a country that can provide an actual instance of an attempt—a crude, barbaric attempt, perhaps, but still an attempt of a sort—in the direction of the division of the land amongst those who work it. And observe that this lesson is not provided by civilized Russia but by the people themselves in their daily lives. We Russians who have absorbed European civilization cannot hope to be more than a means to an end—the yeast in the leavening—a bridge between the Russian people and revolutionary Europe.[37]

Finally, Herzen spoke of people like himself, of their feelings, of the literature they have produced, and of their historical position, in accents that recall Pëtr Chaadaev:

The true character of Russian thought, whether in poetry or speculation, emerges only in a fully developed, vital form after the accession of Nicholas. The distinctive traits of this movement are a new and tragic sense of right and wrong, an implacable spirit of negation, a bitter irony, a tortured self-questioning. Sometimes a note of wild laughter accompanies it, but it is laughter without gaiety. . . . The emancipated Russian is the most independent creature in the world. And what indeed could there be to restrain him? A sense of the past? . . . But then isn't the starting point of modern Russia just the denial of tradition and national sentiment? . . . The only element in our tradition which we accept is that involved in our organic, our national way of life: and that is inherent in our very being: it is in our blood, it acts upon us more like an instinct than like some external authority to which we feel we must bend our wills. We are independent because we possess nothing. There are literally no demands upon our affections. All our memories are tinged with bitterness and resentment. The fruits of civilization and learning were offered us at the end of the knout.[38]

But, as had the Slavophiles before him, Herzen perceived the advantages inherent in Russia's backward and benighted state. Authority in Russia was naked force; the cards were on the table. The Russian revolution would never replace Tsar Nicholas by a multitude of "other Tsars," and by this Herzen meant the disingenuous, hypocritical, and repressive apparatus of the bourgeois republic. "Russia," he proclaimed, "will never be Protestant. Russia will never be *juste-milieu.*" And he concluded on a note of mingled hope and pessimism: there were the Russian masses, still in the apathetic slumber of those who had long been oppressed; and there were those few like Bakunin and Petrashevsky* who had made efforts, as had Herzen himself, to advance the cause of liberty in Russia. Clearly Herzen believed, as had Ivan Kireevsky, that the virtue residing in the people could found the new society only with the assistance of people like Bakunin and himself—with the help, in effect, of the intelligentsia.

By 1851, Herzen's exile had begun officially: he had decided some months before not to obey the government's orders to return to Russia and had thus automatically become an émigré. In that year he published both *The Russian People and Socialism* and a much lengthier discussion of the same issues, entitled *On the Development of Revolutionary Ideas in Russia.* The first two editions were in French; it appeared in Russia for the first time when it was clandestinely printed by P. G. Zaichnevsky, a particularly militant student radical of the early 1860s. Significantly, the translation was dedicated to the students of the University of Moscow.[39]

At the outset of the book, Herzen spoke of the departure from Russia that was to begin his lifelong exile, although of course he did not know that at the time. He described the peasant villages that he was leaving: tiny clusters of huts, dwarfed by the great forests and the vast, snow-covered plains. And he turned quickly to the character and style of their peasant inhabitants, whose way of life, he observed, had changed very little since the horsemen of Genghis Khan had surprised them so many centuries before —a way of life, as he put it, somewhere between geology and history. He spoke of the gulf that separated the village from both gentry and bureaucracy, and of the qualities of the peasant him-

*M. V. Butashevich-Petrashevsky was a junior official in the Russian Foreign Ministry and a disciple of Fourier. His "circle" was broken up by the police in April 1849. Petrashevsky died in Siberia in 1867.

self—still a "barbarian," but of the kind whose historical life had not yet begun, rather than of the kind whose historical role had come and gone.

He has been conquered but he is no lackey. His rough, democratic and patriarchal language has not been schooled in ante-chambers. His qualities of masculine beauty have endured the dual slavery of tsar and landlord. The peasant of Great Russia and the Ukraine has a most penetrating intelligence and an almost southern vivacity, which one is astonished to find in the North. He speaks well and much; the habit of being always with his neighbors has rendered him communicative.[40]

And Herzen went on to compare the two posting stations on either side of the Russian-Livonian border: the Russian one chaotic and disorganized, with a Russian officer shouting for service, threatening the lackadaisical peasants with all sorts of visitations and retributions from the higher authorities, and eventually exhausting himself, while the peasants dealt with him in the time-honored manner: confessing their derelictions in a singsong tone, accepting the abuse, and waiting for him to exhaust himself in futile threats. The Livonian station, by contrast, was neat and clean, dominated by a middle-class Lutheran spirit of tidiness, efficiency, adherence to regulations, and German patriotism, with a strong dose of servility. Across the Russian border, the indigenous inhabitants had remained savages while their Baltic German masters oppressed them tenaciously but with a defensiveness that revealed a loss of vitality and an isolation from the main paths of historical development. The communal institutions and spirit of Russia were lacking. However disorganized and—for the upper class—inefficient the Russian village and posting station may have been, it contained a vitality and a communalism that stamped it as having a historical destiny. The oppressive but faded world of Germany was—behind its orderly and impressive facade—already a thing of the past. The Baltic Germans had a "fixed morality," the Russians a "moral instinct." The Russians, in the diluted Hegelian argot of the day, were a "young" people, the Germans an "old" one. And Herzen grandly extended the contrast: it was not merely the Baltic Germans or the Germans, but all of Europe that was "old," that had played out its historical role; it was "the Slavic world" that was "young." Only in America, Herzen suggested,[41] might the great ideas of European civilization yet be realized, on a soil "less encumbered with ruins."

Concluding his introduction of "Young Russia," Herzen sketched the rise of Russian power since Peter the Great—a rude, coarse, demanding power that seated itself uninvited at the council table of Europe. And he then had the "temerity," as he put it, to suggest that, at bottom, those millions of Russians and the working masses of Europe were at one: without knowing it, they had a common enemy, "the old feudal and monarchical edifice," and a common aspiration, "the social revolution."

The Emperor Nicholas can at will execute designs, the sense of which escapes him, humiliate the sterile arrogance of France and the majestic prudence of England—we do not have the least pity for those invalids. But what he cannot do is prevent the formation of another league behind his back. He cannot prevent Russian intervention from being the coup de grâce for all the monarchs of the continent, for the entire reaction and the beginning of the armed social struggle —terrible and decisive.

The imperial power of the tsar will not survive that struggle. Victor or vanquished, it belongs to the past; it is not Russian, it is profoundly German—byzantinized German. So it has two titles to death.

And we have two titles to life—the socialist element and youth.

"Sometimes young people die too," a most distinguished man said to me in London, as we were discussing the slavic question.

"Certainly," I answered, "but what is far more certain is that old people always die."[42]

Herzen's view of Russian historical development from the Middle Ages was strikingly close to that of Khomiakov:[43] both depicted medieval Russian society as isolated, local and communal in its social organization. Herzen, like the Slavophiles, now viewed the prince in Old Russia as benevolent, patriarchal, and limited in his functions, but Herzen laid heavy stress on the prince's lack of an organic connection with the territory over which he ruled.* For the Slavophiles, of course, Christianity was at the very heart of Old Russian culture and intimately bound up with the communal order, while Herzen saw the Christianization of Russia as just one more of those cataclysms that periodically affected Russian society, like the Mongol invasions or Peter's Westernization policies.

With the consolidation of power in Russia by the city of Moscow and the eventual creation of the unified Muscovite Tsardom, a new stage in Russian development began. Herzen, like Khomiakov, admitted "the necessity of centralization," but in the next breath said vaguely that had events not decreed otherwise, the cosmpolitan and "free" city of Novgorod might have united Russia in quite a different fashion, in which the communal institutions of society might have been preserved. Like the Decembrists before him, Herzen found the commercial and oligarchical city-state of Novgorod a possible basis for a very different kind of national evolution (a highly dubious proposition—rather as if a German radical had suggested that the commercial bourgeoisie of Bremen or Lübeck might have united Germany).

Herzen regarded Muscovite absolutism as rooted in two important historical developments: the Mongol conquest of Russia in the thirteenth century and the attachment of the Byzantine clerical establishment to Russia after the fall of Constantinople in 1453. In combating the Mongol hegemony over Russia, the Muscovite tsars took over a good deal of the absolutist pretensions of the Mongol khans. And the new wave of Byzantine influence that followed the end of the Eastern Empire led to the investment of the Tsar with the quasi-divinity that had previously characterized the Byzantine Basileus.

Meanwhile, the condition of the common people continued to deteriorate. Serfdom was introduced, and the last vestiges of popular liberty were obliterated. Henceforward the peasantry became apathetic under their impossible burdens, but flared up periodically into savage revolts whenever the power of the cen-

*In this connection, Herzen stresses the so-called rotation system, in which princes of the Riurik dynasty moved from city to city, according to their seniority within a single generation. While the system functioned, it did help to prevent princes from developing strong local ties.

tral government seemed momentarily weakened. At the same time, the communalism of the Russian people and its institutions survived, submerged but not broken. So Herzen retained the dichotomy between society and the state that the Slavophiles had suggested, but he made the separation much more explicit. And he saw Christianity not as a crucial component of peasant society but, in its Byzantine garb, as an essential ally of the absolutist state. The Muscovite autocracy had achieved unlimited power over the other cities of Russia and, in the economic realm, the landlords had achieved a similar authority over "their" peasants.

Herzen regarded Peter the Great, as had the Slavophiles, as a "crowned revolutionary," the first emancipated individual in Russian history. To the Slavophiles, his appearance was a national tragedy. Herzen is ambivalent. On the one hand, Peter swept away the musty, stagnant, deadly old Byzantine Russia and introduced a more mobile and fluid society—at least at the top. Russia became a society more open to individual talent and more secular. On the other hand, Peter extended the sway of the state even further, and its oppressive power became even more terrible for the bulk of the population. At any rate, we can see that whatever Herzen may have felt about the nineteenth-century bourgeoisie, his concern for individual liberty and his secularism in particular link him closely with the dominant values of eighteenth-century radicalism. Here his contrast with the Slavophiles is sharpest. His socialist communalism must incorporate and transcend the values of the eighteenth century, not repudiate them.

Herzen quite properly observes that for the most part the radicalism of eighteenth-century thought was deprived of its bite and seriousness in Russia, becoming a fashionable irony and skepticism about traditional values and institutions, a luxurious sensuality, but largely failing to produce a militant and critical spirit. Nevertheless, in particular during Catherine's reign, both Russian culture and the upper echelons of Russian society were to a degree humanized, and the ground was prepared both for the great flowering of Russian literature in the nineteenth century and for the development of a critical and humanitarian radicalism in a segment of the Russian elite, the initial manifestation of which was the Freemasonry of Nikolai Novikov.

Meanwhile, among the peasantry, the memory of Stenka Razin persisted in folkloric form and helped shape the massive revolt of Emel'ian Pugachëv, which broke out in 1773. The notion that one might understand the revolutionary nature of the Russian people through a study of its folklore was taken up by a good many Populists, as we shall see when we turn to the career of I. A. Khudiakov, one of many Populist ethnographers. These radical Romantics looked to the oral tradition as a kind of unselfconscious history of the *narod* by itself. The key to the militant and rebellious nature of the peasant lay in the tribulations visited upon it from above, and in the great spasms of popular revolt that had previously shaken the country. Thus the folklore of Razin and Pugachëv was largely the discovery of these radical ethnographers; previous collectors had not wanted to find such things. The Slavophile analogue of these Populist collectors was Pëtr Kireevsky, Ivan's brother, who tried to find what he regarded as the religious, peaceful, and communal archetype of the peasantry in *his* monumental investigations.[44]

At the end of the eighteenth century, Herzen believed, the Russian government remained *the* revolutionary force in Russia. The nineteenth century changed that decisively. The entire Russian nation rose against the French in 1812 and drove them out. The peasants reaped none of the rewards of their heroism and returned to their former condition. But elements of the Russian elite were not so accommodating. A "chivalric sense of honor and personal dignity," hitherto unobserved among Russia's pseudo-aristocracy, was born out of the Russian triumph, which meshed, for many military officers, with the realization that much in Russian government and administration needed reform. When Alexander I would not listen to these proud Napoleonic veterans, they went underground and formed the series of secret societies that ended in the Decembrist Revolt of 1825.

In one sense, the Russian government had lost its position of revolutionary leadership (revolutionary in the sense of Westernizing). In another sense, it had not, for it continued most arbitrar-

ily to enforce its will on the helpless body of society. But apart
from a broad commitment to monarchical stability the government of Nicholas did not base itself on real past traditions or on
its own previous legislation: what it decreed today, it might
sweep away tomorrow; what it ordered in one province, it might
forbid in another. The "revolutionary" tradition of Peter the
Great was alive, but in a purposeless and mutilated condition.
And here the Slavophile Ivan Kireevsky would certainly have
agreed: like Herzen, he found the Russian government not really
"conservative," but no longer revolutionary.

Pavel Pestel and his Decembrist colleagues, despite their failure and despite the fact that they had no real connection with
the peasantry, were the first real Russian revolutionaries, or, as
Herzen not quite accurately put it, the first to consider involving
the people in the revolution. They set a precedent; they became
a symbol; they founded a mythology. Above all, they broke the
silence, they shattered the passivity that had so long dominated
the Russian elite, and at this crucial point in Russian history, the
Russian government finally and definitively lost its function as
the bearer of progress. Russia's future was henceforth to be in the
hands of others—at first of her writers.

Under the sterile despotism of Nicholas, a new figure appeared
in Russia, the so-called superfluous man, alienated from his repulsive surroundings, profoundly bored, with no outlet for his energies except in empty and frivolous amusement, which only half
diverted him and left him with his incurable feelings of boredom
and disgust. Pushkin's Evgeny Onegin was the first and greatest
artistic statement of this type; Lermontov's Pechorin, the demonic protagonist of A Hero of Our Time, was his "younger
brother." And many other renderings followed. These figures
could neither live in Nicholas's Russia nor find any effective
means to oppose it, and this particular combination of revulsion
against their society and lack of the inner force necessary to take
action against it was their signature.

So while the deadening and meaningless government of Nicholas engaged itself in the exhausting game of self-preservation,
Russian literature did its subtle work of undermining and expos-

ing, creating a gnawing sense of discontent and dissatisfaction. And beneath the surface, the Russian people, who took no part in the intellectual movement, also began to stir. Incidents of insubordination, minor revolt, attacks on landlords, began to increase. To Europeans, Russia appeared a bastion of stability, an impregnable colossus. But the old regime was dying—profoundly, if semiconsciously, aware of the fact—and new historical forces were maturing. Subversive ideas circulated, especially among young people. Moscow, and particularly the university there, became the center of this still tentative dissidence. The opposition between Moscow and St. Petersburg, now more than a century old, had changed its essential character. Moscow was the center of the young and the innovative. St. Petersburg, once the center of Russia's progressive forces, now became the sterile bastion of the *status quo*, the barracks, parade ground, and chancellery of Nicholas's drama of self-preservation.*

The quickening of Russia's intellectual life, in particular its critical aspect, almost imperceptible at first, became perceptible in journalistic form, despite the government's unceasing efforts to destroy or at least castrate these publications. Herzen discussed a good many of the representatives of the journalism of the 1830s and 1840s, whom he knew so well from his youth and early manhood: Vissarion Belinsky, "the type of studious Moscow youth, the martyr of his doubts and thoughts," palpitating "with indignation and trembling with rage at the eternal spectacle of Russian absolutism."[45] And then there was Osip Senkovsky, the editor of the *Library for Reading*, a pliant sensualist, without convictions, but who undermined the government unintentionally with his epicurean cynicism. Most striking of all these symptoms was the appearance, in 1836, of Pëtr Chaadaev's famous *Philosophical Letter* in the Moscow *Telescope (Teleskop)*.

---

*The historian Nicholas Riasanovsky recounts an anecdote about Nicholas's childhood that seems to confirm Herzen's analysis more graphically than a description of the policies of the mature man. "Even as a child, 'whenever he built a summer house, for his nurse or his governess, out of chairs, earth or toys, he never forgot to *fortify* it with guns—*for protection.*'" And Riasanovsky adds that "he grew to be the chief military engineer of his country, specializing in fortresses, and still later, as emperor, he staked all on making the entire land an impregnable fortress." See Nicholas Riasanovsky, *Nicholas I and Official Nationality in Russia, 1825–1855* (Berkeley and Los Angeles, 1969), p. 10.

Chaadaev indicted Russia for having fallen away from the Roman Catholic Church and hence from the mainstream of Western history; as a result, he concluded, Russia had no past and no future. Chaadaev was officially declared mad by Nicholas and ordered to undergo medical treatment in an institution. (Russian governments, from that day to this, have had difficulty deciding whether their opponents are criminals or madmen, a problem by no means resolved as these words are written.)

In his final chapter, Herzen turned to the great intellectual drama of the 1840s: the debate between the Slavophiles and the Westerners. He began by noting that "the time of reaction against the reform of Peter I has come, not only for the government, which has retreated from its own principle and renounced Western civilization, in the name of which Peter I had trampled on [Russian] nationality, but also for those men whom the government had detached from the people, under the pretext of civilization, and whom it began to hang when they became civilized."[46] So Herzen approved of the posing of "the national question," and he again revealed his deep ambivalence about the work of Peter the Great.

He did not approve of the way in which the Slavophiles dealt with "the national question," feeling that it was neither possible nor desirable to return to the stagnant despotism of the Muscovite tsars and the Byzantine Church. Herzen defended Peter I against the broadsides of the Slavophiles: Peter's work had been in part beneficial, not only because he had opened Russia to the cruel but bracing process of Westernization but also because he had struck out remorselessly against what was stagnant and decrepit.

Herzen vehemently denied the tie between the Orthodoxy of Byzantium and the communal social organization that he and the Slavophiles both cherished. The Byzantine Church never championed the cause of the people; on the contrary, Herzen observed, it instructed the Russian tsars in the ways of despotism and commanded the people to blind obedience. The Russian people did not wish to exchange their German bondage for the old Byzantine one, said Herzen; they wished to liberate themselves.

Having indicted the Slavophile program, Herzen was quick to distinguish the Slavophiles from out-and-out government spokesmen. They were both revolutionary and conservative, and hence they could never really define their relationship to the autocracy on the one hand, or to their Westernizing opponents—Herzen himself and Belinsky—on the other. The Slavophiles understood much of the bloodstained futility of Western history, but they made a fatal mistake: they confused individual liberty—for Herzen one of the ultimate desiderata—with a narrow egoistic individualism. Here again we strike one of the great differences between communalism of the Right and Left: that of the Left insists on the preservation of the individual freedom gained in the liberal, "bourgeois" period of human development, seeking to expand it and reconcile it with communal values at a higher level. Communalism of the Right is disposed to deny liberal individualism outright, rather than looking to transcend it, to retreat to an idealized tableau of the past, rather than to imagine the future with the help of the past. The future must be won through struggle, Herzen cried, but the Slavophiles, despite their discontent, preached submission. Finally, the Slavophiles found the *narod* passive and God-fearing; the Populists, looking to the revolutionary future, *had* to find it rebellious. The Populist view of the destiny of Russia demanded the participation of the masses in its creation in a way that the Slavophile vision did not.

And yet Herzen's final words are healing and reconciling and testified to the historical and even personal kinship that he felt with the Slavophiles: "The socialism which so profoundly, so definitively divides Europe into two enemy camps—do not the Slavophiles accept it as we do? It is the bridge upon which we can clasp each other's hand."[47]

In this important essay Herzen had taken the reactionary utopia of the Slavophiles and made of it a mythology both radical and nationalist.[48] Europe was exhausted. The Russian people were "young," in the sense that their real history had not yet begun. The government, like Orthodox Christianity, was an alien, outside force, imposed upon the people, and almost no one, outside of the autocrat and the upper bureaucracy, had any stake in its preservation. Unlike Europe, Russia was free of the past because the Russian *people* had none. Furthermore, they had never accepted European law, in particular private property. The peasant commune, that "free association of equals," with its periodic redistribution of land, pointed the way to the socialist future, a crucial part of which would be the reconciliation of Western individual liberty with the communal spirit of the Russian people.

Before the death of Nicholas, it was very difficult for Herzen to get these ideas into Russia. Furthermore, there was no very large audience for them. When Herzen established himself as a publicist in London, his first audience was Western European. But after the death of Nicholas, the situation changed in Russia, and Herzen's vision became relevant to the new hopes that were stirring in the educated public.

At this point, it became apparent that Herzen's attitude to the Russian Emperor and state was more ambivalent than it had appeared during his most radical phase, in the late 1840s and early 1850s. Herzen did admire the Westernizing program of Peter the Great, and even regarded the Russian state between the time of Peter and that of Alexander as "revolutionary." Only under Nicholas had the Russian state lost its sense of direction and become *merely* a millstone around the neck of the people. When Alexander II undertook to emancipate the serfs, Herzen came to feel that perhaps the "revolutionary" mission of the state was not altogether exhausted, and so he took to encouraging and cajoling the Emperor as well as threatening him. In this development lies the heart of the "moderation" that was characteristic of Herzen's publicism in the late 1850s and that was to be so bitterly attacked by younger radicals, once they had become disillusioned with the "Tsar Liberator." And as Herzen grew older and in his way "successful," his enthusiasm for revolution diminished.

Finally, a few words should be said about a rather confusing term that any investigator of the 1860s will be bound to encounter: "nihilism." Some historians have used the term to describe the radicalism of the 1860s as a whole,[49] contrasting it thus with the Populism of the following decade. This usage is misleading because it unduly emphasizes the separateness of the two periods and does not reveal the intellectual (and even psychological) continuity between them. Sometimes the term is used to designate style—what would certainly be referred to today as a "radical life-style"—or a set of radical attitudes, elitist and scientistic, prominent in the 1860s and less so afterward.

Most historians have found the purest expression of nihilism in the journalism of Dmitry Pisarev and some of his collaborators on the *Russian Word (Russkoe slovo)*. Pisarev drowned at the age of twenty-eight, but he packed an astonishing amount of activity into so short a life. His journalistic career began in 1859, when he went to work for the first serious and political women's magazine in Russia, *Daybreak (Razsvet)*. Over the next nine years, as editor of the *Russian Word* and (after serving a four-year prison sentence) as a free-lance writer, he achieved a political-journalistic prominence second only to that of Chernyshevsky.

One of the most notable aspects of what was called nihilism was its elitism, which obviously conflicted with the egalitarian tendencies of the Populist vision of Herzen and his successors. Nihilist attitudes always involved a strong belief in the unfettering of the individual, a *personal* revolt against societal standards that were regarded as backward and oppressive. These attitudes might coexist (a bit uneasily) with various forms of belief in the peasantry; often, especially in the mid-1860s, they did not.[50]

Mainstream Populism always implied (and sometimes stated in no uncertain terms) that "the West" had a good deal to learn from Russia, especially from Russia's peasant institutions. Pisarev and his colleagues believed no such thing, nor did they have any faith in the creative capacity of the peasant masses. They wanted to liberate the inhabitants of the Russian village in a variety of ways, but they believed that the first task was to bring into existence an elite of "critically thinking individuals" who would take the lead in transforming Russia. They regarded themselves as supreme realists; they were contemptuous of *anything* that smacked of art or culture for its own sake. In their hands, Pushkin became, for a brief time, a negative figure: a sort of high cultural grandee who had to be brought low, much as a German radical might turn on Goethe. To oppose the exaltation of "art," which diverted people from the real tasks at hand, they made a cult of the exact sciences. Believing that their own emancipation and development were the prerequisites for a new Russia, they cultivated an aura of bitter militancy, ironic superiority, and general extremism: a kind of materialist Byronism. Their ethics were programmatically utilitarian.

In a general way it is clear why this sort of nihilism was so prevalent in the 1860s—flowering, it should be noted, *after* the euphoria of the Emancipation had waned. A self-conscious, zealously fostered elitism was an understandable response to the isolation of Russian radicalism, to the feeling that those who wanted to change things had only themselves to depend on. In some ways, nihilist attitudes were the intellectual counterparts of the Jacobinism and putschism that were also characteristic of the period and that we will discuss later. Certain nihilist attitudes were also very important in helping to demarcate the identity of the younger radicals from that of the earlier generation, from old fossils like Herzen, whose essential being had been formed by the bad old world that had to be destroyed. But in another way, people like Pisarev were the direct descendants of the Westerners of the 1840s. Although they denigrated art and believed in science, they inherited from the 1840s a faith in enlightenment and a belief in the developed individual. By contrast, they ridiculed the Slavophile-Populist belief that the Russia of the future depended on peasant values or institutions.

Nihilist *style* was what contemporaries noticed most often, however; in the memoir literature of the 1860s (particularly the recollections of moderates and conservatives), one finds the word generally used not to refer to Pisarev's radical elitism but to denote shocking and extreme behavior in general. Emancipated women, to take a case in point, were frequently referred to as *nigilistki* (female nihilists). Outside of radical circles the term had an application as broad as "Bolshie" in England after World War I or "Commie" in the America of the 1950s.

Ambiguity was present in the use of the term from its inception. Although it had been infrequently employed by a variety of writers in the early nineteenth century, it was introduced into the political arena by Ivan Turgenev in *Fathers and Children*, with reference to the hero Bazarov, who is, in his power, complexity of motivation, and final mystery, one of the great literary portrayals of a European radical. Much of the response from the Russian Left of the early 1860s to both the man and the term was negative, but Pisarev took it upon himself to champion and identify himself with both. The term was in a descriptive sense not accurate; Bazarov did not believe in "nothing," although he claimed to acknowledge no authorities. Indeed, he professed a passionate belief in the power of people like himself and in the possibilities of science. But the notion that radicals believed in nothing was an enticing one for conservatives; "nihilist" sounded enigmatic, sinister, but at the same time rather fascinating. And so the term became increasingly vague and meaningless.

Still, we must not overlook the more precise meaning of nihilism in the 1860s, as exemplifed by Pisarev. Although in a theoretical sense it conflicted with certain aspects of Populism, it did not do so absolutely. After all, from the Slavophiles to Lenin, the vanguard role of *some* educated group ("the middle gentry," "the intelligentsia," "critically thinking individuals," the Party) was almost always recognized as central to social transformation. The nihilists emphasized that role more powerfully and explicitly than did other 1860s radicals.

The conflicts and arguments within the radical camp over nihilist elitism were continued in the 1870s—and on into the twentieth century. Was there some crucial advantage to "backwardness" or not? How large a role in the revolution should be played by a revolutionary elite? Repeated disappointments with "the people" were to magnify that role, with far-reaching results for Russia.

In thinking generally about the central myths of Populism, one must be careful not to overlook the variety and complexity of the views of individual Populist radicals, as well as evolution within

Populism, taken broadly. The Slavophile tone and feeling that was at moments so evident in Herzen's writings (and in those of other radicals of the 1860s and 1870s) gradually weakened and became more diffuse. Chernyshevsky was temperamentally a Westerner to whom Russian nationalism was largely alien and Herzen's aristocratism was anathema. Chernyshevsky's interest in the commune was a good deal more practical than Herzen's, and he studied it more thoroughly. Moreover, Chernyshevsky lacked that strong hostility to the modern state that was common to the first generation of Slavophiles, to Herzen, and to the mainstream of Populist radicalism. He was concerned, in fact, with the problem of how a (revolutionary) state should nurture and develop collectivist economic institutions, communes and cooperatives. And Chernyshevsky's ethics, like those of Pisarev, were egoistic and utilitarian.

If we concede, then, the existence of recurrent elitist impulses and formulations that both blended and conflicted with Herzen's legacy, and we further note that the most influential radical of the decade was by no means a straightforward continuer of Herzen's key ideas, how can we justify treating them at such length? How can we justify the commanding position given Herzen in these pages: that of the founder of a movement with sufficient unity and coherence to deserve the name?

These difficulties have been highlighted by the recent publication of a considered monograph asserting a quite different framework for considering Russian Populism. In *The Controversy Over Capitalism*, Andrzej Walicki, a distinguished Polish scholar, relegates Herzen and even Chernyshevsky to the role of forerunners. He views "classical Populism" as a phenomenon of the 1870s, which took shape primarily in opposition to Marxism; expressing the "standpoint of the small producers," it was above all an attempt to arrive at a noncapitalist model of economic development—revolutionary in some variants.

It is certainly true that in the 1870s a major preoccupation of Populist radicals became forestalling the horrors of bourgeois industrialization, in making the revolution *before* a rapacious and exploitative bourgeoisie on the European model could de-

velop in Russia. Walicki is to this extent correct in sharply sepa-
rating the two periods.

One's justification for treating the Slavophile inheritance, radicalized by Herzen and Chernyshevsky, as crucially shaping must
lie in the mythic inheritance that Populism received from the
earlier period: the focus on the peasant and his institutions; the
view of the Russian state as oppressive and "non-Russian," imposed from outside onto the organic life of the people (an extremely non-Marxist belief!); the social messianism, the belief
that Russia had a unique destiny, a special entrée into the modern world that would avoid the agonies of class conflict through
which Europe had been passing since the French Revolution.
The broadest formulations of Populism and a great deal of its
feeling and tone predate the arrival of Marxism in Russia, however Pëtr Lavrov, Nikolai Mikhailovsky, and other Populist theo-
rists of the 1870s may have responded to the power of the Marxist
view of history.

Although the presence of Marxist formulations in the writings
of individual Populists is apparent, it was not until the 1880s (and
in an acute form in the 1890s) that a unitary kind of Marxism
became a competitor for the loyalties of Russian radicals. Even
at this point, however, the Populist vision was not vanquished; in
a somewhat updated form, it became the doctrinal base for the
Socialist Revolutionary Party and survived into the 1920s.

When one looks at the history of Marxism in Russia, one naturally finds a variety of currents, interpretations, "applications" of
Marxist doctrine to Russian reality. Yet we are justified, at times,
in speaking inclusively of Russian Marxism. Of course Herzen's
writings never had the doctrinal authority that surrounded those
of Marx, nor would anyone claim for Herzen the depth, power,
and scope of Marx. And yet the radical vision that Herzen did so
much to formulate had the same kind of power over the minds
of thinking Russians for a time that the writings of Marx enjoyed
in a later period, even if no one spoke of "Herzenism." If anything, Populism had a more pervasive influence on educated
Russians than Marxism ever did, although it is harder to pinpoint.
Lacking the scientific and universalist claims of Marxism, Popu-

lism could neither gain non-Russian adherents nor come up with an authoritative set of texts from which its supporters could "prove" their claims. In the heyday of Russian Marxism, a variety of other intellectual movements competed with it—a revived Populism, neo-Kantianism, and the Orthodox revival of the early twentieth century, to mention only a few. From the late 1850s well into the 1870s, Populist ideas were subjected to no sustained challenge of an intellectual kind.[51] And although the number of educated Russians who accepted the totality of Herzen's views was small, almost no "thinking" person escaped the influence of the Populist gestalt.

The New Era and Its Journalists: Herzen and Chernyshevsky

Russians who have no mountains at hand simply say that the domovoy [hobgoblin] *has been smothering them. It is perhaps a truer description. It really seems as though someone were choking you; your dream is not clear, but it is very frightening; it is hard to breathe, yet one must breathe twice as hard, the pulse is quicker, the heart throbs fast and painfully. . . . You are hunted; creatures, not men, not visions, are at your heels; you have glimpses of forgotten shapes that recall other years and earlier ages. . . . There are precipices and abysses, your foot slips, there is no escape, you fly into the void of darkness, a cry bursts from you involuntarily and you wake up. You wake up in a fever, sweat on your brow; choking for breath, you hasten to the window. . . . Outside there is a fresh, bright dawn, the wind is rolling the mist away to one side, there is the scent of grass and forest, there are sounds and calls . . . everything that is ours and earthly. . . . And, pacified, you fill your lungs with the morning air. . . . Long live Reason! our simple earthly reason!*

—Alexander Herzen, *Alpendrucken*[1]

So great was the government pressure on Russian intellectual life in the reign of Nicholas, and so well attested by great writers has that repression been, that it is easy to overlook the important changes in Russian culture between 1830 and 1855. In a general way, one can say that *obshchestvo* became larger, somewhat better educated, more self-conscious—and more critical of the government.[2] Russian literary culture began the great flowering that was to continue beyond the century; the works of Gogol and the early fiction of Turgenev, Dostoevsky, and Tolstoy appeared under Nicholas, together with the criticism of Belinsky and a good body of less important but serious literature. By 1855 the cultural despair of the 1820s and even the 1830s ("Where is Russian literature? What is the matter with us that we have no literature?") had lifted.

Despite a student body of less than four thousand in 1855 and a succession of political and cultural traumas (especially after 1848), Russian universities were far more important in the life of *obshchestvo* in 1855 than they had been in 1825. After 1830, the universities began to become a refuge for the most cultivated segment of gentry youth, who in the previous reign would have been educated at home by tutors. And although Russian university faculties continued to provide a home for professors of limited abilities and questionable pedagogical capacities, the overall quality improved. Timofei Granovsky, together with Herzen and Belinsky the leader of the Westerners, with his chivalric sweetness and moderate Hegelian view of Western history, became a real intellectual force at the University of Moscow in the 1840s and 1850s; until his premature death in 1855, he continued to attract able young men into the ranks of the professoriate. The leading figures of the intellectual Right, Stepan Shevyrëv and Mikhail Pogodin, did not have comparable influence, but in a more limited way they, too, helped to make the university a real center of Russian cultural life.

Every student of this period is familiar with several of the famous cases when on some trifling pretext Nicholas and his censors shut down a periodical and sent the editor to jail, a mental institution, or simply off to his estate. Some may even recall the piquant comment that Nicholas scrawled in the margin of a request for permission to found a new journal: "There are many without this one." Certainly it expressed his deepest attitude toward journalists and all their works. Nevertheless, the best evidence[3] is that the number of periodicals, their variety, and the reading public for them increased during his reign, and the situation with respect to books was similar.

Finally, one may hazard the vaguer and more risky generalization that within this periodical-reading public of some twenty thousand to thirty thousand people can be discerned, between 1840 and 1855, a definite predilection for vaguely "critical," vaguely "liberal," vaguely reformist ideas and points of view. One sees this in the success of the two principal Westernizer journals of the 1840s, the *Contemporary (Sovremennik)* and the *Annals of the Fatherland (Otechestvennye zapiski)*, which together achieved close to seven thousand subscribers by the eve of 1848.[4] The depth and toughness of this point of view should not be exaggerated. Purely frivolous journals, like the *Library for Reading (Biblioteka dlia chteniia)*, and government-oriented publications (some scurrilously so) retained some popularity.

Russia at Nicholas's death was scarcely seething with suppressed radicalism. Still, it is clear that an important segment of *obshchestvo* was independent and critical-minded (however timidly so); such people were influential in journalism, represented in the universities and even, apparently, to a lesser extent, in the schools. Within the bureaucracy itself, attitudes were changing. Younger bureaucrats tended to be better educated, and devotion to the interests of the state as an entity was more widespread than among the older generation. In a number of ministries and other state agencies there was a cautious interest in reform.* But most important of all, virtually the whole of *obshchestvo* was sick of the stagnation and oppression which they felt had been their lot since the panic days of 1848.

The five years (1856–61) between the end of the Crimean War

---

*A number of recent books and articles have pointed out that the bureaucracy under Nicholas was neither static nor to be understood purely mechanically. For a brief discussion of the sociology of Nicholas's administration and the relevant citations from the recent literature, see Richard Wortman, *The Development of a Russian Legal Consciousness* (Chicago and London, 1976), pp. 4–6.

and the Emancipation Edict saw a spectacular change in the
mood and style of both *obshchestvo* and peasant Russia. The
death of Emperor Nicholas, the accession of Alexander II, and
the end of the Crimean War kindled the hope in Russian society
that a freer and less stifling life might be at hand. The sense of
relief following Nicholas's death on March 1, 1855, seems to have
been almost instantaneous; it was coupled, not surprisingly, with
a vague mix of hopes and fears about the future. Vera Aksakova,
the daughter of the well-known writer and critic, wrote in her
diary on April 11, 1855:

In general there everywhere prevails a kind of bewilderment, an
uncertainty as to what the government wants and what it will be.
Everyone feels that things will be easier somehow, with respect both
to clothes and things of the spirit. F. I. Tiutchev has aptly designated
the present time as a *thaw*. Precisely. But what will follow the thaw?
If spring and an abundant summer follow, that will be fine, but if this
thaw is temporary and the freezing weather returns, then it will seem
even harder to bear.[5]

Despite widespread uncertainty, however, the impression seems
to have been general that an era had in fact ended, that things
would never be the same again. As Nikolai Shelgunov, subsequently a prominent radical, wrote in his memoirs:

The sovereign had died; his successor ascended the throne without
shakings or disorders; the war ended; the peace seemed honorable
enough; everything was quiet and peaceful and things might have
reverted to the old and traditional, with a few small changes and
reforms. It might have seemed in order just to rejoice and breathe
freely after our military exertions and losses at Sebastopol. But in
actual fact, the old could no longer repeat itself; everyone felt that
some nerve had been broken, that the road to the old was closed. It
was one of those beginning historical moments, for which not years
but centuries prepare, and they are just as inevitable as avalanches
in the mountains or heavy rains at the equator. In such cases, the
individual will disappear and everyone, from top to bottom, is mastered by one general burst of vital energy. It is at first instinctive, like
a deep breath after a lethargic sleep, like the first lucid awakening
after a fever; but then, after the unconscious, instinctive movement

of the spirit, a condition of clear consciousness gradually develops, people come to themselves and with new strength devote themselves to new work.[6]

This view, of course, is both radical and retrospective. But the Slavophile Aleksei Stepanovich Khomiakov, writing to his friend Konstantin Aksakov shortly after the accession of Alexander II, gave a similar, although more cautious, estimate of the mood in *obshchestvo:*

Affairs are taking a new turn, but this turn is not without danger. A certain spirit of life and liberty has been awakened, evidently provoked by the government. . . . What will happen? All those who kept silent, all those who acquiesced in bondage when we alone dared to demand liberty and to protest against official repression—they are all excited, shouting and singing hymns to liberty of thought.[7]

The issue that more than any other defined the content of the "new era" and dominated Russian intellectual life for the next half-dozen years was the emancipation of the serfs. The crescendo of debate, discussion, and excitement really began with the speech of Alexander II to the Moscow gentry on March 30, 1856. The Emperor stated that although he did not plan to free the serfs "immediately," he was sure that his audience would agree that it was better to abolish serfdom from above than to wait until it was abolished from below. As the government moved toward emancipation—slowly, awkwardly, agonizingly— excitement mounted. Among the peasants, the promise of *volia* (liberty) appears to have manifested itself in a steady increase in disorders and disturbances. According to the calculations of the Third Section (political police), there were 86 major episodes in 1858, 90 in 1859, and 108 in 1860. Terence Emmons, an American historian of the Emancipation, remarks of these escalating figures that

to some extent [they] merely reflected the growing nervousness of government officials, but undoubtedly rumors about the promised emancipation contributed to peasant unrest. It was widely believed, for example, that the Tsar had already declared the peasants free, but that the *chinovniki*, or officials, and the *pomeshchiki* [serf owners] were not allowing the transmission of this news. The large majority of the disturbances in any year continued to result from peasant refusal to fulfill obligations, especially *barshchina*.* Also, numerous attempts by the gentry to reduce peasant allotments, to transfer peasants to poorer lands, or to otherwise increase their demesne lands in anticipation of emancipation, must have had their effect on the rate of peasant disturbances.[8]

The excitement in *obshchestvo* was comparably great, although of course its manifestations were quite different. L. F. Panteleev, who was a student at the University of St. Petersburg between 1858 and 1861, remembered his contemporaries as being virtually obsessed with the development of plans for emancipation. The subject dominated nearly all informal group discussions. Real knowledge of peasant life and hard economic facts about a settlement were rarely encountered in these discussions; it was simply assumed that the former serfs should be provided with "economic security." What so excited a large portion of *obshchestvo* (and the students in particular) was the notion of giving the serfs "liberty," making them human beings in the full sense of the word. "Liberty" then seemed a kind of supreme good, from which a host of subsidiary benefits might be expected to follow.

In fact, a haze of naive optimism suffused the entire period: nothing had as yet been seriously undertaken; no "contradictions" had as yet appeared. Little was known in *obshchestvo* circles about what peasants were actually like, nor was there any quick or easy way of finding out. To most proponents of emancipation the government appeared benevolent, if timid and vacillating. The full depth of the conflict of interest between the gentry landowners and the peasantry was quite obscure. Most landowners presumably sensed but could not articulate it, while their most literate and intelligent spokesmen were extremely cautious in their public utterances, since emancipation was the declared will of the Emperor.

The range of possibility seemed so boundless, largely because nothing had yet been done. Nicholas I had been a thoroughly

*Labor dues, roughly equivalent to the French corvée.

known quantity; his successor and his successor's government were not. The motives behind Alexander's decision to emancipate were not then (indeed have never been) very well understood, vital as that decision was. In fact, the Russian government did not really know what it was or where it was going. The Emancipation itself was a "leap in the dark," compared to which the Second Reform Bill in England was the merest trifle. And the Russian government was experimenting in other areas as well: easing travel restrictions and trying out a more tolerant and permissive attitude toward the universities. Small wonder if the young and reform-minded grew jubilant and confident, while the older and more conservative drew back in uncertainty and dismay, unable even to express what they felt, since it was the autocracy—their bulwark—that was sponsoring the new era, however haltingly and incoherently.

In examining the forces that helped to shape and express the upsurge in social optimism of the late 1850s, it is important not to exaggerate the importance of radical *ideas* in this process. Primacy should certainly be given to the inchoate change in the mood of *obshchestvo* triggered by the loss of the war and the death of Nicholas. Nevertheless, *obshchestvo*'s growing receptivity to radical ideas and the emergence of key tenets of Populism are aspects of the drama that cannot be omitted. They provided something quite essential: a vocabulary for people's aspirations.

Journalism as a whole was enlivened by the social mood of the mid- and late 1850s, especially by the debate over Emancipation. For young, intellectually inclined people, journalism became one of the few obvious alternatives to a career in the universities or the imperial bureaucracy, and the relaxation of the censorship made serious, critical journalism seem more viable. Between 1856 and 1860, the total number of periodical publications in Russia increased from 110 to 230,[9] even though many of these new journals failed to last for more than a few issues.

Of all the journals that expressed and, in turn, influenced the social mood of Russia in those years, initially the most important was Alexander Herzen's *Bell (Kolokol)*, which began its career in 1857. Published in London, the *Bell* was smuggled into Russia in hundreds, and for a short time in thousands, of copies per issue. The ferment in Russia was homegrown; but the *Bell* helped the Russians of the new era to express their hopes and aspirations. One cannot minimize its importance: virtually every memoir of the period mentions it at some length, with hatred or approbation, depending on the viewpoint. The *Bell*, fundamentally, did two things: it provided the only free forum for criticism and discussion of the realities of Russian life in the reform period, in particular with respect to peasant emancipation, and it introduced young Russians to the constellation of ideas that Herzen called "Russian socialism" and that we know as Populism.

The *Bell* grew naturally out of Herzen's earlier publishing ventures. He tells us himself that the idea of creating an uncensored Russian press occurred to him as early as 1849, but it was not until his involvement with continental radicalism was largely over and he was settled in London that he devoted himself seriously to the task. With the assistance of several Polish radicals, he founded in 1853 the Free Russian Press. Herzen had provided his Polish colleagues with financial backing for their propagandistic publications; in exchange, they made available to him Cyrillic type that they had acquired in Paris. By April Herzen was writing to a friend that "there will be a press, and if I do nothing more, this initiative in the direction of public discussion in Russia will be appreciated some day."[10] On May 20, Herzen proclaimed in the émigré *Polish Democrat* that he intended to create a free tribunal outside the boundaries of the country. "The founding of a Russian press in London," he wrote, "appears to be the most practical revolutionary action that a Russian can take, in the expectation of being able to do other, better things."[11]

Having made this decision, Herzen was most concerned with the matter of *contacts* in Russia, both in the technical sense of being able to reach Russians with what he wrote, to get his material into the country, and in the sense of finding an audience with whom he could make intellectual contact. His first thoughts, in the latter respect, turned to his old "Westerner" cronies of the previous decade, and for the next two years Herzen tried to get in touch with them, both through personal letters and through pamphlets, some of which were smuggled into Russia through Poland.

The results were discouraging. Of Herzen's old friends, only the historian Granovsky showed any initial enthusiasm for the Free Russian Press and its works. The reasons for this apathetic and sometimes hostile response are not difficult to discover. Since his emigration to Europe, Herzen had moved away from the ideals that he had shared with the Westerner group of the 1840s. He had repudiated the middle-class liberals and radicals of the West. He had become more sympathetic to violent revolution as a condition of progress in Europe and in Russia. And his Russian socialism had obvious Slavophile elements in it. Some of his former friends, like the critic Vasily Botkin and the literary doctor Nikolai Ketcher, were so upset by Herzen's radicalism that they would not write to him. When the actor M. S. Shchepkin took the trouble to pay Herzen a visit in London, he ended by advising him to abandon the Free Russian Press and go to America.

Granovsky's reaction was more ambiguous. On occasion he expressed cautious approval. But in the fall of 1855, he wrote a letter to a mutual friend, K. D. Kavelin, in which he accused Herzen of childishness and impracticality; Herzen was, he said, posturing before the radicals of Western Europe by exaggerating the strength of oppositional forces in Russia. There was some truth in this charge. Wounded vanity, personal and national, played its part in the formation of Herzen's Russian socialism. But Granovsky's accusation was scarcely the whole truth, nor did it constitute a serious answer to the ideas Herzen was developing. In view of the old debate between the Slavophiles and the Westernizers, it is not surprising that it was the Slavophile component in Herzen's views to which Granovsky really took exception, in particular what Granovsky took to be Herzen's hostility to Peter the Great, who remained a hero to Granovsky and others of the old Westerner group for whom he spoke.*

*Writing in the 1870s, another Westernizer, P. V. Annenkov, developed a more fair-minded view of the relationship. The Slavophiles, he wrote, "managed to bring into the field of vision of the Russian intelligentsia a new subject, a new active element of thought—the people, to be precise; and after [their] preaching neither scholarship

In his reply to Granovsky, Herzen indignantly denied any kinship with the moribund religiosity of the Slavophiles, but he did
admit—as he later did to Turgenev—to an interest in "certain of
their thoughts." He was rather vague about this interest, referring only to their belief in the Russian peasant. But there is no
question that Herzen was stung by Granovsky's linking him with
their old enemies from the salon debates of the previous decade.
One feels that he protested a bit too much as he heaped on the
invective: the Slavophiles, he concluded, were false, dangerous
"Orthodox Jesuits." Still, he was interested in "certain of their
thoughts."[12]

The audience for his words before 1856 was small, and it was
extremely difficult to get his publications into Russia. And yet,
among the press's earliest productions were some of Herzen's
most memorable pamphlets, *St. George's Day! St. George's Day!
To the Russian Gentry** and *Baptized Property*, a full-dress attack on serfdom. But as time passed, it grew harder and harder
to carry on. Herzen recalled this discouraging period in his memoirs in the following terms:

Three years of life in London had fatigued me. It is a laborious business to work without seeing the fruit from close at hand; and as well
as this I was too much cut off from any circle of my kin. Printing sheet
after sheet with Chernetsky and piling up heaps of printed pamphlets in Trübner's cellars, I had hardly any opportunity to send anything across the frontiers of Russia. I could not give up: the Russian
printing press was my life's work . . . with it I lived in the atmosphere
of Russia; with it I was prepared and armed. But with all that, it wore
one out that one's work was never heard of: one's hands sank to one's

---

in general, nor the science of government in particular could avoid considering it
and taking it into account in their various political and social solutions. This was
the great merit of the party, whatever its cost. Later, and already abroad, Herzen
understood very well the importance of the structure which the Slavophiles had
erected, and he used to say, not for nothing: 'Our European Westernizer party will
acquire the position and the significance of a social force only when it masters the
themes and the problems put into circulation by the Slavophiles.'" *The Extraordinary Decade,* quoted in Nicholas V. Riasanovsky, *A Parting of Ways: Government and the
Educated Public in Russia 1801–1855* (Oxford, 1977), p. 292.

*St. George's Day *(Iur'ev den')*: in the fifteenth century, the custom arose that on or
about St. George's Day a free peasant could move, provided he had no outstanding obligations to his landlord. The association with both peasant liberty and gentry acquiescence in
it is clear.

sides. Faith dwindled by the minute and sought after a sign, and not only was there no sign; there was not *one single* word of sympathy from home.[13]

Under these dispiriting circumstances, the death of Nicholas was an enormously exciting and hopeful event. Martin Malia has provided a memorable description:

... it was a day in March, 1855, during the Crimean War when Herzen learned the news that after thirty years the Tyrant had at last passed from the scene amidst the ruin of all his policies . . . the perfect embodiment of autocracy; whom he had seen only once, at the coronation in 1826, when as a boy of fourteen he had beheld the imperial hands "still red with the blood of the Decembrists," but who had dominated his whole life since the Sparrow Hills, first as a symbol, then as a reality. When Herzen learned this news, with a truly Russian broad nature (for it was not yet eleven o'clock in the morning), he summoned in his émigré friends, uncorked his best champagne, and to the London urchins who gaped at this scene through the garden gates he threw pieces of silver, calling to them to shout through the streets the tidings that meant a new and more "human" life for Russia: "Hurrah! hurrah! Impernikel is dead! Impernikel is dead!"[14]

Even with "Impernikel" gone, however, not much was to be expected from his old friends, and Herzen did not conceal his anger and disappointment. He soon decided, however, to expand the activities of the Free Russian Press and put out a journal; the result was the *Polar Star (Poliarnaia zvezda)*, whose name was chosen to stress the continuity of his activity with that of the Decembrists, several of whom had published a short-lived journal of the same name. In the summer of 1855, the first number of the journal appeared, and in an article entitled "To Ours," Herzen roundly scolded his old friends: "Your silence, we frankly confess, in no way shakes our faith in the Russian people and its future; we merely doubt the moral strength and capacity of our generation."[15] In this notable first number, Herzen also published Belinsky's famous "Letter to Gogol," several chapters from his memoirs, and his "Letter to Alexander II," in which he

set out what was to become his "minimum program" over the
next six years: freedom of the word in Russia, abolition of corporal punishment, and—most important—the emancipation of the
serfs with land.

The death of Nicholas and the liberalization measures undertaken by Alexander II proved the turning point in Herzen's
career as Russia's tribune. His countrymen began to be less afraid
of contact with him. The liberalized travel restrictions meant
that many more Russians went abroad, and some got as far as
London. Growing numbers bought, read, and even smuggled
back into Russia the publications of the Free Russian Press.

To respond to the greater volume of communications reaching
him from inside Russia, Herzen undertook to publish periodic
anthologies which he called *Voices from Russia (Golosa iz Rossii)*.[16] These anthologies, which included a variety of points of
view, give a vivid sense of the intellectual ferment in Russia that
began with the new reign. Most notably, *Voices from Russia*
contained several contributions by two academics who are generally considered the leading spokesmen for Russian "liberalism"
in this period: Boris Chicherin and Konstantin Kavelin.

It is doubtful that the point of view articulated by these two
men, which overlapped with Herzen's goals in the latter 1850s,
deserves the name of liberalism. It certainly had little to do with
the Manchesterian doctrines that formed the basis for early liberalism in Western Europe. Neither Chicherin nor Kavelin was—
or could have been—sympathetic toward the idea of the "night
watchman state." They were, in fact, moderate Westerners who
hoped that the Russian state would resume the progressive role
it had played before it had become separated from the *narod* by
the bureaucracy—an idea that, as Terence Emmons recently
noted, was widespread in the Russia of the late 1850s, "[being]
shared by the conservatives, by many radicals (at least in their
weaker moments), by the peasants (who on a few occasions were
able to express it in quite modern terms . . .), and even by many
liberals with bureaucratic experience who might have been expected to look at domestic policies in different terms."[17]

To get a sense of this "liberal" view, one cannot do better than turn to one of Boris Chicherin's contributions to *Voices from Russia*. "But what should be understood by the term liberalism?" he asks rhetorically, and then gives a seven-point answer:

1. Freedom of conscience . . .
2. Freedom from serfdom . . .
3. Freedom of public opinion . . .
4. Freedom of the press . . .
5. Freedom of teaching . . .
6. Publicity of all government activities whose exposure is not harmful to the state, and especially of the budget of state revenues and expenditures . . .
7. Publicity and public conduct of legal procedures.[18]

It may strike us that Chicherin has produced a list of concrete reforms rather than a statement about Russian liberalism. Chicherin's statism, invariably expressed in Hegelian language, suggested that liberal reform would come from above, through the monarchy's recovery of its Petrine legacy to rationalize and humanize Russian life. But neither Chicherin nor Kavelin nor any of the other Hegelian liberals could describe a coherent liberal program; nor could they devise a way to work for the realization of their concrete plans, beyond urging the government to bring them into existence.

Once the general euphoria of the latter 1850s was over, Chicherin found himself isolated between the radical intelligentsia, whose socialism he hated and feared, and the government, which refused to adopt the progressive policies for which he had hoped. His "liberalism" gives us another slant on the constricted, unreal quality of *obshchestvo* politics, as well as on the absence in Russia of any social stratum with a material stake in liberal ideas.

Even in the 1850s, Chicherin came to believe that Herzen was an irresponsible and dangerous demagogue—despite the fact that his "liberal" demands were extremely close to Herzen's minimum program. Both Chicherin and Kavelin spoke against Herzen's socialism, and were especially antagonistic toward his view of the commune as the basis of the Russian society of the future. But Chicherin was more fervent and doctrinaire in his hostility to socialism—as he had earlier been to Slavophilism. Kavelin's views were less firm, and he admired Herzen as a writer and a critic. In fact, the unity of Russia's two "liberal" spokesmen was a precarious affair that was not to survive the end of the decade.

In 1855 and into 1856, Herzen succeeded in getting a few copies of the *Polar Star* into Russia through his Polish contacts, and he even approached the Russian delegates to the Paris Peace Conference in 1856. But toward the middle of 1856, demand for the *Polar Star* and his other publications began to pick up, and the trend continued into 1857. By April 9, orders had been placed for three hundred copies, and Herzen was reckoning on two hundred more by May 1.[19] At this point, the publications of the Free Russian Press could be obtained in several continental cities, as well as in London—and probably elsewhere, too.

It was not only the rise in sales that was encouraging to Herzen in early 1857. In mid-1856, he had received an anonymous letter, which he published in the May 1857 number of the *Polar Star:*

Your "Polar Star" [it ran] has appeared on the Petersburg horizon, and we greet it as the Bethlehem shepherds once greeted that holy star which burned over the cradle where freedom was born. If you could see with what enthusiasm it is read, its articles copied, its contents reported, your very phrases repeated, it would give you more than one sweet moment in your melancholy exile. Every noble heart among the younger generation . . . sympathizes with you.[20]

An exhilarating letter for Herzen to receive! Here was his audience, and no mistake! Here was the future of Russia.

It was in this atmosphere of rising hope and excitement that the *Bell* was born in the spring of 1857. The idea apparently came from Nikolai Ogarëv, Herzen's old and close friend, who had joined him in London as a collaborator a year before. Herzen seized upon it with alacrity. The *Polar Star,* they thought at the time, should continue as the vehicle for major theoretical works, the republication of out-of-print or suppressed classics, and the like; the *Bell* would be a kind of supplement, whose material should be "lighter," more newsy, and which could respond with greater rapidity and flexibility to the drama beginning to unfold in Russia. But soon the *Bell* became the major vehicle, while the *Polar Star* simply petered out.

The *Bell* was an immense success. Between 1857 and 1862, its circulation rose to something over twenty-five hundred copies per issue;[21] the upward curve of the *Bell's* circulation figures coincided precisely with the springtime of the post-Nicholaevan period, with the general intellectual ferment that carried through the Emancipation.

On occasion the *Bell* featured theoretical articles by Herzen on Russian socialism; Ogarëv contributed both prose and poetry. In a section called "Is It True?" *(Pravda li?)*, rumors and sometimes established facts of scandalous behavior by the government or individual landowners were printed. A great deal of the material was from anonymous individuals or groups within Russia, people who have generally been referred to as Herzen's "correspondents." Sometimes these correspondents had a personal message; sometimes they wished to comment on an issue of the day, most frequently the peasant question. Sometimes the correspondents were to Herzen's right; sometimes he was criticized from the Left. According to Herzen's stated policy, only two kinds of correspondence were not printed: what he judged to be material from cranks or of no general interest, and literature that was frankly government-inspired or reflected the official government point of view.

The importance of Herzen's correspondents suggests the degree to which Herzen conceived the *Bell* not merely as his organ —or his and Ogarëv's—but as an enterprise in which all the voices of the new era were involved. His countrymen were not merely to listen to the *Bell*, said Herzen, they were to ring it themselves. He wanted to create a chorus, not merely a single note.[22] And in this he largely succeeded.

At the outset, Herzen made a momentous decision with respect to what he hoped the *Bell* would accomplish. Despite the publication of a good deal of material pertaining both directly and indirectly to peasant socialism, he intended to have as great an effect as possible on the Emancipation drama. The decision was momentous because it led the *Bell*—with many a twist and turn, to be sure—away from the more systematic radicalism that Herzen had professed in the early 1850s and led him to address Alexander II directly—and not merely in apocalyptic and accusatory tones. He was willing to plead, cajole—and, on occasion, to flatter and congratulate. The most famous such incident occurred on February 15, 1858, after the publication of the so-called "Rescript to Nazimov" had publicly committed the government to some kind of major reform. In the current number of the *Bell*, Herzen published a congratulatory "Open Letter" to the Emperor that began with the words "Thou hast conquered, O Galilean." This exultant apostrophe was eagerly seized upon by Herzen's young radical opponents, to whom it flagrantly exhibited his moderation, credulity, and reliance on a melodramatic and dated rhetoric. Taken out of context, the words seemed particularly ridiculous, and the episode was damaging.

The question to what extent the *Bell*'s concentration on the minimum program (freedom of the word, abolition of corporal punishment, and Emancipation of the serfs with land) was merely a tactic and to what extent Herzen actually became "more conservative" is one over which historians have been battling from that day to this. It is of course true that if one puts forward one's minimum program over a period of years—successfully—what began as a tactic may become something more —if not quite a conviction. Nor should Herzen's view of the historical evolution of the Russian monarchy be left out of account: he saw it as an ambiguously progressive force in Russian life between Peter the Great and shortly after 1815. Only under Nicholas had the dynasty become wholly retrograde. So it was not so difficult for Herzen to believe on occasion that the monarchy might again take up the burdens and responsibilities it had abdicated under Nicholas. And Herzen also continued to entertain hopes of the gentry—or at least a progressive portion of it. Should the monarchy prove equal to the task of reforming itself, the collaboration of a certain portion of the gentry would be essential. Or, if the need should be for a social and political struggle against the crown, the "progressive" gentry might be an indispensable force for change. During the latter 1850s, although Herzen periodically informed his readers that the only alternative to a generous emancipation was a bloody peasant uprising, one senses that he gradually lost whatever taste he might once have had for such a holocaust. He was too cultivated, too attached to so much of Russian life and culture, to dream the passionate dreams of apocalypse that some of the younger generation were soon to express.

Herzen's only firm conviction was that radical change in Russia had to come about, in some sense, *through* the people; it could not be done exclusively *for* or *to* them. As he wrote in an essay of the early 1860s:

Only the man who, when summoned to action, understands the life of the people, while not losing what science has given him; only the man who voices its aspirations, and founds on the realisation of them his participation in the common cause of the people of the soil, will be the bridegroom that is to come. . . .

Who will be the destined man?

Will it be an emperor who, renouncing the Petrine tradition [that is, antinational revolution from above], combines in himself Tsar and Stenka Razin? Will it be a new Pestel? Or another Yemelyan Puga-chëv, Cossack, Tsar and schismatic? Or will it be a prophet and a peasant, like Antony Bezdninsky?*

It is hard to tell: these are *des détails,* as the French say. Whoever it may be, it is our task to go to meet him with bread and salt.[23]

Initially, Herzen's minimum program was as successful as he could have hoped. Now unmasking concrete abuses, now publishing "radical" but constructive proposals as to how the emancipation should proceed, now opening his pages to a wide variety of opinions and information from inside the country seems to have corresponded exactly to the needs of the moment. The *Bell* was read not only by young radicals like Nikolai Dobroliubov, but by far broader strata of the population. Herzen once remarked that he wanted to be read "in the Winter Palace." His ambition

*Herzen refers to Anton Petrov, the "leader" of the only considerable peasant disturbance that followed the Emancipation, in the village of Bezdna. Petrov's status as a "prophet" is open to some doubt.

was gratified, and indeed the contents of the *Bell* were as well
known to some members of the upper bureaucracy as they were
to radical students. A. M. Unkovsky, a gentry "liberal" from Tver'
province, went so far as to say that in the city of Tver', "Herzen's
influence was so powerful that there was not a house [in gentry
and bureaucratic spheres] in which the *Bell* was not to be
found."[24] This is probably an exaggeration, and yet it suggests the
Bell's interest for cultivated people of different political persuasions. After all, it contained an extraordinary amount of interesting *information*. With a press as constrained as Russia's was,
portions of the *Bell* could be read as a kind of gossip sheet. And
in reformist Tver', an amorphous kind of progressivism was increasingly chic. Having a copy of the *Bell* around the house lent
most establishments a certain cachet. As far as the students were
concerned, the progressive publicist N. A. Mel'gunov wrote to
Herzen at the beginning of 1858: "our youth prays to you, keeps
portraits of you and even refuses to abuse those whom you, evidently by design, do not abuse."[25]

By the end of 1858, Herzen had done far more than woo his old
Westerner friends back into the fold: he had created an all-Rus-
sian audience for the *Bell*. And getting the *Bell* and other contraband literature into the country was becoming much less difficult. This was in part due to the considerable increase in the
number of Russians traveling abroad—and to the interest that
many of them had in Herzen's message. In December 1857, the
Third Section compiled a list of the outlets in Western Europe
where one could buy the *Bell* and other contraband literature.
Cities in which there were one or more booksellers stocking such
literature now included London, Vienna, Hamburg, Berlin, Brus-
sels, Breslau, Poznan, Leipzig, and Paris; an outlet soon appeared
in Dresden. Nor was Herzen entirely dependent any longer on
returning travelers. Certain foreign booksellers smuggled in
publications of the Free Russian Press with false covers pasted
on, along with shipments of licit reading matter; others inserted
caches of books in shipments of clothes or hats; still others merely
resorted to the time-honored practice of bribing the authorities.
(Nor did the *Bell* come in only through Western Europe. There

was a considerable illegal traffic in more ordinary forms of contraband from Athens and Constantinople to Odessa; from Chinese cities into Irkutsk.) Herzen even sent copies of his journal through the regular mail to highly placed personages in Russia, who presumably would not be damaged if it were discovered that the *Bell* had arrived with the morning post.[26]

Ordinarily, one calculates that each copy of a subscribed periodical is read by one or two or three people. The *Bell*, however, was different. A good many copies found their way into networks of students in universities and other higher institutions, and even gymnasia. If a student-run library stocked the *Bell*, it seems plausible that scores of students might read all or part of a single copy. Among students and elsewhere in society, copies were frequently passed from hand to hand, and on numerous occasions individual articles and even entire issues were reproduced and distributed, usually by students—even in provincial cities like Voronezh. Thus, although no precise figure can be given as to how many people "read" the *Bell*, it was obviously far more than the several thousand copies being printed; indeed, one must assume that at least in the major cities of the empire, anyone who was willing to make a serious effort could get hold of a copy of the *Bell* without much difficulty.

The Russian government worked away at countering what was regarded in most quarters as Herzen's sinister influence. They attempted to put pressure on foreign governments, where there was a chance that such pressure might be effective. They sent spies abroad; they adopted such measures of domestic vigilance as they were capable of at home. Yet the government effort was not only ineffective and inefficient but also a bit halfhearted. A good many highly placed people read the *Bell*, either as a scandal sheet or because they found its unmasking of abuses useful. Iakov Rostovtsev, the chief bureaucratic emancipator, took out a subscription for the Editorial Commission, the central bureaucratic agency in the drafting of the Emancipation legislation.[27]

To Alexander and the upper bureaucracy, the ideological position of the *Bell* was noxious, but the journal had its uses, especially to those working on the Emancipation reform who wanted to deal as generously with the peasantry as seemed politically and economically possible. No doubt some effort was made to keep the *Bell* out of the country. But had the government been more determined, a great deal more could have been done, in particular to keep it from circulating widely within Russia's borders.

Toward the end of the 1850s, Herzen's house in London became a center of Russian life abroad. The stream of Russian and Polish radicals and other refugees from the continent increased, and to it was added a motley group of Russian travelers, not all of whose motives were political or even in any way serious. One of his collaborators on the *Bell,* V. I. Kel'siev,* has left us an exceptionally vivid picture of the more social dimension of Herzen's activity:

The visitor to London generally informed Trübner [Herzen's London publisher] of his desire to have the honor of making Herzen's acquaintance. Trübner would give him the address and offer to write a note. In answer to this note, Herzen would arrange a meeting, either at his place or at that of the visitor, if the latter for some reason did not want to be seen in Herzen's house. Such cases were very frequent. . . . People did not use their real names in Herzen's house, or used them very rarely. Whoever did not wish to conceal his visits gave his own name; with those who were uncertain or asked that their names not be given out, we either changed them (which, incidentally, happened rarely) or dealt with indiscreet questions by saying that we didn't remember, didn't know, it was a difficult name, etc. And in fact it was hard to remember all those who came to worship, there were so many of them. They flashed by, one after the other; they came in, trembling with reverence, heard every word of Herzen and engraved it in their memory; they gave him information, either orally or in the form of prepared notes; they expressed their sympathy to him and the sympathy of their acquaintances; they thanked him for the benefits conferred upon Russia by his unmasking and for the fear which the *Bell* inspired in everything dishonest and unclean; then they took their leave and disappeared. Whom did I not see at Herzen's in my time! There were governors, generals, merchants, litterateurs, ladies, old men and old women—there were students. A

*The passage is taken from what is known as Kel'siev's "Confession," made after he returned to Russia and threw himself on the mercy of the government. The description seems accurate enough, however.

whole panorama of some kind passed before one's eyes, really a cascade—and all this without taking into account those whom he saw *tête à tête*. Many a time, standing at the fireplace in his study in Fulham, I laughed inside to hear some retired captain, who had travelled to London expressly to see Herzen from some backwater like Simbirsk or Vologda, declare his sympathy, explain that he was not a reactionary.[28]

As Herzen succinctly put it in his memoirs, "we were in fashion."

How great was the *Bell*'s influence on Russian society in the late 1850s? We do know that despite some interest by Rostovtsev and other bureaucrats at the highest level of government, the *Bell*'s direct impact on the creation of the Emancipation Statute was negligible. Its indirect influence, one might argue, was somewhat greater, but in view of the small number of men actually involved in drawing up the statute, and their *relative* insulation from public opinion, it would be a mistake to ascribe either much praise or blame to Herzen for the final shape of the settlement.

His influence on broad strata of public opinion was obviously much greater, but to say with any precision *how* great involves one in the most basic questions of the relationship between ideas and other, less clearly defined social forces in a developing historical situation. Herzen, a man of great energy and publicistic talent, was ready from his base in London to channel the aspirations and express the hopes of an emerging, shapeless, optimistic body of public opinion in Russia, eager for change and forward movement after the stagnation of Nicholas's reign and Russia's defeat in the Crimean War. His failure to find an audience in Russia before 1856 shows that his later success depended on the times, on the public mood, on the initial actions of Alexander II. But Herzen capitalized brilliantly on his opportunity. His mix of ideological socialism, veneration of the peasant, sardonic unmasking of individual and bureaucratic abuses could not—at least initially—have been better designed to express the developing social mood. His irony, flamboyance, and righteous indignation had a special appeal for Russian youth, desirous of change, disposed to be angry with its elders and to regard itself as the hope of the future—yet without much sense of practical politics or the possibility of developing a coherent, practical program of reform. The number of young radicals who kept pictures of Herzen, their hero, suggests that his image and personality, as well as his ideas, were important to them. As Russian youth became more experienced in the ways of radicalism, less hopeful, more cut off and isolated from the surrounding society, however, the personality of Herzen became less attractive to those whose hatred of the established order was greater, and in some cases whose origins were humbler.

Of course, there were many vague progressives in the late 1850s, students and nonstudents alike, whose "awakening" was a kind of springtime that passed, a sowing of wild oats. They had their brief fling at radicalism or even revolution, "looked into" the *Bell*—and were absorbed, one way or another, by the changing society around them. Many older men and women were attracted by the social ferment, applauded the Emancipation, but became politically apathetic, absorbed by family and career in the 1860s. Many—more than one would like to believe—undoubtedly found the primitive, chauvinistic bromides of reactionary journalists like Mikhail Katkov a satisfactory substitute for Herzen's brilliant rhetoric.

"Die, if necessary," wrote Herzen in one of his passionate appeals to the younger generation, "for the preservation of the *equal right of every peasant to land*—die for the communal principle."[29] Only a few would take such advice at face value and act upon it when public opinion was less well disposed, and ironically enough they were just the ones for whom the persona of Herzen, with his irony, literary ambition, and long cultural baggage train, was soon to become suspect. For despite Herzen's theoretical socialism, which was sometimes to be seen in the pages of the *Bell,* the whole thrust of his minimum program was to draw him close to the moderate reformism of liberal professors like Konstantin Kavelin or, for that matter, Ivan Turgenev. Boris Chicherin criticized Herzen's socialism in *Voices from Russia,* but, for the most part, moderate public opinion had little difficulty in "accepting" Herzen's minimum program and the means through which he hoped to realize it.

In 1859 Herzen faced for the first time what one may roughly call a challenge from the Left. At the root of this challenge lay the fact that the inchoate political optimism that characterized the beginning of the new era was developing some rudimentary structure, and Herzen's desire to be realistic and effective had pulled him toward the center.

By that year, nuclei of a much more intransigent attitude toward the old order in Russia already existed both on university campuses and particularly in association with the St. Petersburg periodical the *Contemporary (Sovremennik)*, of whom the most important editor was Nikolai Gavrilovich Chernyshevsky. Most of the group around the *Contemporary* had been deeply influenced by Herzen. But their Herzen was the radical Westerner of the 1840s and the author of the incendiary books and pamphlets of the early 1850s—not the pragmatic and canny editor of the *Bell* who wanted to be read in the Winter Palace.

The *Contemporary* was one of Russia's most venerable journals. Founded by the poet Aleksandr Pushkin and his friend P. A. Pletnëv in 1836, it had come under Pletnëv's sole control when Pushkin was killed in a duel a year later, and it had remained his journal until 1846. Pletnëv, a man of purely literary interests, cared nothing for the social and political debates of the 1840s, and during his tenure the *Contemporary* came to be regarded as an honorable anachronism, a relic of the golden age of Russian poetry that had passed. In 1847 the journal was bought by the critic I. I. Panaev and the poet N. A. Nekrasov. Under their leadership it published several of Vissarion Belinsky's final and most engagé articles, and even during the worst of the post-1848 reaction it maintained a cautiously Western and progressive orientation. By 1855 its circulation had grown to about three thousand,[30] a considerable figure for the time. And in that same year Chernyshevsky began his close association with the *Contemporary*, an association as important to the history of Russian radicalism as that of Herzen with the *Bell*.

Chernyshevsky came from a long line of village priests of the central Volga region. He was born in 1828 in the provincial city of Saratov, where his father was the priest of a considerable

parish and a person of consequence in the ecclesiastical affairs of
the region. Chernyshevsky's father, Gavriil, according to William
F. Woehrlin, a recent biographer,[31] was far from the stereotypi-
cal narrow-minded provincial ecclesiastic so often portrayed in
the pages of nineteenth-century Russian novels. He was a man
of considerable education and a large fund of "Christian kindness
and humanity." Family life was warm and pleasant, and until
young Chernyshevsky arrived at the University of St. Petersburg
he showed little of the rebelliousness that was dramatically to
characterize the remainder of his life. He was shy and provincial,
an omniverous but disorganized reader, solitary and still committed to the Christian views of his family.

Between 1846 and 1851, Chernyshevsky's political and religious
views underwent a total change. He came to know several members of the Petrashevsky Circle, the only radical grouping of any
importance at the time, and several other critics of the government. He read François Fourier and Ludwig Feuerbach, observed the revolutions of 1848 with attention. By 1850 he considered himself a philosophical materialist and "remarked that he
valued Herzen above all other Russians and that there was nothing he would not do for him."[32]

After several years as a teacher, most of the time in Saratov,
Chernyshevsky began the career as a journalist that was to end
only with his arrest in 1862. He might have continued his teaching—who can say for how long—had it not been for the rejection,
in 1855, of his master's dissertation, "On the Aesthetic Relations
Between Art and Reality," in which he coolly denied the importance of technical aesthetic questions and advocated an art that
would pose vital moral and political questions, questions that in
Russia could be posed in no other way. As Venturi has remarked,
Chernyshevsky was consciously engaged in recovering and developing the tradition of engaged criticism that Belinsky had begun.

At first, Chernyshevsky divided his critical contributions between the *Contemporary* and the *Annals of the Fatherland (Otechestvennye zapiski)*, but he soon committed himself to the former, where he became, by dint of hard work, reliability, and a
certain amount of flattery, completely indispensable to Ne-

krasov. In 1855, with an academic career seemingly ruled out, Chernyshevsky took full charge of the literary and later the socio-political sections of the *Contemporary*.

Almost from the beginning, Chernyshevsky's call for a socially engaged art met opposition from the variously talented group of writers who were the literary mainstays of the *Contemporary*—most notably from Leo Tolstoy and Ivan Turgenev. The quarrel has been frequently treated in historical literature;[33] what is important for us is that the dispute between writers like Turgenev and Chernyshevsky has its similarities with the more political conflict between Chernyshevsky and Herzen, which came to a head in 1859.

Basically, there were two things about Chernyshevsky to which Turgenev and the others objected. One was his relative indifference to literary craft and to the autonomous value of art. The other was the more nebulous but extremely important question of his personality, manner, and *style*. These were matters that were also at stake in the disputes between Herzen and the followers of Chernyshevsky in the 1860s.

Any reader who follows the trail of quarrels between Chernyshevsky and his opponents is likely to be struck by the unusual vehemence of the latter—especially the more aristocratic ones. Their hostility was not mere snobbism, although there was plenty of that. (Tolstoy, whose reaction to Chernyshevsky was particularly extreme, referred to him as "this gentleman who smells of bugs," and there is plenty of other evidence that Chernyshevsky's plebeian origins were held against him. How dare this bedraggled creature from the seminary bandy words with a Tolstoy—or a Turgenev!) Chernyshevsky offended against a whole nexus of values, many of which were as dear to a "radical" like Herzen as to an apolitical gentry novelist (as he then was) like Tolstoy. Many of these values related to character traits that were specifically male and specifically aristocratic. Chernyshevsky had little sense of *culture*—in the sense that a cultivated man of the world ought to be familiar with certain places, books, and situations, ought to have ritualized his behavior in certain ways. He was concerned with what interested him. He was narrow and single-minded. He did not care about good manners. He could be a bore.

In a society that still valued masculinity and animal vitality, Chernyshevsky was shy and diffident and even slightly effeminate. He was made ridiculous by his wife, a vain and shallow woman for whom he entertained a slavish and hopeless passion. There was nothing martial about him, nor was there much evidence of that passionate love of physical nature so obvious in Turgenev, for instance.

In a more intellectual vein, his ethics were utilitarian. He believed in what he called "rational egoism"—that proper ethical conduct consisted in interpreting the pleasure-pain calculus to bring the greatest benefit to society as a whole.

Chernyshevsky was not an ignoble person. On the contrary. Those who knew him best all attested to his tender heart, his benevolence, his selflessness. His conduct throughout his journalistic and "political" career certainly demonstrates that he did not lack courage. But it was the courage of the clerk, not of the warrior. Compared with Herzen, he seems pure—but also bloodless and somewhat arid. When his enemies accused him of stinking of the seminary, they were not altogether mistaken: he possessed that subtle combination of arrogance and humility so often characteristic of priests, and not only in Russia; he is a figure out of Russian religious history, despite himself. Thinking back on the 1850s at the end of his life in exile, he wrote that "My memories of Turgenev and the others are incapable of arousing in me any other feeling than a longing to sleep. . . . These people had no interest for me. . . . I was a man crushed by work. They lived the usual life of the educated classes, and I had no inclination for that."[34] The smug dismissiveness helps explain why so much of *obshchestvo* disliked Chernyshevsky in so visceral a way.

Chernyshevsky's conversion to materialism was an intellectual one. From the standpoint of character, ethical *behavior,* and tone, he underwent no sharp break with his early spiritual and intellectual formation. What Nicolas Berdyaev, a great student of the Russian intelligentsia, wrote of nihilism in general is specifically relevant to Chernyshevsky:

[Nihilism] grew up on the spiritual soil of Orthodoxy; it could appear only in a soul which was cast in an Orthodox mould. It is Orthodox asceticism turned inside out, and asceticism without Grace. At the base of Russian nihilism, when grasped in its purity and depth, lies the Orthodox rejection of the world, its sense of the truth that "the whole world lieth in wickedness," the acknowledgement of the sinfulness of all riches and luxury, of all creative profusion in art and in thought. Like Orthodox asceticism, nihilism was an individualist movement, but it was also directed against the fulness and richness of life. Nihilism considers as sinful luxury not only art, metaphysics and spiritual values, but religion also. All its strength must be devoted to the emancipation of earthly man, the emancipation of laboring people from their excessive suffering, to establishing conditions of a happy life, to the destruction of superstition and prejudice, conventional standards and lofty ideas, which enslave man and hinder his happiness. That is the one thing needful, all else is of the Devil.[35]

Small wonder that to Tolstoy, who at that time embodied "creative profusion in art" and "the fulness and richness of life," Chernyshevsky appeared a canting priest, an ill-smelling Savonarola.

His asceticism seemed to convey not only a programmatic joylessness but the desire to deprive others of pleasure, to narrow life, to make it gray. Turgenev found his dissertation, subsequently published in the *Contemporary,* to be "disgusting carrion."[36] Although Turgenev's hostility was less violent and total than that of Tolstoy (on occasion he was capable of finding Chernyshevsky "useful"), he never really modified his underlying dislike, and he finally broke with the *Contemporary* altogether in 1860. Although Chernyshevsky preached the equality of the sexes and in some ways lived his doctrine with remarkable consistency and character, love and sex were in practice a humiliation and a torment to him. He did not enjoy good wine, sensual, unprogrammatic conversation. He was a Russian Roundhead, and his enemies were Cavaliers, even if they were in favor of a generous emancipation settlement or thought that all virtue resided in the Russian people.*

*Of the generation of the 1840s, only the plebeian Belinsky was at all similar to Chernyshevsky in stylistic effect, but he was singularly lacking in Chernyshevsky's dryness. But then there was no "young generation" to be concerned with such things.

But a generation was growing up in Russia that would pass a very different judgment on Chernyshevsky and the values and style he embodied. They would rightly see in his manner a far more vigorous repudiation of the past than it was in Herzen's power to make. They would condemn the useless cultural baggage that Herzen—like other "older people"—carried around on his back like a turtle's shell. And they would fervently embrace the sexual equality for which Chernyshevsky and others so firmly stood. What to the young Tolstoy was joyously male behavior, they would find repulsively exploitative. Turgenev with his hunting, Tolstoy with his wenching, Herzen with his fine conversation, his fancy phrases in five languages—all of them embodied the values of *obshchestvo,* however intellectually critical they may have been. Chernyshevsky not only repudiated those values, he gave the younger generation a living model of something else, something to oppose to those who became known, after Turgenev's novel, as "the fathers."

Turgenev himself understood the new mentality very well; his feelings, like Herzen's, were far more ambiguous than those of Tolstoy. Turgenev captured a good deal of the "younger generation" in a famous speech that he gave Bazarov, the hero of *Fathers and Children:*

But then we realized that to talk, to talk everlastingly about our ulcers is not worth the labor, that it only leads to platitudes and doctrinairism; we also saw that our wise men, the so-called advanced people and accusers, were good for nothing, that we were occupying our minds with rubbish; we were talking about art, about unconscious creation, about parliamentarianism, about the bar, and the devil knows what else, when it was really a question of daily bread, when we were being smothered by the crudest of superstitions . . . when the very freedom the government was making so much fuss about would hardly be of any use to us, because our peasant is glad to rob himself just in order to get drunk in the tavern.[37]

Chernyshevsky recognized his enormous intellectual debt to the Westerners of the 1840s, to Herzen and Belinsky in particular. But he did not love them as Herzen did, nor did he identify with them. Herzen took a kind of pleasure in running his fingers over those intellectual sores; there is a perceptible morbid rapture in his discussion of the "superfluous men" and their life under Nicholas.

But to Nikolai Dobroliubov and others of Chernyshevsky's younger followers, what had come by 1859 to seem most striking about the older gentry "rebels" was their self-pity, their uselessness, their incapacity for day-to-day work. The mood of the time made this generation gap inevitable. The gulf in consciousness between the pre- and post-Crimean period had become—in less than five years—enormous, virtually unbridgeable. Herzen told the younger radicals that they didn't know what it was like to live under Nicholas. Of course they didn't! But who could care about that in 1859?

The new era had something of the same effect on the fortunes of the *Contemporary* as it had on those of the *Bell*. Between 1856 and 1860, the *Contemporary*'s subscribers increased from three thousand to sixty-five hundred[38]—and this despite the defection of the literary stars who had made the journal what it was. Nekrasov's faith in Chernyshevsky was amply vindicated by the developing social mood of the latter 1850s.

The withdrawal of the Turgenevs and the Tolstoys gave Chernyshevsky the opportunity to staff the journal with collaborators of his own choosing. The most important of these was Nikolai Dobroliubov, a young man from a background similar to Chernyshevsky's but far less happy and tranquil. Dobroliubov shared Chernyshevsky's general outlook—they were intellectually at one to an extraordinary degree—but his temperament was quite different.* Chernyshevsky's behavior toward his "liberal" enemies was, on the whole, far from provocative—despite their frequent and venomous accusations and sallies. (He made, in fact, a notable effort to avoid a total break with Turgenev, and for a considerable time he succeeded.) Dobroliubov's hatred of the old

---

*See Alfred Kuhn's perceptive remarks about how similar Dobroliubov felt himself to be to the lazy, procrastinating, indecisive Oblomov-type he so violently attacked, in "Dobroliubov's Critique of Oblomov: Polemics and Psychology," *Slavic Review* 30:1 (March 1971), pp. 93–109. There is also an excellent biographical sketch in E. Lampert, *Sons Against Fathers* (Oxford, 1965), pp. 226–71.

order was, if not more thoroughgoing than Chernyshevsky's, sharper and more visceral; he was a very unhappy young man, consumed at times both with self-hatred and with loathing of the world around him, and delighted to throw down the gauntlet to those he disagreed with. Dobroliubov's challenge to his enemies was as explicit as it could possibly be.

Dobroliubov's connection with the *Contemporary* lasted just five years. In 1856, while still a student at the Pedagogical Institute in St. Petersburg, he became an occasional contributor. After his graduation in 1857, he became a regular member of the staff; soon he virtually took over the criticism section, which allowed Chernyshevsky to devote himself primarily to social and political matters. In 1859, Dobroliubov founded a satirical supplement to the *Contemporary* entitled the *Whistle (Svistok)*, which contained the most biting and barbed criticism of gentry Russia and particularly of "liberal" Russia that had ever appeared in public print. The *Whistle* drew an immediate response from militant university students. One wrote to Dobroliubov that "after reading your fine *Whistle*, I have the desire to heckle the university wisemen, the Olympian professors, together with the newly born university 'police,' i.e., the rector, inspector and subinspector."[39]

It was Dobroliubov who finally provoked Turgenev into a total break with the *Contemporary* in 1860, with a harsh review of the latter's *On the Eve*, entitled "Will the Real Day Ever Come?" Exhausted by a long battle with "scrofula" (tuberculosis of the lymph glands), Dobroliubov died in November 1861. His death was an enormous blow to Chernyshevsky, who had not only agreed with his opinions and sponsored his career but loved him with a kind of tenderness that only a handful of those who were close to him realized he possessed.

In 1857 and 1858 the political line of the *Contemporary* was almost identical with that of the *Bell*. Both hailed Russia's intellectual awakening; both spoke for a coalition of all progressive forces in the country. Chernyshevsky hailed the public commitment to emancipation in terms almost as rhapsodic as those of Herzen. Like Herzen, he defended the village commune as a socialist nucleus for the future; like Herzen, he pressed for an emancipation *with land*. But in Chernyshevsky's defense of the commune, the Slavophile feeling was far less pronounced than with Herzen. There was no talk of the Russians being "young" and the West "old"; there was no sense of Russia's mission to "save" the West. Instead of Herzen's glittering (but sometimes rather abstract) paeans to the Russian village, Chernyshevsky "looked upon the *obshchina* as an elementary and primitive form of cooperative, which could develop into a more modern variety and thence into an agricultural collective."[40] But like Herzen and the later Populists, Chernyshevsky hoped that the survival of the commune could enable Russia to move directly to socialism, or at least enormously reduce the length and misery of the intermediate stages of development. "History," he said, "like a grandmother, is very fond of its grandchildren."[41]

Chernyshevsky was concentrating on "practical" and minimal goals, much as Herzen did. He worked at making a case for the advantages of free labor to gentry Russia. He devoted much time and space to trying to persuade the makers of the Emancipation that the peasants should not have to pay too dearly for the land they would receive—although his personal conviction was that the peasants should receive all the land they presently farmed and pay nothing for it. Quite as much as Herzen, he was engaging in the politics of the possible.

But by mid-1859, Chernyshevsky had grown more pessimistic about the possibility of an emancipation that would be, from the peasant's point of view, even tolerable. A progressive coalition was no longer useful, he thought; indeed, it was dangerous and harmful. What was needed was to create a real radical constituency for the future, since the peasants would certainly not be satisfied with what they would receive, and major disorders—even revolution—became a real possibility. Herzen, far away in London, did not seem to understand the situation and continued with the old politics of cajoling, praising, and threatening the government by turns, perhaps because he had known Nikolai Miliutin and other reformers, and felt that they were fundamentally on the right side. If there had ever been any point in being read in the Winter Palace—Chernyshevsky might have thought to himself—there certainly was none now.

Characteristically, it was Dobroliubov and not Chernyshevsky himself who provoked the breach. Back in 1856 and 1857, it will be remembered, Dobroliubov had idolized Herzen in a way that Chernyshevsky had long since ceased to do. But in the course of 1858, Dobroliubov's attitude seems to have changed. There is some evidence to suggest that by the middle of that year he was beginning to be bothered by Herzen's conciliatory attitude toward Alexander. Furthermore, he had a personal bone to pick with Herzen, as the latter had not printed Dobroliubov's second lengthy denunciation of disciplinary abuses at the Petersburg Pedagogical Institute. In the summer and fall of 1858, Herzen received a number of letters from Russia criticizing him for entertaining such high hopes of Alexander.[42]

What actually brought about the quarrel, however, were several pieces that Dobroliubov published early in 1859. In essence, he castigated the "liberals" for their illusions and denounced the kind of accusatory literature that the *Bell* had been printing for several years. Denunciations of specific abuses were of no use, he said, and were even harmful, insofar as they helped a rotten system maintain its equilibrium for a while longer.

Herzen's ire was thoroughly aroused. On June 1, he published a reply in the *Bell* entitled "Very Dangerous!!!" in which he defended the efforts of moderate reformers and the usefulness of the broad coalition of progressive forces against which both Dobroliubov and Chernyshevsky were now directing their attacks. Herzen was especially stung by the notion that the "superfluous men" of his own generation were now of no further use—a charge he was to hear with increasing frequency over the next ten years—and that the torch was passing to a new and more vital generation. Herzen accused the *Contemporary* of playing the reactionaries' game by trying to shatter the coalition that had been the driving force for reform.

Intellectual differences were then exacerbated by personal ones. Nekrasov was concerned for his journal and for the consequences of a total rupture with the *Bell*. He persuaded a reluctant Chernyshevsky to travel to London in late June to attempt to heal the breach. The one meeting between Herzen and Chernyshevsky was not a success, and although no consecutive and really credible description of their encounter has survived, the difficulties seem to have been at least as much a matter of style as of policy.[43] Herzen, it seems, behaved with an Olympian hauteur, to which Chernyshevsky responded characteristically by commenting on how tedious Herzen was. "To remain longer would only have been boring," he wrote to Dobroliubov. "It is true that the journey was not useless, but if I had known how boring it would be, I should not have come. . . . My God, I had to say a few things. . . . He is a Kavelin* squared, that is all."[44] And to the editor of the *Russian Word*, Chernyshevsky observed ironically that Herzen still believed he was breaking lances with Khomiakov in the fine drawing rooms of Moscow.

Relations between London and St. Petersburg changed very little until mid-1861, when Herzen quickly came to realize the full inadequacy of the final Emancipation settlement, and the *Bell* gave vent to the full-throated opposition to the settlement for which Chernyshevsky had been hoping. During this period neither Herzen nor Chernyshevsky wished for a noisy and irreparable breach. Chernyshevsky certainly detested Herzen (especially for having attacked Dobroliubov) and probably felt that he had been deliberately humiliated by him. He probably had been. But the impulse at the *Contemporary* to expose Herzen was counterbalanced by the sporadic desire to radicalize him, to win him over. Herzen, after all, could not quite be equated with the detestable "liberals," and the tactical significance of the *Bell* could not be ignored.

In March 1860, the *Bell* published an anonymous "Letter from the Provinces"; the author's identity is uncertain, but the point of view was that of Chernyshevsky and Dobroliubov. The "Let-

---

*Konstantin Kavelin, in Chernyshevsky's view, was one of those credulous liberal professors who expected the dynasty (or "the state") to bestow liberty on Russia more or less painlessly, without violence or struggle.

ter" contained a passionate plea that Herzen not be taken in by liberal fantasies.

You will soon see [the letter ran] that Alexander II will show his teeth, as Nicholas I did. Don't be taken in by gossip about our progress. We are exactly where we were before. . . . Don't be taken in by hope and don't take in others. . . . No, our position is horrible, unbearable, and only the peasants' axes can save us. Nothing apart from those axes is of any use. You have already been told this, it seems, and it is extraordinarily true. There is no other means of salvation. You did everything possible to help a peaceful solution of the problem, but now you are changing your tune. Let your "bell" sound not to prayer but for the charge. Summon Russia to arms.[45]

The "Letter" was signed "one of your friends."

Herzen struck the same note of passionate but friendly disagreement:

We differ from you [he replied] *not in ideas* but in methods; *not in principles* but in ways of acting. You are only *the extreme* expression of *our* own position. We understand your one-sidedness. It is close to our hearts. Our indignation is as young as yours, and our love for the Russian people is as alive now as it was in the years of our youth. But we will not call for the axe, for that oppressive *ultima ratio, so long as there remains one reasonable hope of a solution without the axe.*[46]

The emphasis on youth and age is worth noting. For when Herzen returned to the offensive that fall in an article entitled "The Superfluous Men and the Bilious Ones," it was again the curt dismissal of his contemporaries (and himself) that angered him most. The ingratitude! The lack of a feeling for old struggles or even an interest in them! Herzen predicted that the "bilious" generation would quickly give place to something healthier, better rounded, more life-affirming. The "superfluous men" had admittedly been mutilated by Russian reality, but the younger generation was equally, if differently, malformed. How many older radicals have felt similar sentiments when confronted by their intellectual heirs and successors!

When Soviet historians deal with the quarrel between Cherny-shevsky-Dobroliubov and Herzen in 1859–60, the principal point is to contrast Herzen's "vacillations" and "liberal illusions" with the revolutionary militancy of Chernyshevsky and Dobroliubov. In so doing, they are celebrating the emergence of an unflinch-ingly revolutionary viewpoint among the intelligentsia, a devel-opment they (no doubt accurately) consider an important stage along the way to 1917. For historians of a different perspective, the significance of the episode dwindles and becomes more a matter of tone, style, and feeling. Still, there is no question that by 1859 Chernyshevsky had come to feel that Herzen was far too optimistic about what might be expected from the Emperor and too close to the spineless and trivial liberals (Chicherin and Kave-lin), whose pathetic belief in the monarchy Chernyshevsky felt needed to be exposed in order for a resolute, realistic radical position to become a reality. The siren song of the moderates, hoping for a generous and peaceful solution to the peasant ques-tion "from above," was confusing and disorienting to progressive opinion and had to be exposed.

But the quarrel between Herzen and Chernyshevsky is most important in the history of Russian radicalism because it is premonitory, because it heralded the appearance of a new, mili-tant, and irreconcilable radical spirit. But its importance at the time should not be exaggerated. To read some accounts, one might imagine that public opinion was occupied with little else than sorting itself out into two neat "camps": one genuinely radical and plebeian, grouped about the *Contemporary,* the other made up of gentry "liberals," waverers, and a host of futile and well-intentioned people who continued to believe, against all evidence, in the goodwill of the Emperor and in the possibility of serious reform from above. But in going through the memoir literature on the period, one does not receive this impression. The disagreements between the *Contemporary* and the *Bell* were of immediate importance to only a small number of people, most of whom were closely connected with one side or the other. Most politically aware contemporaries continued to think of Herzen and Chernyshevsky as allies—as, to a degree, they did themselves. The notion that the amorphously progressive coalition suffered a fatal blow in 1859 is largely the work of historians who view the quarrel in terms of later developments within Russian radicalism.

In 1861 and 1862, progressive Russians were occupied with other things than journalists' tactical disputes. The Emancipation Edict was finally promulgated, and after a brief moment of euphoria, Herzen joined Chernyshevsky in bitter condemnation of it—all the more bitter, perhaps, because he had continued to hope for so long. And although the peasants were clearly disenchanted with the terms of the Emancipation, which most of them found utterly incomprehensible and many of them thought did not represent the real will of the Tsar, disorders were scattered and did not threaten social stability. Meanwhile, elements of the gentry were showing somewhat more spine than Chernyshevsky had expected—and university students also seemed prepared to defy the government in substantial numbers. The result was that since the peasants did not seem, for the moment, to be reaching for their axes, while individual gentry were at least beginning to formulate demands for political compensation for their economic losses, Chernyshevsky took a less negative view of the political potential of *obshchestvo*. He was encouraged by the ferment among Russian students but was well aware that escalating disorders might trigger reaction, rather than revolution.

Another factor that helped heal the breach between London and St. Petersburg was the attempt to create a revolutionary organization that would unite the diverse oppositional nuclei that now existed throughout the country. This organization was the first Land and Liberty *(Zemlia i volia)*. Neither Herzen nor Chernyshevsky seems to have been directly involved in the rather amateurish organizing efforts that went forward in 1861–62.[47] The lead was taken by Ogarëv in London, and particularly by a number of younger Russian radicals, almost all of whom had close ties to Chernyshevsky. The *Bell*, despite Herzen's ambivalence about creating a conspiratorial organization, was important in defining and publicizing the broader aims of the organization. Chernyshevsky was distracted by the death of Dobroliubov and weighed down by his obligations to the *Contemporary*. His organizational role appears to have been a very limited one. But of course he had substantially influenced the intellectual formation of young radicals like the Serno-Solovëvich brothers and others of the active organizers, and he certainly rendered advice and support.[48]

The importance of Land and Liberty is largely that of a harbinger. The Central Committee, with its shifting personnel and vague program, never succeeded in creating a national radical network. And with the failure of peasant discontent to grow into major disorder, the exhaustion of the reforming mood of *obshchestvo*, and the government's offensive against the Left in the summer of 1862, such structure as had existed soon collapsed.

Land and Liberty was a transitional organization. Its program was sketchy, its component parts only casually and sporadically in touch; it aimed to unite what already existed, to provide assistance and guidance for the anticipated peasant uprising. The groups that followed upon it were more tightly organized, more intellectually cohesive, more militant, and more turned in upon themselves. Nevertheless, Land and Liberty provided many Russian radicals with their first organizational experience. It also brought the *Bell* and the *Contemporary*—whatever the inner reservations of their editors—back into the arena together, for the last time. The active career of Chernyshevsky ended with his arrest in the summer of 1862, while Herzen's career ended in a long, slow decline. After 1862 his broad, amorphous, and moderate constituency disappeared. Most of "progressive" *obshchestvo* became more conservative and nationalistic in the wake of the insurrection in Russian Poland. Herzen's support for the Polish rebels is often cited to explain his loss of influence over broad strata of public opinion in Russia. No doubt it was important. But in addition the Russian radicalism of the 1860s was dominated by extreme and militant young men and women who idolized Chernyshevsky and repudiated Herzen. The *Bell* had been the organ of the reforming coalition that existed between 1857 and 1862. It had no real base of support in the very different period that followed.

University Students
in the New Era

"Oh Lord! Gracious goodness! Here they are, here they are!" screams Lyuba with her face glued to the window.

Sure enough, there is Volodya sitting in the phaeton with St. Jérome but no longer in his dark blue coat and grey cap but in the uniform of a University student with its blue-embroidered collar, three-cornered hat and short gilt sword at his side.

"Oh, if only she were alive!" cries grandmamma, seeing Volodya in his uniform, and falls into a swoon.

—Leo Tolstoy, *Boyhood*

In a country that is being "modernized," however poorly this painful process may be understood by all concerned, the university, and higher education generally, is in a central but deeply ambiguous position. On the one hand, institutions of higher education are necessary in molding and training the personnel necessary to run a modern state. On the other, the university is almost certain to produce a variety of criticism, ranging from the purely technical sort to the radical moralism of the intelligentsia point of view.

Student political activists are drawn naturally, if far from exclusively, to intelligentsia attitudes. Even upper-class students, who have a definite stake in the existing order, may not, at that early stage of their lives, perceive their interests rationally, clearly, or selfishly. Nor are they likely to understand the duration, difficulty, and social cost of political change. As Donald K. Emmerson, a perceptive recent commentator, has written:

Righteous in tone, symbolic in content, student politics tend to differ from "adult" politics in the sense that it is more often the art of the impossible. This emphasis on style over program and commitment over compromise is at once the weakness of student movements and their strength. Student political leaders cannot always escape criticism for the irrelevance of their conceits, for dissipating their energies in proclaiming and protecting ideal images of self and society while ignoring the complex, mundane, "low-payoff" tasks of incremental reform. Yet in those very images—in the credibility of the myth of student innocence, in the purity of their rage against evil—lies the fragile chance to effect basic change, albeit not singly or directly but by triggering or accompanying larger forces into action.[1]

The student movement was of fundamental importance in Russian politics, from the late 1850s on—precisely the period in which the situation in the universities became of major and practical concern to the Russian government. Both Alexander I (in his late years) and Nicholas I had worried about subversive ideas in the universities. But under Alexander II, the old prophecy of Joseph de Maistre seemed to be taking on flesh: what Russia had to fear was not the specter of peasant insurrection, not Pugachëv, but "a Pugachëv of the university."

The Russian universities in the mid-nineteenth century were of comparatively recent origin. The oldest, in Moscow, had been founded only in 1755. Kharkov and Kazan' received universities in 1804, St. Petersburg in 1819, and Kiev only in 1834. (The two non-Russian universities of the Russian Empire, Dorpat and Vilna, are somewhat peripheral to our concern with social ferment in Russia, as is the University of Odessa, which came into existence only in 1865.

The relationship between the Russian gentry and the universities had always been uncomfortable. In fact, until after 1825, the gentry never took to the educational institutions the state had created, in large part for them. The student body in Moscow remained very small throughout the eighteenth century. (In 1764 there were only forty-eight students in residence, of whom eight were members of the gentry. At the end of the century, there were still no more than a hundred.[2]) Tutors and foreign universities were the rule for most gentry who cared about ideas and culture; those who cared less, but wanted a service career, often attended military academies, which gave them a high rank upon graduation. Despite the fact that the university was heavily plebeian in social composition (its students being largely the sons of lower officers, priests, free peasants, and even serfs), it failed to democratize the ruling elite because of its small size.

Under Alexander I and Nicholas, the situation grew more complex. Alexander was determined to reconcile the gentry to the universities, three of which were founded under his reforming auspices, and Nicholas showed signs of wanting to restrict university education to them, despite his fears of a gentry *Fronde.* Alexander's reforming minister, Mikhail Speransky, changed the situation with his Education Act, which became law in August 1809. This decree made the achievement of the eighth rank in the service hierarchy (which conferred nobility) dependent upon a certificate from a university "testifying to the successful study of sciences appropriate to his branch of civil service." If the candidate could not produce such a certificate, he had to go to the university and pass an examination to the same effect. The Education Act thus went some distance toward restoring "the Petrine bond between education and state service."[3] Despite this blow to aristocratic dilettantism, however, it was not until after 1825 that the thinking members of the gentry, at any rate, really embraced the university. With the increasing mistrust between the monarchy and the more cultivated and speculative members of *obshchestvo* (particularly those who approached an intelligentsia mentality), the university became the refuge of the latter and thereby took on a respectability and prestige it had never before enjoyed in gentry circles—as evinced, for instance, in the quotation from Leo Tolstoy's memoirs that heads this chapter.

Despite Nicholas's distrust of the gentry, an attitude that was permanently exacerbated by the Decembrist Revolt, he was even less inclined to the idea of raising up substantial numbers of the lower classes through the educational process. Although in theory the universities were open to all the free estates of the realm (in 1827 serfs had been forbidden by statute to attend), the talented plebeians who had previously used the university to advance their fortunes now found new obstacles placed in their path. Secret ministerial directives sharply qualified open admission to the university in practice. The gentry-dominated gymnasia, with their classicized curriculum, became, if not the only means of entrance, by far the easiest way into the university, not least because they were in part given over to direct preparation of the student for university entrance examinations. Tuition fees had been introduced in the last years of Alexander I. In 1845, they were raised, not so much out of financial need as for reasons of social control.

Nicholas also divested the universities of a great deal of their internal autonomy. All educational levels came under direct bureaucratic supervision and control; the universities were placed under the administrative authority of the curators of the educational districts in which they were located. The governance rights of the university councils were sharply curtailed, and the curator might dismiss "unreliable" professors. A substantial number of inspectors, often of military background, kept tabs on the intellectual, political, and moral situation in both schools and universities, including student church attendance and reception of the sacraments.[4] The total number of gymnasium and university students remained small, and the rate of growth modest. By 1848, university enrollment had reached only 4,566, and gymnasium enrollment 18,911.[5] In the immediate aftermath of the upheavals of that year, the number of university students dropped by one fourth.

The year 1848 had other negative consequences. The University of Moscow was the only Russian university that had begun to develop the kind of tradition and *esprit de corps* so characteristic of the ancient universities of Western Europe. And although the center of the Slavophile-Westerner confrontation had been the Moscow salons, the university had been a forum, too. But in the fear and then torpor that prevailed in intellectual circles after 1848, the university lost much of this intellectual vitality. Philosophy, under perennial suspicion in the nineteenth-century Russian university, disappeared again from the curriculum, as did the public law of the states of Western Europe. The remaining rights of the university councils were further curtailed; rectors and deans were no longer elected but were made agents of the Ministry of Education, and their functions were conceived by the government as identical with those of the detested inspectors. As the reign of Nicholas drew to a close, both faculties and students were passive, demoralized, and opportunistic. Apathy and careerism seemed totally predominant.[6]

As in so many other areas of Russian life, the Crimean defeat quickly convinced the government that "improvements" were necessary: the quality of education had to be improved and the quantity of educated men increased. So the new era began quickly in the universities, and a stream of decrees and administrative changes were launched after 1855. The universities were opened up to all those who could pass the qualifying examinations, and a dramatic increase in enrollment resulted. Between 1854 and 1859, the population of the universities increased by more than half. St. Petersburg almost tripled in size. Formerly proscribed subjects were reintroduced. Travel restrictions and the ban on the importation of scholarly materials were relaxed. Many of the military bully boys who had occupied the crucial posts of curators and inspectors were replaced by milder men with civilian backgrounds, and even more important was a general relaxation of "supervision." After 1858, student inspectors were relieved of their supervisory responsibilities except within the walls of the university.

The response of the rapidly growing student body to these changes—and to the feeling of liberal drift that accompanied them—was rapid and pronounced. Students seem to be particularly sensitive to the inner strength and self-confidence of the authorities whom they "confront." So it is no wonder more and more Russian students sensed that neither Alexander nor his subordinates had a clear sense of what they wanted to achieve, beyond the broadest possible commitment to "improvement." Indecision at the top translated itself down the chain of command. Curators, inspectors, rectors, and the older professors lost their sense of the situation and some of their self-confidence. And the students were not slow to take advantage of this development. Beards, mustaches, and long hair—formerly strictly forbidden—made their appearance, then as now symbols of liberation.

The situation in which the students found themselves fostered the dramatization of certain adolescent behavior patterns—specifically what Jean Piaget has called the "constant mixture of devotion to humanity and acute egocentricity." The adolescent, writes Piaget,

thanks to his budding personality, sees himself as equal to his elders, yet different from them, different because of the new life stirring within him. He wants to surpass and astound them by transforming the world. That is why the adolescent's systems or life plans are at the same time filled with generous sentiments and altruistic or mystically fervent projects and with disquieting megalomania and conscious egocentricity. . . . The adolescent in all modesty attributes to himself an essential role in the salvation of humanity and organizes his life accordingly.[7]

If a propensity for messianic elitism is characteristic of able young people, a number of factors in the Russian situation contributed to its luxuriant development. One was that there were so few students—still fewer than five thousand in 1860–61. Then there was the importance the new Tsar clearly ascribed to the university and its personnel. To be a student was to be in the vanguard of progress, to be the hope of the nation; to the students from lower-class backgrounds, there was the additional feeling that they were joining this new elite, rather than merely assuming their natural place within it. And around them they perceived an inchoate or articulated sympathy; *obshchestvo* wanted to "believe in youth," especially in university youth, especially at the dawn of the new era.

No other social forces could contest the students for their self-assumed role as the nation's hope. The government had been disastrously defeated in war, and Nicholas was dead. A substantial modern middle class was still decades away; the Great Reforms had yet to do their work. And the students were geographically concentrated; their developing *esprit de corps* could easily assume tangible and organized forms.

Until very recently, it has been customary to rely heavily on social factors to explain the growing radicalism of Russian students in the latter 1850s and 1860s. Alexander's measures to democratize the universities, so the argument runs, brought plebeian elements into *obshchestvo* (or at least into its vicinity), resulting in quite substantial changes in the quality and texture of Russian culture within a surprisingly brief period. These people—the children of priests, doctors and medical functionaries, marginal landowners, and lower bureaucrats—received the now-famous label of *raznochintsy* (literally, "the people of various ranks"), those who could not or did not fit into Russia's disintegrating caste system. Soviet historians, analyzing the alleged replacement of "feudalism" by "capitalism" on the historical stage, often periodize the history of the intelligentsia similarly, indicating that at some point around 1861 the gentry ceased to be the dominant social element in the intelligentsia and were replaced by the *raznochintsy*. Many Western historians have endorsed this general view, without claiming a comparable sociological precision: "From Gentry to *Raznochintsy*" or some similar phrase indicates that Chernyshevsky is about to be introduced in textbook or lecture.

That much of the intellectual leadership in Russian radicalism in the 1850s and 1860s was in the hands of *raznochintsy* cannot be denied. In such an aristocratic culture as Russia was, the appearance of so many sons of priests on the social and intellectual scene could not fail to make a deep impression, and it is perhaps not surprising that historians often characterize the entire period as *raznochintsy*. To the most obvious names of Chernyshevsky and Dobroliubov one could add a score of others. Certain of the seminarians pioneered a militant and uncompromising style and image that proved deeply attractive to several generations of

Russian radicals. With the broadening of the social base of the universities, upper-class students came to be more immediately aware of the poverty of their lower-class confreres, and in the atmosphere of the period diluted their snobbery with a volatile mixture of compassion and admiration. This opening up of the university, despite periodic attempts by the governmnt to limit or even reverse the policy, proved irresistible, and it undoubtedly hastened the demise of the educated gentry's virtual monopoly over Russian intellectual life.

Still, despite the leadership provided by Dobroliubov and Chernyshevsky and the prominence of seminarians at both the *Contemporary* and the *Russian Word,* there is little evidence to suggest that *raznochintsy* students as a group were decisive in the growth of student dissatisfaction and radicalism.[8] Nor does the figure of Chernyshevsky seem to have been more attractive to the sons of priests or poor army doctors than to the children of gentry landowners. Indeed, the reverse may be true. To an upper-class student, tormented about his privileged position and exploitative social role, and determined to repudiate them, the persona of Chernyshevsky could have a special appeal—based on militant moralism and cultural strangeness. Despite the appearance of a number of *raznochintsy* in prominent positions, the evidence suggests that most lower-class students were simply trying to "make it" in the upper world of Russian society, whose doors were now at least ajar.

The two great Russian novels about the radical politics of the 1860s, Turgenev's *Fathers and Children* and Dostoevsky's *The Possessed,* suggest opposite answers to the question: Were the young radicals of the 1860s rebelling *against* the values of their "parents" (the gentry liberals of the 1840s) or simply acting out those values in a more vigorous, extreme, and uncompromising fashion? Turgenev stressed rebelliousness, and his version of the generation gap has been more generally accepted. It is certainly true that in any period of impending social change or upheaval, generational conflicts are exacerbated, which is one reason why Turgenev's vivid portrayal of those differences has always seemed so compelling.

But it might be argued that Dostoevsky's view of the situation was more profound, however idiosyncratic his demonic portrayal of 1860s radicalism. Stepan Trofimovich Verkhovensky, the 1840s Westerner (and a caricature of Granovsky), is the father of Pëtr Verkhovensky, the radical of the 1860s. Their values are ultimately identical; the younger Verkhovensky is merely more thoroughgoing and consistent, less timid and sentimental. What Dostoevsky saw less clearly is that the Slavophile ideas that affected him so powerfully had themselves contributed to the satanic social doctrines against which he fought so hard.

The fact is that we do not know enough about the backgrounds of individual radicals to generalize as to whether they were rebelling against the personal values of their families or putting those values into practice in a more consequent and militant fashion, a question that has often been raised with respect to more recent "young radicals."[9] A comparison of Chernyshevsky and Dobroliubov suggests the difficulties of the question. Up to a point, the backgrounds of the two were remarkably similar. They were both the sons of priests, both had demonstrated piety and intellectual precocity as children, and both were from provincial backwaters. But Chernyshevsky's biography suggests a substantial carryover in basic values from childhood to maturity, from the bright, ascetic, repressed child of the provinces to the radical of St. Petersburg.[10] One has the sense that Chernyshevsky's rejected Christianity gave him the emotional basis for his radicalism and guided him in his first intellectual formulation of moral principle. Nor does Chernyshevsky seem to have regarded his intellectual break with the values of Russian society as a repudiation of his parents. "More and more," Chernyshevsky wrote in his diary at the age of twenty, "I recognize a similarity between [my father] and me in the best moments of my life, or, in any case, between him and what I consider to be the best in man."[11]

Dobroliubov's case was very different. If Chernyshevsky's childhood was idyllic, Dobroliubov's was grim. Dobroliubov's father, far from being generally respected, beloved, and permissive, seems to have been an irritable tyrant with a penchant for bootlicking. Chernyshevsky was sent by his family to the University of St. Petersburg, but Dobroliubov broke with his father when he left the seminary for an intellectual career in the capital. The stages in Chernyshevsky's biography flow into each other, while Dobroliubov's brief career speaks of tremendous repression,[12] followed by a frenzy of revolt and permanent instability.

An unquestionable precondition of the growing student radicalism of the late 1850s was the mood of "liberal" reformism unleashed by Alexander II's educational reforms and most of all by the coming of Emancipation. In general, this link between student attitudes and broader and more diffuse social moods seems characteristic. A determined radical minority can pursue its activities for some time without broad social sympathy, but a large-scale student movement depends on its participants feeling that they have substantial—if halting or inarticulate—support outside the walls. When the social mood changes drastically, as Americans have recently had occasion to observe, student attitudes are likely to alter correspondingly. Perhaps it is best of all to be able to feel that you are doing the right thing, that most people know you are, and that they admire you and wish you well, although they are too timid or socially encumbered to join you, despite the belief, shared by all thoughtful parties, that the future is on your side. For a time in the late 1850s, Russian students—or at least an activist minority—were in that happy position.

Student movements also need non-student figures with whom they can identify—members of the faculty or other individuals within the university, or figures from the larger world of journalism or politics. Russian students, in fact, had both. There were the remote but glamorous figures of Herzen and Ogarëv in London, and the increasingly influential group around the *Contemporary*—above all, Chernyshevsky. Nearer at hand were sympathetic and popular "liberal" professors, like Konstantin

Dmitrievich Kavelin, professor of law at the University of St. Petersburg. L. F. Panteleev, whose memoirs illuminate the period vividly, recalled Kavelin in the following striking terms:

He tried to become close friends with his students; all those of any talent could count on being received at Kavelin's Sunday morning receptions, which were specially arranged for students. He always expressed his opinion without the least hesitation, without nervous or sidelong glances—whether it was agreeable or not—while at the same time he knew how to listen attentively to any objection, without ever attempting to intimidate a young opponent with his authority. At the receptions, scholarly questions were discussed, as well as the latest in literature, but primarily the phenomena of our contemporary domestic politics. Principally, of course, this meant the liberation of the peasants. Being very well informed as to the course of the reform, K.D. informed us of its most trifling details and the difficulties which it was encountering. . . . It was first from K.D. that we learned of the initial preparations of N. A. Miliutin for the creation of the zemstvo institutions,* and it was also K.D. who explained to us the full significance of the transformation which was being prepared, not only from the economic point of view, but the social. . . . Through his broad contacts, K.D. was *au courant* with everything which then had social significance, and he gladly shared it all with his interlocutors. There was only one boundary which K.D. never crossed: even I, a student enjoying his particular favor (when he left for the country in the summer, he entrusted me with arranging the juridical chronicle in [the journal] *The Century,* one of whose editors he was)—even I never saw *The Bell* at his place, although he undoubtedly received it. He did, however, often tell us interesting things from it.[13]

Kavelin was probably the most influential of the activist, reform-minded professors of the late 1850s, but at the climax of student unrest and disorders in 1861–62 he ran into trouble. His was the basic dilemma of all moderate progressives in periods of acute disorder. He did not provide the kind of uncompromising support the most militant students demanded, while the more moderate and conservative authorities held him responsible for the breakdown of order. Kavelin always prided himself on being able to communicate with people of radically different persuasions:

*The zemstvos were organs of local government that were introduced after the Emancipation.

the Slavophiles, conservative bureaucrats, Herzen, Dobroliubov. In that respect he belonged to the 1840s, not the 1860s. And when the political situation polarized beyond a certain point, he ended by being acceptable to no one.[14]

The relationship between what one might call "campus issues" and the dramatic development of reform at the national level was complex. Undoubtedly, most student activists focused on local rather than national concerns, although the excitement of the Emancipation drama had a catalytic effect. What people seem to have noticed first was that students seemed to be thinking and feeling more as a group, that class and regional differences seemed to be diminishing, and that the students who arrived at the universities in 1858 seemed to be distinctly more interested in politics than their predecessors had been.

Soon the greater cohesion of the students began to create "we-they" situations. Since the attitude of the university authorities—the curators and rectors—was now uncertain or even sympathetic, student organizations began to spring up: libraries, scholarship funds (financed by the richer students for their poorer colleagues), social clubs, and a spectrum of periodicals— ranging from quite acceptable scholarly journals to badly printed imitations of the *Bell*. As student corporatism developed, clashes with the police began to be more serious, if not actually more frequent. In the old days, these clashes seldom had had serious consequences. Increasingly, after 1856, students viewed the beating or maltreatment of one of them as an offense against the entire body, and they met, often in large numbers, to seek redress. Sometimes they succeeded, particularly at first, as neither the university nor the civil authorities were accustomed to dealing with crowds of determined students. Under Nicholas the educational bureaucracy would automatically have had recourse to Draconian measures. Now its officials hesitated—either because they simply had lost their bearings, or because the signals they received from above were confusing, or because elements among them were touched with the sympathy toward reform, so common to *obshchestvo* in general. As Anthony Graham Netting, a perceptive student of Russian public opinion, wrote a few years ago, "political and cultural revolutions depend less on their dedicated partisans than on the apparent enemies who in crucial moments partly give way. It was this involuntary reserve army that liberal *obshchestvo* [had assembled] under the very guns of Nicholas I."[15]

Sometimes the animus of the students was directed at university officials, particularly the prying and officious student inspectors. After a rather nasty case at Kazan' in 1857, which began with a parietal violation, a number of students were expelled, but the inspector resigned and so, eventually, did the curator.[16] A rather similar case occurred at Kharkov in the same year, when one of the curator's minions struck a student in the course of "arresting" him for appearing on the street in an improper uniform. A series of tumultuous student meetings ensued, in the course of which the curator felt himself forced to resign. Both of these incidents, and others like them, were regarded by the students as victories and whetted their appetites for more.

Incompetent, indifferent, or authoritarian professors (some were all three), who were regarded as holdovers from the bad old days of Nicholas, were frequent targets. To achieve their removal was not merely educationally desirable but took on a political coloring as well: it was part of the task of reforming Russia. Students answered back to these professors in class, petitioned against them, boycotted their lectures, or resorted to systematic harassment (clapping, whistling, and so on). These incidents, too, were likely to escalate, and the administration frequently found itself in the middle, between an outraged and defensive faculty majority and an aroused student body. In the spring of 1859, Prince Viazemsky, the son of the great poet who was Pushkin's friend, became curator of the educational district of Kazan'. He replaced a man who had been driven out by just such an episode —an attack on a professor, which had led to a series of boycotts, expulsions, and general chaos.

For better than two years, Viazemsky managed to keep matters under control. He was cognizant of the relationship between "student unrest" and social reforms being carried out elsewhere, and he did his best to be reasonable, accessible, and not to overreact and make things worse. Conservative officials tended to feel that he was not reacting at all.

But even an intelligent and tactful conservative like Viazemsky was not immune from the pressures of the day. The Kazan' students had tangled with an Italian professor of geography in 1859; although he was an eminent scholar, his Russian was so bad no one could understand his lectures. In the tumultuous fall of 1861, the students began to work on him again. This time, Viazemsky and his hitherto tactful and discreet inspector let the matter get completely out of hand. The university was closed for several months in the late fall and winter, and the buildings were briefly occupied by troops. Several scores of students were expelled, and after two separate investigations, one of them involving an elaborate government commission, Viazemsky was replaced in June 1862.

The principal means of mobilizing student support in one of the frequent *istorii* ("histories") was the so-called *skhodka*. The term was of peasant origin, significantly; it meant the meeting of the village assembly and was taken over by the students to designate their own meetings. As the 1850s wore on, *skhodki* became ever more common and often unruly. In most instances, they were unauthorized, although rules governing *skhodki* were at least hazy; in some instances (St. Petersburg), the curators and rectors had initially encouraged them, thinking to draw the students into orderly and practical cooperation in their own governance. But the *skhodki*, like other forms of student assemblies, came to be regarded by the authorities as dangerous in the extreme, and they were forbidden by law in May 1861, unless specifically authorized, as was "all bargaining with them through deputies or mobs."[17]

Although the primary focus of the students' discontent was on their own position in a university badly in need of reform, a few were getting more interested in radical solutions to national problems; after 1858, the loose congeries of ideas that would become known as Populism was more and more attractive to a minority of the students, although not necessarily to the most militant. Everyone had something to say about Herzen's *Bell*.

Newssheets and "journals," some printed and some handwritten, began to make their appearance in the universities during and after 1858. In St. Petersburg there was the *Herald of Free Opinion (Vestnik svobodnogo mneniia)* and the more radical *Little Bell (Kolokol'chik)*. Venturi notes that in Moscow alone at least four manuscript newspapers were circulating in 1858: the *Spark,* the *Living Voice,* the *Echo,* the *Unmasker.*[18] Kharkov had its *Free Word.* Finally, at Kazan', St. Petersburg, and elsewhere, the corporate, student-run libraries became centers for the accumulation and distribution of the *Bell* and other illegal literature. Most of the students' own newspapers were largely oriented toward what was taking place on campus, but there was a distinct subcurrent of interest in national politics, and the hostility toward local figures spilled over into criticisms of the government and Alexander himself.

Toward 1860, on most university campuses, groups were forming who cared only about the national arena and who utilized campus issues primarily to radicalize the student body. Also at Moscow was the so-called Library of Kazan' Students, from whose ranks were drawn some of the most dedicated and extreme radicals of the 1860s, among them P. E. Argiropulo and P. G. Zaichnevsky,[19] the principal author of the extremist Jacobin manifesto *Young Russia.* The Library of Kazan' Students undertook a considerable venture in clandestine publishing, beginning in 1859; extensive selections from Herzen appeared, followed by Ludwig Feuerbach's *Essence of Christianity* and Friedrich Karl Büchner's materialist tract *Force and Matter.* Only Zaichnevsky's arrest in 1861 prevented the publication of P. J. Proudhon's *What Is Property?*[20] The University of Kazan' gave rise to the so-called Kazan' Circle in 1860, whose membership included the radical ethnographer I. A. Khudiakov. The ultimate goal of the group was to induce a peasant insurrection; in the short run, the circle tried to keep the student body "aroused and alert to attempts to deprive it of its 'rights.' "[21] There was a "secret society" at the University of Kharkov that as early as 1856 was vaguely discussing extremely radical ideas: how to make a political revolution, the revolutionary potential of the cossacks, and even the question of regicide. A decision was grandly taken to extirpate the imperial family, although no one actually did anything.[22]

What is the best way to get at the relationship between student discontent within the university, spilling over into national politics, and the larger question of the development of Russian radicalism? Was the radical literature, to which the students had access in the late 1850s, actually important in their development? An even harder question to answer: What was the nature of the radicalizing experience that many of the Russian students underwent in the five-year period following the death of Nicholas?

To the first question, Soviet scholarship has given a fairly simple and unequivocal answer: student discontent was an important part of the larger upheaval that brought about Emancipation in 1861 and inaugurated the "capitalist period" of Russian historical development. Like the ideas of Herzen and Chernyshevsky, student unrest was in the final analysis a "reflection" or "echo" of the so-called crisis of serf agriculture and the rising curve of peasant disorder.[23] But this "explanation" is quite inadequate. Perhaps the notion of "reflection" is never adequate to explain the relationship between ideas and an economic substructure. Still, it is true that peasant unrest helped generate the excitement of the late 1850s. The Kazan' Circle believed that a peasant insurrection was a distinct possibility, and the expectation of an "inevitable" peasant insurrection was a recurrent motif in radical thinking into the 1860s. Still, this belief was basically a fantasy of the disenchanted portion of the Russian elite, and it often was more a function of their own powerlessness than anything else. The largely self-generated excitement that animated *obshchestvo,* and the students in particular, had more to do with their own altered situation than with any frightening or challenging upheaval from below. The government and many of the landowners certainly worried, among other things, about a peasant uprising, but the students saw themselves bestowing a full humanity on the peasants; their attitude was generous and rather patronizing.

The significance of literature and ideas as radicalizing agents has been much discussed, both by Soviet and particularly by Western historians. Certainly the cluster of ideas, feelings, beliefs, and prejudices that eventually became known as Populism has a genuine intellectual content, and as the 1860s went along, people spoke and wrote in this vocabulary. But one should not exaggerate the direct, unmediated role of books and ideas. The ground must be prepared and the times right. Büchner's *Force and Matter,* which seems to have shattered so many Russians' faith in revealed religion, now seems to educated readers, even to radicals, not only a cramped and pedestrian tract but a new form of metaphysics. Even in Russia its vogue was brief, if powerful. The books that "influence" us this year may fail to move us two years hence. Intellectuals, and students in particular, are notably susceptible to fashion or, to employ a more complimentary term, to "the intellectual currents of the day." To say this is not to deny the sincerity of the commitment of the radical minority, but merely to stress their vanguard role; the commitment of most students to the "intellectual currents of the day" was "broad, rather than deep," as Panteleev remarked of the influence of the *Contemporary.*[24]

Very rapid and at least superficially "extreme" shifts in political allegiance were common in the late 1850s. Many students who had never really had any political views at all became "radical" quite quickly. But this characteristic of the period, attested to both by contemporaries and historians, should not be exaggerated. The movement of some students to the left was gradual and rather hard fought. Such moderate, vaguely "liberal," and Westernizing journals as the *Russian Herald (Russkii vestnik)* and the *Annals of the Fatherland* also had student adherents. The *Annals,* in particular, appealed to students who retained a pronounced bureaucratic mentality, who wanted orderly reform from above, and who continued to dream of brilliant careers within the limits of *obshchestvo* Russia as it then seemed to be evolving.* Such students, who were likely to regard Cherny-

*Dmitry Pisarev was such a student in 1858. See A. M. Skabichevsky, *Literaturnye vospominaniia* (Moscow-Leningrad, 1928), pp. 107–17. Panteleev remained an adherent of Katkov's *Russian Herald* until the very end of the 1850s. See his *Vospominaniia* (Moscow, 1958), p. 145.

shevsky and Dobroliubov as rabble-rousers, were in a real sense not "typical" of the times, but they, too, applauded the Emancipation and, from time to time, looked into Herzen's *Bell.*

Nor is it anachronistic to discuss the matter of "image," so important in American politics today, not least in student and radical politics, in the Russian radicalism of the 1850s and 1860s. Men like P. N. Rybnikov and especially P. I. Iakushkin helped by their lives and examples to create the figure of a Populist-ethnographer, wandering among the people and becoming part of them. That this image is not an adequate rendering of these men does not matter to the student of the 1860s. What matters is to understand how an influential minority of their contemporaries regarded them.

Part of the declining appeal of Herzen to Russian youth and his replacement by Chernyshevsky has more to do with the two men's images than with the ideas they put forward. The "younger generation" of Russian radicals in the late 1850s and 1860s was powerfully attracted to Chernyshevsky's puritanism, asceticism, deliberate lack of charm, and social ease. His whole bearing was an affront to the existing order, and he conveyed the impression that he would not make the slightest social concession: to smile and murmur a few ceremonial words to put an interlocutor at his ease would be, somehow, to betray his whole position. Sincerity was everything. He insisted on being accepted exactly as he was. Herzen, on the other hand, was a "gentleman," even an aristocrat. He loved good food, good wine, and brilliant conversation. He was charming—or could be—and however much he might criticize the existing order, he was clearly a product of it and was bound to it by a myriad tangible and intangible ties—not least the substantial sum of money he arranged to have brought out of Russia when he emigrated. Chernyshevsky conveyed none of this sense of attachment to the old. Both he and Dobroliubov embodied the most militant rejection of the old and the determination to create something new.

Much of this collision of images emerged in an open letter to Herzen, which was written by a young radical in France in 1866. I quote it at length, not because it is fair or accurate—probably

very few of even the most extreme and embittered Russian radicals would have endorsed its rhetoric except in the heat of battle
—but because it conveys so well the way in which Herzen's
image, persona, and style, rather than his ideas, were being rejected.

I have long since ceased [wrote Alexander Serno-Solovëvich] to read,
or at any rate to be interested in your sheet [the *Bell*]. Hackneyed,
long familiar sounds; rhetorical phrases and appeals, ancient variations on an ancient theme; witticisms, sometimes fairly clever, but
more often flat; commonplaces about "Land and Liberty"—all this
has become too tedious, too boring, too repulsive. . . .

Yes, the young generation has understood you. Having understood
you, it has turned away from you in disgust; and you still dream that
you are its guide, that you are "a power and a force in the Russian
state," that you are a leader and representative of youth. You our
leader? Ha! Ha! Ha! The young generation has long outstripped you
by a whole head in its understanding of facts and events. Failing to
perceive that you have been left behind by events, you flap your
enfeebled wings with all your might; and then, when you see that
people are only laughing at you, you go off in a rage and reproach the
younger generation with ingratitude to their teacher, to the founder
of their school, the first high priest of Russian socialism! You are a
poet, a painter, an artist, a storyteller—anything you please, but *not*
a political leader and still less a political thinker, the founder of a
school and a doctrine. . . .

So you were the complement of Chernyshevsky! You marched
shoulder to shoulder with Chernyshevsky! Such an idea I never expected even from you, and I have studied you closely. . . . You the
complement of Chernyshevsky! No, Mr. Herzen. It is too late now to
take refuge behind Chernyshevsky. . . . Between you and Chernyshevsky there was not, and could not be, anything in common. You
are two opposite elements which cannot exist side by side or near one
another. You are the representatives of two hostile natures, which do
not complement, but exterminate each other—so completely do you
differ in everything, not only in your philosophy of life, but in your
attitude toward yourself and to other people, not only in general
questions but in the minutest details of your private life.

Conceit is your great misfortune, it completely blinds you. . . .
Come down to earth; forget that you are a great man; remember that
the medals with your effigy were struck not by a grateful posterity,
but by yourself, out of your blood-stained wealth. Look more closely

at what is going on around you, and you will then perhaps understand that dry leaves and paper snakes interest nobody . . . that you, Mr. Herzen, are a dead man.[25]

Few, if any, students of the late 1850s and early 1860s consciously modeled themselves any longer on Herzen, while Chernyshevsky was personally fascinating to many. Leo Tolstoy thought that "a bilious, spiteful man is not normal," but increasing numbers of radical students did not agree. In an aristocratic society like that of Russia, smelling of bugs was an excellent way of proclaiming one's disaffection. Good manners and reasonableness not only bound one indirectly to the established order, they were among the essential guarantors of liberal impotence.

Many contemporaries and historians noticed the intellectual shallowness of the radicalism of students (and some older people) in the late 1850s. In one sense they were correct. Very few of the students had really mastered Büchner, Moleschott, Proudhon, or Fourier, and their radical impulses most often found expression in sloganizing. (The arguments of their opponents, one might add, were not ordinarily on a higher level.) But intellectual influences are a secondary consideration here. Most people do not become radicals because of the books they read—although they may appeal to books and draw sustenance from them. To understand the radicalizing experience that students underwent in the late 1850s, one must look instead to the sharp break with the past that occurred in 1855-56 and the *consciousness* it helped induce, a consciousness that men were not wholly impotent with respect to their environment, that things might be changed, ought to be changed—and were about to be changed. One must look to the special qualities of youth and adolescence, and to the privileged and isolated position of Russian university students. Various Western intellectual currents helped to provide a language for expressing these feelings of mission: German materialism; the utilitarianism of Bentham and Mill; the socialism of Saint-Simon and Fourier. And many of the ideas and preoccupations that had animated both the Slavophiles and the Westerners in the 1840s were reappearing now as guiding motifs of the new radicalism, although not in a form that was intelligible to the older generation.

Some students understood these ideas, made a deep commitment to them, and contributed in turn to their development. For others they remained satisfyingly shocking slogans that corresponded to the emotional needs of the moment and gave them an important but fleeting sense of themselves and their generation. Some students went on to a deeper involvement with radicalism and the revolutionary movement; for others, radicalism was merely their kind of wild oats. But those whose radicalism could survive the withdrawal of the inchoate, "liberal" support of the late 1850s were a minority.

The view that institutions of higher education became, from here on out, the nursery of Russian radicalism is a theme of recent Western scholarship on this period.[26] But which students were likely to be radicalized at the university? Behind this question of university radicalism lies the larger general question of secondary education in Russia. The seminaries, the gymnasia, and the military schools were all harsh in their discipline, primitive in their pedagogical methods, and notably lacking in creature comforts. Most memoir literature that tells about these schools in the time of Nicholas is bloodcurdling, even to the reader who has cut his teeth on *Tom Brown's Schooldays.** But until much more systematic study has been made of secondary education under Nicholas, no serious discussion will be possible.

In fact, no background discussion of causal factors and circumstances can take us very far in analyzing what went on in Russian universities in the late 1850s and early 1860s. What happened there had a rhythm of chronological development that was de-

*In an admittedly impressionistic survey, Alain Besançon has taken note of the bitter memories that many Russian radicals had of their secondary education, and contrasted it with the warm nest from which most of them had emerged. More concretely, he stresses the Manichaean attitudes that were nurtured in the gymnasium: the hatred of authority, the vague democratic tendency, the beginnings of a culture of student solidarity. The harsh conditions in these schools must also have contributed to the popularity of the small number of "liberal" or "modern" secondary-school teachers who managed to survive under Nicholas. Their concern for the students and/or their hostility to the prevalent scholastic teaching methods appears to have won them a sympathy that no intellectual radicalism could then have achieved. See *Education et société en Russie dans le second tiers du XIXe siècle* (Paris and The Hague, 1974), pp. 16–49.

termined in part by national politics and in part by the logic of events within each university. These patterns were similar in a rough kind of way, but there were many local variants. The "student movement" at the University of St. Petersburg was the most tumultuous, in part because the excitements of national politics were greater in the capital than elsewhere, in part because there was greater support for student attitudes and activities, both within the university and in its immediate surroundings, in *obshchestvo*.

The situation at Kharkov was complicated by the many Polish students there—better organized than the Russian students, but rather suspicious, even separatist, in their attitudes. Their complex relationship sometimes reminds a contemporary American professor of the difficulties that black and white student radicals encountered in the late 1960s in working out a concerted campaign against that "common enemy," the university administration. In fact, Polish nationalism sometimes made the Russian and Ukrainian students more moderate in their actions and demands.

Another variant is provided by the University of Kazan', the most remote and, in a sense, isolated of the Russian universities. There the faculty was considerably less competent than at the other universities.* Kazan' students, furthermore, had a tradition of rowdyism and indiscipline, so it is not surprising that many disorders at Kazan' developed around bitter encounters between professors and students over the intellectual qualifications and performance of the former.

Soviet historians generally employ the term "student movement" as if there had been some kind of coordinated leadership and formally agreed-upon program—as if the students' encounters with the authorities were an organized political movement.[27] But despite a good deal of interuniversity contact, the ferment and the disturbances developed autonomously. One crucial difference between the Russian student movement of the

---

*An exception might be made for the discipline of chemistry, and of course the great mathematician Nikolai Lobachevsky had spent his life at Kazan' as professor and rector. But his brilliant work on non-Euclidean geometry was recognized in Russia (and Europe) only subsequently.

1850s and 1860s and the student radicalism in America a hundred years later has to do with the means of communication. Geographical mobility and in particular the electronic media gave American student politics of the 1960s a national and even supranational unity that was far removed from anything possible in the nineteenth century. The spread of radical politics on American campuses was often abetted by the gnawing feeling of inferiority that many students began to feel if their campus had remained relatively tranquil, while nightly news programs showed building seizures at Stanford and Columbia and a bombing at Wisconsin. Russian students simply could not be anything like so aware of what their confreres elsewhere were up to.

But one should not treat each university as a separate and unrelated story: the drama was far too similar. The national excitement and the government's attitude were unifying factors; and students moving from one university to another did help push the movement along. Fundamentally, however, structural similarities, rather than "influence" of one institution upon another, made for similarities in their histories during this period.

5

The University of
St. Petersburg

The hopes and enthusiasms of the new era were most powerfully felt in the capital, where student messianism could feed on being in the place where decisions were actually being taken, in a cosmopolitan city where students could on occasion fraternize with this or that "reformer" in the houses of a numerous and progressive *obshchestvo*. The career of the "student movement" in St. Petersburg was more dramatic and in the end more explosive than in other university cities; in that sense it was not typical. But there is much to be gained by observing the dynamics of a general process where the outlines were clearest and most extreme.

Stirrings were apparent as early as the winter of 1856–57. Lev Modzalevsky, a prominent figure in the early *skhodki* and subsequently a well-known and respected liberal educator, had this to say about the university, which he entered from a St. Petersburg gymnasium in 1856:

At the beginning of Alexander's reign all of Russian society *(obshchestvo)* experienced decided difficulties in the abrupt transition from the rule of Nicholas to the abundant new life, rich in the most iridescent hopes. The wall between Russia and Western Europe suddenly fell; the dead formalism collapsed, together with many of its constraints; everyone caught a whiff of greater freedom of thought and word. Together with the government, *obshchestvo* itself dashed toward the reform which had to precede the verification of new principles and the repudiation of the old delusions and defects. Our university, which had only 350 enrolled students, soon took on up to 1,000 new members of every estate, calling and age—and life became more noisy, precisely *more noisy,* since peace and quiet are necessary for study. The most merciless rejection, necessary for the renewal of the old life, penetrated the university from *obshchestvo* and found there the most fertile kind of soil. We—youth—boldly and triumphantly denied previous principles of morality and citizenship, although new ones had not yet been found. And in fact no one was in a hurry to find them and all energies were expended on rejection. If in fact new principles were taken on, then they still had to be verified,—and then we sought their realization in life, sparing nothing that they might triumph. . . . Employing the freedom which had been granted to us, to which we were as yet not accustomed, we soon stopped attending the lectures of strict and boring professors, who gave us their knowledge in some kind of dead form, and came into the lecture hall only to hear those who tried to apply their knowledge to the solution of essential questions, to the destruction of the old evil, and to the disclosure before us of new, fresh ideals, on the most rapid realization of which depended, it appeared, the entire happiness of our governmental, social, family and individual lives.[1]

Writing many years later, Modzalevsky laid heavy stress on the idealism of his contemporaries, their strong sense of mission, and their developing sense of a corporate identity. He rather dryly noted another characteristic of the movement, which other observers have noticed in other student activists: ". . . we gradually got out of the habit of all quiet, hard work which was not flashy, which did not bear fruit quickly."[2]

Prince G. A. Shcherbatov, the curator of the educational district, was unusually sympathetic to moderate student "activism"; he introduced the *skhodka* to the St. Petersburg student body himself. He hoped to make use of these periodic gatherings to guide and control the rapidly expanding student body. As long as the *skhodki* were regarded as a species of school assembly, there was no very obvious student enthusiasm for them. But soon *skhodki* were being convened by students involved in various projects, without the explicit urging—or even consent—of the curator, and interest in them picked up.

By the end of the year, a new student solidarity could be observed in the widespread concern for the lot of poorer students. A journal entitled *Miscellany (Sbornik)* was established to publish student literary and scholarly works, the proceeds to go into a fund for their needy compatriots; a series of public lectures by prominent professors was arranged to the same end. The liberal and meritocratic atmosphere from which the *Miscellany* emerged can be gauged from a speech that Modzalevsky, one of its moving spirits, gave to a *skhodka* of students from the faculty of Oriental languages on October 20, 1857.

Culture [Modzalevsky told his audience] does not belong to one class. In our century—the century of the destruction of monopoly and all exclusive rights—still less must it have an exclusive character. To the man of science there are no estates, no titles, no uniforms and thank God we already have a sphere where the external affiliations of a person do not swallow up the person himself. . . . It seems to us, that is to say, that the university is a sphere in which there must be only seekers after knowledge, not *petite bourgeoisie,* not merchants, not officials, not officers, not Russian aristocrats.[3]

At first the authorities took a benevolent and even an active interest in these proceedings. Government facilities were made available for the printing of the *Miscellany,* and the Empress donated three hundred rubles. But this rather tame experiment in student journalism soon fell victim to changing times. The students who came to the university in 1857, and especially those who arrived in ·1858, were perceptibly more radical and political than their predecessors; the bland, "scholarly" fare provided by the *Miscellany* did not appeal to them, and the journal died a lingering death. But it served as a rallying point for student corporatism and solidarity at the time. And even in the spring of 1857, the *skhodki* that were called to deal with the *Miscellany's* business were harbingers of the more political and obstreperous future, as A. M. Skabichevsky, one of the participants, recalled:

Although the *skhodki* were convened to read articles for the miscel-lanies and decide whether they were suitable for publication, I some-how do not remember a single such reading; I remember endless conversations, youthful dreams and quarrels, I remember readings of new issues of Herzen's *Bell,* this or that suppressed poem or article, circulated, at the time, abundantly in handwritten copies. For instance, it was at one of these *skhodki* that I first became acquainted with Nekrasov's poem, "Belinskii." Our classmate, Vsevolod Krestovskii, in turn, read his ultra-radical poems.[4]

L. F. Panteleev was an activist among the students who arrived in the fall of 1858, and he confirmed that his contemporaries were rather more interested in social and political matters than their predecessors had been. Doubtless exaggerating the watershed nature of 1858, Panteleev divided the older students into two categories: those who drank, horsed around, and behaved more or less consciously like German *Burschen;* and those who worked hard but narrowly and unimaginatively at their defined course of study, without "social interests" or the passion for periodical reading that was to be so typical of their engagé successors. Among the first students whom Panteleev met upon his arrival at the university was the son of a peasant woman, like himself from Vologda. He had come in first on the entrance examinations, but to Panteleev's astonishment he was not at all interested in the emancipation of the peasants and did not read either Nekrasov or Turgenev.[5]

A more enduring example of student solidarity and concern for their colleagues in need was the *kassa,* or mutual aid fund. An offshoot of the *Miscellany,* the *kassa* came into existence formally in December 1857. Funds were solicited from the more well-to-do and were also brought in by theatrical performances, lectures, concerts, and the like. After a discreet investigation of the circumstances of the recipient, the students would either grant him the money outright or give him a loan. Formal criteria for defining eligibility were never agreed upon, and a means test seemed "degrading." Between December 31, 1857, and June 1, 1859, the *kassa* raised and distributed nine thousand rubles; in the same period the government dispensed only seven thousand rubles in aid.[6]

Student assertiveness was more evident in 1857-58. Long hair and particularly mustaches were in evidence for the first time, and some students simply defied the authorities, who demanded that they shave them off. Students also defied the ban on smoking within the university; after a certain amount of fuss they were given a smoking room. "All these things were trifles," Skabichevsky recalled, "but they somehow raised our spirits and inspired us. The university became especially attractive. You would walk around within its walls and feel, with every step, as if your heart were beating more and more strongly within your breast. You were expecting something new, special, bravura. Everyone felt an irresistible longing to show his worth in some desperately courageous, heroic action."[7]

Excitement mounted steadily throughout the year, as it did in the other Russian universities as well. For weeks at a time there was some kind of *skhodka* nearly every day. Petitions to the authorities became more and more frequent; they seemed to be circulating almost constantly. Many related to clashes with the police, frequently stemming from student noise and disorder in St. Petersburg. Although they were not as yet political, the students responded as a body: they fought back physically, they petitioned the university and the city authorities—and they rightly believed that they had public opinion on their side. The arrogant city police were not popular with any group in St. Petersburg.

Rumors began to circulate—that a revolution was coming, that the capital was going to be moved to Kiev, that Grand Duke Konstantin, the Emperor's liberal brother, was already writing a constitution, that there would be orthographic reform! The very uncertainty of the authorities spurred the students on. They *did* achieve redress in several encounters with the police—which simply made ordinary high-handed police behavior seem suddenly more intolerable than it ever had before. When the authorities proved unable to enforce the ban on long hair and in effect connived at this small breach of regulations, the entire structure of rules that they embodied and represented lost some of its legitimacy. There were sharp encounters between faculty members and students, although nothing really serious yet. Interest in self-government grew rapidly; a number of *skhodki* were given over to a project for turning the university into a republic, run by elected legislative and judicial bodies.

It was also just about this time that the students first began to be aware of real divisions in their own ranks—between those who, in one way or another, clung to the old way of doing things, and those who embodied the new. On the side of the old were the mock-German students, the generally indifferent, and those who studied narrowly and compulsively with their careers in mind. The students of the new era grouped themselves, in 1858, in a rough fashion around two handwritten journals: the relatively moderate *Herald of Free Opinion* and the more radical *Little Bell*. The differences between the two groups seem to have had more to do with style than substance. Both were sharply critical of the students, faculty, and administration; neither made direct reference to national politics, but both gave clear evidence of a generally disrespectful attitude toward authority. A copy of the *Herald* eventually found its way to Emperor Alexander, via the Third Section, and he was quite upset. Prince Shcherbatov summoned the editor and contributors to his office and praised the journal profusely, but went on to say that he thought it might be better if he were accepted as a kind of adviser and collaborator who would be able to advise the students in cases where they might be misinterpreted by the nervous authorities beyond the university walls. So impressive was his gentleness and sympathy that the students did not feel it possible to oppose him directly; but the addition of this august representative of the administration to the editorial board robbed the *Herald* of much of its charm, and it did not long survive.[8]

The students at St. Petersburg—and elsewhere—became more and more possessed by missionary zeal. They wanted to proselytize beyond the walls of the university, to begin their mission of creating a new Russia. This was the great era of the Sunday Schools—voluntary institutions for the instruction of illiterate peasants and urban workers in the rudiments of reading and writing. Most of the instructors in the Sunday Schools seem to have been students, although there was broad participation by "liberal" *obshchestvo*. Some teachers engaged directly in the propagation of radical ideas, and the Sunday Schools, which had come to number over three hundred, were closed by the police in 1862. But while they lasted (and at one time there were twenty-eight in St. Petersburg) they were an important outlet for "enlightening" impulses.[9]

Many students, in addition, had one or more tutees, generally drawn from the ranks of the well-to-do. For the poorer students, these tutorials were a matter of economic necessity, but some undertook what they considered the education of the country's future elite for missionary, rather than financial, reasons. And in 1859, many members of *obshchestvo* were quite willing to have their children educated by radical (or cryptoradical) students; moreover, they often sat in on the tutorials themselves. As Skabichevsky, a former tutor, remembered the experience:

It was quite natural that with the increasing excitement of society's mood the very air, it seemed, was alive with the thirst for progress and enlightenment. A couple of students had only to appear in some rural neighborhood, and even if they did not want to busy themselves with the education of young ladies, proposing instead to tramp through the woods and shoot partridges, the young ladies of the neighborhood would themselves draw them into the enterprise, bombarding them with a mass of questions, demanding explanations, importuning them with violent quarrels, asking for serious books, etc.

Such phrases as "ridding oneself of vulgar, obsolete prejudices," "putting off from oneself the old man," "awakening to a new life" became highly fashionable. The novels of the time could not begin in any other way than with the sudden appearance of "him," who struck "her" with the breadth of his knowledge and erudition, the depth of his ideas and the dizzying novelty of his daring views.

Mummy and daddy were still not frightened then by the appearance of the "new man" at their estate. The springtime of Russia's renewal was still radiant with the most iridescent colors. Mummies and daddies themselves had nothing against playing liberal and seating the young apostle of progress in a prominent place at their table, together with the tutor, who, in his turn, tried to strut his own stuff in front of the student and show that he was not old hat. In all of this there was something genuinely naive and touchingly bucolic.[10]

He goes on to observe, however, that the "enlighteners" were not yet the embittered enemies of the existing order that many of them became after the struggles and political polarization of the years 1861–63. By the mid-1860s, "mummy and daddy" had a quite different attitude toward the apostles of progress.

It is no accident that in his little drama of education in the provinces Skabichevsky made the tutees women. For the late 1850s in Russia saw the real beginnings of what was to be called the "woman question": the lengthy debate over the role of women and their place in Russian society.[11] Radicals of Herzen's generation had been interested in Saint-Simonian ideas on the subject, and the novels of George Sand had enjoyed a distinct vogue, but the question of the emancipation of women became an important social issue only in the new era. The most influential early posing of the question from a pro-feminist point of view was an article by the prominent doctor and educator Nikolai Pirogov, entitled "Questions of Life." Pirogov had been largely responsible for the organization and utilization of female nurses at the front during the Crimean War, and in the postwar period he went on to devote considerable effort to bringing the question of women's education before the public.

Small wonder that the mood of the new era touched women as well as men. For until the late 1850s the role of women was conceived entirely in domestic terms and there was no higher education for them at all. Nadezhda Destunis, one of the first women publicists, related her arguments about women's education directly to the atmosphere of the post-Crimean period: "Can it be [she wrote in a letter to the Slavophile periodical, *Russian Colloquy*] that in our time when everywhere, in all of Russian society, there is so much activity, so much seething, so much striving forward—can it be that the Russian woman alone remains a passive, non-participating spectator to all this activity? Cannot some role for her in this common endeavor be found?"[12]

In the late 1850s—and with increasing fervor and better organization in the 1860s—Russian women did begin to redefine their social role, but the struggle was long and difficult. The first periodical devoted to at least a semiserious discussion of women's problems, *Daybreak,* was founded in 1859.[13] Admission to higher education was an obvious place to begin, and soon Russian women began to appear in the lecture halls of the University of St. Petersburg, although they were "free auditors" rather than regular students. Panteleev recalled his first encounter with a woman in the university:

It was the fall semester of 1860 and we second-year law students were sitting in Lecture Hall IX and waiting for Professor Kavelin. The hall, as always during his lectures, was packed: Konstantin Dmitrievich was then at the zenith of his popularity. Kavelin came in on time, but to our absolute astonishment, right behind him appeared the figure of the rector, P. A. Pletnëv, with a young and pretty woman on his arm. Pëtr Aleksandrovich courteously seated the young woman in an arm chair, sat down himself, and Kavelin, as if nothing were out of the ordinary, read his lecture. I do not think, however, that on this occasion we all listened to the lecture with our customary attention. The same thing happened at the following lecture; then Kavelin himself escorted the young lady several times and then she began to appear alone in the lecture hall, carrying a notebook to write down the lecture and seating herself, in expectation of the professor, in one of the regular chairs. The young lady was of a quite markedly Italian type, of no great height, always wearing a black wool dress of a simple sort; her hair was cut rather short and gathered in a net.* She was Natal'ia Ieronimovna Korsini, daughter of a rather well known St. Petersburg architect. . . . Her mother, no longer alive at that time, had taken some part in literature in the 'forties and at the beginning of the 'fifties and was an acquaintance of Pletnëv.[14]

Korsini soon began to attend other classes, and her example was followed by other women, until, by the end of the second semester, women in university lectures were a generally accepted phenomenon, no longer worthy of note, as other issues dominated the attention of the community. It is worth pointing out, however, that the University of St. Petersburg was altogether more enlightened on this subject than the University of Moscow. There, the University Council voted against the admission of wcmen as auditors, with only two professors recorded as favoring

---

*The simple black wool dress and the short hair would seem to indicate that Korsini considered herself a radical, although the fact that she was escorted by Pletnëv probably meant that she was a rather respectable one.

their entrance. In the furor of the early 1860s, the admission of women to the university came to be regarded as genuinely "radical," and in 1863 all women were forbidden to attend. Not until the 1870s were women able to achieve their own courses at the university level, and for a good deal longer their status was highly uncertain.

Throughout the academic years 1858–59 and 1859–60, the temper of the students grew steadily more self-confident, independent, and boisterous. The university was becoming unrecognizable to the students of a mere half-dozen years before. Part of the change was due to the increasing number of outsiders who swarmed to the lectures and simply hung around. The women auditors were the most spectacular addition, but people from all walks of Russian life—officers, government employees, professional people, priests—were simply "there" and contributed, directly and indirectly, to the chaotic vitality of the scene.

In the course of my five-year stint at the university [Skabichevsky recalled], it went through such a radical change as to be unrecognizable. Instead of the old dead silence of empty corridors through which small groups of frightened and well turned out students shyly moved only in the interval between lectures, now, from dawn until dark, the university was as noisy as a beehive; you had to fight your way through its corridors and lecture halls.[15]

The university was more and more fashionable and at the center of things, and this fact augmented the students' sense of their own importance. The explosions that rocked the universities in 1861–62 cannot be understood without taking into account the uneven momentum that had been building for the previous several years.

Skhodki became, more and more, a regular and accepted part of one's daily life. They accustomed the students who gravitated toward them to argument and debate, to noise and unruliness, to deciding issues, in some sense, on their merits and in the open. They affected the *consciousness* of the students in a fashion most hostile to the essentially passive ideal of student behavior that the authorities had unreservedly held until recently and upon which they would soon fall back. A steady stream of incidents, some involving the authorities, others having to do with disputes among the students, increased the numbers and disorder at the meetings.

Another extremely important aspect of the *skhodki* was that the students came to use them as quasi-legal instruments—to police their own organizations and to render judgment on those accused of violating the trust of the student body or misusing its funds. A kind of demystification of the students' attitude toward law seems to have occurred. Their hostility toward decisions rendered from on high, toward the arbitrary, toward mere order-keeping—as well as toward obvious injustice—was greater and nearer the surface.

The student community's evolution toward a more open and, in a sense, Western system of legal regulation culminated in what the American historian Thomas Hegarty calls "the first public jury trial in all Russia,"[16] which took place on March 5 and 6, 1860. The defendant was Nikolai Butchik, treasurer of the student *kassa* at St. Petersburg, who was accused and convicted of having embezzled student funds. He was sentenced to pay a fine equivalent to the sum he had taken and to be expelled from the university. Professor V. D. Spasovich, a political moderate, favorite of the students, and specialist in criminal law, served as chief justice. There were prosecuting and defense attorneys, and the verdict was rendered by a five-man jury and immediately announced to all the students at a *skhodka*. The curator gave his permission for the trial, and Spasovich helped the students with the procedures. The university authorities seem to have had little idea how "radicalizing" such an experience was likely to be for Russian students.

It is therefore scarcely surprising that the line demarcating university issues from national issues became somewhat attenuated and student interest in the larger issues of national politics increased. At the same time, radical attitudes on those issues became more common among the students—in a sense, more normal. Thus the more timid and conformist among the students could express such attitudes with less fear of censure;

indeed, in certain circles, radicalism was fashionable and even de rigueur, always an auspicious development for the growth of a student "movement."

One convenient gathering place for the radical and activist minority was the student library, which had been established on a subscription basis by two students in 1858. After passing through a series of managerial crises, it was operating, by mid-1859, "under rules drawn up by the student body at large" and was responsible to periodic *skhodki.* "The room occupied by the library," as Hegarty notes, "grew into more than a place for locating necessary reading materials. Students turned it into a club, where particularly in the evenings they came not so much to read and study as to talk over important issues affecting both the university and the nation. Librarian Iakovlev took pains to provide copies of Herzen's *Bell* for the students; discussions often centered on the issues which it had raised."[17]

The fall of 1860 was rather quiet—in part, apparently, because of a certain disenchantment with the chaotic regime of *skhodki,* in part because many of the activist students were occupied with teaching in the newly opened Sunday Schools. But this was merely a lull before the storm, and a series of episodes in the second semester restored the momentum that had been building in the previous year.

In February, the university administration excluded a speech by Professor N. I. Kostomarov from the program of a university celebration because they believed the subject of the Emancipation was likely to be broached. A spontaneous demonstration broke out at the close of the ceremony, forcing the rector to flee, although he later was compelled to return to the rostrum, where, shaking with terror, he promised the students that Kostomarov would give his speech that evening in the great hall of the university.[18] Kostomarov did, and was carried in triumph from the hall on the shoulders of the students.

Far more serious was the sequence of events that followed the death of Taras Shevchenko, the great Ukrainian nationalist poet, on February 26; the funerals of oppositional figures were ideal occasions for the expression of antigovernment sentiment. Shevchenko's, on February 28, turned into a massive, if orderly, political demonstration—of a rather vague and unfocused kind. It also provided the occasion for a *rapprochement* between the leaders of the Russian student corporation and some of the most active Polish students, who had hitherto tended to stand aside from the activities of their Russian colleagues. A few days later, the funeral of an in no way noteworthy Polish student who had died of natural causes became at the last minute a requiem for five Polish students who had been shot several days earlier by Russian troops in Warsaw. Russian and Polish students attended in large numbers, and they were joined by a number of Russian, Ukrainian, and Polish faculty members and by a crowd of sympathizers from St. Petersburg society. Toward the end of the service, the Poles broke into a "patriotic anthem," which could not be drowned out by the organist. All present, Hegarty reports, "were deeply moved."[19] When it was rumored that only the Poles were to be held responsible for the demonstration, three hundred Russian students signed a statement that they, too, had taken part in the requiem. Although the curator came to the brink of resigning, he did not, and no students were punished. Relations between the Russians and Poles further improved, and the student body reckoned that they had won yet another victory. Each of their triumphs generated further momentum and a willingness to seek out and tackle the next issue.

While all of these changes were taking place within the university walls, the attitude of the government, and particularly of Alexander II, was undergoing a very different kind of evolution: from enthusiasm to anxiety to positive hostility. Alexander had made the key decisions that were so important in initiating the ferment in the universities and in *obshchestvo* at large. On the one hand, no one can doubt the genuineness, however limited, of the Emperor's reforming impulse. But Alexander was neither strong nor decisive; even with respect to the Emancipation—in all its ambiguity his major achievement—he often prevailed through a kind of muddled stubbornness rather than through foresight or firmness. Furthermore, his "liberalization"—nowhere more than in the universities—represented a leap into the unknown. Not only did he have no real idea of what his measures would lead to, he had only the vaguest idea of what he wanted. So it is not surprising that his initial optimism and "belief in the students" did not prove durable; and once it was shaken, he tended to take refuge in the belief that a group of ill-intentioned persons had formed a subversive conspiracy against him. His father's propensity to believe in conspiracies had already become legendary, and the tendency was strong in a good many high government officials.*

At first, Alexander was skeptical. During the academic year 1857–58, the governor-general of Moscow sent him a telegram, concerning a rather minor incident, saying that in effect a "revolt" had occurred among the Moscow students. Alexander replied coldly that he did not believe this to be true and referred instead to the "crude actions" of the police;[20] his phrase was the contemporary equivalent of "police brutality." But Alexander's confidence in the students was already being eroded. In September we find him making anxious inquiries, via the head of the political police, as to whether the students of the University of St. Petersburg were behaving themselves and whether things were "in order." He received a soothing reply from the minister of education: the students were showing proper respect for authority and not gathering in unruly groups for discussion. But the Emperor was (quite properly) not entirely convinced by his minister's words, noting in the margin: "I wish that it were so."[21] A few weeks later, after a petty disorder at Kazan', Alexander issued an imperial decree forbidding the students to show pleasure or displeasure at lectures. The employment of an imperial decree to regulate cheering and booing during university lectures indicates how serious a view of the situation Alexander took.[22]

Throughout 1859 and 1860, Alexander continued to feel—and behave—ambivalently toward the universities. He took steps to

---

*In 1862, the Russian government closed the Sunday Schools; Alexander had been prevailed upon to believe that they harbored a full-blown radical conspiracy. Soviet historians tend to accept that conclusion; for quite different reasons they, too, are desirous of discovering conspiracies, which they adduce in support of the revolutionary militancy of various areas of Russian society in the 1860s. So the picture that emerges from the work of many Soviet historians, citing tsarist governmental sources, is of a much more "revolutionary" situation than in fact existed.

clarify the fact that when outside the university walls students were in fact subject to police regulations, just as were all other citizens. Admissions were stiffened, apparently with a view to admitting a more "studious" and orderly element, and on several occasions Alexander expressed concern about order within the walls and about the infusion of the lower classes into higher education. At the same time, the process of liberalizing and enriching the curriculum, which had been going on since the beginning of his reign, continued. Philosophy was restored as a field, new chairs were awarded in both Moscow and St. Petersburg, and—most striking of all—in May 1860, all universities were granted the right to receive scholarly books and journals from abroad without having to submit them to the censorship.[23]

By the spring of 1860, Alexander had become extremely concerned about the state of the universities, and his anxiety deepened steadily over the course of the next twelve months. In the summer of 1860, he established a commission to look into the question in detail and to ascertain whether E. P. Kovalevsky, the moderate and rather sensible minister of education, had not been too permissive and rather derelict in fulfilling his supervisory responsibilities. The commission presented its report the following April. Not only was it deeply critical of Kovalevsky, it suggested vaguely that the student disturbances were interconnected—a notion that ministered to Alexander's deep fears of conspiracy.

Kovalevsky counterattacked vigorously and managed, for the time being, to save his job. But Alexander remained convinced that the situation in the universities was fraught with subversive and disorderly potential; the Emancipation of the serfs had finally been proclaimed, and the government was highly uncertain about the economic and political future of the country. The upshot was that yet another commission was appointed, this one including Kovalevsky and presided over by Count S. G. Stroganov, an intelligent moderate conservative who enjoyed excellent personal relations both with the imperial family and with numerous Russian intellectuals. Stroganov had been curator of the Moscow Educational District during the 1840s and was given much

of the credit for the modest intellectual renaissance it had enjoyed at that time. The recommendations of the Stroganov Commission, incorporating further criticisms by Kovalevsky and re-
worked in part by the Council of Ministers, became the famous
"May Rules" of 1861, which finally brought the disturbances at
the University of St. Petersburg (and elsewhere) to a head and
concluded the first phase of the student movement's involvement in Russian social and political life.

Most of the propositions set forth in the May Rules were complex and specific. Two factors were of the utmost importance to
the students and were primarily responsible for touching off—
not causing—the disorders that ensued. In the first place, it was
clear that the authorities, from Alexander down, intended to end
the corporate institutions that had sprung up in the universities
over the preceding five years and the unruly and insubordinate
spirit that had accompanied them. Surveillance of the student
body was reemphasized, and those who did not adhere to the
rules were to be dismissed. All *skhodki* not specifically authorized by the authorities were forbidden, as was all bargaining
with "mobs." At the same time, Admiral E. V. Putiatin, a brusque
and rigid disciplinarian, replaced Kovalevsky as minister of education and a decision was taken to introduce the new regulations
not gradually, but "at once."

There is no question that the decision to eliminate student
corporate institutions would have been extremely difficult to
implement without serious disorder, even had the executors of
the new policy been endowed with an unprecedented combination of tact, sensitivity, and forcefulness. But the implementation
of the May Rules deserves to stand as a monument of how not to
introduce a policy that is sure to be deeply unpopular with an
excited student body. The students left for their summer vaca-
tion in early June knowing nothing about the content of the new
rules but with rumors of the most diverse kind in the air. Soon
after they left, Putiatin decided to introduce the new rules all at
once. He then ordered that the *kassa* and the library were to be
taken over by the university authorities. On July 20, Alexander
decreed that the student uniform was to be abolished, with the

decisions made, and then, he set off for a lengthy and well-earned rest in the Crimea.

The result of all this activity was that when the students reconvened in the fall, they did so in a mood of pessimism and bitterness, but without having any precise idea of what was going to happen.[24] Nor did it occur to Putiatin that it might be useful to enlist faculty support, least of all from contemptible liberals like Kavelin and Spasovich, whom he considered nearly as unreliable as the students. During the previous spring, Curator Ivan Delianov had turned to Kavelin and three other professors and asked them to draw up a code that would effectively regulate student behavior. The professors were pleased to be asked and responded quickly. They made use of elected student deputies in an attempt to ensure that their results would be acceptable to the student body as a whole, and ended several months' labor with a proposal that confirmed the student institutions but regulated them rather strictly: the *skhodka* was to meet under the chairmanship of a professor and elect officers who would be in charge of the *kassa,* the library, the *Miscellany* (should it survive), and other student organizations. Only a committee, made up of the elected student officers, should be able to convene the *skhodka* and bring business before it. A special court would be set up to judge student offenders, and further proposals provided for strict rules against disruption by students within the university.[25]

The May Rules meant that the proposal of the Kavelin Commission was doomed. The professors, however, still thought they might cushion the shock of the new regulations and help the students through the transition period as they were introduced. Then it became clear that there would be no transition period, and although the University Council elected a group of professors to help implement the rules, most of their suggestions were ignored. Of the few that *were* adopted, one turned out to be a fatal mistake. The idea was that the new regulations should be included in a booklet that would also contain the student's residency permit, grades, and library card—something along the lines of the German university *Studiumbuch,* known at the University of Dorpat as a *Matrikel* and in Russian as a *matrikul.* Thus a convenient symbol of the oppressive new order was dreamed up by the liberal opposition and issued by the reactionary authorities. And the administrative situation could not have been worse in the fall of 1861: Delianov had been replaced as curator by General G. I. Filipson, an inexperienced tool of Putiatin; Pletnëv, the rector, was in Western Europe, and his replacement, I. I. Sreznevsky, did not have the old man's moral authority.[26]

Thus, when the university formally convened on September 17, the students still did not know the content of the May Rules, and the faculty, which did know them, had become thoroughly alienated from the Ministry of Education and the acting curator. From the moment that the convocation prayer was over, large crowds of students met in daily *skhodki* to decide what to do. A number of the more activist and radical students—among them N. V. Shelgunov, E. P. Mikhaelis, and M. P. Pokrovsky—founded a "secret committee" to ensure that the growing student protests would be properly channeled and directed. Several of these leaders were close to Chernyshevsky.

The administration, after trying to ignore the *skhodki* for several days, ordered a partial lockout in an attempt to deny the students a place to meet. The virtually inevitable result was that the students broke into the main auditorium, had their *skhodka*, and decided that they would not accept the *matrikuly*, which were supposed to be distributed in the near future, as a symbol of their rejection of the new rules—whose content they still did not officially know. Putiatin reacted by closing the university—without, of course, consulting the faculty—and as a result there occurred the first mass action by the student body. By midmorning on September 25, a crowd of about a thousand students had assembled in the courtyard of the university. It was rumored, and widely believed, that some student deputies had been arrested. Violent and inflammatory speeches were made, and the crowd suddenly decided to confront Curator Filipson at his apartment, where the students (wrongly) believed him to be.

It was a beautiful September day. The sun shone brilliantly on the long lines of the student procession, the head of which was already approaching Palace Bridge while the tail had just emerged from the gates of the university. Along our route there were crowds of girls, auditors of university lectures and a great many young people having some connection or other with the students or simply sympathizing with us. We arrived at Nevsky Prospekt without noticing anything particular around us. Upon our appearance at about Morskaia Street and further along Nevsky, the French hairdressers ran out of their shops and with animated faces and sparkling eyes, rubbing their hands together delightedly, they cried: "Révolution! Révolution! V'la ça commune! ça y est! Voyons! Voyons!," etc.[27]

By the time the students arrived at Filipson's apartment, they had been joined by a substantial contingent of mounted police and troops. When Filipson heard what had happened, he returned to his apartment and negotiations began. Eventually he was accompanied by the students back to the university. The atmosphere was very tense, but nobody did anything violent. While the students remained in the courtyard, a deputation waited on Filipson. The students put forth, essentially, two demands: that they be allowed to use their library while the university was closed; and that the May Rules and the *matrikuly* be abolished. Filipson rejected both demands, and the students finally dispersed.[28]

Two other bodies met that evening: the University Council and the so-called Ruling Council, which Alexander II had constituted to make decisions on his behalf while he was away from St. Petersburg. The members of the University Council refused to take responsibility for formally introducing the May Rules, to which most of them were opposed. The meeting was angry, and Filipson withdrew to consult the ministry. The Ruling Council informed the students that if they engaged in further disorderly behavior, troops would be used against them, and ordered that the "most guilty" students be arrested. By the morning of September 26, thirty-two students were in custody.[29]

But the arrests did not have the desired effect. Not only did they not bring home to the students the reality of their powerlessness, they induced demonstrations of sympathy from Petersburg *obshchestvo:* professors, young officers, medical students, and other sympathizers flocked to what was becoming a virtually continuous *skhodka* in the university courtyard. On September 27, the courtyard was surrounded by troops, and the governor-general of St. Petersburg informed the students that if they did not disperse immediately, he would order the soldiers to open fire. Absolute pandemonium ensued, but the students remained, screaming that they would die for their rights and for their arrested comrades if need be. Then, reported an eyewitness,

on a pile of lumber appeared the tall, dark figure of one of the women auditors who was most respected by us and most devoted to intellectual matters, and to the student body, Mar'ia Arsen'evna Bogdanova, who subsequently became a well known educator. Her eyes were full of tears, her face was red and extremely agitated. She began to persuade us that they certainly would not fire on us, since they would not dare, on their own initiative, to cut down two thousand students; the police and cossacks would simply plunge into the crowd, beat us with whips and seize individuals. We were in no position to fight against crude physical force and apart from being beaten up and arrested we would achieve nothing. "For this reason," Bogdanova concluded her speech, "we all, the women here present, beg you, dear comrades, for the sake of our common honor and general welfare, to concede the obvious impossibility of opposition, to disperse immediately, in order to be able to turn to the thinking society of Petersburg for the defense of our just cause." These words had a strongly sobering effect on us and after some brief argument and discussion it was decided to enter into discussion with General Ignat'ev about the conditions for capitulation.[30]

For the next several weeks the situation remained deadlocked, with Alexander incommunicado in his Crimean resort. Negotiations, punctuated by disorders and further arrests, continued. As the professors refused to distribute the *matrikuly* to the students, an arrangement was concocted by which students could order them through the mail. Some six hundred-odd did so, but when the university was reopened on October 11, class attendance was minuscule. Then students who had not accepted their *matrikuly* were formally notified of their dismissal.

On October 12, the bloody confrontation finally occurred. Several hundred ex-students stormed the main university building;

others were drawn in, and a wild battle with police and soldiers ensued in which many students were badly beaten up and hundreds more were arrested. Between then and December 20, when the Emperor closed the university, it was in a state of semiparalysis, opening briefly and then closing again several times. Despite the fact that the most radical and disruptive students were presumably exiled, consigned to the Fortress of St. Peter and St. Paul, or simply left the city, *skhodki*, protests, and sporadic violence continued. On December 25, the disastrous reign of Putiatin ended, but not before Kavelin, Spasovich, and several other faculty "liberals" had resigned. A. V. Golovnin, a canny moderate, became minister of education in January 1862. But the university remained closed until August 1863.

While the tide of student militancy was rising, the rebels received powerful if diffuse support, not merely from radicals like Chernyshevsky but from broad strata of Petersburg *obshchestvo,* who helped maintain their élan by treating them as the vanguard in the struggle for a new and more humane order, outside the university as well as within it.

Just where did the support come from? We must depend on the most impressionistic kind of source material—primarily memoirs—to arrive at even the beginnings of an answer. The sympathizers certainly included other, nonuniversity students—studying medicine or preparing for a teaching career. Even some gymnasium pupils became involved. Prestigious political support came from the radical journalists of the *Contemporary* and the *Russian Word* and their more moderate counterparts on *Annals of the Fatherland,* who were less influential and whose support was more sporadic. And there was Herzen, whose influence was at its zenith. Viewing the tumult of the fall of 1861 from London, Herzen announced to his readers that the torch had passed to the students, who, he said, *"alone are pure.* The idea of Russian citizenship has been bred in the universities."[31] The same veneration can be detected in the words of Elena Andreevna Shtakenshneider, the daughter of a well-known St. Petersburg architect and a keen observer of the intellectual and social scene in the capital. "Events occur ceaselessly, irrepressibly," she wrote (somewhat incoherently) in her diary on September 28, 1861, "controlled by no one. *Obshchestvo* shies away from them fearfully and only the younger generation looks them right in the eye, like acquaintances, and unafraid, break their young heads to use them as stepping stones to the coming day."[32]

The Shtakenshneiders entertained on a lavish scale, and their house was among the most notable gathering places for Petersburg *obshchestvo* sympathetic to the new era. There one might find government officials, army officers, artists, theater people, musicians, and university professors. A similar locus was the house of N. L. Tiblen, a wealthy and progressive editor and sometime artillery officer. Panteleev, who was often at Tiblen's, met Chernyshevsky there, as well as the historian Kostomarov, the chemist N. N. Sokolov, Pëtr Lavrov, who was to become one of Russia's most notable radicals within a few years, and a whole galaxy of Russia's literary and journalistic talent.[33] Yet the minister of the interior, S. S. Lanskoy, was also a friend of Tiblen. Generally speaking, the early 1860s marked the end of such mixed gatherings, which had characterized Russian intellectual life so markedly for the previous half century. Political antagonisms were soon to become too powerful; indeed, it is remarkable that Lanskoy was still able to visit a house where Chernyshevsky was cordially received.

The students, Panteleev informs us, were eagerly sought after by Petersburg society in the fall of 1861, particularly those who had been several months in the Fortress of St. Peter and St. Paul for their part in the disorders. "The mood of society was extraordinarily elevated," he wrote, describing the last few weeks of 1861:

Wherever you went there was noise, talk, lively disputes, but the main thing was the general expectation that something of enormous significance was going to happen, perhaps even in the very near future. As far as we, the former students, were concerned, we not only had a hearty welcome everywhere, but, it appeared, were much sought after guests. It must be confessed that we accepted all this as a proper tribute for our behavior in the fall of 1861. But since youth always conceives of the future in a somewhat more rapid tempo of development, we certainly did not consider that our song was sung. We were convinced—and we gave others to understand—that the events of the autumn were only the beginning of that social role to the fulfilment of which "we" were called; and indeed the general chorus echoed our belief that we—namely the "younger generation" —were destined to make the "good word" into living reality.[34]

6

A New Left and a New Right

Public proclamation of the Emancipation Edict came in late February 1861. Those who remembered the occasion in their diaries and memoirs have left us the most varied descriptions of how the great day went in the principal cities of the empire. Some could recollect scenes of wild rejoicing; others remembered that it was business as usual; still others recalled the dire (and accurate) premonitions about the future that possessed them and a few other farsighted observers.

The government was concerned most of all with how the peasants would take their liberty. The settlement was by any reckoning immensely complicated, and the edict was written in the most stilted and arcane kind of bureaucratic language, full of elaborate and pious formulas—perhaps in the semiconscious hope that the peasants would be so exhausted by the effort to understand it that they would have no energy left for rebellion. And it was released during Lent, at which time the makers of high policy banked on a penitential atmosphere; indeed, an outside observer might well conclude that such an Emancipation had been visited on Russia's former serfs as a penance. And apparently the efforts of the government were crowned with success in at least this respect: it took peasant Russia a long time to make head or tail of what had happened.

In retrospect, historians have expressed surprise that the Emancipation went off as quietly as it did, in view of the enormous disappointment that the hopes of the peasants sustained.

But the view was different in the fall of 1861. There had been a big disturbance in the village of Bezdna the previous spring, resulting in the massacre of several hundred peasants by government troops, and there had been many smaller disorders. Most educated people believed that the peasants had not finished expressing themselves about the Emancipation: some rejoiced at the prospect, others regarded it with trepidation.

By the time the students were released from prison in December 1861, St. Petersburg was in a highly strained, nervous, and expectant state. Public support for them was running high; they and their liberal sympathizers were anticipating new developments in the village and perhaps elsewhere. Land and Liberty, the first real revolutionary organization of the 1860s, began to take shape in late 1861, and it was predicated on the notion that peasant revolts on a large scale were inevitable within a year or two and that the "people's friends" and sympathizers among the educated classes had better be ready to guide and assist the spontaneous expression of the people's rage.

Moreover, in 1861 and early 1862 so many revolutionary manifestos were printed and distributed that Soviet historians have sometimes referred to the period as the "era of proclamations." Probably the best known was entitled *To the Young Generation*, written by Mikhail Mikhailov and Nikolai Shelgunov.[1] Although Herzen did not approve of the operation, his Free Russian Press in London printed it, and six hundred copies were smuggled into Russia in the summer of 1861, a great many of which ended up in St. Petersburg, in part because some of the student leadership helped distribute it. *To the Young Generation* was in fact addressed directly to the students. Its message was simple and straightforward: "Imperial Russia is in dissolution." The only vital forces in the country were the peasants, the intelligentsia, and the students. The Romanovs were no longer needed; a popular republic, based on the communal institutions of the peasantry, should replace them. The manifesto did not talk about seizing power, but certain of its phraseology expressed direct hostility toward Western Europe and its economic doctrines; the distinct echo of Herzen's Russian socialism could be heard.

The *Great Russian (Velikoruss)*, three issues of which appeared between July and October 1861, was even vaguer and considerably more moderate. It was, in essence, an appeal to *obshchestvo* to prevent the bankrupt government of Alexander from creating a massive peasant insurrection. In a somewhat roundabout way, the *Great Russian* prescribed a more generous settlement for the peasants and a constitution for the country, together with the liberation of Poland. The tone of the *Great Russian* was moderate; it was couched as an appeal to Alexander to put himself in touch with the living forces of the country, rather than a demand that those forces make an end of him.[2]

These were only the most notable of the barrage of anonymous appeals, programs, and denunciations that appeared on the streets and in the mails within the space of a few months. Some were written by students—appeals not to accept the *matrikuly*, and so on—and even these generally had some broader political content, if only an exhortation to work together for "the people's freedom." And the number of entreaties to the troops not to fire on Russian peasants or on Poles indicated that some radicals were hoping for support among the soldiers. These appeals were particularly unsettling to the government.

Even the foreign political events of 1861 brought hope to those who were hoping and working for change and upheaval. The Russian government's attempt to combine moderate reform with moderate repression in Poland was not working very well; the situation there was tense and disorders frequent. Garibaldi's march on Rome had led to hopeful speculations about the emergence of a revolutionary Italy and even the destruction of Austria.[3] Relations were strained between Austria and Prussia, and there was some ground for hope that the Finns might contribute to the Russian government's problems. Was not a Franco-Polish war of liberation against Russia at least a possibility? Even the American Civil War seemed a hopeful sign. Thus the proponents of "movement" in Russia looked west and believed that they saw the forces of order and repression everywhere on the defensive. Just as American radicals in the 1960s had a vision of a Third World revolutionary force, led by China, overwhelming the rigid and unjust order created by American power and the cold war stalemate, Russian radicals needed to envisage their struggle as part of a larger and more powerful movement for change. Even Herzen, prone to caution in such matters, "to some extent" believed in a "rising of the peasants and the army."

The seemingly powerful combination of a militant minority of students (or at least young people) and a vaguely expectant public opinion seems to have endured in the capital until spring. Stirrings of discontent among the gentry, many of whom thought they had been victimized by the Emancipation, helped keep the pot boiling. Ten days before the Emancipation Edict was promulgated in 1861, the British ambassador reported to London that

the necessity for the assertion by the nobility of some sort of political rights in exchange for those of which the Emancipation will deprive them, is a theme which is loudly and publicly discussed at places of public resort in Moscow and the interior cities, and which in various ways, in spite of the Censure, finds its echo in the public press. A desire in short for a Representative Government is very openly expressed.[4]

In February 1862, a gentry group from Tver' province "insisted on the need for an independent judiciary, on 'publicity' for all acts of the government and administration, and again spoke of an 'assembly of delegates elected by the country without distinction of class in order to create free institutions.' "[5] And indications of a similar spirit were evident elsewhere in the country. In June 1862, P. A. Valuev, the minister of the interior, submitted a memorial to Alexander entitled *On the Internal State of Russia*. Valuev pointed out that the government was dangerously isolated. The nobility, or, he wrote acidly, "what is customarily called by that name, does not understand its true interests, is dissatisfied, aroused and somewhat disrespectful, shattered into a plurality of divergent tendencies, so that it nowhere represents a serious support." Even loyalty to the Emperor, Valuev felt, was uncertain. It was absolutely necessary for the government to regain support in *obshchestvo* by encouraging "constructive"

activities, particularly in the economic sphere, thus providing a
range of useful occupation for potential frondeurs.[6]

In the capital, the government continued to be alarmed,
throughout the winter and spring, at the ceaseless flow of incendiary leaflets and proclamations. A "free university" (much like
those that appeared on or near American campuses in the 1960s)
continued to keep student consciousness high, although it
bogged down in a welter of recrimination over the question of
whether lectures should be suspended to protest the arrest of
Professor P. V. Pavlov, one of the moving spirits behind the
Sunday School movement. At the height of the acrimony, the
whole enterprise was terminated by the government.

But the kind of public support that students, and the Left as
a whole, enjoyed in St. Petersburg (and elsewhere to a lesser
extent) was a volatile and uncertain thing. It was based on no
solid tie of social or economic interest. Once the general feeling
of relief at the end of Nicholas's despotism had abated, "liberal"
public opinion was sustained primarily by the Emancipation
drama and the hopes that it engendered. Now Emancipation had
been accomplished, however disappointingly, leaving a certain
feeling of anticlimax. Public opinion turned out to be disconcert-
ingly dependent upon the *mood* of *obshchestvo,* compounded of
a general desire to "move forward" (whatever that might mean),
a certain intellectual ferment, and a shallow intoxication with
fashionable ideas. The more radical and serious students and
members of the intelligentsia did not realize how isolated they
were—or, at any rate, might shortly become.

Being insecurely rooted and inadequately grounded, the public opinion of the day was particularly vulnerable to weariness
and discouragement. Since the salon "liberals" had very little
concrete stake in the new era, it would be easy enough for them
to feel that "things" or students "had gone too far." And after a
time, people get tired of constant excitement and of heroic but
somewhat abstract causes, and yearn again for tranquillity, careerism, and the everyday round. Only if their vital interests are
at stake can they persevere indefinitely. Outside the capital—in
Moscow, for instance—the level of public support for students

and radicalism was generally lower, and both the activities of the students and their public resonance had been more circumscribed.

One might argue, then, that public support for the Left would soon have diminished in the capital even without the catastrophic events that were soon to occur. Two developments only might have averted a change in the mood of the public: the outbreak of a major peasant disturbance or a striking political success of some kind for reformist *obshchestvo*. If the gentry had been sufficiently organized and able to agree upon a program for wresting a share of political power from the government, the course of events would have been very different. But in fact they were easily cowed. And despite some disorder, the monarchism and docility of the peasants survived the disappointments of the Emancipation. For all of their élan, the activist students had very little idea of what to do next in the winter and spring of 1862, and neither the gentry nor the peasants came to their rescue.

What in fact took place was a series of events that deprived the students of the respect—indeed the veneration—that they had hitherto enjoyed, split their movement, and helped a nationalist "New Right" emerge in Russian society. Disenchanted moderates and conservatives who had hitherto grumbled fearfully in small groups or confided their anxieties to their diaries found it suddenly respectable to do so in public. A. V. Nikitenko, professor of Russian literature at St. Petersburg and a politically moderate censor, wrote in his diary on March 19 that

the prospects before us are becoming gloomier and gloomier. If a certain party prevails, then good-bye to all reasonable, liberal and moderate principles, and the representatives of those principles will be crushed by the crowd, smashing and trampling everything in its path. And what then? A new yoke, new despotism.

And again, on April 14:

All these ultra-progressives are preparing a terrible future for Russia. And what do they want? Instead of gradual but prompt reform, they want an immediate overturn, a revolution, and are attempting to

produce an artificial one. Crazy blind men! They want to posture on
stage, want to play at History. . . . Really, does Russia need the kind
of revolution they are dreaming up?[7]

Not only was this sort of viewpoint heard in public in the latter
spring, but the abruptness of the change in society's mood suggests that public support for the Left had already begun to decay
from within.

The catalytic events began with a series of fires in St. Petersburg that broke out on May 15–16 and lasted into early June,
although the worst seems to have been over by May 28. A contemporary[8] noted eighteen more or less serious fires, scattered
throughout the city, within that period of less than two weeks.
Because of the prevalence of wooden buildings, the damage was
enormous, some estimates running as high as sixty thousand silver rubles.[9] The culmination came on May 28, when two of the
biggest markets and trading points in the city—the Apraksin
Dvor and the Shchukin Market—went up. Thousands of shop-
keepers and petty traders suffered heavy losses. Prince Peter
Kropotkin, then a member of the Corps of Pages in the capital,
has left us a vivid description:

The Apraxin Dvor was an immense space, more than half a mile
square, which was entirely covered with small shops,—mere shanties
of wood,—where all sorts of second and third hand goods were sold.
Old furniture and bedding, second-hand dresses and books, poured
in from every quarter of the city, and were stored in the small shanties, in the passages between them, and even on their roofs. This
accumulation of inflammable materials had at its back the Ministry
of the Interior and its archives, where all the documents concerning
the liberation of the serfs were kept; and in the front of it, which was
lined by a row of shops built of stone, was the state Bank. A narrow
lane, also bordered with stone shops, separated the Apraxin Dvor
from a wing of the Corps of Pages, which was occupied by grocery
and oil shops in its lower story. . . . Almost opposite the Ministry of
the Interior, on the other side of a canal, there were extensive timber
yards. This labyrinth of small shanties and timber yards opposite took
fire almost at the same moment, about four o'clock in the afternoon.
    If there had been wind on that day, half the city would have
perished in the flames. . . .

I was that afternoon at the Corps, dining at the house of one of our officers, and we dashed to the spot as soon as we saw from the windows the first clouds of smoke rising in our immediate neighborhood. The sight was terrific. Like an immense snake, rattling and whistling, the fire threw itself in all directions, right and left, enveloped the shanties, and suddenly rose in a huge column, darting out its whistling tongues to lick up more shanties with their contents. Whirlwinds of smoke and fire were formed; and when the whirls of burning feathers from the bedding shops began to sweep about the space, it became impossible to remain any longer inside the burning market. The whole had to be abandoned.

The authorities had entirely lost their heads. There was not, at that time, a single steam fire engine in St. Petersburg, and it was workmen who suggested bringing one from the iron works of Kolpino, situated twenty miles by rail from the capital. When the engine reached the railway station, it was the people who dragged it to the conflagration. Of its four lines of hose, one was damaged by an unknown hand, and the other three were directed upon the Ministry of the Interior. . . .

It was the crowd, the people, who did everything to prevent the fire from spreading further and further. There was a moment when the Bank was seriously menaced. The goods cleared from the shops opposite were thrown into the Sadovaya street, and lay in great heaps upon the walls of the left wing of the Bank. The articles which covered the street itself continually took fire, but the people, roasting there in an almost unbearable heat, prevented the flames from being communicated to the piles of goods on the other side. They swore at all the authorities, seeing that there was not a pump on the spot. "What are they all doing at the Ministry of the Interior, when the Bank and the Foundlings' House are going to take fire? They have all lost their heads!" "Where is the chief of police that he cannot send a fire brigade to the Bank?" they said. . . .

The Ministry itself was not on fire; it was the archives which were burning, and many boys, chiefly cadets and pages, together with a number of clerks, carried bundles of papers out of the burning building and loaded them into cabs. Often a bundle would fall out, and the wind, taking possession of its leaves, would strew them about the square. Through the smoke a sinister fire could be seen raging in the timber yards on the other side of the canal.

The narrow lane which separated the Corps of Pages from the Apraxin Dvor was in a deplorable state. The shops which lined it were full of brimstone, oil, turpentine, and the like, and immense tongues of fire of many hues, thrown out by explosions, licked the roofs of the wing of the Corps, which bordered the lane on the other side. . . .

About three or four in the morning it was evident that bounds had been put to the fire; the danger of its spreading to the Corps was over, and after having quenched our thirst with half a dozen glasses of tea, in a small "white inn" which happened to be open, we fell, half dead from fatigue, on the first bed that we found unoccupied in the hospital of the Corps.[10]

From very early on, arson was suspected. Nikitenko mentions rumors to that effect in his diary entry for May 24,[11] but they were almost certainly afoot before then. On May 25, five separate fires broke out in St. Petersburg, and anxiety began to turn into hysteria: criminals were to blame, agents of Palmerston (!), the Poles. Panteleev heard a remarkable rumor that a general had coated his back with some flammable substance and gone around the city rubbing his back against the walls of buildings, which would then burst into flames.[12] Among the lower classes of the city, recalcitrant gentry who would not accept the Emancipation were sometimes accused.

But most often the working people of St. Petersburg blamed the students, relating the tumult in the streets over the preceding months to the fires. Again the notion that the students were *opposed* to the Emancipation was heard. The students continued to be regarded as enemies of Tsar and people; it was suddenly crystal clear how poorly the message of the university radicals had been understood by the objects of their concern. What seems to have counted most was that the students were upper-class, idle, and privileged, a particularly obnoxious manifestation of the Russia of landlords and bureaucrats. At the height of the panic it was not safe for students on the streets, and some appealed to the police for protection.[13]

The fires were absolutely terrifying to the population of St. Petersburg, most of all to the lower strata, who lived in wooden houses packed together in a labyrinthine maze of crooked streets and alleys. No one could say when or where disaster would strike next. Skabichevsky, an eyewitness, described the general panic, which could be seen in the fact that wherever you went you saw suitcases, baskets and parcels, in which poor people and those of modest means had tied up everything that was dearest and most valuable to them, waiting for the first alarm to swiftly carry away their tied-up things. At every apartment building, in addition, there were night watchmen—domestic sentries taking shifts. At the same time, on the streets at night, especially in the outlying districts and out-of-the-way places, volunteers from among the local inhabitants set up nightly patrols. It got to the point that there was some danger in traveling the streets at night. If you looked as if you might be an arsonist, you could be dragged off to the police station and even beaten up, particularly if any kind of suspicious fluid were found on you. . . . I myself saw, on a beautiful morning on Nikol'sky St. where we lived, how a crowd of local householders was walking along and scrutinizing every unusual stain on the fence, every dab, evidently made by some passing painter, trying out his brush or colors. These spots were thoroughly planed off, since there was a rumor that the arsonists had oiled the walls of houses with some kind of stuff which would ignite the walls when the sun's rays fell on it.[14]

What is more surprising, perhaps, is how quickly and naturally many educated people assumed that the fires were part of a left-wing political conspiracy emanating from the university. In government circles and among conservatives, such an assumption was to be expected, but how is one to account for the fact that many political moderates—people who were loosely known as "liberals"—also blamed the students, and without a shred of hard evidence? One might expect such a turnabout from the most shallow and fashionable radicals: Kropotkin reported that

a few days after the conflagration, I went on Sunday to see my cousin, the aide-de-camp of the Emperor, in whose apartment I had often seen the Horse Guard officers in sympathy with Chernyshevsky; my cousin himself had been up till then an assiduous reader of "The Contemporary." . . . Now he brought several numbers of "The Contemporary," and, putting them on the table I was sitting at, said to me, "Well, now, after *this* I will have no more of that incendiary stuff; enough of it,"—and these words expressed the opinion of "all St. Petersburg."[15]

Even more remarkable is the fact that Ivan Turgenev came to the conclusion that radicals were behind the fires, as did Konstantin Kavelin. Kavelin had resigned from the university a few months earlier, and no doubt the frenetic and, in the end, disappointing activities of the last several years had taken their toll on him. His influence over the students had waned; he had lost his job on their behalf, and he seems to have felt keenly their ingratitude—Kavelin often felt that his activities, particularly his sacrifices, were unappreciated. "Can this be called progress?" he wrote to his colleague V. D. Spasovich. "Good God! Such progress merits only buckshot and the gallows. It's clear that people will never become wiser. If reaction now rears its head in triumph, will it be any wonder?"[16] The presumption is strong that well before the outbreak of the fires Kavelin felt that the students had "gone too far"; certainly he assumed their guilt as soon as the fires began.

Of course, the presumption was not altogether absurd. The nerves of *obshchestvo* were strained almost to the breaking point. There was a widespread, if rather indefinite, expectation of either revolution or some major cataclysm. Was it not natural to interpret the fires as being the prelude to upheaval? And in addition, the initial outbreak of the fires coincided with the appearance of a new proclamation, only one of the steady stream that had been appearing, but the most bloodcurdling and extreme by far: the manifesto entitled *Young Russia,* which we will consider below.

With respect to the working-class population of St. Petersburg, one should note that the panic fear of the fires focused hostility on those toward whom the population had previously been antipathetic: the Poles and the gentry. The fact that students were the *dominant* group upon which suspicion fell and against which hostility was directed suggests that they had already become targets of popular antipathy.

Clearly, the *emergence* of this hostility to the students (and to the other scapegoat candidates) was related to a sense that the usual order of things had broken down. The city had been visited by a mysterious catastrophe, before which the authorities, no less than the victims, were helpless. This sense of the inadequacy of regular institutions and normal ways of understanding what was happening helps account for the extraordinary rumors, like that of the inflammatory general. The rumors, in turn, helped to explain the apparently inexplicable and to induce various forms of self-help, mutual aid, and vigilante activity.

The reaction of *obshchestvo* was somewhat more measured and less activist than that of the working people, but it, too, exhibited a release of latent hostility, an abnormal credulousness and susceptibility to rumor. Many of those who had been happy to question the social order suddenly found themselves much attached to it when it seemed jeopardized by mysterious malefactors. And this sense was easily translated into political conservatism of a gut kind. The fear of upheaval, for many, seems to have replaced the more superficial excitement and sense of liberation previously associated with prospects for dramatic social change.[17]

The appearance of the *Young Russia* manifesto certainly helped along this change in *obshchestvo* opinion. *Young Russia* was signed by something called the Central Revolutionary Committee. It was actually the work of a young student radical, P. G. Zaichnevsky, who had been expelled from the University of Moscow and arrested in the summer of 1861 for propagandizing the peasants of his native Orël province, and a few of his friends. It was written in the relatively lax atmosphere of a Moscow prison of the day, smuggled out, and distributed. Zaichnevsky was nineteen at the time of his arrest, twenty when he wrote *Young Russia*. He was to have a long career as a radical, but his finest hour came early on.

If the *Great Russian* of the previous fall had urged the vital and progressive forces of the country to take action to prevent a *Pugachëvshchina*, *Young Russia* gloried in the prospect. Zaichnevsky and his friends saw the country as divided into two absolutely irreconcilable camps: that of the ruling class and that of the people, with nothing substantial in between. The most bitter kind of struggle was inevitable, a struggle in which "rivers of blood will flow." Recalling the revolts of Stenka Razin and Pugachëv, the authors predicted "a revolution, a bloody and pitiless revolution, a revolution which must change everything down to the very roots, utterly overthrowing all the foundations of present society and bringing about the ruin of all who support the present order."[18]

The postrevolutionary vision expressed in the manifesto was in a general way Populist: Russia was to become a decentralized federation in which the peasant *obshchina* and communally run factories would organize production. There were to be free education, the emancipation of women, and the abolition of the parasitic monasteries. All nationalities would be given the right to secede from the federated republic that would emerge from the bloody chaos attendant upon the demise of the old order. But a new revolutionary viewpoint and strategy made its appearance: the revolutionary dictatorship of a minority. This "Jacobin" approach to the problem of revolution was to have a long and eventful history in Russia, culminating in the Bolshevik seizure of power in 1917. Jacobinism is frequently the outcome of a situation in which an intelligentsia minority has been powerfully radicalized but despairs of mass support from other elements of society, or conceives of that support as merely negative or destructive. The authors of *Young Russia* believed that the exploited Russian peasant could—and would—sweep away the old order. They believed that the way of life and institutions of the peasantry would be the foundation upon which the new Russia would emerge. But they thought that only a militant minority of students and intellectuals—the most militant and resolute elements of the intelligentsia—would have the vision and the organizational capacity necessary to bring the new order into existence, to harness the destructive force of the upheaval, and to preside over the ruthless liquidation of all residues and traces of Russia's imperial past. Hence, a transitional dictatorship of the intelligentsia would be absolutely necessary, a dictatorship that would "stop at nothing."

What has generally interested historians about *Young Russia* is precisely the emergence of this Jacobin viewpoint, which in many doctrinal guises would recur in Russia until 1917, despite the periodic episodes of revulsion against its antidemocratic elitism and extremism, despite such powerful opponents as Kropotkin and Rosa Luxemburg. Needless to say, public opinion in St. Petersburg and Moscow in May 1862 was scarcely able to view the manifesto in this light. *Young Russia* struck them almost wholly by its bloodcurdling language and its consignment of nearly all of *obshchestvo* to total destruction. It was a document ideally calculated at any time to convince moderates and "liberals" that their future lay with gentle, if not imperceptible, attempts to reform the existing order. Its distribution at the end of many months of extreme social excitement and tension, in conjunction with a series of devastating fires in Russian cities, was ideally calculated to push all but the most extreme and dedicated radicals far toward the right, to reinforce decisively the impression that the new era had been a Pandora's box. In short, it played directly into the hands of the government—as Herzen, Bakunin, and Chernyshevsky all recognized.

On about May 14, a copy of *Young Russia* had fallen into the hands of the authorities in Moscow; at about the same time, the first copies made their appearance in St. Petersburg, circulated both through the mails and on the street. The timing could not have been more perfect. The public became aware of the manifesto precisely at the moment that the first suspicions of arson were being voiced, and the social reaction to *Young Russia* developed in the atmosphere of feverish paranoia induced by the fires.[19] And fire was one of the destructive agencies specifically mentioned by the manifesto. Very rapidly—almost overnight—the attitude of *obshchestvo* hardened against students, radicals, and disturbers of the peace.

Government and conservative circles were at first astonished and frightened, but they soon realized that the situation was propitious for a major counterattack against the forces of insurrection and chaos. On June 10, Count S. N. Urusov, a member of the State Council and head of the Second Section of His Majesty's

Own Chancery (in charge of legal codification), wrote to an influential figure in the Church that

> in recent days we have been worried by the fires. This terrible misfor-
> tune, which has overwhelmed thousands of the poor, has neverthe-
> less had the salutary effect of revealing, in all its force, the devotion
> of the real Russian people to Belief and its fidelity to the Sovereign.
> I myself saw how the people prayed in this terrible time and myself
> heard how moved they were by the presence of their Tsar at the fire
> and by his grief. The Empress deigned to be at the place of devasta-
> tion during the day; I was not there, but everyone told me that at the
> appearance of Her Majesty the rapture of those who had been
> burned out was indescribable. But as powerfully, on the one hand, as
> the people was moved by a feeling of love, their feeling of loathing
> for the enemies of church and state was equally powerful. Those who
> had hoped to find support among the people for their efforts to shake
> all authority have been deeply deceived.[20]

Neither the investigating commission constituted by the government nor subsequent efforts by historians have been able to shed
much light on who was responsible for the fires. No evidence has
been found to connect either radicals, attempting to ignite an
insurrection, or reactionaries, trying to move the country and the
government to the right, with the fires. Either hypothesis *might*
be true. Because the fires so obviously played into the government's hands, some nineteenth-century radicals and Soviet historians came to believe that they were a provocation, contrived
to justify the repressive measures that began on May 28, with the
proclamation of what amounted to martial law in St. Petersburg,
and continued into the summer.

There is a third possibility. It is conceivable that the fires were
the work not of any group with a defined political aim but of
various individuals who for widely divergent reasons contributed
to the wave of arson. Contagion in such things is not unknown.
Once the setting of fires became a recognized possibility, as it
were, many different motives—material gain, individual pathol-
ogy, and so on—may have prompted people to take action. We
know of two such cases: a merchant tried to set a fire in order to
collect insurance, and a "deranged teacher" with vaguely radical

sympathies set several others. S. Reiser, the leading Soviet student of the fires, mentions both cases, but as he is psychologically committed to the idea that the fires were not a manifestation of unbalanced radicalism but of right-wing Machiavellianism, he does not consider the idea that the two arsonists whom the investigating commission *did* discover might have been typical; any more than did the moderate and conservative opinion of the day, which tended to blame the student Left.

The repressive measures that the government undertook in the spring and summer of 1862 provoked remarkably little public outcry; either the fires and the appearance of *Young Russia* had drastically weakened *obshchestvo* opposition to government repression, or the government had seriously overestimated the strength of gentry "liberalism" and radicalism in the aftermath of the Emancipation. In the July 15 number of the *Bell,* Herzen gave a graphic picture of the summer of 1862.

In St. Petersburg there is terror—the most dangerous and mindless kind of all, that of cowardice confused. Not the terror of the lion but that of the calf, a terror in which the demented government, not knowing the source of the danger, knowing neither its strengths nor its weaknesses and hence pontificating nonsense, is helped by society, literature, the people, progress and regress. . . .

The *Day** has been suppressed, the *Contemporary* and the *Russian Word* have been suppressed, the Sunday Schools have been closed, the Chess Club has been closed and so have the reading rooms, the money intended for poor students has been taken away, supervision of the presses has been redoubled, two ministers and the Third Section have to authorize the reading of public lectures; there are constant arrests.[21]

With a qualification or two, Herzen's vivid picture may stand. Not only were the *Russian Word* and the *Contemporary* both closed down for a time, but Pisarev and Chernyshevsky had been arrested—word of this had not yet reached Herzen in London. The arrest of Chernyshevsky, however, appears to have been

---

*The *Day (Den')* was a Slavophile periodical edited by Ivan Aksakov.

long contemplated by the government and was not a hasty step taken in response to the tumult of the spring. Indeed, the government was somewhat less confused than Herzen allowed. Given its fear of social chaos, even revolution, there was nothing irrational about cracking down on the Left in July 1862 if it was politically possible to do so, and the government's rather crude tactics were effective.

What the fires and *Young Russia* had inaugurated, the outbreak of a full-scale revolt in Poland the following January furthered and developed. Polonophilia, long a common feature of European liberalism and radicalism, had a special meaning and a special volatility in Russia. Catherine the Great, after all, had been the principal author of the infamous partitions that had altogether removed a once-great state from the map of Europe. Russian guilt over what the dynasty had done could manifest itself in tearful declarations of contrition and resounding expressions of good intentions—the effusions of Emperor Alexander I to Prince Czartoryski are a case in point. On the other hand, the rivalry and hatred between the two nations was old and deep. Catholic Poles had traditionally gloried in their membership in the exclusive club of European or Western nations; they were prone to remark to Western European visitors that Asia began at the Russian border. After the protracted and bloody conflicts with their Western neighbor, Russians savored the long, slow eclipse of Polish state power in the seventeenth and eighteenth centuries; only in the most cosmopolitan and "enlightened" circles were the partitions criticized. For most of *obshchestvo,* Polonophobia was a deeper and older emotion than the remarks they were sometimes heard to make at dinner that Poland's wrongs ought to be redressed.

Alexander I had given Russia's portion of Poland (the lion's share) a constitution—much to the chagrin of some of his officers, who hoped that he would think first of making his own subjects into citizens—but it had been revoked after the ungrateful Poles revolted in 1830. Since then, Poland had been treated—more or less—like a conquered province.

Sympathy for Poland had become a fashionable attitude in

obshchestvo circles during the new era, and had been notably characteristic of the student Left. There had been well-organized groups of Polish students at most Russian universities in the late 1850s; although the Poles as a group were rather suspicious of their Russian colleagues, there was considerable Russian student support for Polish national aspirations. Many of the more radical Russian students devoted a lot of effort to convincing their Polish confreres that their ultimate goals were not in conflict. The Polish cause was naturally not popular in nationalist circles, but a certain unfocused sympathy for Poland could sometimes be detected among such younger Slavophiles as Ivan Aksakov and Iury Samarin, and among old-fashioned patriots like the conservative historian Mikhail Pogodin.[22] Many of the radical proclamations of 1861–62 had made some mention of Polish liberty.

All this changed abruptly when a major rebellion against Russian rule broke out in January 1863, and Russian nationalism was further exacerbated by the futile remonstrances of England and France, which the Russian government ignored. Guilt and unease gave way to patriotic fervor; the Poles were blamed for the fires of the preceding year, and Polish participation in the student disorders was recalled and exaggerated. The principal spokesman for the aroused Russian national feeling was Mikhail Katkov, Herzen's old companion, a former "liberal" Westerner and editor of the *Russian Herald.* "Between these two co-tribal nationalities, history has always posed the fateful question of life and death," Katkov wrote in an article entitled simply "The Polish Question." "Both states were not simply rivals, but enemies which could not live side by side, enemies to the end. Between them the question was not simply which will gain first place, which will become mightier; rather the question was which of them will exist."[23] Katkov's career as the most influential journalistic representative of extreme Russian chauvinism had begun, and for the moment he carried much of educated Russian public opinion with him. His two journals, the *Moscow Gazette (Moskovskie vedomosti)* and the *Russian Herald,* had a combined circulation of almost eighteen thousand, an altogether exceptional audience for a single journalist at the time.

Those who stood against the tide—and this meant the most resolute elements on the Left—were simply swamped. Herzen was especially identified with the cause of Poland, and from mid-1863 the *Bell* went into a period of rapid decline, its circulation according to Kornilov falling to a mere five hundred.[24]

By the end of 1863, the public mood in Russia was vastly different from what it had been only eighteen months before. Land and Liberty, the first tentatively revolutionary organization in Russia since the Decembrists, had petered out; Chernyshevsky and Pisarev were in jail; there was no real student movement; and even the London *Times* could discern that Katkov was the real spokesman for public opinion in Russia. Times had changed.

Alexander Herzen, with his customary perspicacity, understood how crucial public opinion was in defining what had happened.

There was a revolution in society itself. Some were sobered by the emancipation of the peasants; others were simply tired by political agitation; they wished for the former repose; they were satiated before a meal which had cost them so much trouble.

It cannot be denied: our breath is short and our endurance is long!

Seven years of liberalism had exhausted the whole reserve of radical aspirations. All that had been amassed and compressed in the mind since 1825 was expended in raptures of joy, in the foretaste of good things to come. After the truncated emancipation of the peasants people with weak nerves thought that Russia had gone too far, was going too quickly.

At the same time, the *radical* party, young, and for that reason full of theories, began to announce its intentions more and more impulsively, frightening a society that was frightened even before this. It set forth as its ostensible aim such extreme outcomes, that liberals and champions of gradual progress crossed themselves and spat, and ran away stopping their ears, to hide under the old, filthy, but familiar blanket of the police. The headlong haste of the students and the landowners' want of practice in listening to other people could not help bringing them to blows.

The force of public opinion, hardly called to life, manifested itself as a savage conservatism. It declared its participation in public affairs

by elbowing the government into the debauchery of terror and persecution.[25]

The bridges between nascent Russian radicalism and the rest of
society had been, for the time being, largely destroyed, and the
next phase of Russian radicalism was to reflect strongly the isolated militancy of the extreme Left and its increasing attraction
toward terrorism and conspiracy.

Before turning to the heirs of *Young Russia,* however, we must
take note of the development of a radical consciousness, the
product of the drama of the Emancipation itself, and its anti-
climactic aftermath—as well as the development of a Populist
view of Russia's history, which could provide the "usable past"
so necessary to a persistent radicalism. Afanasy Prokof'evich
Shchapov was Populism's historian of the *narod,* and Pavel
Ivanovich Iakushkin, more than anyone else, created a persona
for the new radicals. It is to their lives that we must now turn our
attention.

7

From Slavophilism to Populism: A. P. Shchapov

> *The state, in its idea, is a lie.*
>
> —Konstantin Aksakov

> *When I studied the history [written by] Ustrialov and Karamzin, it always seemed to me strange that in it one could not find the history of rural* Rus', *the history of the masses, the history of the so-called simple black people. Can it be that this enormous majority is not entitled to culture, to historical development and significance?*
>
> —Afanasy Prokof'evich Shchapov

Much of what was common to Slavophile and Populist aspiration was finally the result of two extremely important historical peculiarities in Russia's development: the cultural discontinuities resulting from the reforms of Peter the Great and Russia's rapid Westernization; and the enormous part played by the state in Russian development—from the programmatic borrowing of navigational techniques and poetic genres in the eighteenth century to the rapid industrial development in the last twenty-five years of the imperial regime. Taken together, classical Slavophilism and Populism are part of a fitful reaction in Russian culture against the state as the sponsor of a modernity regarded as alien. Populism evolved, in part, out of Slavophilism, in the atmosphere that developed after the Crimean defeat, and was vitally conditioned by the social optimism of the first part of the reign of Alexander II. Chernyshevsky gave Populist ideas a more Western orientation by softening the anarchist, antistatist implications of Slavophilism, by virtually eliminating the messianic sense of Russia's "specialness," and by ceasing to speak of her separate path. Although a good many of Chernyshevsky's followers were both more anarchist and more nationalist than he, on the whole it was the Western elements in Populism that were strengthened in the 1870s and 1880s (particularly with the arrival of Marxism as a rival blueprint for the intelligentsia), but it never lost the essential stamp it had received at the hands of Herzen and Ogarëv.

On the more prosaic and concrete level of individual lives, however, the connection between the two was more veiled. Classical Slavophilism as a system of thought had many fewer adherents at the height of its influence than Populism was to achieve. And most of the Populist radicals of the 1860s and 1870s were either indifferent to Slavophilism or hostile to it; what was likely to strike them about it was its chauvinistic potential, its social quietism, and its origins in the gentry salons of the pre-1848 period. And as the gentry culture of the "fathers" (even in its most radical form) became odious to younger radicals, the Slavophile roots of Populism became ever harder to discern. But in retrospect it is clear that most of the Populist Left between 1861 and 1881 experienced Slavophilism in the radical form created by Herzen and developed by Chernyshevsky; this was the intellectual bridge between the Slavophiles and the emerging world of radical Populism.

In certain individual lives, however, one can see how Slavophilism evolved into Populism, how someone moved from the force field of one system into another. One of the most interesting cases is that of Pavel Nikolaevich Rybnikov, one of the most important collectors of folk songs in all nineteenth-century Russia. From a family of Old Believer Moscow merchants, Rybnikov was educated in a Moscow gymnasium, from which he graduated with distinction in 1850. After a lengthy European tour, during which he served a rich family as an interpreter, he

entered the University of Moscow in the fall of 1854, several years
before the general ferment there began.[1]

The Russian merchant class was notably late in achieving
cultural or political self-consciousness; the plays of Aleksandr
Ostrovsky render the social and political "backwardness" of
the merchant class in telling and not unfair terms. Rybnikov's
family, however, was unusually cultivated and self-aware—and
quite well-to-do. They nourished their son's interest in national minorities and regional peculiarities, as well as his special interest in Old Believers. They must also have instilled in
him his love of books; by the time he finished the university
in mid-1858, he was notably well read, not only in folklore, literature, and theology, but in writers of the Hegelian tradition
(including Ludwig Feuerbach and Max Stirner), French socialist thought, and such comparatively obscure figures as Gio-
vanni Battista Vico.

Apparently, Rybnikov was already intellectually and personally close to the Khomiakov family when he arrived at the university. He tutored the sons of A. S. Khomiakov and spent time
during the summer on his estate. He also came to know the
Aksakov brothers and Iury Samarin—friends who were to be
invaluable to him at crucial junctures in his career. But while
there is no question that Rybnikov's initial impulse toward the
study of popular life was actively encouraged by Khomiakov's
view of the peasant as the embodiment of old Russian religiosity
and communalism, by the time we have any hard evidence about
their relationship (around 1855–56), Khomiakov and Rybnikov
had become friendly enemies.

Rybnikov became a leading light in one of the student groups
that first developed a distinctly "Populist" outlook; he and his
friends formed their views in frequent evening discussions,
which often included Khomiakov, Konstantin Aksakov, and on at
least one occasion Samarin. The student members of the group
(which was not closed to outsiders and hence was soon penetrated by the police) called themselves the *vertepniki,* from an
obscure Slavic word *(vertep)* that had come to be an underworld
term for a den of thieves. They met in small student apartments

and attic rooms (most often Rybnikov's) and discussed the social and political issues of the day. They considered themselves republicans; several, including Rybnikov, adopted Feuerbach's views on religion; they had progressive views on the family and the emancipation of women. But the heart of their discussions, even before peasant emancipation became a live issue, was the future of the Russian village and the essential character of the peasantry. Was the peasant, as Khomiakov tirelessly argued, the bearer of a deeply religious culture? Or was he (as the *vertepniki* were reading in the *Bell*) an unself-conscious socialist? It is pleasant to imagine Khomiakov, then in his fifties and accustomed to all the amenities of Moscow salon life, sitting up till all hours with these poor students, drinking tea out of cracked cups and passing the single spoon from hand to hand—patiently, if unsuccessfully, arguing his case against Feuerbach's atheism and for the traditional family structure. All the participants in these evening marathons could agree, however, on the necessity of studying the *narod* at first hand, and everyone could agree on the central importance of the peasant commune.

Other influential *vertepniki* were A. A. Kozlov, who subsequently abandoned radicalism and became a philosophy professor at the University of Kiev, and Matvei Sviridenko, a passionate student of popular folkways, who ran a radical bookstore in St. Petersburg and died in 1864. Rybnikov and Sviridenko were, together with P. I. Iakushkin, the first Russians to put on contemporary peasant costume for their ethnographic expeditions into the countryside. Their peasant dress was more than a collector's strategy—it was a political statement: they were already "going to the people," to use a phrase that came into vogue only later.

In the winter of 1859, after his graduation from the university, Rybnikov was arrested while on an ethnographic foray among the Old Believers of Chernigov province*—under highly suspicious circumstances. He had a commission from a magazine, but he was dressed in peasant clothes; when asked for his (internal)

*The mid-seventeenth-century Schism *(Raskol)* in the Russian Church was occasioned by "corrections" in the prayer books and manuals, ordered by the Patriarch Nikon, a Grecophile. Those of the Russian clergy and laity who refused to accept these changes became known as Old Ritualists or Old Believers.

passport, he could produce only a letter from Khomiakov.* The
government was edgy and intensely suspicious of "ill-intentioned
persons" stirring up trouble among the serfs, who were soon to
be emancipated; and Rybnikov's radical opinions were known to
the authorities. If Khomiakov had not brought his considerable
influence to bear, Rybnikov might well have spent some time in
jail. As it was, he was sentenced to administrative exile in Petrozavodsk, on Lake Onega, several hundred kilometers northeast of St. Petersburg.

Rybnikov remained in Petrozavodsk for seven years. He was
given an undemanding job by the reform-minded governor in
the provincial bureaucracy, and he divided his time between
charming the local society and wandering among the peasants.
In doing so, he made a discovery of enormous importance in the
history of Russian folklore. He found out that the *byliny,* or
epic-historical songs (some of which could be traced back as far
as the eleventh century), were still part of the oral tradition in
the area, and the versions that he published between 1861 and
1867 electrified the scholarly world. Rybnikov transcribed more
than two hundred texts, and the collectors who followed him
added many more.

Neither Rybnikov's radicalism nor his interest in folklore survived much beyond his thirty-fifth birthday. In 1866, thanks to his
Slavophile friends Ivan Aksakov and Iury Samarin, he obtained a
good position in the Russian administration in Poland. Little is
known of his later career, beyond a skeleton of dates. He did come
to be much interested in Tolstoy's ideas, and one writer refers to
him as a "Christian anarchist," although evidently he was a secret
one. He seems to have become progressively more pessimistic
about his country, coming to believe (like Pëtr Chaadaev) that
Russian life was hopelessly lacking in intellectual continuity and
tradition. "It is nauseating for a cultivated man to live in Russian
society" was his final recorded word on the subject.² He died in
1885, a successful functionary but a disappointed man.

---

*According to police reports, Rybnikov was asking the Old Believers about "the
ancient rights and customs of the Russian people." See M. M. Klevensky, "Vertepniki,"
Katorga i ssylka, No. 47, p. 26.

The central point at issue between Rybnikov and his Slavophile friends boiled down to who the Russian peasant really was
—to the *narodnost'*, or national essence, of the Russian people,
in the Romantic vocabulary of the time. In the case of Rybnikov
and other more-or-less radical students of the peasantry, their
sense of this peasant *narodnost'* gradually changed: the emphasis
on the religious and the traditional fell away; the peasant ceased
to be regarded as submissive, becoming dignified and resolute
instead. As the peasant came to be viewed as inherently rebellious, his monarchism was temporarily forgotten; young collectors from the universities began to ask the peasants to sing songs
about Stenka Razin, Pugachëv, and other rebels and bandits.

This intellectual shift cannot be understood without reference
to the general intellectual ferment of the times, to the surge of
social optimism and above all the excitement generated by the
Emancipation. People like Rybnikov did not embrace Populism
by self-consciously turning their Slavophile coats or by moving
from one "camp" to another (to employ the militaristic ter-
minology favored by Soviet historians), but in amorphous and
unconscious ways. They had never been *wholly* "Slavophile,"
and there was not yet a category such as "Populist." But their
view of the peasant, their sense of the essence of the *narod*, was
changing.

Afanasy Shchapov is a more substantial figure in the history of
Russian radicalism than Rybnikov, and a consideration of his
career and writings illuminates a number of these connections.
Shchapov has been a relatively neglected figure among the Russian radicals of the 1860s.[3] Very little of what he wrote dealt with
the social and political problems of the day; he does not seem to
have had a serious connection with Land and Liberty or any
other actively conspiratorial group; furthermore, in 1863 he
rather abruptly abandoned his Populist historical outlook and
became a naive believer in "scientific" history, in the manner of
Henry Buckle, attempting to derive the march of social progress
from race, geography, and climate.

Yet on the basis of his early work Shchapov has an excellent

claim to be called the historian of Populism. More than any other
serious practitioner, he took the key ideas and themes of early
Populism and gave a reading of Russian history in these terms.
And in Shchapov's historical work, the intellectual kinship of
Slavophilism and Populism is as clearly expressed as it is in
Herzen.

Shchapov was born on October 5, 1830, in the small town of
Anga, in the depths of Siberia, not far from Irkutsk. He was the
son of a poor sacristan and his Buriat wife, who would have been
regarded by most non-peasant Russians as a "native." His father's
family was of Great Russian stock; they had migrated to Siberia
at the end of the seventeenth century, or been sent there in
connection with the Schism *(Raskol)* in the Russian Church. His
parents planned to make young Afanasy a priest, so they sent
him, at the age of nine, to the ecclesiastical boarding school, or
bursa, in Irkutsk. Such institutions tended to be the epitome of
material squalor and pedagogical backwardness;[4] the one in Irkutsk was "one of the worst schools in Russia." The little boys
who were lodged there suffered from filth, insufficient clothing,
rats, lice, and mange, poor food, and so on. They had almost no
books, and the school couldn't even manage spoons for the miserable meals. Beatings were the customary form of punishment,
and for an offense of some seriousness the corporal punishment
was turned into a public affair, with not only the students present
but townspeople as well. Any historian setting out to investigate
the prominence of the children of priests among Russian radicals
in the nineteenth century would do well to study such schools.

Shchapov's identification with the peasantry and his hatred of
coercive authority probably owed something to the contrast between his poor but happy home (where his mother "always wore
the local peasant costume") and the oppressive life of the school;
Shchapov's biographer, N. Ia. Aristov, suggests perhaps a bit fan-
cifully that his subsequent sympathy for peasant flight from the
Russian state, as a historical phenomenon, was rooted in his understanding of what motivated the frequent runaways from the
bursa, his first experience with nonfamilial, "external" authority.[5]

Between 1846 and 1852, Afanasy attended the seminary in Irkutsk, which seems to have been an improvement on the bursa; we know very little about his days there, except that he was already interested in history and is reported to have read Nikolai Karamzin's classic *History of the Russian State* while in residence.[6]

In 1852, at the age of almost twenty-two, Shchapov went to the Ecclesiastical Academy at Kazan'; there were four such schools in Russia, and they were the topmost rung of the educational ladder for members of the clerical estate. The young man's remarkable intellectual qualities must already have attracted the attention of his teachers. The academy was run by monks, but most of its teachers were lay, and some of them were rather progressive, in the manner of the Westerners of the 1840s. Interest in Hegel was widespread, and A. F. Gusev, the professor of physics, was putting his students on to Feuerbach—the most direct kind of challenge to the views of the clerical administration.[7] Some students knew the work of Herzen and Belinsky, and copies of the *Contemporary* and the *Annals of the Fatherland* circulated clandestinely.

It is from these years, the early and mid-1850s, that we have our first real impressions of young Shchapov from his contemporaries; he was a most unusual student. He is remembered as extremely naive, childlike, and unself-conscious. He was nervous and lively in his manner, passionately sincere and direct in his conversation, and remarkably untidy, both in appearance and in his manner of life. In a world dominated by hierarchy, he was seemingly unaware of it: he talked in the same sweet, sincere, and unaffected way to the rector of the academy as to his fellow students. He seems to have gotten away with it largely because he was such a transparently good-natured person that everyone could see no disrespect was intended.

Another factor that helped to shield Shchapov from the displeasure of the authorities, and even to some extent from the cruel jokes of his comrades, was his obvious scholarly aptitude and his extraordinary capacity for work. He would be pointed out to incoming students as an academic prodigy, the like of which had never before been seen at the academy. He was supposed to be working seventeen hours a day—perhaps he actually did so. In any case, he was heavily engaged with the classics of Russian history—Karamzin, thick volumes by Mikhail Pogodin—and he threw himself avidly upon each successive volume of Sergei Solov'ëv's monumental *History of Russia* as they appeared in the 1850s. He also ransacked the library for primary sources, and was renowned for having spent countless hours poring over the enormous code of Russian laws, as well as the early chronicles.

Because of this unheard-of zeal and energy, his contemporaries plagued him less than might have been expected, linking him humorously but half-seriously with patristic scholarship and the heroic traditions of Eastern Orthodox asceticism: he was known as "the New Stylite" and "the Blessed Afanasy." An ascetic he certainly was at that time. In addition to his famous work habits, he was known to be frightened of women, shy and awkward in any social situation, and unable to stand the taste—or even smell—of any alcoholic beverage. He considered becoming a monk, he said, because he could see little difference between a monk's life and a scholar's.

Ordinary boys were quite incapable of not teasing such a creature, and from time to time Afanasy had to defend himself in the time-honored fashion. This he was able to do. Although he was practically impervious to the routine of mild ridicule, when he decided that he had been insulted he could lose his temper utterly; on such occasions his usual manner of shy seriousness completely disappeared and he became a formidable fighter.

As far back in Shchapov's life as the historian can penetrate, he was noted for his pride in his peasant ancestry, in a time and place when such an attitude was highly unusual. Most of Shchapov's contemporaries at the bursa and the seminary were also the sons of parish clergy, whose family's way of life was close to that of their peasant flock. Slurs and insults about peasant crudity and stupidity were common enough, both from the monkish administrators and from a few of the more well-to-do students. When such remarks were made, Shchapov was likely to lose his temper and come out swinging. Certainly his sense of identification with the peasantry—and with all of its suffering and neglect throughout Russian history—was something that drew him to Slavophilism and then to more radical and political forms of Slavophile ideas. The Crimean War occasioned, at the academy as elsewhere in Russia, a mood that mixed Russian nationalism with an angry and frustrated criticism of the government. The war seems to have hit Shchapov hard: he wept bitterly, after the fall of Sevastopol, at the senseless death of so many brave Russian peasant boys.

It is difficult to piece together the attitude of the clerical administration toward their young prodigy. The picture of these men that emerges in the skimpy historical literature on the academy is deeply negative. In particular, Grigory, the rector when Shchapov arrived and subsequently archbishop of Kazan', seems to have been an obscurantist bully. Imbued with a deep hatred of all secular culture, he seems to have conceived his job in completely supervisory and police terms: prowling the corridors and classrooms (and occasionally the streets of Kazan') during the day and the dormitories at night, in the nineteenth-century equivalent of sneakers, looking for truants, absentees, smokers, novel-readers, and other violators of the academy's severe and complicated rules. And a number of his subordinates were of a like disposition, if somewhat less vigilant and energetic.[8]

The monks were probably a bit more tolerant of Shchapov's simplicity, spontaneity, and tendency to lose himself in his work (and not show up in class) than one might have expected. Perhaps this was largely the response to his remarkable naiveté and good humor; perhaps they hoped, as schoolmasters do, that their star pupil would bring laurels to the academy and to them. In fact they furthered his career, and at certain moments he got real support from one or two men. Even the much-reviled Grigory took some interest in Shchapov's work and actually suggested what became the topic of his master's thesis: the Church Schism of the seventeenth century.* In 1857, the new rector of the acad-

---

*Although he later criticized it for its deviation from clerical orthodoxy. See N. Ia. Aristov, *Afanasii Prokof'evich Shchapov. Zhizn' i sochineniia* (St. Petersburg, 1883), p. 14.

emy, Ioann Sokolov, became a close friend, advising and counseling the young scholar and trying to help him in the struggle with his developing personal problems.*

Our knowledge of Shchapov's relations with the faculty is only slightly fuller. When he arrived at the academy, the teacher of Russian history was G. Z. Eliseev, who left Kazan' in 1856 to join the young radical writers on the staff of the *Contemporary*.[9] Eliseev and Shchapov subsequently came to know each other quite well in St. Petersburg in the early 1860s, but Eliseev left the academy just as Shchapov was beginning to reach out beyond its conventional clerical world view, and there is no evidence that he played much part in Shchapov's education to radicalism. After his departure, Russian history was taught for a time by I. P. Gvozdev, of whom Shchapov was very fond; he called him "Grampa," although Gvozdev was still a young man. But Gvozdev knew little enough about Russian history; he made competent lectures out of Solov'ëv and other historians of the "state school" for his classes. As Shchapov was busy defining his views *against* Solov'ëv, Gvozdev could hardly have been a real intellectual influence.

A more important figure was S. T. Eshevsky, of whom Shchapov saw a good deal in the mid-1850s. Eshevsky, a student of Granovsky, was then a docent at the University of Kazan'. Subsequently the author of a major study of the relationship between the central government and the provinces of the Roman Empire, Eshevsky seems to have focused Shchapov's inchoate predilection for local and regional freedom in Russia into a more definite contrast between peasant society and state power. He suggested that Shchapov turn his attention to Russian colonization of the northeast, and directed the young historian's attention to the cadastral surveys *(pistsovye knigi)*, compiled at the order of the various regional princes in the Middle Ages, as

---

*A lighter side of the relationship is revealed in an anecdote recorded by Aristov. On one occasion, the two men were out walking together when they met a group of drunken peasants, staggering along, arm in arm, and singing at the top of their lungs. "There's the vital force of your black people [peasants]," observed the rector with a smile. "But they're still better than we are," replied Shchapov. "They don't let each other fall, but even when we're sober we're always ready to trip each other up." *Ibid.*, p. 45.

a valuable historical source. Shchapov later made this stress on colonization a vital part of his view of Russian historical development, in opposition to those historians who stressed the consolidation of state power.[10] Unfortunately, a foolish quarrel over the use of historical documents terminated the relationship between the two men, even before Eshevsky was called to the University of Moscow in 1857. Shchapov was increasingly prone to such quarrels as he achieved greater academic renown.

In 1857, Alexander I proclaimed the coming demise of serfdom and commitment to reform. For the first time in his life Shchapov became interested in contemporary affairs, but not surprisingly he initially interpreted the edict in such a way as to reinforce his belief in the essential benevolence of the Russian Church and state. By the time of his instructorship at the academy, almost two years later, however, Shchapov's belief in the Tsar Liberator was exhibiting signs of strain.

At about the same time as his friendship with Eshevsky was at its height, and rumors of Emancipation were in the air, Shchapov began to be seriously interested in Slavophile views of Russian history.[11] Through 1856, he read the Slavophile periodical *Russian Colloquy (Russkaia beseda)* avidly, and discussed the ideas he found there with anyone who would listen. A highlight of that year in the journal's pages was the controversy between the statist historian Sergei Solov'ëv and Konstantin Aksakov over the meaning of Moscow's "gathering of the Russian lands" and the Muscovite autocracy in Russian history.

To Solov'ëv, the sixth volume of whose monumental *History of Russia* had just appeared, the Russian state and the Russian nation were inseparable; the history of Russia *was* the history of the development of the Russian state. Although positivist in his practice, Solov'ëv believed in Hegel's "world-historical individuals," and it is with the rulers and state-builders that he was principally concerned. Although Solov'ëv criticized Karamzin on many points, both believed in the autocracy: the central role of the state in modern Russian life was faithfully, if variously, reflected by nineteenth-century historians.

In no other Slavophile did opposition to the state take a purer,

more dogmatic, or more utopian form than in the writings of
Konstantin Aksakov.[12] He saw all of Russian historical development as conditioned by the unique relationship between the
state and what he called "the land" *(zemlia)*. At one level, the
distinction was simply between the limited political jurisdiction
of state power before Peter the Great, performing the essential
function of protecting society, and that society itself—religious,
communal, and free. At another level, however, the land embodied the timeless moral truth of Christianity, issuing in peaceful,
communitarian social forms, while the state, in Andrzej Walicki's
trenchant phrase, was an "artificial, mechanical and external
structure."[13] Necessary for the preservation of the land, it represented a "lower" principle, one that was necessitated by human
imperfection, by the fact that man was a fallen creature. Nicolas
Berdyaev is quite correct in noting that "the Slavophils had no
love for the State and authority; they saw evil in all authority.
. . . The monarchical doctrine of the Slavophils fundamentally
and in its inward pathos was anarchist and a product of their
revulsion from authority."[14] Behind Aksakov's static "Christian
people's utopia" lay the Romantic hatred of social and political
rationalism that animated all the early Slavophiles.

In his polemic with Solov'ëv,[15] Aksakov stressed, in a way that
must have appealed to Shchapov, the fact that the common people were absent from Solov'ëv's volumes: such an account of
Russian history was ludicrously incomplete. He was outraged at
Solov'ëv's vague Hegelian optimism: history should be written in
relation to truth and to its national expression, not in accord with
the notion that things were getting better and better all the time
—especially when one meant by that essentially that state power
was growing and consolidating. Aksakov found that Solov'ëv was
ultimately a mere apologist for the reforms of Peter the Great—
which Aksakov believed had destroyed the crucial harmony between state and land, and which he condemned even more bitterly than did Khomiakov or Kireevsky, seeing them as a violent
intrusion of the state into the affairs of the land that led to the
cultural enslavement of the Russian gentry to the rationalist cosmopolitanism of the West.

Shchapov read other historical works with a Slavophile point of view. He was fascinated by the work of Vladimir Leshkov, a now-forgotten legal historian at the University of Moscow. In 1856, Leshkov published a book entitled *The Social Customs of Ancient Russia,* in which he investigated the territorial extent of the ancient Russian princedoms that had been absorbed by Moscow.[16] Two years later, Leshkov followed with *The Russian People and the State,* a most Aksakovian work, over which Shchapov pored for several months. From this period dates Shchapov's fascination with the old Assemblies of the Russian Land *(Zemskie sobory),* which Aksakov regarded as crucial in the relationship between state and land, for at these assemblies, called by the monarch and generally organized by estate—gentry, clergy, merchants, peasants—the spirit and opinions of the land informed and guided the deliberations and actions of the state. Aksakov also spoke of the peasant commune *(mir)* and the urban popular assembly *(veche)* as crucial expressions of the ancient Russian *Volksgeist.*

It was some time, however, before either Shchapov's excitement about the Emancipation or his interest in Slavophile literature found much expression in his work. Perhaps one reason for this circumstance may be found in Shchapov's friendship with Ioann Sokolov, the rector of the academy, who was a strong-minded man, committed to historical scholarship but unsympathetic to "democratism," even of the Slavophile variety.

In 1858, Shchapov's master's dissertation appeared as a book, under the lengthy title *The Russian Schism of the Old Ritualists, Examined in Relation to the Internal Condition of the Russian Church and Citizenry in the Seventeenth Century and in the First Half of the Eighteenth Century. An Historical Essay on the Causes of the Origin and Spread of the Schism.* The thesis was based on a large cache of documents that the fortunes of the Crimean War had brought to Kazan'. The large library collection of the Solovetsky Monastery on the White Sea, an early center of the Old Belief, had been transported to Kazan', apparently for fear it would be damaged by the British, and Shchapov, with his familial connection to the Old Believers and his love of documents, had explored its riches.

The published thesis attracted a good deal of critical attention, although the reviews were mixed, and it quickly went into a second edition.[17] In retrospect, one can see that Shchapov's viewpoint was not only confused but clearly transitional. On the one hand, he tended to dismiss the ostensible cause of the Schism: Patriarch Nikon's reform of the Church books. He regarded the schismatics as social rebels protesting against the consolidation of serfdom, the upper classes, and (subsequently) the innovations of Peter the Great. Nikon's harshly imposed changes in liturgy and service books were the cultural expression of violations of an older order, conceived as communal and harmonious. But Shchapov defended Nikon and the Church establishment. He also linked the Schism to the massive peasant rebellion of Stenka Razin, in which many Old Believers took part, but resolutely condemned this "democratic protest." Small wonder that radical reviewers, like Nikolai Dobroliubov and M. A. Antonovich on the *Contemporary*, found the material fascinating but the treatment confused and, on balance, obscurantist.

Also on the basis of documents from the Solovetsky library, Shchapov published between 1857 and 1861 some ten or twelve articles in the Kazan' academy's own journal, the *Orthodox Interlocutor (Pravoslavnyi sobesednik)*. (Rector Sokolov's influence on this journal was clear: he was determined to give it scholarly integrity and intellectual seriousness, and for a time he succeeded.) Shchapov's articles dealt primarily with monasteries and monastic teachers as disseminators of culture and enlightenment in pre-Petrine Russia, and there is little trace of an oppositional point of view, although the criticism of serfdom is clear.[18] But in Shchapov's performance as a teacher and lecturer at the academy in those years, we get a far more vivid sense of the changes taking place in his intellectual outlook and personality. In the early summer of 1856, Shchapov was offered and accepted a post as instructor *(bakkalavr)* in Russian history at the academy. He worked furiously on his lectures that summer, but with the confidence that his new position gave him came a new sociability. And in order to keep going at his desk for long hours, he began to add rum to his many cups of strong tea—a fateful development, as things turned out.

As a lecturer, Shchapov was an inconsistent performer. On occasion he would produce a completely original, finished, and exciting piece of work that he would deliver to the students with an enthusiasm they found irresistible. But if he had been working all night on an article, he might simply string together a list of facts, or talk off the top of his head about his work, or not show up in class at all. Initially, the students were sympathetic. They knew how hard he was working; indeed, he became dependent on them to bring him new pens and sheets of paper, which he rapidly covered with his almost illegible scrawl, turning out his articles and lectures. His manner, both in and out of class, was simple and direct, and the students responded well.

As late as the early fall of 1858, Shchapov's eccentricities were still under control; his drinking was moderate. But within a year he admitted that he suffered on occasion from delirium tremens, and before the year 1859 was out, he had become an alcoholic. He had always been a passionate and sentimental person, prone to outbursts of weeping and occasional violent abuse. Under the influence of alcohol these aspects of his personality became increasingly extreme. He became more and more arrogant about his intellectual abilities, often exploding into wild and abusive tirades at students or colleagues, or at the miserable state of Russian society. After these tantrums were over, he would weep bitterly over his lonely life, his lack of self-control and penchant for self-destruction.

How his political radicalization dovetailed with his growing personal problems is difficult to spell out,* but they became simultaneously more apparent. He seems to have lost faith in the progress of Emancipation, and more than once spoke of his desire to address the Emperor directly about the misery of the

*One reason for this difficulty is that Aristov's book, our only good source for this period of Shchapov's life, was published in 1883, a politically conservative period when no treatment in print of Shchapov's radicalization was really possible. Aristov had to confine himself to Shchapov's dislike of bureaucracy, concern about the state of the country, and so on. But the drift of his remarks is unmistakable. *Ibid.*, pp. 40–41.

peasantry. He began to denounce the gentry and the bureaucrats in his lectures; the opposition of the *narod*'s sincerity and truth-seeking to the hypocrisy of officialdom—certainly a Slavophile-Populist theme—came to obsess him. At the same time he seems to have become more nationalist, and his conversation was laced with criticism of Western cosmopolitanism. He had never been much interested in European history or languages; his apathy now turned to active dislike. His relationship with his students also deteriorated between 1858 and 1861. By now they were upset by his irregular habits, and groups of them visited him to discuss their grievances. His tantrums grew worse: he would tear his clothes, rip books and manuscripts to pieces, and literally chase the students away. But after these outbursts were over, he would still be capable of periods of sustained work and creativity. Most of what he later published in the periodicals of Moscow and St. Petersburg originated in this period.

Basic to Shchapov's Populist vision was a Manichaean dualism derived from Aksakov's distinction between the state and the land. Aksakov thought the reign of Peter the Great had suddenly shattered the preexistent harmony between the two, but Shchapov read the struggle much further back into Russian history.[19] The whole long process of the rise of Moscow, beginning in the fourteenth century, he believed, was freighted with dire consequences for Russian society.

Russia's "natural" development took the form of a slow process of colonization along the rivers of the north. The small social units that replicated themselves in this process were communal in their internal life and tended to be autocthonous. Trade and handicrafts developed from below, strictly in accordance with local needs. In sketching out this historical development, Shchapov laid great stress on all the communal forms of social decision-making for which any evidence could be found in the sources: the village communal meeting *(mirskoi skhod, skhodka)*, the urban popular assembly *(veche)*, the regional council *(zemskii sovet)*, and at the national level, the Assembly of the Land *(Zemskii sobor)*,[20] which became, during the period of Moscow's triumph, a kind of heir to the earlier forms. During

the so-called Appanage Period (roughly encompassing the thirteenth and fourteenth centuries), when the country was largely
governed by various local princes, a loose, federative alliance of
small units prevailed, Shchapov believed, and the vital and harmonious life of society was not infringed upon by the state. Thus
did Shchapov, with his localism and hostility to the state, glorify
a period that most Russian historians have found at best transitional and at worst repulsive, because of the absence of state
power. (Russian historians, more than most, hate it when their
country is "weak.") But as Moscow began to increase its power
over the other cities and augment the territory under its control,
an alien, "outside" force began to menace the autonomy of society: the centralized autocracy.

Despite the trappings of scholarly objectivity, these articles are
obviously and profoundly of their time; the anarchist spirit that
lurks behind the stress on "regionalism" and "federalism" is close
in spirit to Herzen; no wonder he liked them.* As the German
scholar Josef Wachendorf has perceptively pointed out,
Shchapov's concepts of "federation" and "federalism" are not
really political and certainly not legal; they are heavily laden
with ethical-social content: love, mutual solidarity, equality.[21]
Their basis is the family, the most elementary "federation," and
all the other, more extensive social organizations are permeated
with its spirit. The political power and importance of the princes
is unjustifiably minimized in Shchapov's work; the importance of
the *veche* and other "democratic" organs is grossly exaggerated.
These articles are the work of a nineteenth-century *intelligent*,
trying to establish the historical existence of a libertarian and
communal golden age—with definite implications for the future of Russia. It is as impossible to support Shchapov's view of
Old Russia as to endorse the idealized tableaux of Kireevsky or
Aksakov.

Shchapov believed Russian history in the fourteenth and
fifteenth centuries had been dominated by the struggle between

*Herzen's letter to Shchapov, which the latter received in the fall of 1861, has
unfortunately not survived. Aristov, who had a copy of it, recorded Herzen's praise
of Shchapov's historical articles; Herzen called Shchapov's voice "fresh, pure and
powerful." *Ibid.*, p. 74.

Moscow and Novgorod. In his terms, both contained "federative" elements, but he idealized Novgorod as a "federalistic democracy," taking note of the importance of the Novgorod *veche*,
but failing to see that Novgorod's rule over its large empire was
in significant respects as high-handed as Moscow's.[22]

Shchapov regarded the reign of Ivan the Terrible (1533–84) as
the first great triumph of the state; it was followed, however, by
a major reaction. What happened during the Time of Troubles
(1606–13), in Shchapov's view, was that regionalism—largely in
the form of feuding and civil war, to be sure—reasserted itself
against Muscovite centralization. Crucial to his analysis are the
contacts, agreements, and informal alliances among the cities
and regions of Russia that came to the fore in the struggles
against the Poles and the unruly cossack bands. In 1613, with the
Poles stymied and social chaos, for the moment, in abeyance, the
various regions of Russia reconstituted themselves, through a
Zemskii sobor, into a federal state. Tragically for Russia, however, this momentary success was undone by the reassertion of
Muscovite centralization that followed. Shchapov did not make
clear the dynamics of the process, and he left the way clear to
"blame" retrograde, antinational social elements: the dynasty,
realizing an unnatural dictatorship through the rationalist techniques of Western European statecraft, and the gentry, establishing their regime of economic privilege and power on the ruins
of communal and democratic life.

It must be said that there *was* a regional dimension to the
alliance that repelled the Polish invaders and convened the *Zemskii sobor;* and no doubt more people became involved in military and political decision-making than had been the case for
centuries. But was this not simply an emergency, *ad hoc* federalism, created by the virtual disintegration of the central authority,
rather than the reassertion (whatever processes may be concealed within that global term) of some ancient set of historical
"principles"? The failure of the *Zemskii sobor* and other local
deliberative bodies to achieve a solid institutional base in the
seventeenth century was certainly related to the resurgence of
autocratic power, but an observer not morally and politically

committed to Shchapov's regional and federal principles is likely
to conclude that the autocracy has a better claim to be elevated
to the status of a "principle" of Russian history than whatever
underlay the *Zemskii sobor* or the peasant commune. Solov'ëv's
statism in the end tells us more of Russia's actual historical development than the quite opposite mythologies generated by Slavophilism and (later) Populism.

The increasingly erratic rhythms of Shchapov's life were interrupted, in the summer of 1860, by the first of a series of events
that moved him to a larger stage. On August 3, N. A. Popov, an
associate professor of history at the University of Kazan', was
called to a professorship in Moscow and recommended Shchapov
as his replacement. The appointment, on a one-year trial basis,
cleared the University Council and was approved by the Ministry
of Education.

The University of Kazan' was one of the smallest and poorest
of Russia's institutions of higher education.[23] It served primarily
the Volga region and Siberia (an enormous area), and enrollment
fluctuated between 320 and 400 in the years 1855–61. Although
students of gentry origin predominated, the percentage of lower-class students was higher than at other Russian universities, as
was the percentage enrolled for professional training in the faculties of law and medicine.[24] The Kazan' students seem to have
been exceptionally belligerent during this period; conflicts with
the police were ugly, and relations with the faculty poor, in part
because of the uneven quality of the teaching staff and the presence on it of a number of foreigners who spoke Russian badly.

After 1855, student corporatism in Kazan' developed even
more rapidly than elsewhere, due in part to the small size of
the student body and the constant conflicts with the faculty
and educational administration, which notably lacked the
kind of sympathetic moderates to be found in St. Petersburg.
Student courts and libraries soon made their appearance,
and *skhodki* became the favorite means of discussing issues
and mobilizing the students. The *kassa* for poor students was
generously endowed by the more well-to-do, and handwrit-

ten newssheets and forbidden books became commonplace.

The educational bureaucracy at Kazan' handled the students very badly. They were horrified by the student corporatism, but the severe measures they took were often uncoordinated and they frequently lacked the will to stand behind them; a heavy turnover in personnel ensued. Without any "liberal" and supportive public opinion in Kazan', the students felt genuinely under siege by late 1859. The appointment of Prince Viazemsky as curator eased the strain a bit; he actively and successfully promoted the Sunday Schools as an outlet for student social idealism. But in the fall of 1860, when Shchapov took up his post as instructor in Russian history, tensions were still high.

We do not know whether Shchapov's reputation had preceded him at the university, but he was known at least to the faculty historians and to some of the students. In any event, Shchapov electrified the audience at his first lecture by his first words:

I want to say immediately that I have no intention of appearing on a university rostrum with thoughts on the subject of the state principle or with ideas about centralization, but with ideas about nationality *(narodnost')* and regionalism. In our time the conviction has to all appearances already taken hold that the *narod* itself is the principal factor in history, that the essence and content of history is the life of the *narod.* [25]

A dramatic moment—here was this young seminarian, with his Asiatic features, wild hair, and exalted manner, proclaiming his intention to take on Solov'ëv and all the statist Olympians, past and present, in the name of the *narod!* To the more politically minded of the Kazan' students, scarred by their battles with old fogies, mediocrities, and conservatives on the faculty, Shchapov must have seemed the demiurge of the present moment, and indeed his success at the university was immediate and virtually total.

Shchapov continued his informal ways: students were in and out of his apartment at all hours, talking, eating, drinking, and borrowing books. And initially, at least, Shchapov appeared regularly on the podium, to receive admiration and attention from this more politically receptive (and somewhat less well prepared) audience.

Some of his increasing radicalism found direct expression. One day in the winter, he announced his intention to lecture on the Decembrists—a daring proposition, even at the height of the new era. The students gasped—and word was quickly brought to the administration. On the announced day, one of the curator's assistants walked in and ostentatiously seated himself at the back of the hall. Shchapov pulled a small and rather smudged piece of paper from his pocket, stuck it back in again, then pulled it out, smiled, and talked for an hour in a rather conversational way about the Decembrists, ending, however, with some verses about how the *narod* would bring liberty to Russia in the end. This performance was received with long and stormy applause, and the administration decided to ignore the incident.

On occasion, Shchapov would meet with groups of students in someone's apartment and discuss contemporary ideas and problems with them. One November evening he spoke revealingly about his ideas for a "Russian constitution."[26] His point of view was profoundly antistatist—both "liberal" and Romantic. He spoke of freedom—of thought, speech, and labor—in terms that recalled French Revolutionary oratory. He spoke of a series of regionally based, elective assemblies that would culminate in a revived *Zemskii sobor.* But neither the government nor the intelligentsia would draw up a constitution—the people, which had always been the source of creativity in Russian history, would do that. All the government had to do was free the people, while the intelligentsia might provide some advice to ensure the orderly embodiment of the people's genius in institutional form. The amount of damage that had been done the *narod* by political and economic oppression was something that Shchapov was not then willing to confront, or able to understand.

Sometimes he sounded a genuinely revolutionary note; a constant theme of his evening discussions was his longing for a fusion of the intellectual radicalism of *obshchestvo* with the elemental force of popular democracy, of Western consciousness with homegrown peasant rebelliousness. "Will the time soon come,"

he said in words that recall Bakunin, "that holy time when Pugachëv, the motive force of the popular masses, will give his hand
to the Decembrist Murav'ëv or Pestel or Petrashevsky, when the
grave, sad sounds of the people's songs will blend with the songs
and thoughts of Ryleev?"[*27]

Like that of so many other Populist radicals, Shchapov's interest in ethnography had grown, and he had become almost obsessed with the history of peasant rebellion, with bandits—in fact,
with all manifestations of the *narod*'s hostility to the existing
order. He frequently speculated—that winter when the Emancipation finally became law—on when some new manifestation of
popular fury might take place, and what form it might take.

And yet at other times Shchapov would speak as if a renewal
of the monarchy might yet be possible, as if one might still appeal
directly to the Little Father with some hope of success. The
notion of the Tsar Liberator died harder than it is easy for us to
comprehend. Herzen, Bakunin—even Chernyshevsky, for a moment—entertained it. No educated Russian could be unaffected
by the titanic role played by the autocracy in Russian history;
least of all could its enemies forget what it had done for, as well
as to, Russia.

As the winter of 1861 drew on, Shchapov's mood seems to have
become more gloomy and strained; it is not clear why. Perhaps,
as Aristov suggests, he was growing weary of and cynical about
the political adulation he was receiving, and yearned for the
scholar's workroom.[28] Did disappointment with the terms of the
Emancipation have some part? Or was it simply physical debilita-
tion, stemming from alcoholism? In any case, he put in a request
to the university administration for a year's leave of absence to
work in the archives of Moscow and St. Petersburg, to meet other
historians, and to fill gaps in his historical education. But before
his request could be acted upon, came the news of the shootings
at Bezdna.

---

*Kondraty Ryleev was a Decembrist poet who had been hanged in 1826. The
reference to his "thoughts" also refers to the collection of his poems, *Dumy*,
the Russian word being somewhere between "thoughts" and "meditations."

In April 1861,[29] one Anton Petrov, a peasant from the village of Bezdna, southeast of Kazan' on a tributary of the Volga, set himself up as an interpreter of the Emancipation statutes that had been delivered to the village a few days before. Episodes involving interpretation of the statutes were quite common in the Russian villages, not only because of the prevalent illiteracy of the peasants, the arcane and archaic language of the statutes, and their length and complexity, but above all because the gap was so great between the actual terms of the Emancipation and the "liberty" *(volia)* the peasants believed they were receiving. In many areas the belief was widespread that *volia* had been granted by the Tsar long before but that this fact had been concealed by the "lords," "boyars," or "officials" (such terms generally being employed interchangeably). If the peasants understood a passage in the statutes but did not like what they heard, the reader might be dismissed; it might be said that he read "well enough" but interpreted everything as favoring the lords. In discussing these matters, Daniel Field offers the trenchant observation of the British historian Eric Hobsbawm: for peasants, "the refusal to understand is a form of class struggle."[30]

There was thus enormous pressure on those who read the statutes to the villagers to "find the true *volia,*" to interpret the statutes in a manner that would conform to the expectations of the listeners. In this case, Petrov, a literate Old Believer, claimed to have found "true liberty" in certain of the statistics that studded the statutes, and peasants began to flock to Bezdna, in ever larger numbers, to hear him render the truth of their freedom.

It is immensely difficult to establish, from conflicting reports of involved participants and ex post facto accounts, what the threat of violence actually was, or the degree of insubordination, or even whether Petrov had put himself forward as the Tsar's anointed. He *seems* to have done no more than advocate that the peasants refuse their continuing economic obligations to their landlords. But the government was panicky, troops were sent, and when on April 12 the soldiers confronted some thousands of Petrov's followers at Bezdna, they refused to surrender their leader. Eventually, a series of volleys was fired into the crowd, resulting, it has been calculated, in the death of some two hundred peasants, although no remotely accurate estimate of the number of dead was possible at the time.

Confused reports of this dreadful event were quickly brought back to Kazan', with an effect on the students there analogous in some ways to the impact on American college students of the shootings at Kent State University in 1969, if on a much smaller and more local scale. And, as we have seen, Shchapov (along with many other radicals) had been "expecting" something of this sort. Indeed, there is a curious congruence between his attitude and that of the provincial governor and the other authorities: they all were expecting Pugachëv, however differently they understood what that meant. No one involved in the situation at Bezdna was in a position to respond to events with dispassion, a cool head, or even minimal objectivity.

As soon as the news had gotten back to the city, students from the university and the academy set about organizing a requiem Mass, in which their sentiments of outrage and solidarity with the victims could be expressed in a fashion that would make interference or retribution from the authorities difficult. The requiem took place on April 17, with student-priests as celebrants. Given Shchapov's relationship to the more radical students, it is likely enough that he had a hand in arranging the service (which took place in the city cemetery), but he denied it subsequently. In any event, after the service was over, he stepped forward in a state of violent agitation (perhaps increased by alcohol) and made a brief speech. The most plausible version of it runs as follows:

My friends, killed for the *narod!*
The democrat Christ, heretofore the mythical God created by humankind in Europe, to whose sufferings men will prostrate themselves in the forthcoming holy week, proclaimed communal-democratic liberty to the world in the era of the yoke of the Roman Empire and of the slavery of nations, and for this he was nailed to the cross by Pilate's court-martial, and so became the redemptive sacrifice for the whole world's liberty.
In Russia, for the past century and a half, among the bitterly suffering, dark mass of the *narod,* among you *muzhiki,* your own Christs

have appeared—democratic conspirators. Since the middle of the last century they have come to be called prophets, and the *narod* has believed in them as redeemers and liberators. Once again such a prophet has appeared and you, my friends, were the first to answer his summons and to fall as the redemptive victims of despotism, sacrificed for the liberty that the *narod* has awaited so long. You were the first to disturb our sleep, to destroy by your initiative our unjust doubts that our *narod* is capable of taking an initiative in political movements. Louder than the tsar and more nobly than the noble, you said to the *narod:* let thy servant go in peace. The land you worked, whose fruits nourished us, which you now wanted to acquire as your property, and which has now taken you into its bosom as martyrs— this land will summon the *narod* to rebellion and to liberty. Peace to your dust, and eternal historical memory to your selfless deed! Long live a democratic constitution![31]

As soon as the provincial governor got wind of what had happened, he cabled St. Petersburg about the service and about Shchapov's speech. Tsar Alexander himself took a considerable interest in the proceedings. After extensive discussions among various government agencies, and after the first reports of Shchapov's interrogation in Kazan' had been received in the capital, the Emperor's initial decision was reaffirmed: Shchapov should be arrested. But in order to prevent student demonstrations or other disruptive events, Shchapov was merely told that he was to go to St. Petersburg and justify himself, and the curator, Prince Viazemsky, gave him two hundred rubles for expenses.[32] On April 29, Shchapov was escorted to the dock by a crowd of student well-wishers. When the steamboat reached Nizhny Novgorod, agents from the Third Section came aboard and put Shchapov officially under arrest.

There was nothing the Russian government feared so much, in the summer of 1861, as major peasant disturbances in which intellectuals would take a hand; and what the government feared, many radicals tried to promote. Land and Liberty, the first "national" network of radicals and sympathizers, was put together precisely for this eventuality. This being the case, the interest that the Emperor showed in Shchapov, from the first news of the requiem in Kazan', is hardly surprising. When Shchapov arrived in the capital, he was questioned extensively by agents of the Third Section, and he remained under arrest for almost four months, spending some weeks in a hospital, presumably undergoing treatment for alcoholism. After the initial round of questioning was over and it was beginning to be clear that Shchapov did not represent a well-oiled revolutionary conspiracy, the prisoner was given the opportunity he had long desired to address Tsar Alexander directly.

The rather lengthy letter that he wrote has survived.[33] In analyzing it, one cannot, of course, forget the circumstances under which it was written or lose sight of the elements of hypocrisy and dissimulation that it contains. Nevertheless, the curious blend of naive Slavophile monarchism with a kind of liberalism seems honestly to reflect Shchapov's beliefs at the time—or at least what we might call his "best case" analysis of the situation.

The letter, in essence, summons Alexander to be what he is supposed to be: the father of the *narod*. It calls upon him to end Russia's undemocratic and destructive organization by estate and to create a classless, "democratic" monarchy, in which the long-suppressed genius of the Russian people could flower. Shchapov thought this ambitious goal could be accomplished by liberating the *narod* from gentry-bureaucratic oppression, and then by promoting a modern version of the ancient communal governing forms, plus making a major commitment of capital for all-class schools, universities, and financial and credit institutions —all regionally organized but funded by the government.

With this massive but sketchy (and highly utopian) program, we are at a curious juncture, where Romantic Slavophile-Populism borders on a kind of liberalism not often found in Russia. The Slavophile idealization of the peasantry's capacity, the belief in them as a treasure house of religious harmony, is beginning to look a bit red. The Slavophile monarchy—benevolent, patriarchal, but limited, which does not interfere in the life of society —is to make the resources available for the people's genius to develop; it is not to force or even define the course of that development.

At the same time, Shchapov—as a poor, ambitious scion of a clerical-peasant family—regards the *narod* as a reservoir of all kinds of ability, and stresses the need to create a situation where careers will indeed be open to talent. This kind of social optimism was possible during the flood tide of the time; Shchapov's letter was one of the final attempts by a Russian radical to persuade the monarchy to reform the country—root and branch—from above. In the more bitter and polarized politics of the 1860s, such appeals were bound to come to an end; indeed, the naiveté of his proposal was striking even in 1861.

We can see Shchapov's Slavophilism becoming Populism in another way. When Kireevsky, Khomiakov, and the other early Slavophiles denounce the bureaucracy, they do so in part as representatives of an older landed elite, whose power has been eroded by the rationalizing autocracy and its bureaucratic agents. For them, as for Shchapov, the *narod* has preserved the essential values of religious faith, communal organizations, and a traditional way of life, but they never suggest that the *narod* can develop these qualities by itself, tacitly assuming that an elite of some kind (gentry or intelligentsia) must do that. But for Shchapov the people's genius need only be unfettered and supported to fulfill its destiny. He makes no distinction between new and old landed elites. All are rapacious and parasitic; all have come between the Tsar and his people.

Shchapov denied, at the outset of his letter, that it was a "political address"; "God preserve me from the very thought," he wrote with pious hypocrisy. But his idea for the recreation (or creation) of tiers of conciliar agencies—*narodosovetie,* or popular councilship, he called it—would in fact create a kind of constitutional monarchy. Indeed, the old Slavophile concept of a Tsar who conducted foreign relations but "did not interfere in the life of society" was already very different from the actual Russian autocracy. Any attempt to breathe life into the Romantic, traditionalist phrase was bound to issue in some kind of limitation on existing monarchical sovereignty. Alexander responded predictably. "All this shows what kind of ideas prevail with him," he wrote in the margin of the letter, "and that it will be necessary to watch him carefully when we consider it possible to set him at liberty."[34]

Watch him carefully they did. He was released from custody in August, although the threat of incarceration in the Solovetsky Monastery hung over his head for a time. But Alexander over-ruled the Holy Synod, which had claimed the right to try and to punish Shchapov as a member of the clerical estate. Instead, he was deprived of his position at the University of Kazan', forbidden as well to teach at the Ecclesiastical Academy—and given a job at the Ministry of the Interior! Ironically enough, the notion of lodging him in the midst of the bureaucracy he so detested may have originated in Shchapov's own letter to Alexander. In the concluding paragraph he had asked specifically not to be sent back to Kazan', but for a "little corner" to do his work in St. Petersburg, and a modest sum of money to arrange the publication of his works and to treat "the illness which is torturing me" —presumably alcoholism.

In August, Shchapov went to work in a small office of the Ministry of the Interior, charged with responsibility for the affairs of the Old Believers, under the supervision of the minister himself, P. A. Valuev. He was apparently paid some kind of a salary; according to Aristov, he got six hundred rubles for the eleven months during which he was "employed" at the ministry.[35] Despite the fact that he was free to do research at government expense, Shchapov was not happy. He was enraged by the bureaucrats and the bureaucratic mentality with which he now came in daily contact: he was constantly fuming about the "life-less abstractions" by means of which the desiccated representatives of the central government attempted to understand the Russian people. It is more difficult to get the other side, but it seems that the people at the ministry found Shchapov a naive and finally irritating "crazy" with whom it was impossible to get on. Shchapov's temper was not improved by having to submit all his articles to a ministerial censorship, which came down on his purple prose with a heavy hand. He finally almost ceased coming in to his office at the ministry and did his work in his apartment.

There was all the more reason for him to do so, as his St. Petersburg associations were scarcely such as would commend themselves to Valuev or his ministerial colleagues. The episode at Bezdna and Shchapov's part in it had caused a stir in St. Petersburg radical circles, the more so as his old teacher, Eliseev, was now an influential figure at the *Contemporary*. When it appeared that the Holy Synod might send Shchapov off to the monastery, Chernyshevsky was only the most notable of the radical journalists who were prepared to launch a public campaign on his behalf, should it be necessary. It was not. Shchapov was established as a new literary-political star on the horizon, and he was courted by journalists, writers, and historians who were involved with the opposition. He became friendly with A. N. Pypin, the ethnographer (and brother-in-law of Chernyshevsky), with Vasily Kurochkin, editor of the *Spark (Iskra)*. He had some contact with the historian N. I. Kostomarov, whose views were in many respects close to his own, and who may in fact have had some influence on him a few years previously. His friendship with N. G. Pomialovsky, author of *Seminary Sketches* (that stinging indictment of life in the bursa, which greatly appealed to Shchapov), ended in a stupid quarrel, as did so many of Shchapov's relationships in this period. Perhaps not surprisingly, Chernyshevsky remained aloof, despite Shchapov's frequently expressed desire to meet him. They finally spent a disastrous evening together in December 1861; the exact subject of their marathon disagreement is not known, but apparently Shchapov was kept off the *Contemporary* staff on the grounds that his views were too close to the Slavophiles', particularly his antistatism.[36]

In addition to the "scholarly" articles that Shchapov published in the *Annals of the Fatherland* and other large-circulation journals, he produced a lengthy statement of his political views, undergirded by a certain amount of historical background. This "Letter to Prince Viazemsky," written in October 1861, subsequently turned up in Herzen's archives. It was never published and never submitted to the censor. Hence, although it was written in anger, and the language is even more immoderate than usual, it may be taken to represent Shchapov's political position some five months after his far more circumspect communication with Tsar Alexander.[37]

The letter is striking for its feverish tone and sense of impending apocalypse. It was written just as the universities were going up in smoke and the mood in St. Petersburg was inflamed to a degree. Shchapov clearly expected a major social transformation soon, but despite his harsh words about the Russian autocracy, he did not rule out the possibility that this transformation might proceed under monarchical auspices. He told Viazemsky that Russia was on the eve of a revival of "the land," of the achievement of "popular councilship": communal, regional, federal, and democratic. He gave a confused, angry, and ecstatic evocation of the Russia of the future, governed by a great hierarchy of communes, culminating in the *Zemskii sobor.* The motive force of the new order would be the "new generation," those who had attended the requiem in Kazan': students, intellectuals, peasants, and schismatics.

He then launched into a fervid denunciation of all those forces in Russian life that had so cruelly oppressed the *narod* since the seventeenth century, pouring his sentences out onto the page. The *narod* elected the Romanovs, who then usurped absolute power. The Church lost its communal spirit and became Byzantine and hierarchical. The gentry developed, after Peter the Great, into Germanized petty tyrants whose oppression of the people only increased with the passage of time. The Old Believers, the more extreme of the sectarians, and peasant rebels like Stenka Razin and Pugachëv were the true representatives of the *narod* in its struggle against centralized despotism.

The real focus of Shchapov's denunciation was Peter the Great, who in these pages achieved the status of arch-villain of Russian history that he had occupied in the work of the Slavophiles Ivan Kireevsky and Konstantin Aksakov. Shchapov called him the "German-Russian genius," the first Emperor (as opposed to Tsar), the destroyer of Russia's "natural-historical development." For the "truth of the *narod*" he substituted "truth as the monarch's will."*³⁸ Peter bureaucratized Russia and brought to the country the "abstract," German conception of the state. Senate, colleges, and all those ramshackle Western institutions were imposed on the country, at a moment when Russia's communal institutions should have been developed. (All this happened, Shchapov wrote, in a rather simpleminded way, because Peter was raised by Germans and traveled to the West in his youth, instead of traveling around his own country and seeing how it worked.) So Peter became the Antichrist to large portions of his own people, Old Believers and sectarians.

So what now? If the Tsar were not to face the awful "day of the people's judgment," he must himself restore the communal self-government and self-development of the land. If *narodosovetie* were not proclaimed, if the Tsar did not renounce the Petrine autocracy, a "most terrible Russian revolution" was a certainty.

Such a cry of rage could not, of course, be published anywhere under Shchapov's name, nor was it sent to Viazemsky. Shchapov's friends apparently talked him out of doing either. But it was circulated in manuscript, and a few months later it was sent to Herzen in London (who might have published it anonymously, but did not) by people close to the *Contemporary*.

Much of Shchapov's energies, in late 1861 and early 1862, went into the *Century (Vek)*, a journal edited by Eliseev but run along cooperative lines by an artel of radical writers.³⁹ The *Century* in fact lasted barely ten weeks, but Shchapov was a central figure in the journal: not only did he publish fifteen articles, far more than anyone else, but together with Nikolai Shelgunov and Eliseev, he gave the Century its particular flavor: a perceptibly nativist, Slavophile kind of Populism, with a strong sense of Russia's uniqueness. In his articles, Shelgunov tried to define how Russia's future industrialization might be rural and based on the peasant commune, rather than upon a network of urban factories, as in the West. Eliseev tried to demonstrate the socialist potentialities of the Russian peasant, while Shchapov wrote a

*A reference to Feofan Prokopovich's justification of the Petrine monarchy, *The Justice of the Monarch's Will* (1722). The Russian word *pravda* meant both "truth" and "justice," with just a hint of "law," too.

series of articles on "popular councilship" in Russian history, with
an eye to its recrudescence in the immediate future. Individuals
from *obshchestvo* Russia, he felt, if they were to be midwives to
the new Russia, had to study the *narod* and its history; when they
were sufficiently steeped in it, they might join with the people
in the renewed *Zemskii sobor.*

One of the *Century*'s great difficulties was its political diversity. Among the participants were radical bohemians like P. I.
Iakushkin, and political moderates like the novelist N. S. Leskov
and K. K. Arsen'ev (subsequently the editor of the liberal *Messenger of Europe* [*Vestnik Evropy*]). But there were also would-be
revolutionaries, like Nikolai Serno-Solovëvich, who were interested in the *Century* only because they hoped it might be of
some use to Land and Liberty. The militant but nonrevolutionary nativism of Eliseev and Shchapov was not satisfactory to a
number of contributors, and several criticized Eliseev for being
an authoritarian editor who did not understand the cooperative
principles upon which the contributors had agreed to base the
journal. On April 29, 1862, the last issue appeared.

The most important creation of Shchapov's St. Petersburg period (and arguably of his entire career) was *The Land and the
Schism (Zemstvo i raskol),* which came out in two parts in the fall
of 1862. Despite its rhetorical exaggeration, repetitiveness, and
organizational chaos, *The Land and the Schism* was a major
landmark in the historiography of the Russian Church Schism.
From it are descended not only the numerous Populist and Marxist treatments of the Schism, but really *all* accounts that deal
with it as in some part a social movement. With the advent of
"modernization theory" as a rubric for studying Russian development, Shchapov's point of view has again become influential.[40]

These two small volumes* constitute Shchapov's most enduring attack on the Russian autocracy and its works. In its pro-

---

*Part I of *Zemstvo i raskol* appeared as a small book in St. Petersburg in the fall of 1862;
Part II came out at about the same time in the journal of the Dostoevsky brothers, *Time
(Vremia)*. The latter journal, though reasonably catholic in the material published, was not
in the habit of printing radical polemics or material offensive to the government. The appearance of Shchapov's monograph in *Time* is indicative of its interest to religious and nationalist
circles, as well as radical ones. The entire work is reprinted in A. P. Shchapov, *Sochineniia*,
Vol. I (St. Petersburg, 1906), pp. 451–579.

foundly Manichaean attitude, in its glorification of both schismatics and peasant insurrectionaries, *The Land and the Schism*
stands in sharp contrast to Shchapov's dissertation, *The Russian
Schism of the Old Ritualists,* which had been published only four
years earlier. Shchapov, like other Russian radicals, had come a
long way in that short time.

Although Shchapov was nominally writing about the Schism in
the Church and the dissenters who had emerged from it, the
"schism" with which he was really concerned was a larger and
even more important event: the split between the land *(zemstvo)*
and the increasingly bureaucratized Russian state of the seventeenth and eighteenth centuries. The Church Schism became a
mere symptom, albeit an important one. As he did in other essays, Shchapov began in 1613 with the election of the Romanov
dynasty by the *Zemskii sobor,* when, he claimed, the revival of
the democratic communalism of the land had saved Russia from
social and political chaos. Without much exaggeration, one can
say that in Shchapov's view Russian history had been all downhill
from there.

Most of the damage was done, Shchapov had come to believe,
in the reigns of Tsar Aleksei (1645–76) and under Peter the Great
(1682–1725). Although Shchapov used a very Slavophile vocabulary in indicting Aleksei and Peter, his main focus was on the
accelerating economic, political, and cultural oppression of the
Russian lower orders by the more and more Westernized gentry
elite. As the Romanovs infringed on Russia's benevolent patriarchal, limited monarchy and her regional-communal-democratic
"councils"*—what amounted to an Old Russian constitution, although Shchapov does not use the term—they turned to the
West for help in shaping the new institutions that would buttress
their arbitrary rule: an "abstract" concept of the state, Scandina-
vian and German government institutions, and a culture derived
first from Protestant Northern Europe and then from France.
This way of putting it suggests the kind of attack on Enlighten-

---

*Recent research has not given us reason to believe that any such network of
regional councils existed in the seventeenth century. Peasant communes undoubtedly
did exist, although some of the practices most striking to Populists like Shchapov (such as
the periodic repartition of land) became widespread only in the eighteenth century.

ment cosmopolitanism that was made so often by European Romantics after Burke and adapted for use in Russia by the Slavophiles. But it was not the state that destroyed the boyar aristocracy to which Shchapov was opposed, but the state that had enserfed and cretinized the Russian *narod,* a difference that substantially demarcates the ideological feeling of his attack on "the West" from that of his Slavophile forebears. He dwells on the repressiveness of serfdom; on the increase in taxes; on the development of caste spirit; on the maiming of the old regionalism through the imposition of new and arbitrary provincial and district boundaries.

In their ideological criticism, the Slavophiles subtly echoed the aristocratic social groups who had long ago been defeated by, or drawn into the orbit of, the autocracy; Shchapov performed the same function for the hundreds of thousands of peasants who fled that autocracy in the sixteenth, seventeenth, and eighteenth centuries. He did not exactly speak "for" them (although that was in part his intention), but his democratic Slavophilism would have been impossible without the overwhelming fact of their experience, those "miserable cockroach journeyings," in Gorky's memorable phrase.

Shchapov was of two minds about Russian culture. On the one hand, he wanted to argue that the culture of the *narod* was superior to that of *obshchestvo,* just as the land was morally and culturally superior to the world of *obshchestvo* that the state had created. But he couldn't quite persuade himself of this any longer. In his later work, Shchapov would make no bones about the cultural backwardness in which centuries of serfdom had left the *narod,* and already we can find traces of this point of view in his writing: one minute he is praising the culture of the *narod;* the next he is indicting Peter the Great for the ignorance in which he left the masses.[41]

Faced with this kind of economic and political oppression, the people of the land could do two things: run away or revolt. In fact they did both. They had recourse to brigandage and banditry, for which Shchapov offered a social interpretation: this was one way that the creatures of the state could be resisted. Of the numerous popular revolts of the seventeenth century, he singled out the enormous rebellion associated with the name of Stenka Razin and the abortive rebellion of the traditionalist Moscow guards, the *Strel'tsy* (meaning archers, musketeers, "shooters") against Peter the Great; he stressed the connection of both with the Old Believers. Even more fundamental to the popular response was flight; modern scholarship has amply confirmed the stress that Shchapov laid on those who simply ran away from the heavy burdens of serfdom and military service. Indeed, the cossack hosts, that distinctive Russian phenomenon, were the result of a fusion of two cultures: Slavic peasants, fleeing their governmental and gentry persecutors, and the remnants of the once-powerful Tatar (Mongol) hordes on the periphery of the Russian state.

Rebellion and flight combined and recombined within the Schism. Clerics, peasants, merchants (and a very few members of the upper class) refused to accept the corrected Church books; after revolts, violent resistance, and self-immolation, those who stuck by the uncorrected books either fled to out-of-the-way parts of the realm or adhered to secret religious communities in the larger cities.

The most militant and extreme in this refusal of the Church and the state that supported it were the so-called Wanderers *(Beguny, Stranniki)*. Shchapov had solid grounds for his belief that they were religious, unself-conscious anarchists; modern scholarship has largely confirmed his description of their lives, even if they were less numerous than he supposed. They refused to live in a world that—the Russian Church having fallen into apostasy—they believed was ruled by the Antichrist: in effect, Peter the Great and his successors on the throne of Russia. As they were (literally) homeless in this world, their lives came to be spent on the road, in "wandering" or "running." The effect was to lend an apocalyptic religious sanction to the previously existing phenomenon of peasant flight. Because the image of the Antichrist was stamped on Russian coins, they could not use money, nor for the same reason could they carry the Russian internal passport. (Many of them did carry passports of a kind— often inscribed with a prayer, or a parody of the Antichrist's

passport, or a "letter" from God.) More recently, the Wanderers
had come to be supported by a network of sympathizers who
maintained facilities in their homes or places of business to put
up their more militant coreligionists. At the end of their lives
many of these fellow travelers would sell their possessions and
engage in some kind of (often quite symbolic) "travel," or at least
be carried out into their gardens to die, so that they should not
be "at home" when the end came.

In addition to the Wanderers, others of the extreme Protestant
sects, as well as the Old Believers, were of interest to Russian
radicals in the 1860s and 1870s. Just as the peasant rebels of the
seventeenth and eighteenth centuries were conceived to be
"primitive rebels" (to use Hobsbawm's phrase), the opposition of
these sectarians to Church and state was regarded as a kind of
primitive or unself-conscious anarchism. And the hope of many
intellectuals was, of course, that class consciousness could be
achieved without any loss in militancy; in other words, that not
only could these representatives of the *narod* be won for the
cause of the radical intelligentsia, but that, in a deep sense,
the two groups would turn out to be brothers under the skin and
the split between the *narod* and *obshchestvo* could, through
common opposition to the state, be healed. This was an ingenious
and inspiriting pipe dream, it turned out, but only the ideologically unsympathetic could see such things clearly in 1862. Precisely at this time, V. I. Kel'siev and Ogarëv were putting together a special supplement to the *Bell* in London; entitled the
Popular Assembly (Obshchee veche), it was intended as propaganda for agents of Land and Liberty in Russia, for use among
Old Believers and sectarians; although little came of Kel'siev's
dreams and projects, Russian intellectuals made a number of
similar attempts over the next several decades.

Like most of these *intelligenty*, Shchapov was not, by this
time, interested in the religious issues of the Schism at all; indeed,
he called the actual beliefs of the Wanderers (presumably notions
like the rule of the Antichrist in Russia) "twaddle." Of course,
that was not the point, for beneath the religious phraseology,
within the religious hull, was the social and democratic kernel.

The Schism was *really* a revolt of the most militant members of the land against the reforms of Peter the Great and against the virtual destruction of the old culture of Russia. The Schism was not essentially a religious phenomenon, despite the fact that the land had only a religious vocabulary in which to make its protest. Shchapov called the decision of an Old Believer community not to pray for the Tsar "democratic." As the Wanderers were the most militant and extreme representatives of the land point of view (fugitive soldiers seem often to have gravitated toward the Wanderers and their network of "safe houses"), Shchapov naturally dwelt on them.

Shchapov found proof of the close connection between the land and the Schism in the fact that the culture of the schismatics closely resembled Russia's communal and regional culture before Peter the Great. Discovering on occasion what he wanted to discover, Shchapov found that the Schism gave the land the opportunity of recreating the old world in a real, if limited, fashion: there was a regional element within the Schism, and regional differences between communities; the Schism spread through colonization; and the old communal and conciliar forms appeared within the structure of the schismatic communities. Finally, various regions and communities kept in touch with each other in ways that Shchapov viewed as closely akin to the "federative" principle of Old Russia.

The second half of 1862 was a time of personal stress for Shchapov. The government offensive of the summer, and particularly the closing of the journals and the arrest of Chernyshevsky, affected all Russian radicals, and Shchapov's social life suffered a special blow with the closing of the Chess Club, upon which he had heavily depended for human contact. It may be doubted that he suffered correspondingly as a result of losing his job at the ministry, but his dismissal was politically ominous as well as entailing financial loss. Aristov reports that throughout this period Shchapov's drunkenness grew worse; he may have stopped working almost entirely. When he was lonely and in his cups, Shchapov would simply take to the streets in search of society.

His hatred of uniforms (especially military ones) had grown so great that he would sometimes pursue officers and uniformed bureaucrats upon whom he happened in his wanderings and abuse them drunkenly. On other occasions he would try to find peasants to sing folk songs for him, or talk for hours with cabdrivers, after which he would give them extravagant tips. At the same time he grew more cynical about the *narod* and began to talk about the loss of spirit and initiative that the Russian people had suffered through their long subjection to the state.[42]

Shchapov might have gotten into serious trouble with the law or continued his steady physical and psychological decline had he not finally met the woman who—it is no exaggeration to say—became his salvation, as well as his wife, lover, nurse, and research assistant. Her name was Ol'ga Ivanovna Zhemchuzhnikova, and she was from a clerical family. Her father had been a poor teacher, but she had been orphaned at an early age and raised by a rich and affectionate uncle who had let her go her own way. The way she decided upon included considerable education and sympathy for advanced political ideas, including feminism. Zhemchuzhnikova was an energetic, intelligent, rather plain person—highly sensible and practical, but with a deep sympathy for all unfortunates, most of all for the poor and oppressed. Then as now, such sympathies could easily become radical and political if the atmosphere were propitious. Zhemchuzhnikova had read a number of Shchapov's articles, and on that politically admirable basis she decided she wished to make his acquaintance. Aristov, who introduced the two, reports that she had wept after reading of the plight of the eighteenth-century peasantry in *The Land and the Schism;* he also recalls showing her Shchapov's picture, and that she was impressed by his "long, wavy hair."[43] They met around Christmas, 1862, and their relationship developed rapidly throughout the following year. When Shchapov discovered that he was to be sent to Siberia, she instantly declared her intention to accompany him. Her willingness to share his fate lessened the initial trauma of exile, and, once in Siberia, her presence made life possible.

For Shchapov discovered in the fall of 1862 that the authorities had not forgotten him. The previous July, a pair of Herzen's couriers had been caught entering Russia with letters and messages for a number of people; others were mentioned in more or less compromising ways in letters and documents. Chernyshevsky was the most prominent victim of the "affair of the London propagandists" (although Herzen's message to him was merely the occasion of his arrest, not its cause); Turgenev was also harassed for many months; and some thirty people were eventually brought to trial. One of those who turned up in the police dragnet was a man called Nichiporenko, who appears to have relied on the sheer volume of information he turned over to the police to save him. Among those whom he implicated was Shchapov. As we know, Herzen *had* written to Shchapov; someone, although probably not Shchapov himself, had sent the "Letter to Prince Viazemsky" to London; and in addition there were striking similarities between Shchapov's interests and those of Kel'siev, the most prominent recent addition to Herzen's ménage, in whom the authorities were interested. Still, Nichiporenko changed his story several times; Shchapov faced him down in an oral confrontation, and after a time the investigation seemed to lapse.[44]

Nevertheless, Shchapov had made some new enemies with the publication of *The Land and the Schism*. Andrei Nikolaevich Murav'ëv, an elderly and conservative church historian (with excellent connections in the upper bureaucracy), called Shchapov's viewpoint "real communism" and wrote letters of denunciation to a number of highly placed persons, including the minister of the interior.[45] Before the new year of 1863 was many weeks old, Shchapov had been informed by some government representatives—it is not certain by whom—that if he wished to avoid immediate arrest and exile, he would have to go into the clinic run by Professor Zablotsky (which had facilities for treating prisoners and people uder surveillance) and undergo treatment for alcoholism and general physical debility. For the next few months he was lodged in several hospitals and clinics, under the care of various medical men. He was allowed to visit specific friends by day, but had to be back at night in the hospital. The friends whom he visited had to guarantee that he would return to the hospital.

The year 1863 was a strange one for Shchapov. He collaborated with Eliseev and Antonovich on the short-lived journal *Essays (Ocherki)* while moving from hospital to hospital; his political fate was uncertain. The only real security in his life came from his close relationship with Zhemchuzhnikova. His ideas changed rapidly in this period, as can be seen from a piece that appeared in the *Contemporary Word (Sovremennoe slovo)* as early as January 1863. Entitled "The New Era: On the Boundary of Two Millennia,"[46] the article revealed a new and strong affinity for intelligentsia elitism, and a sharp diminution in Shchapov's veneration for the people. Picking up themes he had broached a year ago in *The Land and the Schism,* Shchapov turned them completely around. Despite the great achievements of the Russian people, he wrote, they stood in dire need of European culture—in particular, scientific culture, which must be brought to them by the educated minority, primarily by the representatives of *obshchestvo* in the two capitals. Shchapov also reversed himself by declaring that of the two intellectual tendencies of the previous generation, he now chose Westernism over Slavophilism, which like the world of the Old Believers was fatally tainted with futile nostalgia for dead forms of life. The educated minority must bring European culture not only to the Russian masses but also to the peoples of the East, who stood in even greater need of it. If the Russian elite were successfully to accomplish this mission, "Europe will recognize Russia as a great nation." (This naive vision of Russia as *Kulturträger* in the Orient curiously anticipates the kind of imperial program later developed by the Sinologue V. P. Vasil'ev and other spokesmen for Russian expansion in Asia, most of whom, like Shchapov, had undergone some kind of Slavophile influence.[47]) By spring, Shchapov was almost obsessed with his own (and the Russian people's) ignorance of the natural sciences—particularly, at that time, astronomy. His journalism of the period reveals an exacerbated scientism: he came to admire Pisarev, and after reading Buckle's historical works, he longed to rewrite Russian history along the lines of the natural sciences—stressing climate, geography, topography, and what Buckle grandiloquently called "the General Aspect of Nature."

Some Soviet historians (the late M. N. Pokrovsky among them) have expressed a restrained enthusiasm for Shchapov's discovery of "historical materialism," but to most observers Shchapov's later work is markedly inferior to that of his Slavophile-Populist period in originality and imagination, if not in energy.

What is one to make of such a rapid and dramatic change of view? Eliseev (who was greatly annoyed by it) quite properly stressed the quality of *conversion* and the naive science-worship with which Shchapov's later work is suffused: "as soon as Shchapov mastered some new scientific fact or other, he was immediately prepared to lay it at the base of Russian history and onesidedly derive all the events of that history from it."[48] It is also true that the times were ripe for elitism: the people were disappointing the Left by failing to revolt, and radicals were now looking to other radicals (or education, or propaganda), not thinking that Stenka Razin would return, at least not any time soon. So Shchapov was in tune with the times. It is the rapidity of his conversion that needs explanation, rather than the new ideas themselves.

Shchapov had been feeling for some time that both he and the Russian people (and his identification of the two was strong) were suffering from provincialism and undereducation (the "ignorance of the seminary," in his own words). It seems likely that this feeling had grown within him as he sought to leave Kazan' for Moscow or St. Petersburg, and it had matured during his stay in the capital. Undoubtedly his semi-incarceration in a series of clinics and hospitals provided a climate conducive to a rethinking of things, and we have Shchapov's own testimony that the doctors with whom he talked greatly reinforced his growing belief in science. It provided a curious note of contradiction in *The Land and the Schism* and finally came into the open in 1863.

The Shchapovs went into exile as a married couple in March 1864. Their initial destination was the village of Anga, Shchapov's birthplace, but they were soon granted permission to live in Irkutsk, where the solitude was slightly less devastating. (Ironi-

cally enough, the Bakunins had been in exile there, but Mikhail
had escaped some two years previously and his wife had joined
him abroad less than a year before.) The Shchapovs had developed an optimistic, compensatory, hopeful view of Siberia as a
healthy place, full of vitality, a place of the future where people
might live in harmony with nature and where the writ of the
state did not run. It was a view more in keeping with the ideas
that Shchapov had abandoned than his new opinions about the
West, science, and the importance of intellectuals; alas, there
were few enough of those in Irkutsk, and little enough science.
He continued to write—voluminously—although lack of access
to libraries and up-to-date information led to abstractness and
intellectual attenuation; his articles and surveys of Russian culture grew in ambition as they declined in specificity. He was able
to go on a number of scientific expeditions to out-of-the-way
regions, and his descriptions are considered a genuine contribution to the ethnography of Siberia.

Until the very end of his life, Shchapov continued to hope that
he might be allowed to return to one of the major cities of European Russia, if not to Moscow or St. Petersburg, but his many
letters to influential people failed to turn the trick. Less than a
year after his arrival in Irkutsk, he was implicated in the activities
of a group of Siberian separatists, although his accuser eventually
abandoned the charge. But Shchapov's name was revered among
the young radicals associated with the Kazan' area; his speech at
the requiem circulated as a pamphlet, and his name turned up
often in the testimony of arrested radicals and in the pages of
letters that fell into the hands of the Third Section.[49] Taken
together with his previous adventures, it is scarcely surprising
that the government kept him in Siberia until the end.

The Shchapovs had gone into exile with substantial funds, provided by Ol'ga Ivanovna's rich uncle. Neither of them was good
at handling money, however, and after her uncle's death they
began a long, downward slide into destitution. Shchapov's travels
and writings for the Russian Geographical Society were of some
help, and Shchapova taught in the Irkutsk gymnasium from 1869
until her death in 1872, which helped much more. But after that,

Shchapov sank into a terrible melancholic stupor, aggravated by hunger and a recrudescent alcoholism. The Siberian authorities were still sufficiently afraid of him to suppress all mention of his death, which came in February 1876, officially of tuberculosis, in the local press. It was many months before his friends back in European Russia knew that he was dead, and rumors circulated that he had died of starvation. In various ways, he had.

His final contact with the world of advanced European ideas came about through the exile of an energetic young radical named German Lopatin in Irkutsk, after he had tried and failed to rescue Chernyshevsky from Siberia. Lopatin hoped to arrange Shchapov's escape, after which he and Ol'ga Ivanovna would join Lopatin and Pëtr Lavrov in Zurich, where Lavrov was just getting his journal *Forward (Vperëd)* started. First Shchapov made difficulties because he didn't think that he could live outside of Russia; then, after Lopatin escaped and set out to arrange matters from abroad, their correspondence went astray through the carelessness of the courier. By the time orderly contact had been reestablished, Ol'ga Ivanovna was dead, and Shchapov refused to leave her grave.[50]

From an intellectual point of view, Shchapov ought to be considered the antipode of Chernyshevsky: he embodied the Slavophile inheritance of Populism most fully, just as Chernyshevsky was the most "Western" of the early Populists. This means, of course, that Shchapov's pre-1863 writings were close to those of Herzen: they emphasized Russia's communal peasant culture, the separateness of that culture from *obshchestvo*, its revolutionary potential. And like Eliseev and other early Populists, Shchapov radicalized Slavophile nationalism into a kind of revolutionary messianism; in this, too, he is akin to Herzen, who stressed the notion that revolutionary Russia would follow a path separate from the West and perhaps redeem Western history.

In other respects, Shchapov anticipated the direction that Bakunin's thought took in the 1860s, after he escaped from Irkutsk and arrived in the West as an exile. (Although Shchapov's name does not figure significantly in the extant literature on

Bakunin, there is some evidence that his political and social interpretation of the Schism and of Stenka Razin's revolt was of great
interest to Bakunin.[51]) For Shchapov's books and articles pushed
Populist ideas further in the direction of anarchism than did any
other body of work prior to Bakunin. The hatred of the state,
characteristic of all the early Slavophiles, found its most powerful
Populist expression in Shchapov and Bakunin. Social and moral
virtue resided in the Russian people and in their communal and
federal social institutions; the state was the tyrannical bearer of
an antinational rationalism.

How important a figure was Shchapov to the young radicals
who came after him? Vera Figner, a prominent member of the
People's Will who wrote extensive memoirs after 1917, listed him,
along with Herzen and Bakunin, as someone whose work helped
her to understand the importance of the village commune.[52]
Georgy Plekhanov's Populist formulations (prior to his emigration and conversion to Marxism) clearly owe a debt to Shchapov,
in the sharpness of the dualism between *obshchestvo* and the
narod, in their historical grounding. When Aristov's biography of
Shchapov appeared in 1883, Plekhanov reviewed it in an émigré
radical journal.[53] Although he was at that time working his way
out of Populism and into a somewhat schematic Marxism, Plekhanov treated Shchapov almost tenderly, as befitted a writer
about whom he had cared. He called Shchapov's historical articles "really influential in the theory of Populism," but contrasted
his naive counterposing of historical "principles" with the sophisticated analyses of Chernyshevsky, which he regarded as a long
step toward the social democracy he was about to embrace.

In a recent book, S. Frederick Starr discussed Shchapov in a
different context, which also deserves mention.[54] In the period
after the Crimean War, the antistatism and hostility to bureaucracy so apparent in one wing of Populism was not confined to
radicals. The creation of the zemstvos—agencies of local and
provincial self-government—was only the principal manifestation of a generally critical attitude among respectable professors
and bureaucrats, who would have been indignant to discover
their names linked with Shchapov, let alone Bakunin! The ex-

traordinary role of the state in Russian national development is a central fact here; in periods when the policies shaped by bureaucratic centralism failed or faltered, various criticisms might emerge which were similar only in their final appeals to local autonomy and popular initiative. And the period after the Crimean War was such a period.

But the power of the state in Russian life was enormous. Just as provincialist ideology and provincial reform failed seriously to tilt the balance in favor of greater popular initiative, the federalist-anarchist emphasis in Populism was challenged in the 1860s (and repeatedly thereafter) by a revolutionary centralism just as despairing of and hostile to popular initiative as the bureaucracy of the Russian ancien régime.

The Emergence of Populist Style: Pavel Ivanovich Iakushkin

The mission of thought is to construct archtypes; I
mean, to point out from among those infinite figures
that reality presents those in which, because of their
greater purity, that reality becomes clearer.
—José Ortega y Gasset, *Meditations on Hunting*

Chernyshevsky's "civil execution" took place on May 19, 1864, at eight o'clock in the morning, on Customs House Square in St. Petersburg.[1] After his arrest in the summer of 1862, he had been sentenced to seven years' hard labor in Siberia and banishment there for life. Despite his influential radical journalism and his involvement with active revolutionary groups, the evidence against him had been insufficient, and the government had been forced to use forged letters from an agent provocateur to convict him. Chernyshevsky had been confined in the Fortress of St. Peter and St. Paul for almost two years prior to his appearance in the square on that rainy May morning.

The civil execution was a barbarous but purely symbolic ceremony. Before a member of the gentry could be punished for a major offense, he had to be formally stripped of his civil rights, guaranteed to him under the Charter of the Nobility issued by Catherine the Great in 1785. The ceremony consisted of the reading of the sentence, followed by the breaking of a wooden sword over the head of the criminal. He was then led off in chains.

Chernyshevsky was very well known in St. Petersburg, and the crowd assembled in the square was large. It was made up of high army officers and fancy ladies and ordinary citizens, many of whom had simply turned out for the show. There was also a large group of writers, students, bohemian intellectuals—many of whom had a precise admiration or vague ideological sympathy for the man who was to be "executed." The scaffold was surrounded by a tight ring of soldiers, policemen, and civil guards. An avenue was kept clear for the carriage that would bring the prisoner to the scaffold. Umbrellas were everywhere, distracting the guards, who pressed the people back. As the sword was broken over Chernyshevsky's head, it began to rain harder.

Suddenly there was an eddy in the crowd; a man was trying to force his way to the scaffold. He was small and wiry, with a pockmarked face, a full beard, and gold-rimmed glasses; he pushed his way almost to the platform before he was apprehended. He was wearing peasant costume: a red calico shirt, and wide velveteen trousers tucked into his worn boots. He explained heatedly, in a loud voice, that Chernyshevsky was a friend of his and he wanted to say good-bye. The guards crowded around him; still arguing, he shouted that everyone wanted to say good-bye, not just he alone.

An officer, who seemed to know him personally, tried to calm him down. "Pavel Ivanovich, Pavel Ivanovich," he soothed, "it's impossible." And he muttered something about arranging to have the man say good-bye to Chernyshevsky later.

Then the bouquets and flowers began to fall on the scaffold. The first one was thrown by a young girl, who was immediately taken into custody and brought to a police station. The little man in the peasant costume followed her there and noisily claimed that he had thrown the bouquet. The policemen looked uncertainly from her to him. The police chief came out of his office and asked her calmly if she had thrown it, and if she had, who had told her to do it.

The girl collected herself and replied distinctly, "Yes, I threw the first bouquet, and I did it because I wanted to."

"Who convinced you to commit this act?" persisted the police chief.

"I decided to express my sympathy with an innocent man through the bouquet," said the girl melodramatically.

"Why do you think that Chernyshevsky is innocent?"

At this the girl became confused. "They said . . . I heard . . . it's generally known . . ."

The man in peasant clothes interrupted again. "As you can see, she's a child," he said impatiently. "She doesn't know what she's doing, taking this guilt on herself, when it was I who threw the first wreath. I order you," he said grandly, "to release her and arrest me."

Several policemen quickly confirmed the girl's account and said they had not seen the man at all. The chief smiled thinly at him. "You, Mr. Iakushkin," he said, "will please take yourself off. If your declaration is confirmed, you will be arrested—depend upon it—and not released."

"But I don't have an apartment," Iakushkin continued to argue. "Where will you look for me?"

"Don't disturb yourself about that. You're so obvious that you'll be found," the chief answered. "Go on, go on, wherever you like. Your declaration will be taken into account," he added ominously.

Iakushkin shrugged his shoulders, muttered something, and left the station house.[2]

That morning's work was, if not typical, at least characteristic of Pavel Ivanovich Iakushkin, ethnographer, writer, drunk, and thorn in the flesh of Russia's police. Iakushkin was a man about whom anecdotes multiplied and around whom legends grew like weeds. His contemporaries saw him as every kind of symbolic figure. To some—like the writer Nikolai Leskov—he was a modern incarnation of the Holy Fool, a pilgrim, a wanderer on the face of the earth. To many of the more general public, this scion of the gentry class who spent his time traveling on foot through rural Russia, collecting songs, talking to peasants, and being arrested was an incarnation of "Old Russia," of the "essence of the Russian people," something little understood but much talked about. To still others, Iakushkin was the first *narodnik*—a man who had discovered that the way to the good life and good society of the future ran through the Russian peasant village. To the representatives of provincial officialdom whom he encountered on his travels in the countryside, however, Iakushkin embodied disorder, democracy—even revolution.

In a way, the provincial policemen who arrested and harassed Iakushkin were quite right. His way of life was a negation of the creed they lived by: order, hierarchy, bureaucratic formality, and petty venality. In a country and a time in which one's dress was an automatic indicator of rank and status, Iakushkin was the son of a landowner who spent his life in peasant costume. His travel documents were never in order, and he rarely had any money. He simply asked people—peasants in the country, students and intellectuals in the city—for what he needed. As he never needed much, he almost always got it: a bed for the night, or a warm room to write in.

Iakushkin had many friends and more acquaintances, although none of the close and lifelong variety. Chernyshevsky, for instance, was scarcely an intimate, despite the vociferous warmth of Iakushkin's public farewell. Iakushkin's "circle" ranged from respected dignitaries like Count Stroganov, curator of the Moscow Educational District, through a variety of writers, professors, and intellectuals of all political persuasions, to the doormen and tavernkeepers of St. Petersburg. And one should add "the Russian people," by which Iakushkin meant the Russian peasantry, from the Caspian Sea to the Baltic and the Ukraine. The peasants were for him a constituency, an object of affection and a source of moral value. Despite the diversity of his associations, Iakushkin treated everyone who crossed his path (except, perhaps, for Jews and policemen) in much the same curious, friendly, and natural fashion. It may be this casual egalitarianism that most deeply offended the official Russia of the day, which retaliated by destroying him.

In the early 1880s, a collection of Iakushkin's writings was published in St. Petersburg, and appended to it were reminiscences
of him by friends and contemporaries. The 1880s were a decade
of stagnancy and reaction in Russia; the presiding genii of the
time were the wintry pessimist Konstantin Pobedonostsev and
the Tsar-philistine Alexander III, who when he thought of the
Jews always remembered the crucifixion. The volume of Iakush-
kiniana appeared at about the time that the *Annals of the Fatherland*—the last and most enduring of Russia's radical journals—
was shut down by the government. It is striking how many of
those who had known Iakushkin twenty or thirty years before,
now, looking back from the reactionary tranquillity of the 1880s,
regarded him as the embodiment of the new era, the fresh hopes
that had stirred Russian society after the death of Nicholas I and
the end of the Crimean War.

The "thaw" is a recurrent metaphor in Russian history, although Russian thaws tend to be of the January variety. And it
was in this "thaw" after the Crimean War that Iakushkin became
a figure, a personage, for a few brief years, before he was mutilated and destroyed by the great events, the high and low politics
of the 1860s. Historians—of the Russian state, the revolutionary
movement, of Russian literature—have by and large failed to
remember him, and with reason. He played no great role, influenced the course of events slightly, if at all, and left no important literary legacy. Only in the history of folklore does he have
a small, if secure, place as a collector. But even the crude outline
of his life can help us feel what it was like to live through this
remarkable period. Who was this "new man" who appeared in
the literary-journalistic world of St. Petersburg in the spring of
1858? Where had he come from?

Iakushkin was born, on January 14, 1822, into a middle-gentry
family of Orël province, several days' ride south of Moscow, in
the heartland of Russia's gentry writers and men of letters.[3] Turgenev, Tolstoy, Leskov, the Kireevsky brothers, Marko Vovchok
—all had their estates in the Tula–Orël area, and Iakushkin grew
up in the rural landscape immortalized in *A Sportsman's
Sketches*. His family, however, was an unusual one, and it

scarcely requires a psychohistorian or a peasant wisewoman to trace some of the scars left by the circumstances of his birth and childhood.

Pavel Ivanovich's father, Ivan Andreevich Iakushkin, provides a notable example of the kind of purposeless and debased life that circumstances made possible for the Russian gentry at the end of the eighteenth century and beginning of the nineteenth. Ivan Andreevich retired from the guards in his youth, after only six years of service, in 1781. In 1813, his elder brother died, leaving him, inter alia, a substantial estate, Saburovo, about seventy kilometers from Orël, where Ivan Andreevich was able to surrender himself to a career of debauchery impressive even in Russian gentry annals. The seduction of serf girls seems to have been his principal enthusiasm, and it was the most resolute and formidable of these peasant women who was Pavel Ivanovich's mother. At the age of fifteen, a peasant girl from Saburovo, one Praskov'ia Faleevna, presented the lord of the manor with a son, Aleksandr; three years later, Pavel was born, on January 14, 1822. Other children by other women were already on the scene, in the works, or yet to be; being illegitimate, none of them bore their father's name. At the time of the birth of his second son by Praskov'ia Faleevna, Ivan Andreevich Iakushkin was sixty-four years old.

For better or for worse, we have no way of knowing precisely how it was that Praskov'ia Faleevna managed to triumph over her rivals—not to mention the temperament of Ivan Andreevich —and become Madame Iakushkin and the mistress of Saburovo. Perhaps the attitude of his neighbors helped the "old bachelor" (as one Soviet historian calls him) to take this step. Perhaps his advancing age was a factor. In any case, Pavel's mother became Praskov'ia Faleevna Iakushkina just before the birth of her third child, Nikolai. Praskov'ia Faleevna—subsequently, at least—enjoyed, by all reports, the "respect" of her neighbors; the only surviving criticism of her character was that she had a tendency to be "despotic" and by no means objected to having the peasants beaten. Much as one might expect.

Ivan Andreevich died in 1832, at the age of seventy-four, hav-

ing sired his final son, Semën, only two years earlier. In view of
the preoccupations of the master, it is not surprising that the
economic foundations of the estate had become shaky. With
Praskov'ia Faleevna's firm and capable hand at the helm, the
situation improved; only subsequently, when Praskov'ia Faleevna was approaching sixty, did unmistakable signs of decay
become evident. No doubt it was Praskov'ia Faleevna's peasant
lack of sentimentality, her hardheadedness—together, perhaps,
with a judicious deference—that so commended her to the local
gentry.

As a writer and as a man, Iakushkin was little given to Romantic introspection and personal reflection; he never told his public
how he felt about his father or his illegitimate birth. Neither he
nor his brother Aleksandr (also illegitimate) was awarded gentry
status; when he entered the University of Moscow, he was
obliged to take with him a special document containing a physical description, as if he were a peasant. This is how we know that
at the age of eighteen Iakushkin was just under five feet four
inches tall, with red hair, dark red eyebrows, a pale complexion,
and gray eyes. His only "distinguishing mark" was a mole on his
cheek.

It is almost impossible to resist the proposition that Iakushkin's
subsequent "going to the people," his love of the Russian peasant, was in some way related to his peasant mother and to a sense
of his own special relationship to the peasantry. But we know
nothing about his earliest years—until he entered the Orël gymnasium at the age of eleven—except the barest skeleton of family
dates. A Soviet historian hopefully surmises a "democratic" childhood: his mother was much occupied with running the estate;
therefore Pavel and his brothers were left with peasant nurses
and peasant playfellows. This is probable enough, particularly in
view of the special gift he showed at the gymnasium for coming
out with long strings of peasant swear words in moments of stress.
But one doubts that there was anything consciously peasant-
oriented in the upbringing that Praskov'ia Faleevna gave her
children; the opposite was more likely to be true. But situations
of this kind are always complicated, and it may well be that

the first peasant songs Pavel heard came from his mother's lips.

At the Orël gymnasium, which he entered in 1833, we have the brief but helpful testimony of Nikolai Leskov, who followed Iakushkin through the school several years later.[4] He tells us that Pavel Ivanovich was a character. He was known to his schoolmates as "Goat," and like many rebels since, he had hair trouble. The director of the gymnasium himself took unfavorable notice of Iakushkin's long hair, which sprouted from his head in unmanageable tufts, and put him on exhibit before the school as an example of how not to look. Pavel (and some of his admirers) were also given humiliating public haircuts for a while, but this kind of pedagogy soon had to be abandoned, since young Iakushkin would invariably resort to his "coarse peasant words," the audience would "die laughing," and the intended lesson would be lost in general hilarity. Furthermore, Leskov tells us, Iakushkin's tufts had an almost miraculous power of growth and renewal. Leskov compared him to a Tungus miracle worker, who could pass his hand over a slit belly and lo! it was healed. Seemingly within minutes of the end of the haircut, the disorderly tufts would reappear, undaunted. Thus Leskov, no doubt with the benefit of hindsight, sees Iakushkin's *prostonarodnost'* (which may be translated as "simple people-ness") as already clear. His German teacher called him a "little peasant doll."

Pavel did well at the gymnasium, although according to one source he had to repeat the seventh class because he was insolent. Whether he had a favorite teacher—the almost stock figure of the "good" (and radical) teacher laboring in the provinces— we do not know. Present on the faculty, however, was a man named V. P. Petrov, math teacher and friend of Alexander Herzen. The Soviet historian A. I. Balandin naturally suspects a connection here and sees Petrov kindling Iakushkin's interest in the sciences.[5] Be that as it may, Pavel Ivanovich left the gymnasium in 1840 and enrolled at the University of Moscow, where his elder brother, Aleksandr, had preceded him.

The university, it soon became clear, was not Iakushkin's milieu, and mathematics was not his subject. It is doubtful that he finished and became a *Kandidat.* Nor did the great ideological

debates of the 1840s, the salon struggle between the Slavophiles
and the Westerners, have much attraction for him. Indeed, at no
time in his career was Iakushkin much interested in abstract
ideas. He once told Leskov that he thought that theoretical socialism was "stupid," but it was really all one to him. "They'll
have nothing to take away from me but my trousers," he observed carelessly. Nor does he appear to have been very interested in the Romantic, anti-industrial utopia of the Slavophiles.
They read too many "little German books," he would remark
contemptuously; he dismissed Konstantin Aksakov's ideas on
government reform simply by remarking that he had "studied
the Germans." To study the Germans meant to enter a realm of
abstract ideas, to submit yourself to tedious philosophical formulations that had nothing to do with "life" or the real needs of
anybody. And yet, despite his apparent ideological indifference
—indeed, his innocence of ideology—there are serious grounds
for considering Iakushkin a man of the "Left," as we shall see.

So the "great debate" of the 1840s—immortalized in Herzen's
memoirs—passed him by. Or, rather, he passed it by. He had
some acquaintance with the luminaries on both sides; he knew
the Romantic-bohemian poet and critic Apollon Grigor'ev, as
well as the "Westernizing" historians Sergei Solov'ëv, Timofei
Granovsky, and Konstantin Kavelin, but he remained obscure
and in the shadows.

In fact, while Khomiakov and Ivan Kireevsky were dusting off
the Eastern Fathers, while Belinsky was anathematizing reactionaries and philistines, Iakushkin was finding his calling. He
was discovering—or rediscovering—rural Russia and the songs
and tales of the Russian people. He came to his vocation gradually, with the assistance of two of the more prominent intellectual luminaries of the period: the conservative nationalist historian Mikhail Petrovich Pogodin and the Slavophile Pëtr
Kireevsky, the first really serious collector of Russian folk songs,
and perhaps the greatest.

Pëtr Vasil'evich Kireevsky was a remarkable man and in an
indirect way an intellectually influential one, but he was so shy
and self-effacing, so devoid of the ordinary forms of ambition and

egoism, that he remains even now in the shadows, as he did during his relatively brief life (1808–56).[6] Like his brother, Ivan, he was a lonely man who found a kind of solace in the communalism of family life and in a few close friendships: with Ivan, with the poet Nikolai Iazykov. But even in these relationships, which were the heart of his emotional life, he was devoid of the assertive and demanding aspect of friendship, and he seemed to seek out a subsidiary role and position in relation to the objects of his attachment and operate from there. He never married, but took his brother's family for his own. When Iazykov was seriously ill for several years in the mid-1830s, Pëtr gave freely of his own time and energies, serving as traveling companion and nurse. Ivan Kireevsky was in many respects similar to his brother in his shyness, his emotional awkwardness, and his inability to complete projects and realize himself intellectually. Both brothers were to a degree overshadowed and intimidated by their brilliant and vivacious mother, Avdot'ia Petrovna Elagina (Kireevskaia by her first marriage), the leading hostess of intellectual Moscow in the first half of the nineteenth century.

Pëtr was important in the creation of Slavophilism, but not as an ideologue. Characteristically, he was never able to form his own Romantic nostalgia into an intellectual structure; he made himself felt only indirectly, by acting on his brother. He participated in the intellectual debates of the 1840s, but mechanically.[7] He was not a debater or a salon lion, and he never felt at home in those brilliant and lustrous surroundings.

Pëtr's lifework was the collecting of Russian folk songs. He began, at first in a desultory way, in the early 1830s, and by his death in 1856 he had amassed a very large body of songs, almost none of which had he published—and many of which remain unpublished to this day. The work absorbed him increasingly, and he was assisted by a large group of friends and acquaintances: great writers, such as Pushkin and Gogol; gentry neighbors, who copied down a song or two because they knew of his interest; students at the University of Moscow, like Iakushkin. In time, Kireevsky's work became well known to all literary Russia. Interest in the collection grew, and songs came in from all sides.[8]

The history of the collection and why so little of it was published in the nineteenth century is itself a fascinating subject,
which has recently been rather thoroughly explored by Soviet
folklorists. No doubt, as they persuasively argue, the regime of
Tsar Nicholas and its censors was largely to blame. But Kireevsky's own passivity and inability to follow through on a project were also factors, as his occasionally exasperated friends often
said. In fact, the massive collection seems to have brought little
satisfaction to those most closely associated with it. Pëtr Kireevsky was deeply troubled by his inability to bring it out; Iakushkin was, for a time, its putative editor, and the project
brought him nothing but trouble.

Although Iakushkin's collecting activities in fact predate his
acquaintance with Pëtr Kireevsky, it was Kireevsky who provided him with encouragement and support for what had been
a casual and amusing activity. At some point in the early 1840s,
Iakushkin learned of Kireevsky's interest and sent the older man
a song he had transcribed. According to Bazanov, Kireevsky
responded with fifteen rubles, an impressive sum for Pavel
Ivanovich at any time. The experiment was repeated on two
more occasions, and the third transaction brought with it an
introduction to the great collector. All this must have taken place
prior to 1843, since by that summer Iakushkin's collecting activity
had already taken on a more systematic and regular form.[9]

From the time of his departure from the university in 1845
until the end of 1849, Iakushkin spent most of his time traveling
and collecting. In addition to the songs—which, of course, went
into the Kireevsky collection—Iakushkin collected proverbs for
V. I. Dal', who did for folk sayings and proverbs what Kireevsky
did for songs (except for the fact that Dal' had no psychological
problems about publishing). Moreover, a certain number of fairy
tales *(skazki)* collected by Iakushkin found their way eventually
into the great collection by Afanas'ev, which is for Russians what
Grimms' *Hausmärchen* is for Germans.[10] Pavel Ivanovich was
supported by Kireevsky and Dal' (and perhaps others) in these
years; thus in a sense he may be called the first "professional"
collector in Russia. Apparently for financial reasons, however,

Iakushkin was forced to curtail his collecting activity in the fall of 1849 and take the examinations that would qualify him as a secondary-school teacher.

In accordance with his Slavophile views, Pëtr Kireevsky had a rather special Romantic and historical attitude toward the songs in his collection. He was looking for traces of an ancient spirituality and religious culture that, he believed, had been sapped and undermined by the Westernization and "modernization" of Russia since Peter the Great. This spiritual culture, and the "organic," patriarchal social life to which it corresponded, had been all but totally destroyed in Russia's upper class, but significant traces still remained in the life of the peasantry. This belief was common to Slavophiles, and so while Ivan Kireevsky and Aleksei Stepanovich Khomiakov occupied themselves with trying to understand Russia's pre-Petrine history and culture in the manner of idealist historians and spiritual anthropologists, Pëtr Kireevsky sought Old Russian culture in old Russian songs. He had, in other words, a preconceived idea of the Russian people in his mind— peaceful, religious, patriarchal in their social forms—and the songs he collected were to vindicate this canvas, to enlarge and deepen it.

Kireevsky paid little attention to modern and regional variants. The more "ancient" the song was, the better. He cared most about songs with religious content and imagery. On the other hand, he was totally uninterested in songs about Stenka Razin and Emel'ian Pugachëv, or in the folklore of peasant revolt in general. This turned out to be Iakushkin's subject, but he got no help here from his mentor.

Iakushkin, we know, expressed a contemptuous lack of interest in Slavophilism later in his life. Whether he took it seriously when he was serving his apprenticeship with Kireevsky we have no real way of knowing. Traces of what might be termed Slavophile attitudes can be seen in certain of his journalistic writings of the 1850s. But it is hard to imagine that such an untheoretical, hard-headed, commonsensical nature as Iakushkin was could ever have really read or even taken very seriously the "little German books" that he subsequently dismissed so flippantly. And Ivan

Kireevsky and Khomiakov were zealous proselytizers in the 1840s; had Iakushkin been in any sense a convert, we should in all probability know about it.

Certainly Iakushkin's more realistic and contemporary attitude toward the song, his lack of interest in constructing an ideal text in which the spiritual message would be most radiantly clear, his fascination with regional variation, with dialect—all this differentiates him sharply from Kireevsky and his spiritual quest.

Iakushkin's other early mentor, the conservative nationalist historian Mikhail Petrovich Pogodin, had a more scholarly and less ideological attitude toward folklore, although this can be said only with reservations. Pogodin—a historian, journalist, and organizer—was a man whose description demands superlatives.[11] He was, to begin with, extremely long-lived, immensely energetic, remarkably varied in his interests. His erudition was on a grand, nineteenth-century scale. He was also boring, bigoted, stubborn, and intellectually limited, to a degree. His more emotional and fulsome pages on the glories of Russia's national past (in particular, on Peter the Great) are hilarious and have to be read to be believed. The seizures and ecstatic constriction of the heart that he experienced when he was shown the house where Peter the Great lived in Holland are a kind of nationalist farce.[12]

Despite Pogodin's titanic excesses, it was he who seems to have done most to guide and define Iakushkin's first serious collecting activity. He helped make what had been pleasant summertime rambles in the country a vocation and (as nearly as the word can be used of Iakushkin) a career. We have, in fact, a remarkable letter, written by Pogodin to Iakushkin in the mid-1840s, in which he formally and fully laid out what should be the young man's mode of activity on a trip to the countryside. "Your primary goal," Pogodin began in his pedantic way,

is to collect folk songs. You ought to have with you Novikov's and Sakharov's collections, to which you should attach an alphabetical catalogue for convenient reference. Having heard the songs from the lips of the people, you will note variations on the printed text, describing precisely where you heard them. You will likewise inscribe the new songs in alphabetical order as they are sung or spoken before you, without any kind of omission. In writing down the songs, you will have occasion to observe differences in pronunciation; these differences are very important as they can serve, together with other more or less important signs, to define dialects and sub-dialects, which in turn help delimit tribes and appanage principalities [the old, pre-Muscovite princely territories] and, perhaps, certain provinces as well.

Here, strikingly, is a less spiritual, more historical approach to folklore than we find with the Slavophile Kireevsky. Pogodin's emphasis was to be taken over by the younger generation of folklorists, who by and large showed a new scrupulousness with regard to the given text and a new interest in its regional variation.

"Of the songs," continued Pogodin, "you will value the historical most highly; since one encounters them most rarely among the people, they are the most valuable. But they are known—that I know for sure. . . .

Ritual songs occupy second place after the historical—for instance the Christmas songs, which display clear signs of antiquity. Šafařík has assured me that he has seen traces of great antiquity in many of our songs. He deeply regrets that our dear Peter Vasil'evich Kireevskii is delaying the publication of his valuable collection.

Finally, direct your attention to the spiritual songs, of which we have a multitude—and they are capital. Every blind man at the fair or outside the monastery will sing you a whole notebook.

For the songs, as equally for your other goals, you must strive to stay as far as possible from towns and great roads, the paths of civilization, so-called, with its depravities. You are nowhere to say that you have come with such-and-such a goal—the collecting of songs or any other. Little by little, inadvertently as it were, between things you must do it, neither appearing a clever fellow nor being confused by any kind of stupidity or banality. It seems to me that it would be best if you grew yourself a beard, put on a red calico shirt with a twisted collar, belted your caftan with a sash—yes, and supply yourself with various wares: earrings, rings, beads, lace, ribbons, biscuits, cakes, and be a trader through the villages. Then you will have the best chance of striking up an acquaintance with the village singers. This is the way of wisdom in collecting songs. By the way, experience will teach you best of all.

And in conclusion, Pogodin enumerated other things that Ia- kushkin was to note, describe, and explore in the countryside:

the sites of ancient towns, burial mounds and their contents. Where are they? Traces of ancient settlements, churches and monasteries. Tradition. Old churches and houses in general, if they are remarkable for originality. Iconostases. Images. Church plate. Collect informa- tion about documents, the manuscripts of books printed in the old orthography in particular. Write down either the location or where you heard of old coins, icons, wooden crosses, figures ín bronze or stone—old things in general,

Pogodin wound up in a burst of enthusiasm. "Learn the names of connoisseurs and collectors and about their collections. The names of traders, and inform us rapidly by mail."[13]

Iakushkin did in fact grow a beard and dress himself—roughly —as Pogodin advised. Still, Pogodin cannot be held responsible for Iakushkin's permanently abandoning every other costume but the red calico shirt, the sash, and the greasy boots. Pavel Ivanovich followed Pogodin's further instructions and frequently disguised himself as a petty trader, dispensing rouge, whiting, lace, and ribbons to peasant women and writing down songs "between things." Very seldom did Iakushkin tell either lord or peasant that he had come to the countryside merely to record peasant songs; when he did, for one reason or another, admit his purpose, the result was often skepticism, incredulity, or suspicion of some more sinister purpose. Particularly as the coming Eman- cipation came to dominate the life of rural Russia and the tem- perature of the body social began to rise, a gentleman journalist collecting folk songs in peasant costume looked more like a dan- gerous political agitator and was treated accordingly. Particu- larly when, as was almost inevitably the case with Iakushkin, his papers were not in order.

Although Pavel Ivanovich wrote a number of what he termed tales and "articles," his most characteristic mode of expression was what he called *Putevye pis'ma* ("travel letters"). Although some of the songs he collected first appeared in this diarist and anecdotal form, most of them either went into the main body of the Kireevsky collection, were published in some other form, or were lost. Apart from the songs, Iakushkin's travel notes dealt extensively with the kind of archaeological and antiquarian discovery that Pogodin had recommended. Burial mounds, old buildings, icons, manuscript collections—these he faithfully (and enthusiastically) tracked down and reported. Intermingled with these reports, however, were the conversations with peasant Russia that are the chief value of the *Putevye pis'ma* and make them such engrossing reading even today. No one in Iakushkin's time, perhaps no reporter in nineteenth-century Russia, took the trouble to listen to the real voice of the people, as he did, or tried to live its real life. On the road, in the poorest taverns and pothouses, in the dank and filthy monastery dormitories where pilgrims slept, in third-class railway cars, in peasant huts, and in the fields, we find him asking the poorest and most numerous class of Russia to tell its stories and give its opinion on the issues that concerned it most.

His fundamental mission (which, characteristically, he appears never to have formulated soberly and straightforwardly) was to find out what the life of peasant Russia was like and to inform *obshchestvo*. He was interested in what the people wore, what they ate, what words they used, and what they suffered. He was fundamentally a realist, in other words, and to be a realist about peasant Russia in the 1850s and the 1860s was to write *"j'accuse."* Perhaps to describe things as they are is always to indict; only under very special circumstances does realism not appear to be "Left." Thus it does not matter that Iakushkin had no real "ideology"; according to Leskov, Iakushkin's social ideal seemed to be a "universal artel, a great vague ideal, which, insofar as I can judge, he never understood himself." This kind of vague communal idealism could be found either on the utopian Right, among the Slavophiles, or on the utopian Left, in the *narodnik* ideology that developed in the 1860s. But Iakushkin's simplicity, his attachment to the concrete, and above all his realism, forbade him either of these spiritual resting places.

Not, one must add, that the powerful political currents of the day had no effect on Pavel Ivanovich. Between the time he first began to scour the countryside for Pogodin and Kireevsky in the mid-1840s and his death in 1871, Iakushkin the man and the journalist underwent a series of subtle changes and permutations; it was as if he were caught in the undertow of the times. The great drama of Emancipation whetted his sense of the exploitation of the peasants and his hostility not only to the Russian bureaucracy but to the gentry—both liberal and conservative—as well. One might have supposed, for instance, that Iakushkin would have found Ivan Turgenev a fairly sympathetic figure—at any rate in the period before he became embroiled in the literary-political controversy that followed the publication of *Fathers and Children* in 1862. It is quite possible that the stories of peasant life that Turgenev published collectively under the title of *A Sportsman's Sketches* had some influence on Iakushkin's own reporting on rural Russia. And yet in his masterpiece, "Great Is the God of the Russian Land,"[14] Iakushkin bitterly assailed Turgenev and "liberals" of his stripe. They were people who believed in "the rule of law," but they had made the law in their own interest, so that it became simply formalized extortion and exploitation. The peasant knew nothing of written law; the very idea of law "in a book" was incomprehensible to him. So he remained true to his own customs and laws of life, dealing with "their law" any way he could. Here Iakushkin displayed an attitude common to both Slavophiles and Populists: the state and its laws was a force alien and exterior to the Russian people; the state had no respect for the traditional customs and values of Russian society. But in this context, the thrust of Iakushkin's criticism of the liberal Westernizer Turgenev was distinctly "Left."

As the 1860s wore on, the archaeological and antiquarian content of Iakushkin's "travel letters" was replaced by realistic observation of contemporary peasant life: descriptions of the functioning of a fishing artel (with special emphasis on the intricate cooperative arrangements of the membership); casual but devastating descriptions of peasant poverty; anecdotes revealing the effect of the new railroads on the lives of peasants and petty traders. Not that Iakushkin ever lost his interest in burial mounds, manuscript collections, and old churches—but there were fewer of them as time passed. He could always be interested by how the local wisewoman cured snakebite. But there was less about wonder-working icons of the Mother of God and more about peasant bandits, not to mention Stenka Razin and Pugachëv. Old attitudes—the love of ancient Russian cities and a pronounced dislike of "German" St. Petersburg—now seemed subtly different. Peter the Great was less the destroyer of a time-honored, indigenous Russian culture than a man who drove and oppressed his people without mercy or limit. The 1860s audience for Iakushkin's realism and peasant orientation tended to be a "Left" audience—and what writer is unmoved by the point of view of his readers, admirers, and publishers?

In 1849, however, all this lay in the future. Then he was still a virtually unknown agent of other men; at the age of twenty-seven, he had published only a brief note on the folklore of bandits and sorcerers in Pogodin's journal, the *Muscovite (Moskvitianin)*. Having passed his teacher's examinations in the fall of 1849, Iakushkin spent the next six years as an instructor in various schools in Kharkov province, in the Ukraine. Our information on this period is even scantier than for his university years, but one thing, at least, is clear. Iakushkin's style and way of teaching did not please either the director of schools in Kharkov province or many other local educators. One might regard it as a foregone conclusion that he would be insufficiently authoritarian, that he would rather tell his students about his adventures in rural Russia than teach grammar, that he would take them on similar expeditions, that he would teach his classes in an "ordinary uniform," rather than in the customary "dress uniform." Indeed, one feels that the local school authorities were lucky to have gotten their young teacher into even an ordinary uniform; when one struggles to imagine the classroom scene, one sees him there (if at all) in the peasant costume in which he had lived as a collector and was subsequently to make famous: the red calico shirt, the long-waisted *poddëvka* coat, and the greasy boots.

One man who saw something of Pavel Ivanovich in the early 1850s was Pëtr Veinberg, subsequently a poet, translator, and editor of the *Century*,* then a student at the University of Kharkov. Veinberg confirms our impression that Pavel Ivanovich had no understanding of what was regarded as necessary classroom discipline, and had a "casual" attitude toward his superiors. The whole teaching business, in fact, "made him sick," Iakushkin confided to Veinberg. This was while he occupied the first of a series of similar posts that he was to hold briefly until he gave up teaching and "retired" in 1856.

Veinberg, a good-humored and conventional man of letters, has also left us a description of Pavel Ivanovich's room in Kharkov; it seems to be typical of Pavel Ivanovich's physical surroundings during the infrequent periods in which he was settled somewhere. "On the bed," reports the squeamish Veinberg,

on top of a filthy and rather ragged blanket (and the bed was completely unmade) stood a broken candle stick containing a tallow candle, and next to it some kind of crockery—a sort of plate—with something like sausage on it. On the table was a heap of all kinds of papers and books in unimaginable disorder, on the top of which lay the notorious "ordinary uniform," rolled up in a ball. In the middle of the floor was an indescribable vessel of slops and under the table was the vodka, while dirt and filth were all over the floor and everywhere in a way in which it is hard to imagine.[15]

Pavel Ivanovich's living arrangements taxed Veinberg's powers of description to the limit: everything seems to have been "unimaginable" or, at the very least, "indescribable." Pavel Ivanovich got angry at his visitor's obvious distaste and called him a "little gentleman."

The two met again a decade or so later in St. Petersburg, after Iakushkin had become a figure of some renown. Veinberg arranged for Iakushkin to take part in a "literary evening"; he was

*Just before it was sold to the writers' cooperative that included Iakushkin, Shchapov, Eliseev, and Leskov.

supposed to bring the occasion to a dramatic close by reading one of his stories. Iakushkin was very drunk by the close of the evening, but he managed to get himself to the lectern, where he intoned the first line of the story: "It happened in a tavern." He was unable to go any further, however, and after repeating the opening line twice more, he uttered one of his "energetic Russian words," threw up his hands, and "somehow left the stage." The audience, Veinberg reported, took it good-humoredly. Literary evenings are often too long, and for some of the audience, at any rate, their guest must have performed about as expected.

While Iakushkin was bouncing from school to school in the Ukraine, the Crimean War broke out, and perhaps out of desperation with his teaching career, perhaps out of some compound of curiosity and patriotism, he attempted to enlist in the militia. He was refused (perhaps his appearance failed to inspire confidence) but proceeded to spend a great deal of time at the military hospital in Kharkov, to which Russian wounded were brought back from the south. He later wrote up his conversations with the soldiers as a series of anecdotes entitled "From Tales of the Crimean War."

In the spring of 1856, Iakushkin returned to Saburovo, apparently already determined to resume his collecting activities full-time. But financial problems intervened. Because of his illegitimate birth, he had no legal claim on the family estate, and Praskov'ia Faleevna apparently already regarded him as a "good-for-nothing"; she had no intention of squandering Saburovo's small resources to send her son junketing and carousing around the countryside. The fact that she was herself a peasant probably made the notion of collecting peasant songs appear all the more frivolous and absurd.

His mother having indicated her disapproval, Iakushkin turned again to Pogodin and Kireevsky, hoping that they could arrange for the Russian Geographical Society to sponsor a trip to the Don region, if they could not finance it themselves. But this idea, too, came to nothing. So for the next two years Pavel Ivanovich remained at Saburovo, spending much of his time with the interesting and congenial types in which the Orël area abounded. Pëtr Kireevsky, his patron, died before the year was out, and Leskov does not seem at this time to have been part of his circle of friends. But there were the interesting Ukrainian writer Marko Vovchok and her husband, A. V. Markovich, and other writers—Pisemsky and Ostrovsky—were also periodically on the scene. Iakushkin's closest friends, however, were not these famous men of letters. His most inveterate cronies were I. V. Pavlov, a university acquaintance of Herzen who subsequently became editor of the liberal *Moscow Messenger (Moskovskii vestnik)*; N. K. Ruttsen, an old schoolfellow whose sartorial disorder seems to have rivaled Iakushkin's; and—in particular— a neighboring landowner, Mikhail Aleksandrovich Stakhovich.

These three men were drawn to each other and to Pavel Ivanovich by the usual mild alienation afflicting rather eccentric men of letters in the provinces, but especially by their interest in the *narod*. All of them had "projects" of one kind or another. Pavlov, who seems still to have professed the "Westernizing" radicalism of his university years, wrote a number of articles on social subjects (bribery among provincial officials was one) that were without exception turned down by the journals to which they were sent. Stakhovich wrote pleasant verses, full of rather decorative, laid-on folk motives and phrases; at one time he set out to do an annotated edition of the *Ancient Russian Poems* of Kirsha Danilov, the first collection of *byliny*, or heroic songs, compiled in modern times. But the group met frequently to talk about folklore, local affairs, and politics, and to make music; Stakhovich was an excellent guitarist, and Iakushkin loved to sing, although a contemporary reports that his voice was "shrill and squeaky" and not suitable for the drawing room.

No doubt, as the Emancipation began to loom on the horizon, the friends spent much time talking about what shape it might assume and what they might do at the local level. Stakhovich, although not a radical like Pavlov, was benevolently and paternally disposed toward the peasants; he was also rich and more influential than his friends and served as the marshal of the nobility in the district. Unfortunately, Stakhovich was murdered by one of his former clerks and an estate manager in 1858; the motive, apparently, was robbery. The province was deprived of a respected and influential proponent of Emancipation, and Iakushkin lost the best friend he ever had.

While Pavlov was writing his articles and Stakhovich was variously distinguishing himself, Iakushkin was working hard on the Kireevsky collection.[16] Pëtr Kireevsky had died on October 25, 1856, a few months after his brother. He left the collection to Ivan's children, whose guardian was the dead brothers' half-brother, Vasily Elagin. The latter had no interest in the collection, and he at first honored the dead man's expressed wish and turned the whole business over to Iakushkin, who seemed to meet all the qualifications necessary for continuing Kireevsky's great work and—perhaps even more important—seeing it into print.

Preparing the collection was a big job; the disorder was greater than the new editor had believed. A great many texts were not to be found; others were in the hands of various friends and sympathizers. Iakushkin and Elagin were eventually forced to publish declarations in various journals that the collection now belonged to Elagin and was being prepared by Iakushkin.

Another problem was presented by the Kireevsky methodology—the attempt to create the "ideal text" out of a number of variants, usually on the basis of antiquity, or simply according to what seemed "best" to Kireevsky. Iakushkin, of course, believed that the editor should simply indicate as fully as possible each variant to the best text, with notes elucidating regional and other variations. These methodological differences seemed so interesting and important that the Slavophile journal *Russian Colloquy* printed samples of the work of both men so that the readers of the future edition should be clear about their differing approaches. In the matter of the separation of genres, however—historical, ritual, lyric, and so on—Iakushkin's plan corresponded roughly to that projected by Kireevsky.

Iakushkin worked extremely hard at his project, assisted from time to time by Stakhovich. The work was mostly done at Vasily Elagin's estate, Bunino, and Elagin provided financial support for Iakushkin while he worked. By midsummer of 1857, the work on the historical songs was virtually complete, and Pavel Ivanovich took the projected volume to Moscow, where a number of folklorists, men of letters, and prominent Slavophiles (Khomiakov and Konstantin Aksakov among them) approved it enthusiastically. It was then up to Elagin to see it through the censorship; by the autumn of 1857, Iakushkin felt he had only two weeks or so of small corrections and polishing to do before the historical songs could go to press.

Then the blow fell. In February 1858, Elagin took the project away from him, and two years later it was entrusted to the Society of the Lovers of Russian Literature at the University of Moscow. An influential literary society, founded in 1811, in the late 1850s it was headed by A. S. Khomiakov and its orientation was strongly Slavophile. Eventually, some songs were published by another folklorist, P. A. Bessonov, upon whom Iakushkin's mantle had fallen. Bessonov's edition was intelligently and most bitterly criticized by Iakushkin.

Various explanations for Iakushkin's exclusion from the project have been advanced: from the idea of a simple misunderstanding of some kind to a wholly ideological theory, based on the opposition of the "reactionary" Slavophiles, who had legal rights to the collection, to the radical democrat, Iakushkin. Although the matter is still far from clear, Iakushkin's most recent Soviet biographer, Balandin, has cleared away a great deal of underbrush. Crucial in the matter seems to have been the dislike and distrust of Iakushkin felt by Pëtr Kireevsky's mother, the seventy-year-old grande dame Avdot'ia Petrovna Elagina, who was still unmistakably head of the Kireevsky-Elagin family. The occasion for her outburst of anger at Iakushkin, early in 1858, was that he planned to publish some material not actually in the Kireevsky collection (and, in return, certain songs from the collection would be given to the Russian Geographical Society). She responded angrily that nothing that was not actually her "Petrusha's work" should appear, and lamented the connection of the "madman" Iakushkin with the project. Considering how many hands had been associated with Pëtr's work, her objection was naively ill-founded. From the unusual invective that she adopted ("madman," "four-eyes"), however, it seems probable that the question of including outside material was little more than a pretext for getting rid of a man whom she found repugnant and incomprehensible (and disrespectful, very likely, as well). Indeed, this imperious, religious, and highly cultivated woman, educated at the turn of the century and a literary aristocrat to her fingertips, must have found Iakushkin vexing to the last degree, with his "energetic Russian words," filthy peasant costume, and complete lack of drawing-room manners. Furthermore, the ease and rapidity with which she had her way suggests that some dissatisfaction with Pavel Ivanovich or his methods already existed. It may have been personal, or it may have been that even his atypically delicate and respectful criticisms of Kireevsky's methodology had given offense. Certainly the Slavophiles still tended to think in terms of people being "ours" or "not ours," and Pavel Ivanovich fell into the latter group. Within the month, a consortium of elderly intellectuals—the majority of them Slavophiles—had been set up to be responsible for the work, and Bessonov had been named editor.

Pavel Ivanovich, for all of his even temper and casualness, could not but take this unexpected turn of events with bitterness. It was, in fact, the great setback of his life up to that point, and he never entirely recovered from it. It probably gave the *coup de grâce* to any prospect that he might "settle down" and become no more than the kind of mild eccentric that most men of his class were prepared to tolerate.

Between the spring of 1858 and April 1865, when the police sent him back to Saburovo, Iakushkin based himself in St. Petersburg but spent the greater part of his time on the road, collecting songs and information about popular life, drinking and talking with whoever crossed his path, and getting into scrapes with the provincial police. He was supported by various journals at various times: the Slavophile *Russian Colloquy* (under its most "liberal" and political editor, Ivan Aksakov) and the liberal-radical *Annals of the Fatherland* and *Contemporary*. In addition to producing for these journals his "travel letters," he also wrote what have been called "tales" and "articles"—the most famous of which is undoubtedly "Great Is the God of the Russian Land," a brilliant collection of satirical anecdotes illuminating the progress of peasant emancipation in rural Russia.

No distinctions of genre can really be made with respect to Pavel Ivanovich's work, however. He had one method, which never varied: he went out and talked to people, and then came back to a more tranquil situation (in this period, St. Petersburg) and wrote down what had happened to him, with whom he had talked, and what had been said. So his work is really—except for his song collecting—one long series of conversations with "the other Russia."

When Iakushkin had a commission of some sort (as he did, for instance, to go to Novgorod and Pskov provinces for the *Russian Colloquy* in 1858–59), he would at some point have to sit down and write up his experiences from the extremely bare notes he had taken in the field—without much joy, for he much preferred being on the road to writing about it afterward. If he did not actually have a prior commission, it was generally financial pressure that caused him to nest in someone's apartment and produce an "article."

Iakushkin's writing habits were the subject of much amusement and occasional consternation among those who knew him. While on the road, he jotted things down on menus, cigarette paper (he was a heavy smoker), and even smaller scraps of paper. When he got these "notes" out, often months later, they were torn and dirty beyond description, and it seemed incredible to his host of the moment that anything at all could be produced from them. On many occasions he had lost a crucial scrap or two, and a good deal had to be done from memory.

Nor was he particularly concerned about the looks of the final draft; it, too, was often written on what was nearest at hand. One of his closer friends was the radical Matvei Sviridenko (Rybnikov's friend), who worked in Kozhanchikov's bookstore in St. Petersburg, one of Pavel Ivanovich's regular haunts. In the store, Sviridenko kept a notebook in which he wrote down donations that customers made to Sunday schools for illiterate workers. On one occasion he was both amused and annoyed to find that Pavel

Ivanovich had taken over this notebook for one of his articles: the logbook was there, it was clean paper in quantity, and it never occurred to Iakushkin that there might be any objection.

"Great Is the God of the Russian Land" was written in Kozhanchikov's bookstore, but it turned out to be shorter than Iakushkin had intended, since he lost all his notes while he was still writing. The piece was delivered to Nekrasov, then editor of *Annals of the Fatherland*, unfinished and untitled. (It was always extremely difficult to tell whether a piece by Iakushkin was finished or not, since the content was simply a string of anecdotes; there was no real beginning or end.) Nekrasov had apparently not regarded Iakushkin as much more than an amusing character until he saw the piece, but he recognized its quality immediately, gave it a name, published it, and paid the author fifty rubles.

Many people whose early lives are spent in straitened circumstances develop an exaggerated respect for cash. Exactly the opposite was true of Iakushkin. Except for the last few years of his life in exile, when his health was deteriorating rapidly, he lived as if money did not matter, and he did so with a success probably unique in his time. When he was in pocket, he spent all he had generously, if not prodigally, on his friends in town or on the peasants he met on his travels. The money was equally likely to be spent, apparently, on food and drink or in exchange for songs.

Pavel Ivanovich spent very little when he was in town, except on food and vodka, since he was always living with a friend and he had literally no possessions except the clothes on his back. Nekrasov tried to train Pavel Ivanovich to live in an apartment of his own, but was not successful. Iakushkin was incurably gregarious and—strikingly—afraid of being alone.

The satirical poet D. D. Minaev met Iakushkin on a St. Petersburg street corner on one occasion when he was trying to write a story and looking for a "corner" to stay in. Minaev invited him to move in for a few days and asked him where his "things" were. Iakushkin just grinned. "When my laundry is so far gone that it simply drops off my sinful body, I buy myself a change and throw the old stuff into the stove," he told his new host. That same

evening, he moved in, wearing a new red calico shirt in honor
of the occasion.

When Minaev and Iakushkin arose the next morning, Minaev
asked his guest whether he took coffee or tea in the morning.

"I don't use either of those liquids," replied Pavel Ivanovich,
"but here's a glass of vodka and a piece of bread—that's something else again." And the offer was repeated every morning, not
for a "few days" but for three weeks.

On this occasion, as on others, Iakushkin had a hard time making himself write; it was much pleasanter to go out and drink all
day and far into the night. Since his frequently euphoric return
at 4:00 A.M. disturbed the servants (Minaev said), his host asked
him either to be more quiet or to get back earlier.

Pavel Ivanovich did not come back at all for the next couple
of nights, so Minaev concluded that he was sleeping elsewhere.
As he was just sitting down at his desk one morning, the maid
came in giggling. She said that the porter had just come from
Iakushkin with a request for cigarettes.

"And where *is* Pavel Ivanovich?" Minaev asked in amaze-
ment.

"In the lodge," the maid replied. "He spent the night with the
porter so that he wouldn't disturb you. In the morning he sent
out for vodka and wrote down some songs that the porter sang
him. A *very odd gentleman!*"[17]

Almost no one seems to have resented what might have been
regarded as outrageous sponging in someone else. This was
in part because Pavel Ivanovich was extremely conscientious
about repaying any actual debts. When he was paid for an article, he would go around liquidating his obligations until the
money was gone, at which point he would start all over again. If
anything was left over after his debts had been paid, he would
often distribute it among the taverns and cookhouses where he
ate and drank; he could then indulge himself without the worry of carrying cash with him, which he very often lost or gave
away. At one St. Petersburg restaurant, Iakushkin was such
an impressive customer that the largest kind of wineglass was
named after him. One can imagine customers telling the waiter

that they were thirsty enough that night for a "Iakushkin."

But people's hospitality to Pavel Ivanovich was more, and more generous, than can be explained by his readiness to pay back loans. In the country, of course, he could rely on the notable hospitality of the Orthodox peasantry, who generally regarded a meal and a bed for the wayfaring stranger as a religious obligation —even when the stranger was as odd as Iakushkin. When he encountered Finns or Germans who had no such gracious attitude, he would report the matter indignantly and scathingly, often sounding like the Russian chauvinist that, at bottom, he was.

Nearly all the city dwellers who reported their relations with Iakushkin mentioned his extraordinary tact and delicacy as a guest—a *sui generis* kind of tact, it is hardly necessary to add. On one occasion, a Kharkov University professor arrived at his house in the evening and was told that a gentleman had arrived a few minutes before and had promptly gone to sleep on the bedroom floor. Iakushkin often slept on the floor, and although he would tell people that he did it to stay in shape, it seems clear that he was using this device to tell his host, among other things, that he meant to be no trouble. If anyone was offended by Iakushkin, it was likely to be the servants employed by his more well-to-do acquaintances. Leskov's German maid, Ida, had hysterics repeatedly while Iakushkin was staying in the apartment. At first he slept on the couch or on a rug in the corner, but since Ida wasn't pleased with that, Pavel Ivanovich moved into Leskov's own bed —which the master did not much care for, but he could do nothing without wounding his guest.

It was not just Iakushkin's tact and unquenchable good nature that caused his friends to put up with him so readily, or his ability to efface himself, or the store of anecdotes that one of his visits invariably provided. He had a kind of innocence and simplicity that charmed and impressed not only sophisticated writers but the much less sentimental petite bourgeoisie of St. Petersburg. "Even the well fed and spoiled doorman of a luxurious and elegant house on the Nevskii Prospekt . . . thought it not beneath his dignity to brush off his threadbare coat, saying 'there's a feather on it, Pavel Ivanovich.' "[18] Unquestionably, many of Iakushkin's friends and acquaintances displayed for him a special tenderness, regarding him—consciously or unconsciously—as a kind of "Fool in Christ." For such a personage, clearly, ordinary social standards were quite out of place, and one might be assumed to have a kind of religious obligation toward him. The tradition of the Holy Fool was far more powerfully alive in Russia than elsewhere in nineteenth-century Europe.

Of course, not everybody who chanced to come in contact with Iakushkin loved and protected him. Leskov adds to his reminiscences that of course many people were offended by him, or felt their self-esteem threatened. They would mutter, "It wouldn't be a bad idea to clean him up"; there were those who felt that his exile (for what offense they did not know) was "a good idea."[19]

One evening in the winter of 1863, Iakushkin went to the opera at the Mariinsky Theater; the company was doing *A Life for the Tsar,* and Pavel Ivanovich was dressed as usual. At the end of the first act, an army general approached him, clearly outraged by his clothes and the negligent manner in which he was leaning against the wall of the stalls, looking out at the audience.

The general swelled with anger. "It is inconvenient of you, Mr. Iakushkin, to stand like that. Everyone is looking at you."

"Let them look," replied Pavel Ivanovich calmly, "on the contrary, I find it very convenient."

"This is no place for you," replied the general heatedly. "Your costume is attracting general attention, and it won't do."

"Let them gape. I am not asking anyone to look at me. This is a Russian opera, and I—may I inform you—am also Russian. Therefore I have come here."

"Yes, yes. Only take yourself upstairs, if you please."

"I can see better from here. I paid three rubles, and I don't plan to sacrifice them to no purpose."

At this point, a friend of Iakushkin drew him tactfully away and the scene came to an end.[20]

The peasant attitude toward Iakushkin is a good deal harder to gauge. His writings provide irrefutable evidence that many of the peasants with whom he came in contact were willing to speak frankly to him, as they could not to an ordinary member of his class. Despite his peasant costume and his considerable mastery of peasant speech, however, the peasants rarely—if ever—took him for one of their own. The most obvious indication of his nonpeasant status was his glasses, which peasants never wore. Iakushkin complained to Leskov about the peasants' attitude on at least one occasion; they regarded him, he said, as some kind of mummer or actor. "What do you mean, an actor?" Iakushkin would argue good-naturedly. "All the same, an actor," the peasant would reply, cordially but stubbornly. At any rate, Iakushkin could console himself that he was not taken for a Persian, as Konstantin Aksakov allegedly was when he walked through a village in his notion of peasant garb. The embroidered shirts and lacquered boots of the Slavophiles smelled of the museum, and the greater "realism" of Iakushkin's literary views was echoed in his costume.

The novelist P. D. Boborykin has left us with the most hostile portrait of Iakushkin except for the one emanating from the police archives.[21] Much of his animosity may be regarded as the result of personal friction: Boborykin was a busy, efficient, and somewhat self-important man, and Pavel Ivanovich was not a reliable colleague. When Boborykin was editing the journal *Library for Reading*, Iakushkin promised him strings of articles, but came to him only "for strengthening," as he put it. But Boborykin's observations on Iakushkin and the peasantry have a ring of plausibility about them that obliges us to consider them seriously. Boborykin contends that the peasants knew Iakushkin was a *gospodin* (master) and they could see that he was just "loafing around" and "chattering." They often made fun of him, and what Boborykin refers to vaguely as "misunderstandings" were frequent. Everything about him, says Boborykin, smacked of the "type of Moscow literary Bohemian," the upper-class student or writer. The segment of "the people" with whom Iakushkin really got along, Boborykin maliciously concludes, were not real peasants but tavernkeepers and the motley people who hung out in the *kabak*. (This last observation we may dismiss: Boborykin never traveled with Pavel Ivanovich in the countryside; Iakushkin's social life in St. Petersburg was quite different from his way of life on the road.)

To these observations of Boborykin, we may add that of the well-known writer A. F. Pisemsky, who knew rural Russia pretty well himself.[22] Stressing how alien Iakushkin's wandering, garrulous way of life was to that of the beleaguered Russian peasant, Pisemsky caustically observed that if Iakushkin had been born in the village, he would have been a *zabuldyzhka*—that is, a stock figure of fun, to whom no responsibility of any kind could be entrusted. The function of the *zabuldyzhka* was to amuse people at the tavern, or at a wedding, where he was always given the first cup so he could start "fooling" as soon as possible. This characteristically brutal judgment is also beside the point: Iakushkin was not a peasant and never claimed to be one.

But after all is said and done, both these hostile critics are pointing out an important fact that transcends the biography of Pavel Ivanovich Iakushkin: Russian society in the 1860s was rigorously stratified, and there was no real place in either *obshchestvo* or the *narod* for a man like Iakushkin. He was neither lord nor peasant; he was neither a genuine Holy Fool nor a revolutionary. He tried, with only partial and temporary success, to create an identity of another kind for himself, and his society could not accept it—no segment of it, really. A peasant in a St. Petersburg pothouse once told one of Pavel Ivanovich's journalist friends that he was a "fine, good" *barin* (lord, gentleman), but "wrong in the head," not all there. Another peasant told the same journalist a totally false but revealing anecdote. Iakushkin's father, said the peasant, had disowned him because he had spent twenty thousand rubles on drink, and had "given" him to the peasants. So, said the peasant, Pavel Ivanovich was gradually turning into a muzhik; only his glasses remained to show that he was a "real gentleman." The kernel of truth in this yarn, remarked the journalist, was that Iakushkin really had squandered his modest resources on peasants, paying them generously for the songs they sang him and wining and dining them without stint.[23] The lack of comprehension of "the people" for Iakushkin's life could hardly be better summed up. They really understood him no better than the bureaucracy did—but it was the bureaucracy and the police who had the power; they were the ones who eventually finished him off.

Iakushkin was a prophetic figure. He may be said to be the first Russian from the gentry class actually to "go to the people," and his reception in that quarter foreshadows the pathos surrounding the more political pilgrims who followed him. The anomalies of his family situation, too, remind one inescapably of another mutilated aristocratic rebel, Alexander Herzen. Denied by the circumstances of his birth a "normal" position in his society, Iakushkin was never able to find a place for himself; he was perhaps less a "repentant nobleman" than a bellwether of the Russian intelligentsia in the decades to come.[24]

On August 22, 1859, Iakushkin was arrested in Pskov, where he was on assignment for Aksakov's *Russian Colloquy*. He had arrived earlier in the day, planning to stay for a time with friends, rest up, and put his notes in order. After an early supper, he stepped down to the police station to register. The official on duty seems, as Iakushkin casually put it, to have been "struck by my clothes." He asked Pavel Ivanovich if he were really "Provincial Secretary Iakushkin" (provincial secretary was the rather low rank in the bureaucracy that he had achieved through his teaching career). Iakushkin said that he was. The man then took his papers into the office. In a few minutes he came out again, accompanied by a constable. There was more conversation about the peasant costume. Iakushkin explained that he was wearing it because of his collecting activity, and produced a letter from Aksakov, explaining his relationship to the *Russian Colloquy*. Other officials, of uncertain rank and status, arrived. "Your papers are forged," said the policeman abruptly. "The signatures are forged. The papers are forged," repeated the first official.

This charge was, in fact, false. But Iakushkin's papers were certainly not in order. Instead of his passport, he had only a copy of a letter stating that it had been lost. With aristocratic hauteur, Iakushkin said that if his papers were forged, they must arrest him. His request was immediately granted. He then asked to speak to the chief of police, but was turned down, since the chief had issued strict orders that he was not to be disturbed after hours.

Iakushkin spent the first part of the evening in a relatively comfortable room reserved for prisoners of the gentry class, smoking and reading the Pskov newspaper. He was guarded by an apparently lethargic soldier who spoke with a heavy Ukrainian accent. In the middle of the evening he tried to open the window, since the room was stuffy and he had been smoking heavily. "Where do you think you're going, you son of a bitch?" roared the soldier, who had been dozing. "You want to jump out the window! I'll . . . ." The duty officer raced into the room, and Iakushkin was put in the so-called *arestantskaia,* a kind of prison dormitory reserved for the lower orders, "in which," the soldier had gravely informed him previously, *"it is impossible to be."* The accuracy of the soldier's words was soon obvious. The *arestantskaia* was a dank and stinking cellar whose filth appalled even the less-than-fastidious Pavel Ivanovich. He spent the rest of the night talking to a peasant boy who had run away from his owner and telling him fairy tales.

At nine o'clock the following morning the police chief, Gempel', arrived and, radiating good-heartedness, told him he was free to go. But Iakushkin, now justifiably on his high horse, stated that he wished to complain formally to the governor's office about his treatment. So he sat for another twenty-four hours in the gentry cell where he had initially been confined. The governor, it appeared, was out of town, and it became clear that there was no prospect of speaking to anyone who would take action on his behalf. So when Gempel' again told him he was free to go, he left.

Iakushkin then spent several days in the nearby town of Ostrov, returning to Pskov only to leave it by train. He had bought his ticket and was sitting in the car (feeling, he said, that all was somehow not well), when he heard a voice in the door of the car explode, "Who's wearing glasses here?" He was dragged out of the train by two of his old acquaintances from the police station; as he departed, he heard someone say sympathetically, "They've got a student."

Iakushkin appears to have been completely mystified by the

reason for his rearrest; he had the confused impression, as he was being taken off the train and returned to the police station, that it was for "changing his clothes." Given the events of the past several days, it no longer seemed absolutely absurd that this might be so. He was further detained for six days and then released. Chief Gempel' subsequently explained that after Iakushkin had been released the first time, he had received a description of a murder suspect that tallied with Iakushkin's physiognomy and clothing. The question of the change of clothes had arisen since the chief had received a subsequent report that Iakushkin had abandoned his *poddëvka* coat (which the alleged murder suspect had also been wearing—the long-waisted peasant coat was a very common article) in "a certain tavern," and had emerged in a "gray tunic." This clever maneuver fanned the chief's suspicions and led to Iakushkin's rearrest. He was released after the director of the Pskov gymnasium confirmed Iakushkin's identity and mission in Pskov province. Gempel' said that Pavel Ivanovich was held for only three days; it was actually for six.

In the Russia of that time, what happened to Iakushkin was by no means an unheard-of event; quite the reverse. But it created a considerable stir and further added to his growing fame. There is no question that the government's anxiety about "agitators" in the countryside in those nervous, pre-Emancipation times lay behind the chief's actions—although at the best of times the behavior of provincial officials was often arbitrary. Since 1857, the Ministry of the Interior had been sending out anxious circulars to local police authorities about the danger of ill-intentioned people "stirring up" the peasants. And Iakushkin's inadequate papers and peasant costume must have seemed all but conclusive to Gempel' and his zealous staff.

But the times were complicated ones. Alexander II and various elements in the bureaucracy were still pushing the Emancipation against a kind of passive opposition from the majority of the gentry and bureaucracy. The government, in other words, was far from monolithic in 1859, and Iakushkin was allowed to present his side of the affair in the columns of the *Russian Colloquy*.

His long letter was a masterpiece of its kind, fully bringing out the arbitrary behavior to which he had been subjected, his own bewildered innocence, and neglecting no small detail that might bring him sympathy: the stench of the cellar where he had spent his first night, the pitiable plight of the peasant boy, the profanity of the police, and the way they had called him by the familiar form *ty*, rather than the more respectful *Vy*. Iakushkin's account, in other words, had the wit, controlled indignation, and mastery of detail that the best liberal outrage always has. No exaggerated self-pity or bathos; something that could make the broadest possible segment of public opinion say, "Why, this could have happened to me!" Gempel', on the other hand, produced a formal, badly written, and evasive reply, full of obvious small distortions and quibbles. He was clearly not a man who was accustomed to justifying himself or his actions in print.

The liberal press seized on the incident joyfully. At the urging of Ivan Aksakov, Iakushkin's letter was widely reprinted. The *Russian Messenger (Russkii vestnik)* led the chorus of those who hailed the exposure of the "Pskov Affair" as the kind of healthy publicity that ought to attend the operations of the police and bureaucracy, which had in the past been able to do their work in secrecy and under cover of darkness. In many of these accounts, as in that of the *Russian Colloquy* itself, there was a good deal of praise and encouragement of the government for having the courage and good sense to criticize itself. Only among thoroughgoing radicals like Dobroliubov was there real skepticism about the value of "publicity" *(glasnost')* in effecting the major changes in Russian society that needed to be made. Iakushkin himself, despite his extremely successful venture into liberal publicism, did not share this slightly self-congratulatory liberal euphoria. Less than two years later, we find him writing (in a batch of "travel letters" that was suppressed by the censor): "wouldn't it be better to call a halt to our publicity? Why bother? Really, our publicity will lead to nothing."[25]

Iakushkin's pessimism on this score had by this time been reinforced by further experience. At the end of 1859 he undertook another foray for Ivan Aksakov and the *Russian Colloquy*—this time through Vladimir and Iaroslavl' provinces to towns like

Vologda and Kostroma, hitherto neglected by students of folk-lore. But this trip had a more "political" aspect to it as well: Aksakov wanted Iakushkin to observe and record the economic situation of the peasantry and their communal forms of organization and self-government, subjects in which Pavel Ivanovich was himself becoming more and more interested.

The expedition never really got off the ground. A continuing problem was Iakushkin's lack of proper papers. Aksakov attempted to facilitate matters by giving him a letter to the vice-governor of Iaroslavl' province, an old schoolfellow. But Aksakov's old friend failed him; becoming nervous about such a notorious guest, he showed his letter to the governor, A. P. Buturlin. The latter, who regarded Aksakov as a greater red than Iakushkin, immediately flew into a rage. When he had calmed down, he called in Iakushkin and told him to get out of the province forthwith and not to come back until he had a proper passport. And thus the trip ended. In addition, Buturlin sent both Aksakov's letter and one of his own to the minister of the interior, in whose spacious offices Provincial Secretary Iakushkin was becoming increasingly well known.

Several other developments should be noted in connection with the interrupted excursions in 1859–60. One was the appearance, in the aftermath of the Pskov Affair, of several "False Iakushkins." The phenomenon of the Pretender is an important one in Russian history. The most renowned Pretenders generally appeared at the head of rebellious peasant and cossack forces in times when the authority of the government (but not the idea of the Tsar) had been deeply shaken in the countryside. The False Iakushkins, however, were different from the False Dmitrys and False Peters of the past. They appear to have been people who thought to extricate themselves from difficulties in the provinces by proclaiming that they were the now-notorious Provincial Secretary Iakushkin. Presumably they hoped that the name alone (and the threat of more liberal publicity) would cause their tormentors to release them without further ado.

Another footnote to the Pskov Affair was the appearance of a picture postcard of Iakushkin, bearing the name Emel'ian Pugachëv, leader of the last of the great peasant uprisings. No one seems to know exactly how this confusion arose, but by the mid-1860s Leskov found that pictures of Iakushkin were selling in Paris as "Pougatscheff." And that, clearly, was how official Russia was coming to regard him.

Finally, the adventures of Pavel Ivanovich seem to have spurred the government to enact stricter laws controlling the movements of folklorists and other "scholars" in the countryside. It is fascinating, tedious, and extraordinary to watch the huge, cumbersome bureaucratic machinery of Russia swing slowly, almost imperceptibly, into action on this secondary question, at a time when the life-and-death matter of peasant Emancipation was evolving toward its final conclusion. Cabinet members came together; the Tsar participated in the bureaucratic minuet; ink flowed in rivers. The final result was embodied in a circular from the minister of the interior, issued on January 4, 1860. In essence it declared that only officially sanctioned learned societies could send agents into the countryside, and then only with much registration, preliminary and otherwise. So much for Ivan Aksakov and the *Russian Colloquy*, if not for Provincial Secretary Iakushkin.

Iakushkin had his say on the Emancipation in his brilliant "Great Is the God of the Russian Land," a heavily censored version of which appeared in Nekrasov's *Contemporary* in 1863. Like virtually everything else that he wrote, it is a sketchy "letter from rural Russia." Its point: How did the various segments of Russian society respond to the prospect of Emancipation? What did the peasants think about their promised "liberty"? How did average representatives of various groups (state peasants, gentry "liberals" and conservatives, the serfs themselves) respond to successive steps? And behind the confused and bitterly humorous scenes and dialogues lay Pavel Ivanovich's eternal theme: landlords and peasants live in different worlds and cannot understand each other.

The landlords with whom Iakushkin talked tended to respond, at first, quite simply: "I don't like it—they're taking my Van'ka away. What will I do?" Serfdom was seen as wrong, but "Why can't they abolish it after I'm gone?"

At a somewhat later stage, provincial gentry were supposed to draft their own Emancipation projects, which would then be submitted to government commissions. Iakushkin attended one such session and found Semën Petrovich reading his draft to an audience of one (Pëtr Semënovich) while everyone else was having a buffet lunch. A few people had drafted projects, but the audience was nonexistent.

"Why is only Pëtr Semënovich listening to Semën Petrovich?" inquired Iakushkin of a man standing at the bar.

"He has to listen," replied the man laconically. It turned out that Pëtr Semënovich owed money to Semën Petrovich.

Iakushkin was quite unsentimental, too, in his description of "the people." He related how the state peasants often regarded themselves as not really peasants at all; he reported on how a group of peasants who had recently been privately freed by their owner told him knowingly that "you can't manage the peasant without a stick."

The most stinging passages were undoubtedly those which described the attitudes of gentry "liberals." Their speeches were generous and full of high-flown sentiment, but these gentlemen believed in "the rule of law." Since the "law" of Russia was utterly alien and incomprehensible to the peasants, its "rule" simply meant the crudest kind of class justice. In these passages, Iakushkin abandoned the casual, half-mocking reportorial style usual to him and spoke directly and with a bitter passion to his audience. Here, for a moment, is the radical moral indignation of the Russian intelligentsia, pure and unalloyed.

Among the funniest and most pathetic passages in "Great Is the God" pertain to the peasant attempts to interpret the final Emancipation settlement. To ensure its utter unintelligibility to the peasant, it was often delivered to various localities only in fragments, so that when it was read aloud in the church, whole sections had to be left out. In one town in Orël province, for instance, twenty copies of the rules pertaining to freed serfs in Bessarabia arrived, instead of one copy of the entire edict. In another town they received the supplementary rules relating to serfs who had been assigned to privately owned mining installations. And to assess the full impact of the arrival of a document of this kind, one must remember that it was being delivered to people who either had absolutely no idea of what to expect or expected something utterly different.

Sometimes it was the priest who was chosen to read the edict; sometimes the job was given to a peasant who was trusted by the community, often someone whose literacy was uncertain. In one village the edict was read by a gardener who was supposed to have "studied in Moscow." He was given a dram of vodka and a ruble and told to begin. It took him two days to read the "liberty" (as the peasants universally referred to the edict). The people listened and slept in shifts.

"And what did you understand of it?" Iakushkin inquired of some peasants who had been through this ordeal.

"What did we understand?" they replied. "That liberty is written on four-columned pages."

Iakushkin then asked them why they had gone through with the reading when no one understood anything.

"But so, dear friend, the law commands," they replied. "And we, dear friend, have nothing against the law."

Even when the peasants understood the literal meaning of the words, the possibilities for confusion were almost unlimited. A group approached Iakushkin and showed him a place where the edict read something to the effect that the peasants ought to cultivate the land and "the fruits of the earth" would be theirs. Iakushkin could not convince them that the passage did not mean that they should have their landlord's orchards—they knew perfectly well that the "fruits" were in those orchards.

On another occasion, an aged priest reading the edict hesitated over the word "overshadow" in the text. If you divide the two syllables of the Russian word, it sounds as if you are saying "about hay." The priest then got the word correctly and went on. But the peasants were convinced that there was something "about hay" in the "liberty" that the priest did not want them to hear. So they gave the edict to the deacon, but he could not find anything about hay either. Then the angry and suspicious peasants, Iakushkin reported, "took the manifesto, left the church, and began to read it themselves."

Iakushkin also discussed the extremely delicate subject of peasant revolt in "Great Is the God"—and more extensively in a separate article, "Riots in Russia," published in 1866.[26] His treatment of the peasant "riot" (he uses the German word *Bunt,* which had become common in Russian) is related to a common literary theme of the period: the "imaginary riot." The notion of the imaginary riot was employed by writers like Leskov and Pisemsky, who were consciously opposing the radical Populist view that the Russian countryside was the arena of a bitter class struggle between gentry and peasants. Leskov viewed the rural scene as more or less harmonious, but was troubled by the fact that good men on both "sides" often could not understand each other: the grotesque misunderstandings that resulted could then escalate into riots that were "imaginary" in the sense that their sole cause was the lack of a common language between the two parties.

Iakushkin accepted the idea of the imaginary riot, but he was under no illusion about any basic community of interest, gentry benevolence, or peasant "loyalty." He agreed with Leskov and Pisemsky that the gulf between the village and the manor was so great as virtually to preclude communication, but he located the "cause" of peasant disorder as much in gentry rapaciousness and bureaucratic brutality as in any failure of communication between the two worlds. How, he asked, could the peasant be brought to accept the alien "law" of the landlord's world, when so often in the past it has been simply an official seal on exploitation and gentry arbitrariness? The landlord's law generally arrived in the village like an avalanche, overwhelming whatever customary arrangements might have prevailed there. In such a situation, nomenclature took on a surreal significance for the peasant, as he sought to understand his relationship to an alien government. Iakushkin reported how one "riot" originated in the wish of a village of state peasants to be called, as they had been in the past, "one-homesteaders," a designation that had become obsolete by the mid-1850s. The peasants did not clearly understand what the terms actually meant, although they (rightly) associated the older category in a vague fashion with better days. When the village met and solemnly confirmed its desire to revert to the "one-homestead" designation, the soldiers were called.

Peasant distrust of the landlord even (or perhaps particularly) when he came bringing gifts was brilliantly sketched in Iakushkin's anecdote about the gentleman who came down from town to make "improvements" in several of his villages. A meeting was called, at which the master appeared.

"Well, brothers, how do you live?" the master inquired of the meeting in a friendly way.

"Thank you, little father, by your mercy we live—glory to God," answered someone in the crowd.

"Live well, brothers," answered the master heartily. "You live well now, you will live well—I'm going to make things even better."

At once, Iakushkin reported, everyone at the meeting fell on his knees.

"Little father! Don't make things better. Even now, things are so good that life is short; if they get better, it will be impossible to live at all."

So when a "misunderstanding" developed, or the landlord broke faith with his peasants, he might define the situation as a "riot." The decision was his because he was the one with access to the world of police and soldiers. The peasants had only the option of digging their heels in and resisting passively ("rioting on their knees," as the phrase had it), or at the most taking a wild swing at the nearest tormentor. "It is remarkable," concluded Iakushkin, "how educated people try to give a particular sense to everything. Misunderstandings, requests—it's all *Bunt* to them. There's no other word in their dictionary."

Thus, according to Iakushkin, it was the landlords and officials closest to the peasants who generally "began" the riots—by pronouncing the word "riot," whether out of fear or calculation. Iakushkin underlined the conservatism (or realism, depending on your point of view) of this interpretation by adding that the kinds of radical manifestos and proclamations that had recently

begun to appear "had not the slightest influence on the people."
They were written by people who were strangers to the world
of the village, and at times in a style so bad that even people with
some education could not fathom what they meant. Iakushkin's
treatment of riot and revolt among the peasants disappointed
Soviet historians, who view the aroused countryside as a powerful force—perhaps *the* powerful force—propelling the government into a period of major reform. Nor do they care for Iakushkin's denigration of radical manifestos and brochures, the careful
analysis of which is such an important part of their work.

By the summer of 1864, Iakushkin had become extremely well
known to the Third Section, as well as to the Ministry of the
Interior and various police chiefs—Gempel' in Pskov, Annenkov
in St. Petersburg. The Pskov Affair back in 1859 had been followed by his expulsion from Iaroslavl' province; in the wake of
these adventures, Pavel Ivanovich had been subjected to constant, if not very intensive, police surveillance, and his articles
were subjected to the most intensive scrutiny by the censor.
Some, like "Great Is the God of the Russian Land," were eventually allowed to appear; others were suppressed altogether. As
early as 1860, for instance, Iakushkin had been contemplating an
article on the recruitment of peasant soldiers. It finally appeared,
in a truncated form, in a military magazine, the *Russian Veteran
(Russkii invalid)*, in 1864.[27] When an officer acquaintance with
whom he had discussed the idea years earlier complimented him
on the "truth" of the finished product, Pavel Ivanovich laughed
angrily. "You're full of it, brother," he said. "Half of it was
scratched out. What kind of truth is half a child? I spit on that
kind of truth."

The year 1864 brought Iakushkin's relationship with the police to a boil. First there was the business of Chernyshevsky's
civil execution in May. Then, two months later, an agent assigned to Iakushkin intercepted a letter to Alexander Herzen
in London. Herzen had commented extensively on the Pskov
Affair in the *Bell* and had also described Iakushkin's farewell
to Chernyshevsky. Now proof of a connection was established:

Iakushkin's letter spoke of an article he was to have submitted to the *Bell* but had decided to publish elsewhere. Balandin believes that the projected article probably had to do with the unpolitical subject of Bessonov's edition of Kireevsky's songs. His surmise is very likely correct, but the police did not know this. And the further question remained, both for them and for the historian: How much other information had Iakushkin sent to Herzen?[28]

The Third Section was not able to take immediate action against Iakushkin; the discovery of his correspondence with Herzen took place just as he was setting off for the big Nizhny Novgorod Fair, which he was to cover for Boborykin's journal, the *Library for Reading*. It was his scandalous behavior at the fair, on top of his long record as the incarnation of disorder and the friend of state criminals, that led to his ruin.

Iakushkin left for the fair on August 1, with the Third Section still undecided as to what precisely to do with him. The Nizhny Novgorod Fair was one of the biggest and most impressive of the Russian trade fairs; it had also become an event much patronized by writers, artists, and students of "popular life." Iakushkin traveled there with Boborykin, but their very different styles of life dictated that they find separate quarters at the fair.

The Third Section, having ensured that Iakushkin would be under police surveillance at the fair (through a letter to Ogarëv, the provincial governor), sat back and waited. On August 23, the first report came in. It was short and sweet. "Iakushkin arrived here," wrote the unknown agent,

with inadequate identification papers, given to him by the Orël police on the occasion of the loss of his card. He staggers through the taverns, is constantly drunk, and was brought to the police station, where he remained for two hours. He tells everything exaggeratedly and wishes to write his Pskov article No. 2 again, but he has only himself to blame. Then, continuing his drunken wanderings, he began to appear at the court of arbitration for fighting and disputing; he plays at pitch-and-toss, etc. Things have come to such a pass that Ogarëv has expelled him from Nizhnii-Novgorod Province.[29]

Pavel Ivanovich, clearly, was in search of the Russian people in his usual way. A local folklorist and antiquarian, A. S. Gatsissky, gives us a more intimate look at one of the less sordid scenes. "We got into a boat," he reported,

with the idea of going to the camp of the Volga fisherman; however, we did not get to the camp, but confined ourselves to a trip along the Volga, which had lost, however, much of its poetic charm, since the dust of the fair hung over it in a thick cloud. The soul of our small company was Iakushkin, who enjoyed himself particularly at the expense of the economist [Vladimir Pavlovich] Bezobrazov, who had located, in his recent researches, a dock—on an unnavigable river. There was, however, a serious point to Iakushkin's sparkling mockery: we study popular life without seeing it at all; the research is undertaken by gentlemen in white gloves, who approach their subject with their noses in the air. At the end, far removed from it—as they had been at first—they see in it what they wish—as they had at first—rather than what exists in reality.

"Yes," said Iakushkin, "here we have these overdressed researchers who learn about popular life in three days and write it up in one —nothing to it. Here we've gone to the fishermen, didn't see them at all—but look! Tomorrow Vladimir Pavlovich will be describing in detail his conclusions about fishing on the Volga, the fishermen's way of life and—if someone will only explain it to him—the difference between the Volga word for fisherman and the regular one."[30]

Apart from his general disorderly behavior, two characteristic events led directly to Iakushkin's departure from the fair. On the first occasion, he got drunk at a dinner (held to bring together the merchants and the men of letters who had come to the fair), interrupted the speaker, and had to be removed from the hall. The second incident has been preserved in the stern prose of Colonel Koptev of the Third Section:

On August 17, Iakushkin met Captain Perfil'ev in Nikita Egorov's hotel. Neither of them knew the other, and the occasion for a conversation arose when Captain Perfil'ev was talking to Nikita Egorov (the former chef of the Nizhnii-Novgorod Club). He was asking him how business had been since he had been managing the hotel and maintaining a table at the railroad station, when the drunken Iakushkin, with a glass of vodka in his hand, interrupted the conversation, saying to Perfil'ev "why do you say *ty* to Nikita when he says *Vy* to you? My ears can't stand it." At this, Perfil'ev guessed that he was speaking with Iakushkin and had a conversation with him, in order to gain some understanding of this personality. When he had gone, Nikita Egorov told Perfil'ev that Iakushkin would insolently approach guests who were completely unknown to him, in order that he and they might go into other rooms and amuse themselves with garrulous drunkenness.[31]

On that very evening, Colonel Koptev concluded, Iakushkin had had a similar encounter with another officer, who had reported him to the governor on the following morning; this incident led directly to Iakushkin's expulsion from the fair and the province.

Pavel Ivanovich, in fact, had already had an interview with Governor Ogarëv several days earlier, apparently after the governor had received letters from the Third Section about him and perhaps from the Ministry of the Interior as well. Ogarëv subsequently gave a sober and somewhat guilty account of why he had not taken stronger action on the Iakushkin case on this prior occasion. Iakushkin had convincingly explained to him, he said, the necessity of his peasant costume and his frequenting of taverns, with respect to his work. He had told the governor of his commission from Boborykin and promised to behave himself in the future.

V. I. Mel'nikov, an agent of the Ministry of the Interior, who was working with the governor on other business, gave a very different version of the interview, which he had from Iakushkin himself. According to this (admittedly tainted) version, Ogarëv had "gone into ecstasies" when he learned that Iakushkin collected folk songs; he had dashed to the piano and accompanied his disorderly guest in spirited renditions of songs. Upon parting, he had embraced Iakushkin warmly and said fatuously, "I love learned men." The scene reads like something out of Gogol, but Ogarëv was a good-hearted, emotional, and not very clever man —something like Mel'nikov's version might well have occurred if Iakushkin had turned on the charm.

But the governor was not to be had twice. Following Pavel

Ivanovich's new escapades, Ogarëv sent him back to St. Petersburg in the company of two agents, where, it was now clear, the Third Section was eager to see him. In doing so, Ogarëv cited Iakushkin's lack of proper documents, his riotous behavior, and gave extremely vague hints about inciting the peasants. He also recommended that Iakushkin be confined to his "customary place of residence" and not be allowed to wander freely around. This viewpoint was shared by N. V. Mezentsov, the director and chief of staff of the Third Section, and he wrote to this effect to Annenkov, the Petersburg police chief—himself an old friend of Pavel Ivanovich. After spending two weeks in the hospital, apparently for delirium tremens, Pavel Ivanovich remained in the capital, under strict police supervision, until he was sent to his mother's estate in April 1865. He was then forbidden to leave Saburovo; he was to remain there, still under the watchful eyes of the police.

Balandin does not entirely concur with what might be called the cumulative theory of Iakushkin's exile to Saburovo. He has combed the archives and the memoir literature of the period for indications of new outrages—and he has found a few, for Iakushkin lived his usual Petersburg life between his return from the fair and his departure for Saburovo.[32] But the truth seems to be that the authorities just wanted to be rid of him. They—rightly—regarded him as incorrigible; he was a permanent source of disorder. His way of life, his very existence in the capital, was a public criticism of "official Russia," a slap in the face of right-thinking people, and a bad example to the young. Furthermore, the government—with the Emancipation now an accomplished fact—was moving to suppress much of the dissent it had tolerated a few years earlier as a kind of necessary, if distasteful, pressure on the most conservative elements of society. And at the same time, opposition to the government was taking more extreme and organized forms. Given this situation, what could be more reasonable than to ship Pavel Ivanovich Iakushkin to the provinces and keep him there? There he could parade around in his unsightly rags to his heart's content, and the danger and offensiveness of the performance would be greatly reduced.

According to Annenkov, the idea came from Iakushkin himself, in mid-March 1865.[33] The reason alleged for the move to Saburovo was that it would be easier for him to maintain himself there than in the capital. We have no way of knowing if Iakushkin actually made such a request. In view of his unmistakable distaste for the project at every later stage, it seems more likely that Annenkov developed it himself out of a complaint by Iakushkin that he was having trouble making ends meet in the capital; after all, his wandering had been his sole source of income.

In any event, Pavel Ivanovich departed by train for Orël and Saburovo on April 22, 1865, under guard, and arrived safely and without incident several days later. His departure was a gloomy one. He was worried about the reaction of his mother when he turned up as a political exile; although he did not say so, he was probably just as worried about what it would be like to live under her roof for the foreseeable future.

An observer in St. Petersburg police headquarters described Pavel Ivanovich's final appearance in those familiar surroundings. The two bulky knapsacks of A. P. Shchapov (that other notorious troublemaker, also being sent into exile) had just been carted off, when Iakushkin appeared "with a little bundle under his arm." Turning to the duty officer, he announced "loudly and carelessly, 'I have the honor to present myself. Here I am, ready for whatever Palestine you have in mind.' Two policemen marched over to him: 'Where, Mr. Iakushkin, are your things?'" Thus the ritual question was asked, as it always was by friends and enemies alike! And Pavel Ivanovich replied as he always did, "'here they are'—indicating the bundle—'I am all here.'

"'Then you will go with them,' said the duty officer, pointing to the policemen.

"'Gladly. I'm bored with your Peter [St. Petersburg] and pleased to be travelling at government expense.'" And they went out.[34]

A group of Iakushkin's friends had gathered at Kozhanchikov's bookstore, hoping for a final farewell. A small parcel was waiting for him, containing medicine and a little money. But the carriage drove past them down the Nevsky Prospekt without stopping; the friends merely caught a glimpse of him, between the guards.

Before moving on to the melancholy history of Pavel Ivanovich's last years, a few more words ought to be said about what Soviet historians call, with characteristic abstractness, Iakushkin's "sociopolitical views." His contemporaries gravitated toward one of two interpretations, neither of them very well defined. One of them was that Iakushkin was not political at all. You could argue for a "man of God," a Holy Fool, a "typical broad Russian nature"; if your view of Pavel Ivanovich was negative, he could be a bum, a tramp, or a "good-for-nothing." This was how Pisemsky regarded him. Leskov, the most articulate proponent of the "unpolitical" view, was extremely unsympathetic to the radicals of the 1860s and no doubt disposed to minimize his friend's intellectual affinity with them. For example, when a split developed between the two leading "progressive" journals of the day—the *Annals of the Fatherland* and the *Contemporary,* which, under the powerful influence of Chernyshevsky, was moving to the Left—according to Leskov, Iakushkin not only refused to take sides, break off relations, and do all the things that radical intellectuals were expected to do under these circumstances, but refused even to understand the disagreement. Here were the "little German books" again!

The other theory was that at one time Pavel Ivanovich had been a Slavophile (or at least "under the influence of" the Slavophiles) and that later he had somehow become a radical. This view seems to have been based more on an analysis of his journalism and his "public career" than the unpolitical thesis, although some people who knew him well, like S. V. Maksimov, announced vaguely that he had been "deeply influenced" by the Slavophiles, and further muddied the waters by adding that he was, of course, not a Slavophile himself in any "narrow" sense. All very unhelpful.

The historian who follows the life and adventures of Iakushkin is struck by a marked shift in the political views of his *friends,* if not in his own. By 1861, Pavel Ivanovich was pretty well out of touch with anyone who might be called a Slavophile. There were, of course, nonpolitical reasons for this: his quarrel with the Elagin family over the Kireevsky song collection; his removal from editorial responsibility; the fact that by 1860 there was no longer a real Slavophile "group" or even a coherent Slavophile point of view, as there had been in the 1840s and throughout most of the 1850s. Although Iakushkin continued to correspond with his old teacher Pogodin, he was not close to him, and he seems to have had nothing to do with Ivan Aksakov after 1861.

We have no evidence of any kind that Pavel Ivanovich deliberately broke off relations with nonradicals at the time of Emancipation. Rather, it became progressively harder for anybody except the increasingly radical and "Populist" intelligentsia to appreciate his work and even to be friendly with him personally. Before, the Tory democracy and orientation toward the peasantry that were characteristic of classical Slavophilism—to say nothing of its historical and folkloric interests—had at least given Pavel Ivanovich points of personal and intellectual contact here. But after the death of the Kireevsky brothers and Khomiakov, the intellectual content of Slavophilism became more and more difficult to distinguish from vulgar Russian nationalism—both radical and religious—and from Pan-Slavism. As the Slavophile impulse was weakened and distorted, it lost its basic hostility to the established order, along with its coherence.

(The other forms of "conservatism" with which Pavel Ivanovich came in contact had no intellectual content at all: they could be summed up by such slogans as "Serfdom is immoral, but Emancipation is too dangerous now" or, more simply, "Stop!" These kinds of conservatism Iakushkin encountered in the police stations of Pskov and St. Petersburg, and in the provincial gentry assemblies where he observed the progress of the Emancipation. "Conservatives" of this stripe were not attracted by anything about Pavel Ivanovich. Their attitude was well summed up by the words of the indignant general who found Iakushkin's presence at the opera in peasant costume "inconvenient.")

Then, too, there was Iakushkin's realism. To describe peasant Russia in the 1860s was to indict official Russia. Who read and was moved by such indictments? The radical sympathizers with Chernyshevsky, who were devoted to the literature of "unmasking." Who was really interested in the realities of rural Russia? Who "cared about" the peasants (or professed to)? Mostly, after 1860, the young *narodniki*, some of whom were developing the ideas of Herzen and Chernyshevsky into a full-blown revolutionary ideology. It was they who were interested in the peasants' communal way of life: in the mir, in how an artel of fishermen really worked, in the attitude of the peasant toward the land.

And Pavel Ivanovich himself was changed by the Emancipation and the social radicalism that developed with it. His historical and antiquarian interests receded into the background; the romance of picturesque "Old Russia" was overshadowed by the iniquities of the present. He became less of a pure reporter and more the peasants' advocate before the bar of public opinion. And as he moved in this direction, he found his audience taking shape around him. Radicals like Nekrasov and Chernyshevsky were recruiting for their journals in this period, in part because of their growing estrangement from writers like Leskov and Turgenev, who were more moderate politically and unwilling to submit to the utilitarian and propagandistic spirit emanating from the *Contemporary,* the *Spark,* and the *Whistle.* As Iakushkin's audience changed and developed, its demands pushed him farther in the same direction. He had never much cared for people who called themselves "liberals," anyway—with their tendency toward a complacent "moderation," their hypocrisy, and, above all, their Westernism and lack of sympathy for the values of rural Russia.

And of course "official Russia" helped his evolution along by rejecting him, by spying on him, by throwing him into prison, by posturing before him in military uniforms, clanking its medals menacingly. How could Iakushkin not have felt that to a large extent the enemies of the peasant had become his as well?

Still, there were limits to how far to the left Iakushkin could move. Even the most zealous Soviet scholars concede that he never became a revolutionary activist, although they hope (and sometimes persuade themselves to believe) that he distributed revolutionary propaganda. In May 1862, for instance, Iakushkin went by train from Moscow to Leo Tolstoy's estate, Yasnaya Polyana, between Tula and Orël. Apparently traveling with Ia-kushkin was a radical student; the Third Section subsequently received a denunciation from a passenger, Prince Evgeny Cher-kassky, according to whom Iakushkin and the student had of-fered him a "proclamation." Several Soviet historians have speculated that the proclamation was none other than Zaich-nevsky's extremist, Jacobin *Young Russia* manifesto.[35]

Their interpretation of the episode is wildly improbable. Ia-kushkin's *Weltanschauung* had nothing in common with the bloody fantasies of *Young Russia*. But even more significantly, *if* Iakushkin (or anyone else) had been distributing *Young Russia,* he certainly would not have handed it out jokingly to Prince Evgeny Cherkassky on the train. Even Pavel Ivanovich would have had more sense than that. Nor are we certain that Iakushkin and the student had not just met on the train; we do not even know for a fact that what they were handing out was radical literature. It is curious that the conclusions of sober Soviet schol-ars often resemble those of the tsarist police agents, for which they have such contempt. Both groups show an almost desperate anxiety to prove that the objects of their concern are dangerous revolutionaries.

Iakushkin, in fact, expressed his firm conviction that the radical propaganda distributed in the countryside was for the most part worthless and unintelligible to the peasants. He had an anti-intellectual streak and more than once intimated that the radical intelligentsia was almost as out of touch with village realities as the official Russia it was trying to change. Had he ever turned his realistic eye on the radical intelligentsia—as Pisemsky did—he might have produced something pretty scalding. But he did not, and his abstention was in a way a political decision.

Serious revolutionaries, of course, did not trust Pavel Ivano-vich—and with reason! How could a man as notorious as Iakush-kin, one who called attention to himself so spectacularly, be an effective member of a revolutionary underground? I. A. Khudia-kov, a fellow folklorist and a real revolutionary, liked and admired Iakushkin, who, he felt, "had done much good." But he noted regretfully that nothing serious could be entrusted to a man who drank like that.

Another radical activist, N. V. Shelgunov, had an interesting and acute view of Iakushkin. Shelgunov saw him as essentially trapped between Slavophilism and Populism—which accounted for his passivity and lack of any real political program (beyond "what the people want," and so on). Iakushkin, said Shelgunov, abandoned Moscow for St. Petersburg, but he never entirely escaped from Moscow or really knew what to do in St. Petersburg. Thus, in his contradictions, he represented the period 1855–61. People like Iakushkin had to give way to what Shelgunov rather guardedly called "practical Populism"—by which he meant revolutionary Populism. Shelgunov did not even consider Iakushkin a "realist"—presumably because Pavel Ivanovich did not regard the peasant as a revolutionary force in Russia. For Shelgunov and those like him, the period when it was sufficient to "unmask" and "expose" Russian reality ended in the early 1860s.

Somewhat apart from the question of Iakushkin's politics or lack of them is the matter of his symbolic significance to the young radicals in the 1860s. Gleb Uspensky, the noted radical writer (like Iakushkin a realist, even a pessimist), believed that he was something of a bellwether to young men of the period who were beginning to turn to the peasants—to study their folklore, to help them make a revolution, but perhaps above all to find out from them how to live. In his "Memoirs of a Former Student," one Vladimir Sorokin wrote about the impression that Iakushkin and his Pskov adventure had made upon him in his adolescence. After Iakushkin had first interested him in rural Russia, wrote Sorokin, "a great many of our comrades traveled through the countryside in the summer, collected folksongs, tales and popular traditions there, studied the people's way of life, taught them to read and write."[36]

For some of these young men, their fascination with village life was a pleasant episode in their student years that left them with no more than a few memories and a vague sympathy for an alien

and exotic kind of existence. Yet when one considers the pervasive idealization of the peasant, so characteristic of educated
Russian society in the latter nineteenth century, one is forced to
recognize the significance of even these fleeting experiences of
late adolescence. Not only Russian radicalism developed a strong
peasant orientation in this period; Russian "liberals" and reactionaries often shared with them a hatred of something that they
called the "bourgeoisie" and the capitalism and individualism of
the "West." And this romance with the peasantry (usually carried
on from afar, to be sure) played a fateful role in Russian political
and economic development right up until 1917.

Of course, it was really to the young radicals, the future *narodniki,* that Pavel Ivanovich could appear as a possible model, as
the harbinger of a new identity, almost as a "new man." The only
thing he could not give them was a political program, but by the
time of Chernyshevsky there was no lack of ideas on that front.
But he conveyed the *image,* the way of life, the style of the
narodnik, and his personal failure foreshadows the failure of
Russian Populism.

The final seven years of Iakushkin's life were grim ones. Deprived of both his St. Petersburg friends and the possibility of
travel, he fell prey to depression, illness, loneliness, and the con-
solations of the bottle. His relations with his mother were especially agonizing for him, as his correspondence with old Professor
Pogodin makes clear. "I could not tell her why I was brought
here," he wrote to Pogodin, "and my mother, as you know, is not
only my mother, but a most respectable lady. Can there be a
worse punishment than to quarrel with one's family, with one's
mother? And I am punished with that punishment."[37] Praskov'ia
Faleevna could not understand her son at all. She must have
thought often of her own long struggle for respectability, economic success, and a place in the world. And with those battles
virtually won, her son first revealed his disgusting tendency to
"revert" (or so it must have appeared to her) and then became
a "state criminal." Nor could he offer any account of himself that
would have begun to appease her. The running of the estate was

more and more burdensome and difficult, and here was Pavel Ivanovich, forty-three years old, dressed like a peasant, sick, alcoholic, and under police surveillance, moping around Saburovo. Useless, incomprehensible, and self-destructive.

During his three years at Saburovo, Iakushkin published a few pieces in various journals; his life gave him ample time to write. The first half of "Riots in Russia" appeared in the third number of the *Contemporary* after considerable difficulties with the censorship. In 1868, the *Annals of the Fatherland* published a bitter and pessimistic sketch entitled "Clean Teeth or They'll Call You a Peasant."[38] The title has a double meaning: "cleaning teeth" also means hitting someone in the teeth, which was an approach favored by both gentry and peasants in rural Russia. Iakushkin met a peasant schoolboy on the road who had misunderstood the phrase from one of his books, but he and other peasants assured Pavel Ivanovich that "cleaning people's teeth" was the way to get ahead.

Pavel Ivanovich's growing isolation from Russian intellectual and social life is attested to by his correspondence, which grew in volume after 1865 (a kind of evidence in itself) but declined in interest. Two requests are repeated over and over again in the letters he wrote both from Saburovo and from his subsequent place of exile on the northern shore of the Caspian Sea: send money and send books (and periodicals). He wrote to old Pogodin, he wrote to Aleksandr Ostrovsky, he wrote to Nekrasov; his correspondence with the latter in particular is almost devoid of content, save for terse descriptions of financial distress and intellectual isolation.

As his domestic unhappiness and his ennui deepened, he drank harder and more purposefully, which led, in turn, to further deterioration in his health. He suffered increasingly from catarrh and soon conceived the project of going to Moscow for treatment; even before the year 1865 was out, he had written to Annenkov in St. Petersburg, asking for permission. Despite Pavel Ivanovich's overriding desire to escape from Saburovo (which played an important part in everything he said or did), his medical complaint was genuine.

Iakushkin's request went from Annenkov back to the local
authorities in Orël, back to St. Petersburg, and back to Orël, in
characteristically time-consuming fashion. It was finally turned
down by the minister of the interior himself, partly because of
the new fear of, and hostility toward, radicalism, brought on by
Karakozov's attempted assassination of Alexander II on April 4,
1866. Iakushkin also wrote, without success, to the Third Section
and to his old acquaintance, Governor Ogarëv of Nizhny Novgorod. His mother wrote to the governor of Orël province to the
same effect, but her letter was never answered.

By the end of 1866, Iakushkin appears to have given up the
attempt to achieve his aim directly; instead, he set out to get
permission for a short trip into the neighboring district of
Mtsensk to consult his younger brother, Viktor, who was practic-
ing medicine there.* "Again," Balandin notes, "the bureaucratic
machine was set in motion."[39] The governor's office in Orël, the
Third Section in St. Petersburg, and the Ministry of the Interior
solemnly deliberated and consulted. On March 25, 1867, Pavel
Ivanovich was given permission to make the trip, provided that
he was kept under close surveillance by the police of the two
districts.

The results of the government's bureaucratic indulgence
were, perhaps, predictable. Pavel Ivanovich did no more than
touch base with his brother. He refused to indicate a regular
place of residence to the local authorities, resumed his customary
nomadic existence, and soon turned up in Orël, where the police
picked him up, drunk in the street. He refused to return to
Saburovo and expressed his determination to continue his "treatment" in Moscow. On April 26, he was brought back to his
mother by two police agents. The whole affair was carefully
memorialized by the Orël police department in a document
resoundingly entitled "On the Unwillingness of Provincial Secretary Iakushkin to Leave the Town of Orël."

Back at Saburovo, Pavel Ivanovich renewed his efforts, writing
letter after weary letter. The year dragged on. When it became

*It may have been Viktor Iakushkin upon whom Turgenev based Bazarov in *Fathers
and Children*.

unmistakably clear that Moscow was not a possibility, he asked for Riazan'; his mother offered to guarantee him two hundred rubles a year support. But the minister of the interior, in St. Petersburg, was not to be moved. He saw no reason for the change, and he was unwilling, he said, to burden the governor of Riazan' province with the trouble and expense of looking after a difficult man who had no local connections or "interests."

In his despair, Iakushkin even hoped to be formally tried by the courts—anything to achieve some kind of resolution to his "case." Whether the idea originated at Saburovo or in St. Petersburg, nothing finally came of it. He wrote repeatedly to Pogodin, his most influential remaining friend, begging him to do all he could to have him sent somewhere, "anywhere," away from Saburovo.

Then, in February 1868, Iakushkin simply appeared in the governor's reception room in Orël. "Do what you like with me," he announced with miserable defiance. "If you take me back to the country, I'll run away again in two hours."[40] By this time, the authorities, too, were ready for a policy change—largely for reasons of fatigue. Governor M. N. Longinov of Orël wrote a notably nasty letter to the minister of the interior, Valuev, about Iakushkin's bad influence throughout the province, and there appeared to be general agreement that exile to a remote part of the empire should be the next step. The ministry suggested Astrakhan province, and a small town called Krasnyi Iar, in the Volga littoral near Astrakhan, was decided upon. After spending a few days in the hospital at Orël, Iakushkin—accompanied by his usual two-man escort—left for the Caspian, via Voronezh.

Iakushkin described the lengthy trip in his last published set of "travel letters." From Voronezh, he and his escort traveled down the Don, crossing over to the Volga at the city of Tsaritsyn and continuing by boat to Astrakhan. He was delighted to be on the road again, even under these circumstances, and the letters exude much of his old zest, albeit with a perceptible undercurrent of bitterness about his fate and a marked dislike of his police escort.[41]

The journey provided Iakushkin's most sustained contact with cossacks, and it is scarcely surprising that he found them most congenial. They were independent and democratic and possessed a natural and winning courtesy. Their sense of human dignity was derived, he believed, from a solid sense of their own worth—prerequisite for recognizing the dignity of someone else. The cossacks had escaped not only serfdom but its crippling and long-lived psychological consequences.

The most interesting conversations between Pavel Ivanovich and his cossack traveling companions centered around the great peasant rebels Stenka Razin and Pugachëv. The letters—which he jotted down in a third-class railroad car between Voronezh and Tsaritsyn—are among the most valuable evidence on popular attitudes toward them, a century after Pugachëv was drawn and quartered.[42]

Pugachëv was described as a great warrior, a Don Cossack and a friend of the people who crossed himself "the old way"—a reference to his sympathy for Old Believers, who supported his rebellion in great numbers. He was a just man, but the justice for his enemies was summary—a wink of his eye and they would swing. Stenka Razin, to Iakushkin's cossack informants, was a more complex figure, toward whom there was greater ambivalence. Like Pugachëv, he was a great fighter, but he was also a "heretic"—that is, a magician. The social revolutionary motif emerges clearly with respect to both men, who championed the poor peasant, mistreated or ruined by the landowner, but Pugachëv was not described as a pagan and magician. When Iakushkin asked one of his cossack traveling companions what kind of a "heretic" Razin was, he was answered as follows:

This is what kind. They were going to put him in prison. Good. They bring Stenka to the prison. "Your health, brothers!," he shouts to the prisoners in the stocks. Hello, our father, Stepan Timofeevich! For everyone knew him already. "Why are you sitting here? It's time to be getting out." "But how can we get out," say the prisoners, "we can't manage it ourselves. But by your wisdom?" "By my wisdom, if you please, by mine." He lies down, rests for a little, gets up. "Give me," he says, "the charcoal." And he takes this charcoal, draws a boat on the wall with this charcoal, puts the prisoners in this boat, splashes the water; the river flows away from the prison to the Volga itself. Stenka and his boys burst out singing—right to the Volga.[43]

No one can stand before Stenka: he becomes virtual lord of Astrakhan, terrorizes the governor, and conducts his own rather rapacious foreign relations with Persia. But Stenka is a democrat, a lover of Russia and his free life on the Volga. When he tires of the daughter of the sultan of Persia (he is also a great womanizer), he dumps her in the Volga, jewels and all, and sails back to Russia.

Stenka was also a great enemy of the Orthodox Church—more so than Pugachëv and later Robin Hood types—like the bandit known as Trishka the Siberian, whom Iakushkin also discusses. Stenka's hostility to the Church went beyond Robin Hood's hostility to the "fat priest," for Jolly Robin was no sorcerer or enemy of Christianity. "He was such a heretic," continued Iakushkin's cossack, "he bewitched all Astrakhan, he held everyone in thrall, except one bishop."

The bishop in Astrakhan was then Joseph; Joseph began to talk to Razin: "Fear God! Stop, Stenka, your hereticking!" "Be silent," shouted Stenka Razin, "be silent, father! It's none of your business." The bishop to Stenka again: "it's a great sin to live in heresy." But Stenka sticks to his guns: "Be silent, father! Don't meddle where you're not asked. I'll smite you, bishop," he says. The bishop has his and Stenka his. The bishop again to Stenka Razin: "Think of your soul, how it must answer to God in the other world." Stenka winked to his men, and they took him to the fortress, on to the wall, and from those walls they threw him to the cossacks, on to their spears. Thus Bishop Joseph gave up his soul to God.[44]

The anecdotes about Stenka and the Church were told and received with real awe and some mixed emotion.

Iakushkin was much less well disposed toward the Jews he encountered on the trip (and elsewhere) than he was toward the cossacks. He was aware that the Jews in Russia had been badly mistreated, and, in his opinion, there was such a thing as a "good Jew"—an *evrei*—as well as the "Yid"—the *zhid*. But most Jews seem to have inspired in him an almost physical loathing. He was not in the least interested in them or in their way of life; in

general, Iakushkin showed almost none of the sensitive curiosity
about non-Russian nationalities that he displayed toward his own
people. He was clearly disposed to consider the peasant's hostility toward the Jewish tavernkeeper as sensible and well founded
as his attitude toward the gentry landowner.

Iakushkin arrived in Krasnyi Iar on April 29, 1868. The final
decision as to the precise location of his place of residence within
the province lay with the governor. It has been suggested that
Iakushkin's conduct in Astrakhan (peasant costume, leaving the
city without permission, and so on) persuaded the governor that
he should not be allowed to stay in the capital. Balandin appears
to have shown, however, that the decision to get him out of
Astrakhan was made almost immediately upon his arrival, on the
basis of his record rather than any fresh exploits.[45] So he found
himself—quite simply—at the end of the world. Although the
agony of living under his mother's roof was now ended, he had
traded his life in what was, after all, a relatively populous central
Russian province, within a few days' journey of Moscow, for the
almost total isolation of a tiny fishing community on an island in
the bleak and savage salt marshes of the northern shore of the
Caspian. It was only about twenty miles from Astrakhan, but he
was not allowed to make the trip even when the road was open
—which for large portions of the year it was not. By boat and
carriage, the journey took about twelve hours. The mails were
inefficient and irregular, and Iakushkin's periodical subscriptions
—an increasingly crucial part of his life—were particularly so.
For the first twelve months of his stay, not a single issue of the
Annals of the Fatherland arrived.

As Pavel Ivanovich walked through Krasnyi Iar on his first
morning, the realization of his situation began to sink in. He soon
saw, as he put it, that his new home differed from all other towns,
in that it had no inhabitants. There was simply not a soul to be
seen. The windows were shuttered; gates were locked and
barred; the only living creatures he saw were crows. The tone of
his reflections was bitter in the extreme. When he failed at first
to spot the town jail, he began to reflect upon how in Russia one

could deduce nearly all the crucial information about a village, town, or city from its prison facilities: an old town had a jail and a monastery, but a new town had only a jail; the jail in a provincial capital was larger and functioned more complexly than the jail in a district capital; and so on.

Continuing through the silent and deserted streets, he was struck by a "terrible sadness"; he returned to his apartment, but the four bare walls soon drove him out onto the street again. He set off in search of the bazaar, but found that it functioned only irregularly; a little desultory fish-selling was all that took place on most days. The area around the bazaar was surrounded by taverns, most of them empty. How could the invisible population support so many? Where were the patrons that kept them going? Finally his wanderings brought him to the river, where he found "the same deathliness. Several vessels of various types were standing at the bank; several boats were tied up at the bank . . . but as for people, it was as if Mamai* had passed through. There was not a soul to be seen."[46]

Life in Krasnyi Iar was simply unbearable. It was broiling hot for twelve hours and then, abruptly, freezing cold for twelve. Police supervision was constant and intrusive—especially after one of his co-exiles escaped to Geneva. The police had been so fascinated by Pavel Ivanovich that they totally neglected his apparently well-behaved and orderly compatriot, who simply walked away. Above all, there was nothing to do. And so Iakushkin renewed his requests to the Ministry of the Interior for a new location.

The weary round of letter-writing continued. Finally, in May 1870, Iakushkin was transferred from Krasnyi Iar to Enotaevka, a river port north of Astrakhan on the Volga. By this time, he was suffering from chronic fever, rheumatism, and scurvy. His new location was an improvement, but he still had his heart set on Moscow. The Third Section asked the governor of Orël if he would take Iakushkin back, but the governor declined. Praskov'ia Faleevna evidently wanted Pavel Ivanovich back, for

---

*Mamai was a great Mongol general and the personification to a Russian of destruction and desolation.

Saburovo was sunk in debt, and of the Iakushkin brothers, Aleksandr had been sent to Siberia and Viktor was fatally ill with tuberculosis in Rome.

Apparently convinced that Iakushkin no longer represented a serious danger, the Third Section decided in June 1871 to offer him a choice of where he wanted to live—with only the Moscow and Orël areas excluded. Iakushkin immediately chose Tver', but after official consultation it was decided that Tver' was too near Moscow, so he was transferred to Samara in the fall of 1871.

In Samara, Iakushkin found himself in relatively congenial surroundings for the first time since his departure from St. Petersburg in the spring of 1865. The most important factor was that he had a provincial governor on his side for the first time. Grigory Aksakov, the brother of Ivan Aksakov, Iakushkin's editor and friend, was a cultivated and humane man, sympathetic to folklorists and intellectuals, and a great admirer of Pëtr Kireevsky. Relations between Aksakov and the local intelligentsia were unusually good. He mediated delicately and effectively between Iakushkin and the authorities, citing Iakushkin's now obviously deteriorated health as a convincing argument as to why he should be allowed to remain in Samara, rather than being shipped off to some out-of-the-way village or town.

Pavel Ivanovich found other supporters and well-wishers in Samara. There was Modest Ivanovich Pisarev, an actor of considerable reputation, whose company was performing in Samara with great success; he had known Iakushkin through their mutual friends Apollon Grigor'ev and Aleksandr Ostrovsky. And there was also Veniamin Osipovich Portugalov, who had known Iakushkin at least *en passant* in the mid-1850s in Kharkov. Portugalov, the son of a Jewish merchant, had been drawn into oppositional circles by his perception of the plight of Russian Jewry; he had become a doctor and had spent the decade of the 1860s in exile, with a few months in the Fortress of St. Peter and St. Paul in 1862. Portugalov had been in Samara for only about six months, after having spent several years in places nearly as

remote and unappetizing as Krasnyi Iar. Although his liberal
sympathies appear to have remained strong, his behavior had
been correct enough in the eyes of the police for a considerable
period; he was removed from surveillance altogether in 1876.
Portugalov was serving as an intern in the city hospital, which
was run by the newly established zemstvo. He described his
meeting with Pavel Ivanovich in the following terms:

One tedious and rainy autumn evening, at the end of September,
1871, the maid *announced* to me that someone had arrived who was
neither a *barin* nor a peasant. Receiving the unexpected guest, it was
easy to guess the essentials of the situation when the visitor pronounced his celebrated name: Pavel Ivanovich Iakushkin! Within a
few minutes, he was already no longer a guest, but a dear member
of the family; without ceremony, with easy intimacy, he was telling
us the cause of his abrupt appearance.[47]

Iakushkin's living accommodations, arranged by Portugalov and
approved by Aksakov, were all that he could have desired. He
lived in the hospital but treated it essentially as an apartment,
with the proviso that he return by ten in the evening, a measure
dictated by his health rather than by reasons of security. So he
wrote a bit in the mornings (he started a play), spent whole days
with Pisarev's theater company on occasion, but generally based
himself at Portugalov's apartment. There he mingled with the
"liberal" society of Samara: zemstvo and government officials,
journalists, and at least one other political exile, M. D. Muravsky,
who had been involved with Portugalov in a rather amateurish
"conspiracy" at the University of Kharkov in the 1850s. Unlike
Portugalov, Muravsky, who was known as "Uncle Mitrofan," was
a real revolutionary. He became an active organizer in Orenburg
province, was arrested and tried in the famous "Trial of the 193"
in 1878. After receiving a ten-year sentence, he soon died in
prison.

So Iakushkin was, however briefly, in his element again. As was
usually the case with vaguely Populist circles of this kind, interest
in ethnography—and particularly in folk songs—was high. Por-

tugalov remembers Pavel Ivanovich sitting at the piano and singing:

> We will drink and we will play
> And when death comes we'll die.

And death came all too soon.

Iakushkin enjoyed himself among his new friends, regaled them with accounts of his wanderings, but as usual engaged in no public introspection. If Portugalov is to be believed, Iakushkin pooh-poohed the idea that there had ever been anything political about his life. But if he still had hopes for the future, he said nothing about them, nor did he engage in vain regrets about the past. He took each day as it came, emerging from the hospital, generally, around midday and going to see Pisarev or Portugalov. His wanderlust was either in abeyance or altogether gone. Did he know he was dying?

At the end of November, Iakushkin caught a fever in the hospital and became seriously ill. He hung on for a while, but his constitution was too weak for the ordeal. When Portugalov had first examined him, he had found him suffering from palpitations of the heart, asthma, a terrible cough; at that time, Iakushkin was drinking so much that he simply carried a bottle with him wherever he went, and of course he had been a heavy smoker for many years. In a few days he died—as Portugalov put it, from exhaustion. Upon performing an autopsy, Portugalov found what he thought was "fatty degeneration" of some brain and heart tissue; the heart was also "enclosed in a thick layer of fat." The lungs were in the worst shape of all: they were simply eaten up with huge, ulcerous sores.

His friends buried him, with as much honor and ceremony as they could muster between them (Pavel Ivanovich, of course, had no resources at all), on January 10, 1872. They even managed music, a highly unusual circumstance at the funeral of a private person.

On the day of the burial, a letter and check for fifty rubles arrived from Nekrasov, who seems to have been uncharacteristically generous with Iakushkin. Modest Pisarev sent the money back to Nekrasov, with a letter describing Iakushkin's brief life in Samara. Characteristically, Pavel Ivanovich had been much disturbed by two ten-ruble debts that he owed, one in Krasnyi Iar and one in Enotaevak, and Pisarev gave the names of those to whom the money was due to Nekrasov, as he had promised Iakushkin he would. Otherwise, "when I think back on my past," Iakushkin said just before his death, "I cannot reproach myself for anything."[48]

Russian Jacobins

The generation of which Herzen was a part has been the final manifestation of the liberalizing nobility. His doctrinaire radicalism was a flower of the conservatory, which grew and blossomed in an artificial atmosphere which gave it life but which withered when it was first exposed to the free air and real atmosphere of practical action. The men of that generation criticized, mocked the actual social order with the caustic skill fashionable in the salons and in a dated poetic language. This critique became an occupation for them. They were content with their role.

—Sergei Nechaev, *Obshchina*

The Russian radicalism of the early 1860s was supported by a messianic social optimism that had been building since the death of Nicholas I, two components of which were particularly important in keeping the "movement" going. One was the support of a significant part of educated public opinion, of *obshchestvo*. The other was progressive *obshchestvo*'s belief that the Russian peasantry constituted a revolutionary force that would at some point rise up and sweep the old order away, and whose social institutions would provide the foundation for a new, free, and humane society in Russia.

But by 1863, as we have seen, the situation had altered considerably. "Liberal" support had largely evaporated; progressive public opinion was exhausted by years of social turmoil, terrified by the fires of 1862, and roused to patriotic ire by the Polish rebellion. It was clear that no significant portion of the gentry was going to press hard for a constitution. And although belief in the institutions of the peasantry as the basis for a socialist (or merely democratic) future remained, the peasants were obviously not going to explode into revolt right away. For the next few years, the most militant of the Russian radicals were thrown back on themselves.

Until 1862, potential divisions within the Left had been to some extent held in check by the movement of events themselves and the optimism they generated. Now, as public opinion moved to the right, Russian radicalism began to fragment. Several of the younger veterans, now living the squalid existence of political émigrés, launched a fierce attack on Herzen, whom—in their isolation and despair—they came to regard as a despicable relic of the old order, living in London or Geneva like a lord, amid the ruin of their hopes. In the words of Isaiah Berlin, the younger radicals thought of Herzen as

a self-indulgent sceptic, too rich, too civilized, too elegant, too much a gentleman, too comfortably established in the West to sympathize with the harsh realities of the Russian situation, and dangerous, too, because prone to sound a note of disillusion, even of cynicism, and so to weaken the sinews of the revolution—liable to become ironical and, worse still, entertaining, at a time when serious men must decide to commit themselves to one side or the other without so much fastidious regard to their private consciences and scruples.[1]

One can see the split foreshadowed in the younger generation's veneration of Chernyshevsky and their growing aversion to Herzen's style, if not his ideas, by 1860. But the violent and open breach took place only in the demoralized atmosphere that followed the Polish revolt and the arrest and condemnation of Chernyshevsky.

Nor was the younger generation's hostility to Herzen the only instance of dissension on the Left. In 1864–65, a fairly serious dispute erupted between the only journals in Russia that were still vehicles for radical opinion: the *Contemporary*, which had been allowed to resume publication after eight months, and Dmitry Pisarev's *Russian Word*.[2] The essence of the dispute lay in the *Contemporary*'s fidelity to a broadly Populist position, while Pisarev stressed the importance of a well-educated, scientifically oriented, reforming elite. Only a dedicated and self-conscious leadership could get on with the serious business of liberating the masses from the eternal cycle of misery and deprivation from which they had suffered so long. Pisarev had little belief in "popular wisdom" and—in the discouraging atmosphere of the mid-1860s—he became irritably impatient with those who still believed that the peasants might be a revolutionary force or even bring about their own liberation. He was a strong advocate of industrialization and the spread of scientific ideas; he thought the notion that the survival of the peasant commune might provide Russia with a "separate path" to socialism and modernity was simply ridiculous.

On the other side, the mood at the *Contemporary*, bereft of the leadership of Chernyshevsky and Dobroliubov, was bitter and weary. Saltykov-Shchedrin, the satirical writer, attacked "turncoat nihilists" and revealed a new pessimism about that younger generation in whom all progressives had so recently seen the salvation of Russia. Furthermore, M. A. Antonovich and other *Contemporary* editors produced a string of Populist articles that contained a semimystical strain of peasant-worship, more akin to the writings of Shchapov or Herzen at his most rhapsodic than to the more realistic and economically sophisticated views of Chernyshevsky. Disunity on the Left could scarcely have been more complete.*

Except for some few of Pisarev's followers, the young radicals who became politically conscious between 1862 and 1866 entertained very little hope for reform. Thus the kind of violent, bloody, and total revolution envisaged in *Young Russia* began to

---

*To an extent, the physical contraction of the Left may be seen in the circulation figures for the *Contemporary*; in 1862, there had been seven thousand subscribers, but by the end of 1864 there were only about four thousand. See M. Lemke, *Epokha tsenzurnykh reform* (St. Petersburg, 1904), p. 192n.

seem less "extreme": was this not the only way that Russia could be renewed? Most young radicals stubbornly refused to give up the idea of reaching the people, but clearly the process would be protracted and full of danger, and would demand a lengthy commitment to hard and frustrating work. In the face of this situation, it was natural for intelligentsia radicals to believe that they would have to do more to bring about the revolution, both by raising the consciousness of the peasantry and—some came to feel—by actually setting an insurrection in motion and guiding it, through conspiratorial means.

In the increasingly nerve-wracking, underground, and conspiratorial existence into which they had moved by 1865, Russian radicals were keenly aware of their isolation. They felt the unreliability of those around them—sometimes even that of their own comrades. Leaders began not only to keep a keen eye on possible weakness or deviation among their followers, but to resort to deliberate deceptions to convince their comrades that—despite appearances—they were part of a powerful nationwide (or even Europe-wide) movement. The naive consciousness of a liberating mission was replaced by the belief in the necessity for secret organizations, designed not only to continue the struggle against the government but to ensure that the faithful remained committed.

This sort of development was by no means unique to the Russian radicalism of the 1860s. It was to be found in the secret societies of Restoration Europe (1815–30); more recently, we have seen how the extreme Left in America in the 1970s has gone underground and resorted both to terrorism and to revolutionary fantasy in the effort to keep the "movement" alive in the face of public apathy or hostility.*

Between about 1863 and 1871, Russian radicals lacked a serious,

---

*Isolated acts of terror—assassinations, bank robberies, or kidnappings—such as those engaged in by small groups like the Symbionese Liberation Army advertise the lack of a real program or constituency. The fantasies of the National Caucus of Labor Committees reveal a desperate need to hold their membership together, through subjection to a charismatic leader, by means of intense pressure on the membership to believe in a worldwide conspiracy headed by the Rockefeller family—and by force, if necessary. On the emergence of the National Caucus, see *The New York Times*, Jan. 20, 1974, pp. 1, 51, and the *Boston Phoenix*, Jan. 29, 1974, p. 3 *et seq.*

ongoing, and organized contact with a constituency. They felt, of
course, that the *narod* was their constituency, but most of them
were sooner or later brought to recognize that they were not yet
recognized as the people's spokesmen by anyone but themselves
—and a few nervous functionaries in the political police. They
could not yet speak the language of the people, nor could they
really lead it—although many hoped at least to channel its rage
into a revolutionary and socialist direction. The government remained committed to reform (however it might be mingled with
repression), but with the erosion of the mood of reforming optimism that had characterized the preceding years, recruitment
was often (though not always) more difficult. Furthermore, the
world into which one went, when one became a radical, was now
a distinctly subversive one—which, of course, had attractions of
its own. But one could no longer dream, as even Herzen had, of
heading some kind of reform ministry. Although there are a few
striking exceptions—people for whom 1860s radicalism was wild
oats, later forgiven—the only reasonable supposition for incipient radicals was that the task at hand was to subvert or overthrow
the government from outside. The "we-they" attitude had become total.

Russian universities and other institutions of higher learning—
particularly in the capitals—had become the principal loci for
radical recruitment. But in general the large mass of the student
body was less amenable to radical ideas than it had been; correspondingly, the hostility between committed radicals and "liberals" or moderates grew stronger.

The social composition of radical groups also changed. The
majority of the most active and engaged seems still to have been
drawn from the gentry. But more and more of them were from
the provinces, from outlying parts of the empire. And there was
a growing mix of *raznochintsy:* the sons of priests and lower
officials, the children of army officers from the lower ranks—and
even an occasional representative of a merchant family or a
peasant. And last, but certainly not least, one finds a small but
active group of women taking part in the revolutionary struggle,
in a number of cases leading it. By the end of the 1860s, the

radicals had come to regard the outside world as more and more hostile and less amenable to anything but violent and cataclysmic action. And that violence was increasingly turned on the membership itself.

A convenient place to begin our discussion of this period is the year 1863 and the publication of Chernyshevsky's novel, *What Is To Be Done?* Seldom has a book had so immediate (and indeed so protracted) an effect upon the audience for which it was intended. One is forced to turn to the most threadbare cliché: the novel was in fact the Bible of Russian radicals for many years, although its impact was most powerful on its first generation of readers. And indeed there can have been few Russian Christians of the nineteenth century who read the Bible and attempted to live the Sermon on the Mount with the passion and commitment with which Chernyshevsky's young disciples attempted to live out his communal prescriptions.

Considered formally, as a work of fiction, *What Is To Be Done?* is maladroit and in places laughable, but that has never mattered to its readers. Chernyshevsky himself said—for our purposes—all that need be said, remarking in the preface that "I don't have the shadow of an artistic talent. I even use the language badly. But that's not important."[3] Chernyshevsky is not going to give the reader poetry but, he soon confesses, truth.

The importance of the novel lies in Chernyshevsky's portrait of the men and women who were trying to build a new society —and the power that portrait had for Russian radicals from the mid-1860s into the 1890s, and even beyond. Georgy Plekhanov, the "founder" of Russian Marxism and a man of a later generation, wrote in a frequently quoted passage that "we have all drawn [from the novel] moral strength and faith in a better future"; at the very end of the nineteenth century he concluded that "from the moment when the printing press was introduced in Russia until now no printed work has had such a success as *What Is To Be Done?*"[4]

In 1905, the anarchist Prince Peter Kropotkin wrote of the novel that "for the Russian youth of the time it was a revalation [*sic*], and it became a programme. . . . No novel of Turgueneff and no writings of Tolstoy or any other writer have ever had such a wide and deep influence upon Russian society. . . . It became a watchword of Young Russia, and the influence of the ideas it propagated has never ceased to be apparent since."[5]

Kropotkin was not the only Russian radical who referred to *What Is To Be Done?* in scriptural terms. Pëtr Tkachëv, one of the principal shapers of Russian Jacobinism between 1865 and 1875, referred to the book as the "gospel" of Russian radicalism;[6] and Nikolai Ishutin, an archetypal 1860s radical with whom we will be concerned later in this chapter, is supposed to have recognized only three great men in history: Jesus Christ, St. Paul, and Chernyshevsky. Even so unsympathetic an observer as the novelist Vladimir Nabokov, who treated Chernyshevsky as a peculiar joke on Russian culture, admitted that the novel was read "the way liturgical books are read."[7]

What Is To Be Done? performed several essential services for young radicals of the 1860s. It gave them a rough sketch of a program—the creation of artels and other communal institutions —at a time when the euphoria of the pre-reform period was gone and the prospect of peasant revolution was becoming more remote. Timing is important here; the novel appeared serially in the *Contemporary* in 1863, just as the expectations of Land and Liberty were being dashed and the organization, such as it was, had collapsed. Chernyshevsky was already achieving the status of a martyr; the poet Nekrasov had compared him to Christ crucified. Never did the inveterately inefficient Russian censorship make a greater mistake than by allowing *What Is To Be Done?* to appear, first in the pages of the *Contemporary*, then (incredibly) in book form.

Secondly, the novel provided what in today's academia would be called "role models" for an incipient movement that as yet had none. It was subtitled "Tales About New People"; in Rakhmetov, Vera Pavlovna, Lopukhov, and Kirsanov, Chernyshevsky produced not abstract formulas but pictures of how people should live and what they should do. The new people are rational (almost insanely so), militant, and at war with the existing order—which is scarcely described at all, except when "bad" characters soliloquize about how the corrupt environment made them the pathetic villains they are. At the same time, as soon as the "good" people understand how socialist ideas can transform the world, they are possessed by a heroic resolution that always sees them through; they are never defeated by moral complexity or force of circumstances. Nor is there any difficulty in communication between *obshchestvo* and *narod;* for the "new people" (and for you, dear reader, says Chernyshevsky), starting a cooperative or reforming a prostitute is easy, if only you *will!*

Lopukhov pushes upper-class men off the sidewalk, instead of deferring to them, but Rakhmetov, the most explicitly revolutionary, exemplifies the need for strength and toughness in the service of the *narod.* He eats raw beef and sleeps on a bed of nails; he gets to know the people by traveling all over Russia on foot, serving as a barge hauler and a laborer; his extraordinary strength is celebrated by the people in epic terms, and so on. This physical prowess, which Chernyshevsky himself so strikingly lacked, is controlled and directed by Rakhmetov's complex, elaborate, and rigid system of rules for life. For example, he will eat only what the *narod* eats (except for the essential raw beef), which leads him always to refuse apricots and sardines and to eat oranges only in St. Petersburg. In the provinces, oranges are found only on the tables of the privileged.

However lifeless and caricatured these figures may seem to most twentieth-century readers, they supplied what Che Guevara was to provide for a more recent generation of student radicals: a fusion of ideals, program, and style. In the words of Lenin, a great admirer of the novel: "Chernyshevsky not only showed that every right-thinking and really honest man must be a revolutionary, but he also showed—and this is his greatest merit —what a revolutionary must be like, what his principles must be, how he must approach his aim, and what methods he must use to achieve it."[8] Finally, Chernyshevsky's portraits of women and his description of the sexual equality that the "new people" were trying to achieve had a particular impact on the generation of the 1860s. Although Chernyshevsky's female characters are as

wooden as his males, they raise vital issues intelligently: the need
for a room of one's own, the need for a job outside the home. In
the history of the emancipation of women in Russia, Chernyshevsky and his novel have a special place.

It soon became clear that Chernyshevsky, in his life and in the
pages of his novel, had begun the creation of a radical identity.
The Manichaeism, the exultation of will, the whole-souled,
puritanical (and rhetorical) repudiation of "possession," in
human relationships particularly—all these renewed the courage
of young radicals in the 1860s. And although the heroines and
heroes are intellectually anti-Romantic (they are "rational ego-
ists" and materialists), there is a sentimental high-mindedness
about their personal relations that appealed to a broad segment
of Russia's youth. But above all, Chernyshevsky's "new people"
made the society of the future imaginable, and therefore possible. Neither Herzen, with his cult of the Decembrist rebels, nor
Turgenev, with his magnificent, ambiguous portrait of Bazarov
in *Fathers and Children*,[9] had been able to achieve anything
comparable. With the appearance of Chernyshevsky's novel and
the development of his personal cult, young opponents of the
established order in Russia had at least a rudimentary sense of a
way of life, a culture, a set of convictions upon which they could
base their challenge to the ancien régime. As they did so, they
were able to distinguish themselves from "liberals" and radicals
of Herzen's generation more sharply; hostility to their forebears
became, for a time, part of their sense of themselves.

Judging by the memoir literature and other eyewitness testimony, it was much less clear in the late 1850s and early 1860s what
a "radical identity" might be. The lines between political positions were quite fluid. In a way that is not easy to describe, one
became a radical in the mid-1860s and began to develop a quasi-
tribal relationship to other radicals. Becoming a radical tended
to be a more total experience; at some point it involved a conscious repudiation of the existing order. It was more like a religious conversion. And following the break, the new recruit could
find a self-conscious grouping of people, with ideals imbedded in

a way of life, to receive him or her. In other words, there was now an embryonic radical community, developing most obviously where there were large numbers of students.

Both because of the development of a radical identity and because of the hazardous nature of radicalism after 1862–63, one suspects that the younger generation of radicals was made up increasingly of people who had, from early on, defined themselves, or been defined, as "outsiders." Let us now turn to the most important radical grouping of the mid-1860s and examine their ethos and activities in some detail.

The most important of these "Jacobin"* groups came into existence toward the middle of the decade; after it had crystallized, it became known, appropriately, as Organization *(Organizatsiia),* and the principal figure in it was Nikolai Ishutin.

There is very little information, unfortunately, on Ishutin's early life.[10] We know that he was born in 1840 in a town on the Volga near Saratov; his father was a prosperous merchant, and his mother was from a gentry family. He lost both parents when he was only two years old, however, and was brought up by the Karakozov family, relatives of his father. Dmitry Karakozov, whose attempt on the life of the Emperor was to lead to the destruction of Ishutin's group, was his cousin. After a childhood marred by periodic ill health, he arrived at the University of Moscow in the fall of 1863 to be an auditor. Even before Ishutin left Penza, where he had attended the gymnasium, he had been at least marginally involved in radical activity, distributing pamphlets in the countryside. Although their precise content is not attested, the presumption is that they were the work of Land

---

*The term "Jacobin," of course, derives from the French Revolution. In the Russian context, it was generally employed to designate those who did not believe that the *narod,* left to its own devices, would be able to make the revolution, that the radical intelligentsia would have to take a more or less leading role. Very few of the "Jacobins" of the 1860s denied the *narod* an important role, both in the destruction of the old order and—through popular communal spirit and institutions—in the creation of the new. But as the decade wore on, many intellectuals came to believe that the people's primitive socialist consciousness would have to be developed by nonpeasant radicals and that the people would need intelligentsia leadership in organizing the postrevolutionary society. In an extreme form, then, Russian Jacobinism could be seen as genuinely analogous to French Jacobinism, with a Russian "Committee of Public Safety" making the revolution by decree from above.

and Liberty.[11] Ishutin appears to have had considerable attractive force, although he was "neither eloquent nor learned" and
was sometimes described as a hunchback.

The beginnings of the group that gathered around Ishutin
emerges rather mistily from student politics and the life of the
Moscow University community in the early 1860s. We know that
the students from Penza and several other Volga provinces had
organized into a so-called *zemliachestvo,* an informal social
grouping with a regional base, with certain fraternal and cor-
porative functions.[12] Although the *zemliachestvo* was in no way
a political organization, it contained a number of students who
were prepared to be—or who already were—politically involved. The treasurer, from early on, was D. A. Iurasov, subsequently one of the prime movers in Organization.

More directly, in the words of the eminent Soviet authority
E. S. Vilenskaia, "the core of Ishutin's circle consisted of natives
of Penza province, who finished the gymnasium or the gentry
institute in Penza at the end of the 'fifties or in the early 'sixties."[13] Dmitry Ivanov, another member of Ishutin's circle, recalled the atmosphere at the Penza gymnasium in the early
1860s; despite the schematic and somewhat telegraphic quality of
his remarks, they reveal that some of the intellectual currents
that had been confined to Moscow, St. Petersburg, and the other
university centers in the latter 1850s were reaching the provinces:

Just then . . . a kind of new spirit began to be felt. The traditions of
Belinsky (who was from Penza), *Fathers and Children,* Leo Tolstoy,
Dobroliubov, Nekrasov, Shchedrin, Buckle, Lewes,* *Rotting
Swamps, Who Is To Blame?,*† *What Is To Be Done?,* J. S. Mill, the
liberation of the peasants, the end of state monopolies, the beginning
of the Polish uprising, the introduction of the natural sciences into
gymnasium courses, new history textbooks, new relations between
teachers and students, daring disputes with them in class . . . the
whole atmosphere of school and life caught up [our] youth and sud-

*George Henry Lewes (1817–78), positivist literary critic and popularizer of the ideas
of Auguste Comte. Lewes also wrote several novels and was celebrated for his liaison
with George Eliot.
†*Who Is To Blame?,* a novel by Herzen, written and published in 1846.

denly, after the birch rod, the box on the ears and the scolding, after
Ustrialov's scholasticism, they began to think, to read, to take up
"questions," to argue about ideals, to live boldly, freely, independently.[14]

Several progressive teachers in the Penza gymnasium presumably helped the students find reading of the kind Ivanov mentioned; Ishutin lived with one of them for a while, and the
teacher helped keep his former students in touch with one another.

A number of the future members of Ishutin's group had some
involvement in the university disorders of 1861. M. N. Zagibalov
was expelled from the University of Moscow; Iurasov refused to
accept his *matrikul* and left voluntarily. V. N. Shaganov was
involved but was let off with a reprimand. Pavel Fedoseev was
close to Zaichnevsky and was thus familiar with the way of thinking that had produced *Young Russia.* And there were others
with vague radical associations.

By September 1863, a Moscow circle that may legitimately be
called Ishutin's was meeting for discussions. The nucleus was
provided by veterans of the Penza gymnasium, almost all of
gentry origin. Land and Liberty was still living a shadowy existence, and among the questions discussed was whether the group
should "join" it. A preliminary decision that they should was
apparently taken, but it is not clear whether any real action
resulted.

Informal contacts with other radicals, several of them Poles,
were undertaken right from the start. But whatever fleeting
relations members of Ishutin's circle may have had with members of Land and Liberty and such veteran radicals as V. I. Kel'-
siev should not obscure the differences they rightly perceived in
the situation of the radical Left in Russia at that time. Ishutin and
his friends were—at least initially—under no illusion that there
would be a revolution in Russia in the immediate future; they
had lost the faith that underlay the activities of Land and Liberty
and that had animated the pamphleteers of the so-called era of
proclamations. In the fall of 1863, they were groping for a pro-

gram that would sustain them over a fairly long haul. At first, agitation and propaganda, primarily within the university community, were the order of the day. Then they moved to put Chernyshevsky's program into practice, setting up a variety of cooperative institutions that would both heighten consciousness among people like themselves and begin the formidable task of educating the *narod* to its destiny. The task was wearisome and demanded a staying power that was to prove difficult for Ishutin and his friends.

The mentality of Ishutin's circle is important and is quite distinct from that of any group that preceded it. Franco Venturi observed that "the desire for self-sacrifice was in fact the dominating idea of the group" and noted the spirit of asceticism that animated the hard core.[15] There was almost no interest in education—let alone "culture"—except as a means toward an eventual revolution. The wealthier members—which meant in part those who would one day come into large estates and substantial sums of money—all pledged to donate their resources to "the cause." The natural desire to find material means for their projects and the self-sacrifice that the wealthier members displayed were to take on some rather grotesque forms—at any rate, within the more naive nineteenth-century context with which we are dealing.

In characteristically Russian fashion, the asceticism of the group did not preclude the use of alcohol, and up to a point the group seems to have lived a bohemian life-style, not strikingly different from that of the more emancipated university students of the day. But their detestation of and isolation from the existing order, which grew steadily between 1863 and 1865, clearly demarcated them from other fringe members of the university community. At the same time, there were other groups and individuals, in both Moscow and St. Petersburg, who shared their aspirations and their general mental set. Vilenskaia calls the sum of these groups, who had informal contacts with each other, an "underground," but the term is premature. Most of them still had jobs, or student status, or other connections with the institutions of Russian society. Ishutin himself functioned periodically as a tutor in various subjects. The hard core of his group were roughly of an age—in their early or mid-twenties.

Contacts between what we might call the "new people," after Chernyshevsky, were informal and irregular. But there were pockets of organization, like Ishutin's circle, and the small numbers of really committed "new people" (mostly living a bohemian life around universities if they were not in hiding or exile abroad) felt a growing need for it.

Under such conditions, it is not surprising that members of Ishutin's circle became, in 1864 and 1865, more attracted toward violence. We do not find among his friends that fascination with broad political, social, and even metaphysical issues that has characterized the Russian intelligentsia in so many stages of its existence; discussion of such matters provoked a certain impatience, if it was not regarded as diversionary froth. But Ishutin did like to pose one issue for discussion, both within his circle and when sympathetic outsiders—potential recruits—were present: Does the end justify the means? Ishutin was convinced from early on that it did. Another straw in the wind was a song that was popular among Ishutin and his friends. A kind of parody folk song, it ran as follows:

> The smith's just come from the forge,
> Glory Hallelujah!
>
> And the smith has forged three swords,
> Glory Hallelujah!
>
> The first sword's for the boyar aristocrat,
> Glory Hallelujah!
>
> And the second sword's for the hypocrite priest,
> Glory Hallelujah!
>
> And—with a prayer—the third sword's for the tsar,
> Glory Hallelujah![16]

After a winter of discussion and just getting in touch with people in Moscow, the membership dispersed into the countryside and

to various provincial centers in the summer of 1864. They hoped
for a number of things: to locate individuals and groups who
shared their general view of things and could be, in an informal
way, recruited; to find money to support propaganda; to establish
cooperative organizations; and to engage in a bit of direct agitation among the peasants. Pëtr Ermolov,* the richest of several
members who were well off, started a free school for peasants on
his family estate; it was soon closed down by the local authorities
for purveying ideas hostile to the Orthodox Church.[17] This was
the first of a number of free schools that the *Ishutintsy* were to
undertake. Ishutin himself got a job on a Volga River steamboat,
doubtless emulating Rakhmetov in *What Is To Be Done?*, who
had worked as a barge hauler; from this mobile base he attempted to distribute propaganda among the peasantry, apparently without any great success.

When the group reassembled in Moscow in the fall of 1864,
they had plenty of contacts but nothing that could be called a
serious organization. They constituted a "circle" in the classic
Russian sense: a group of close friends with grand intellectual or
political aspirations. Many of the members knew other individuals and a few "groups" who shared their general orientation and
hopes. That was all. They got involved, that autumn, in a number
of cooperative ventures clearly inspired by *What Is To Be Done?*,
while making firmer contact with others who were trying to do
the same thing. Many of these ventures, with whom one or another member of the group had some connection, were originally quite unconnected to Ishutin. An enterprise like P. A. Spiridov's commune of female typesetters, for instance, arose
independently of the *Ishutintsy*, but various members of the
group, including Ishutin, used to hang out there. Repeated
efforts were made to draw the women more deeply into Ishutin's
political projects, with no success. Several were explicit about
their mistrust of the *Ishutintsy* and their fear of being used.
Although direct evidence about Ishutin's attitude toward women is lacking, it is interesting that there were no women in lead-

*Ermolov, orphaned at an early age, had full control of a large estate in Penza
province, worth between twenty-five and thirty thousand rubles.

ership positions in any of Ishutin's political organizations.[18]

One of the first enterprises to get under way was a bookbinding artel begun by Dmitry Ivanov, also from Ishutin's hometown of Penza but some six years younger. Ivanov and several friends arrived in Moscow in the fall of 1864 with fifty rubles for capital and *What Is To Be Done?* as a handbook; Ishutin soon moved in on this promising project, at first by providing the artel with most of its business. In addition to the gentry student founders, the artel involved four "workers," who stuck with the enterprise until Ivanov was arrested in 1866, but it was never a success either financially or as a venture in "consciousness-raising." Speaking of his attempts to indoctrinate the workers, Ivanov told the court that later tried him (his remarks must therefore be treated with some caution), "We sometimes spoke to these workers about cooperative principles, but they absolutely wouldn't listen to us and could not imagine life without a boss."[19] It would be fascinating to know more about Ivanov's collision with the boss mentality of the four workers, but this scrap of testimony is unfortunately all that we have. We also know very little about the artel's finances, except that it needed periodic inputs of capital from Ishutin.

Altogether a more substantial operation was the cooperative of seamstresses started up by Ivanov's two sisters, Ekaterina and Aleksandra. Ekaterina, the more restless and innovative of the two, arrived in Moscow in November 1864, apparently attracted by what her brother wrote of his experience with the artel of bookbinders. One of her letters to her sister in Nizhny Novgorod gives us a first-rate feeling for the sensibility of a woman radical of the 1860s at the time she was actually making the break with her family and previous circumstances. It was impossible, she wrote, for a woman in Russia to earn an "honest piece of bread" with society constituted as it was.

Is it possible [she continued] that you call honest bread [what is earned by] governesses and teachers in general, who preach to children what they themselves do not believe, or accustom children to lie, advising them not to express before their parents those ideas

which they discuss? Or, perhaps, is it honest to live on a little accumulated capital?[20]

Stimulated by her brother's experience, Ekaterina Ivanova came
to see the organization of a cooperative as something she could
do to change the consciousness of her contemporaries while en-
suring herself that "honest piece of bread." She evidently did not
know that the capital for her artel of seamstresses was put up by
Ishutin: something on the order of two or three hundred rubles
was needed to buy sewing machines, furniture, and such things.
By the time Aleksandra arrived in Moscow in the fall of 1865, the
artel was composed of ten people, a mix of working-class women,
whom Ekaterina hoped to educate and "reform" (as Vera Pavlovna had in *What Is To Be Done?*), and women from the educated upper class; of those who became active in radical politics,
all were from the upper-class group, however. The Zasulich sisters were to become famous in the annals of Russian radicalism
and feminism; two of them were involved in the artel; a third,
Vera, was to become a heroine of the Left by shooting the governor-general of St. Petersburg in 1878 for having a prisoner
flogged. She was subsequently acquitted by a jury and escaped
abroad, where she became a founding member of the first notable group of Russian Marxists in the 1880s.

An incomplete charter of the artel suggests the ideals of its
members—or at least those of the Ivanova sisters.[21] An "elder"
was to be elected by the entire membership to serve a one-year
term, although she could be voted out of office if her performance was deemed unsatisfactory. All incoming members had to
be approved by the entire group, and they were supposed to
bring in ten rubles for capital; should they decide to leave, their
investment would be returned to them. Should a member become sick, the artel would support her for three weeks in the
hospital; a member who needed hospitalization for longer than
three weeks would have to leave the artel. After all expenses had
been taken care of, the remaining proceeds would be divided
equally. There was a common dormitory bedroom, and meals
were eaten together.

But, as with the bookbinding venture, things did not work out according to the model provided by Vera Pavlovna's artel in *What Is To Be Done?* The central problem, as might be expected, was lack of capital. Because they had to buy them in small quantities, materials cost more. One sewing machine was not enough, and the cooperative could not afford a second. As the prices charged by the artel were well below those of ordinary dressmakers, there was plenty of work, but despite the long hours put in by the Ivanova sisters and at least some other members, they barely made enough to pay for food and the rent for their apartment.

It is not surprising that there was considerable turnover in personnel; for this reason, apparently, the "elder" was never elected and the Ivanova sisters provided continuing direction. On occasion, too, they seem to have provided some members with spending money out of their own pockets; in addition, Ishutin and Iurasov contributed additional sums, probably in excess of one hundred fifty rubles. By 1866, the artel's financial position seems to have become truly desperate; a further contribution of one hundred rubles from Ishutin and his friends was judged insufficient to keep it going.

The Ivanova sisters also provided a weekly round of reading and lectures, most of which took place on Sundays. Here again the inspiration was *What Is To Be Done?* After a week of extremely hard work, the members would gather on Sunday to discuss (or be lectured on) popular works of materialism, in particular the *Physiologische Briefe* of Karl Vogt, physiology and geography, as well as novels and essays by Herzen and Chernyshevsky. There was also a smattering of Russian and European literature: Turgenev, Gogol, Goncharov, and Dickens. It would be interesting to know how the working-class women responded to these educational Sundays.

As we have seen, the *Ishutintsy* provided most of the capital for the artel. In addition, many meetings of both groups took place on the premises, at which particular stress was laid on the political role of women in the revolutionary struggle. Personal relations were also close: Osip Motkov, a member of Ishutin's circle, and Aleksandra Ivanova were living together, and the intelligentsia members of the artel were well aware of Ishutin's activities.

The most ambitious of Ishutin's other projects was the attempt to create an iron-smelting factory on cooperative principles in Kaluga province, on land adjoining the properties of one of Russia's largest landholders and factory owners, whose peasants were in a state of discontent over his ruthless management of his many enterprises. But this plan never got off the ground. The *Ishutintsy* were also involved in a second artel of seamstresses; they tried to set up a quilting factory near Mozhaisk; an economic failure, it lasted only a few months.

One of the most interesting and characteristic of the circle's activities was the creation in 1865 of a free school for working-class boys in Moscow, known as the Musatovsky School after its moderate "front man," P. A. Musatovsky, an aristocrat from Vladimir who was a Populist fellow traveler. "We will make revolutionaries out of these little boys," said Ishutin in an oft-quoted remark, and indeed the curriculum was calculated to do just that. Dmitry Iurasov, a twenty-three-year-old dropout from the juridical faculty of the University of Moscow, was the arithmetic teacher, and the following may be considered typical of his teaching methods. Seventy-two million is greater than one, he told his class, and so the seventy-two million people of Russia should have the power that accrued to the one Tsar. Pëtr Ermolov taught natural history; on one occasion he described the eagle as a bird of prey, devouring weak creatures like rabbits; for this reason, he told his class, it was chosen as the symbol of Russian imperial power.[22] The school was closed down after a few months because Ishutin wished to devote its resources to the iron-smelting factory, to the creation of which much of the group's energy was devoted that summer.

Ishutin never stopped trying to realize the program of artels and co-ops sketched out in *What Is To Be Done?* until his organization was destroyed in 1866. Nevertheless, a new spirit began to be discernible among the *Ishutintsy* toward the end of 1865, a spirit we might call revolutionary impatience. Although Ishutin had increased his group's membership and connections among student and other radicals, none of their attempts to set up cooperatives had really succeeded, and their efforts to reach either urban working people or peasants had also failed. As the magnitude and difficulty of the task of building a new society became unmistakably clear, the search for a shortcut became psychologically more and more enticing.

One kind of activity helped the *Ishutintsy* to believe that they were making a real contribution to "the cause": the liberation of political prisoners. Their only real success came in the case of the Polish revolutionary Yaroslaw Dombrowski, who was arrested for his part in the Polish rebellion of late 1864; a few days later he escaped, disguised as a woman. Iurasov hid him for several days in his apartment; later a false passport was made for him, and early in the new year he succeeded in escaping abroad.[23] Then, early in the summer of 1865, Ishutin was informed that N. A. Serno-Solovёvich, at thirty-one a veteran of a decade of radical organizing and pamphleteering, would be passing through Moscow on his way to Siberia. Despite a good deal of discussion, no concrete plan was made on this occasion, and nothing was done. But the episode inspired an elaborate plan to liberate Chernyshevsky—only one of many that were to be hatched over the next fifteen years. (Given his prestige among Russian revolutionaries, it is hardly surprising that group after group was drawn to the notion of freeing him, generally with the idea that he should be set up as a journalist somewhere outside of Russia. To younger radicals who had not known him, his identity was already merging with that of his "mythic" creation, Rakhmetov.) In this instance, Ermolov donated several thousand rubles, and several false passports were procured; conversations took place between the *Ishutintsy,* St. Petersburg sympathizers, several Polish revolutionaries, and various other people. The project was still pending in the spring of 1866.

But Ishutin in particular was sick of talk; propaganda and organization were all very well, but a revolutionary deed was necessary; on one occasion he said to Zagibalov, "All of what we are doing is beside the point; in my opinion—paf, paf" (which seems best translated as "bang, bang").[24] Here we have the first, rather primitive expression of an idea that would periodically recur among the Populists, even after the failure of 1881: that the assassination of the Emperor, perhaps together with that of other high government officials, could provide the spark that would ignite the hitherto apathetic peasantry into revolution. This idea was always most attractive in times when discouragement with the *narod* was greatest; in periods of optimism, it tended to recede. In Franco Venturi's words,

if we follow the strand of revolutionary movements from *Zemlya i Volya* [Land and Liberty] onwards, we are inevitably led to conclude that the pistol shot becomes an exact substitute for . . . [an] appeal to the Tsar (or, after appeal had been proved useless, for the false manifesto used by the Polish revolutionaries to incite the peasants along the Volga). It was when these attempts had failed that the idea of assassination began to take first place. It was both an act of extreme lack of confidence in the State and a confession that the revolutionaries themselves were too immature to replace it with an organization of their own.[25]

The growing interest in regicide coincided with the development of a more extreme psychology and the flowering of the tendencies toward Machiavellianism and mystification that had previously been perceptible within the group.* One also senses for the first time a kind of pessimism, as if Ishutin and his friends felt they might not be around for long and should do something "for the people" on their way out.

---

*Dmitry Ivanov, in his testimony before the government's Commission of Inquiry, noted Ishutin's love of secrecy and mystery, his tendency to speak dramatically of mysterious persons and meetings and to imply the existence of vast, secret organizations with which he was in touch. See E. S. Vilenskaia, *Revoliutsionnoe podpol'e v Rossii (60-e gody XIX v)* (Moscow, 1965), pp. 225–26.

The First Shot

> *Having been occupied with the cause throughout al-*
> *most my entire twenty-five years of life, I either paid*
> *no attention to myself, or at times I detested myself*
> *to such a degree that I was prepared to annihilate not*
> *only all memory of myself, but my very person. In*
> *view of this the reader will understand that I lived*
> *without thinking that I would one day write my*
> *biography.*
> —Ivan Khudiakov, *Attempt at an Autobiography*

At some point in the spring of 1865, Ishutin met a young ethnographer then living in St. Petersburg. His name was Ivan Khudiakov, and although he was fairly new to serious radicalism, he
already had years of study behind him, and a considerable list of
publications on various aspects of folklore and popular education.
German Lopatin, himself just becoming a radical activist,
remembered Khudiakov in 1865 as "short, lean, sickly and extremely nervous, with a high-pitched voice and small, restless
eyes. His small, drawn figure always seemed to be listening for
some sound or exploring some corner with his eyes. An attentive
observer could not fail to see in him a turbulent, active, fanatical
nature," although this fanaticism was "of the sprightly, laughing,
chatty *'bon garçon'* kind," underneath which Khudiakov single-
mindedly pursued his aims, sparing neither himself nor others.[1]
One sign of his nervousness was a little smile that he could not

repress; throughout Khudiakov's life he seems to have been hated by those in authority (in a general, not specifically political sense), and one reason was that nervous, involuntary, "impudent" smile. Another was his courage.[2]

He first met the *Ishutintsy* when several of them had to go to St. Petersburg on some matter pertaining to the Kaluga glass factory, and they needed a reliable contact. Grigory Eliseev, then in Moscow, told them to look up Khudiakov, and they did so. A short time later—in June 1865—Khudiakov came to Moscow to meet Ishutin. They hit it off right away, and for the next year it is proper to think of Khudiakov as closely allied with Ishutin, despite the fact that he continued to live in St. Petersburg. Khudiakov had his small network of radical friends and contacts, but to refer to them *tout court* as "the St. Petersburg underground" (as Vilenskaia and other Soviet historians have done) is to inflate their significance.

Khudiakov, like other folklore enthusiasts, had been pushed to the Left by his interest in the *narod;* and in his intellectual brilliance, his heroic resolve, and his human stuntedness he stands out even in the strange world of the "1860s people." We know his early life largely from his memoirs, a litany of self-revelation, self-concealment, and self-hatred that the historian must use with extreme caution.[3] Khudiakov tells the reader in this small volume that he came into the world at seven o'clock on the evening of January 1, 1842, "with a cry of despair." His family, it was believed, had been resident in Siberia since the sixteenth century; his forebears had been prosperous merchants, but in the last couple of generations the family had come down a bit in the world. His father was a decent, earnest, rather humorless man who had done very well at the Tobolsk gymnasium in the 1820s, but had no money for the university and ended by eking out his living as an educational bureaucrat in towns and cities of north-central Siberia. His disappointments were somehow carried over into his son's life; the young man annexed his father's miseries and frustrations to his own. The father's anger also took a quasi-political form; he became acquainted with several of the exiled Decembrists, and the boy early learned that they were to be pitied and respected, not despised.

Khudiakov spent the first ten years of his life in the town of Ishim, near Tobolsk, where his father was a school inspector. In his memoirs, Khudiakov admitted that his father was a pretty good sort, despite his ignorance of history and gymnastics(!), and that he himself was a well-loved only child. (There is, significantly, no mention of his mother.) Nevertheless, his account of his childhood is basically a tale of woe. He enumerates for the reader a long list of accidents, including a truly spectacular one. When he was a very little boy, Ivan grabbed a horse by the tail and was kicked hard in the testicles. The precise aftereffects of this experience are impossible to ascertain. But he recounts the episode in detail, remarking pointedly that it explains why "with respect to both face and voice" he was subsequently so often mistaken for a castrato. Thus embedded in Khudiakov's account of his own life, the episode takes on a larger metaphorical significance: Khudiakov *felt* that he had been kicked in the balls by Life. It is equally certain that he suffered from some kind of deep sexual uncertainty. His attitude toward women in general and his wife (whom he married in 1865) in particular was equivocal. He was theoretically a strong feminist; he had written an article on "The Woman in Pre-Petrine Russia"; but he was overwhelmed by his wife's (apparently perfectly normal) sexuality, and his view of marriage was that the stronger partner was bound to enslave the weaker. The chapter in his memoirs on his marriage abounds in denunciations not only of his bride but of the tendencies toward greed and flightiness apparent in all women.[4] Maybe they'll improve when they're *really* emancipated, he wrote, but it is obvious that he's not too sanguine.[5] After his arrest and condemnation, Khudiakov forbade his wife to follow him into exile.

In the early 1850s, when Khudiakov was about ten, his father was transferred to a slot in the educational bureaucracy in Tobolsk, and the boy was able to continue his education in a reasonably good gymnasium. He did very well, graduating at the top of his class; still, he complained that the school had "killed" his intellectual and moral force and made him a "physical and intellectual skeleton."*

Khudiakov spent the year 1858–59 at the University of Kazan'. He was subsequently rather vainglorious about his ability to put dull professors down, and sweepingly contemptuous of the faculty, as were many of the brighter and more radical students there. He read Herzen at Kazan' and became an atheist, but his sympathy with the radicals at the university was general, not specific. If only Shchapov had been a professor then, he laments, he might have "found the true path five years earlier." He spent a lot of time on his studies, concentrating on ethnography and folklore; toward the end of the year he decided to pursue those studies in Moscow, under the illustrious Professor F. I. Buslaev, the following year. The second semester in Kazan' ended badly, however; he was unable to take his examinations and seems to have had a kind of small breakdown.

Khudiakov was based in Moscow between 1859 and 1862, studying with Buslaev, the first Russian academic folklorist of real significance and the country's foremost adept of the "mythological school" that derived from the brothers Grimm. The initial framework that Khudiakov learned for interpreting folktales and songs was thus not very well suited for the purposes he soon evolved. Wilhelm Grimm, in 1856, had put forward the central articles of faith: the folktales that were being collected and studied in many parts of the world showed such close resemblances that they had to be derived from a common source in "Indo-European antiquity"; and these tales were "broken-down myths," which could be interpreted only through a proper understanding of the ancient myths from which they derived.[6]

Buslaev, who had begun his literary studies as a student of Stepan Shevyrëv, the regime-oriented nationalist critic, was by this time a firm, if creative, believer in Grimm's legacy. Although Khudiakov soon repudiated Buslaev on political grounds as a teacher and exemplar, he found it much more difficult to emancipate himself from Romantic doctrines of an ancient Indo-Iranian

*Earlier he refers to his extreme piety and his addiction to the prevalent habit of onanism, both of which, he seems to believe, contributed to his feeble health.

people and the mythic base of the folktales he was collecting; not the least of the theory's strengths was that it seemed to account for the remarkable similarities in tales from cultures at the opposite ends of the globe. The seductiveness of mythology complicated and restricted Khudiakov's feeling that much folk material ought to be interpreted as popular history.[7] Unwilling to jettison the broken-down myth idea, he retained it as the base of the tale, which then, he believed, became mingled with and encrusted by the *narod*'s own contribution, in which he was more interested.

From the guarded language that Khudiakov used in his memoirs, it is not easy to get a sense of how his political attitudes developed in these crucial years when it was so easy to be "radicalized." Hostility to religion and a disposition to attribute it to popular ignorance were apparent in his work almost from the first, and strong generational antipathies soon made their appearance as well. After leaving Moscow, Khudiakov came to reject Buslaev as an "archaeologist" cut off from "life,"[8] and he was scathing about his teachers—the older ones most of all. L. F. Panteleev, the Land and Liberty organizer, got in touch with Khudiakov late in 1862, having heard, he later wrote, that Khudiakov was being politicized. But Khudiakov refused to involve himself with Panteleev or his projects.[9] Nevertheless, Khudiakov was already experimenting with propagandistic material in folkloristic form; his *Russian Booklet (Russkaia Knizhka)*, an anthology of proverbs, short tales, and essays, intended to "enlighten" the *narod*, appeared in 1863.

Khudiakov worked hard in Moscow to acquire the tools of his trade, and he began actively collecting folktales, riddles, and songs. The amount he published in his early and mid-twenties is amazing, particularly in view of his concurrent struggles with poverty. Between 1860 and 1863, he produced three small booklets of *Great Russian Fairy Tales*[10] and two collections of *Great Russian Riddles;* his considerable reputation as a collector rests on these volumes. His *Manual of Self-Instruction* (1865, 1867) was a collection of material aimed at peasants teaching themselves to read. It begins with the alphabet, goes on to proverbs (with a certain tendency: for example, "God is high and the Tsar is far away"), and ends with a series of simple narratives with socialist or scientific content. It was one of Khudiakov's favorites among his works; Herzen, Lopatin, and many other radicals liked it, used it in their classes, or took material from it. He also published several volumes containing the biographies of great men and women (Peter the Great, Catherine the Great, Washington, Lincoln, Abelard, Giordano Bruno, Columbus, Galileo, and so on), stressing the power of progressive ideas in history, however their authors may have been scorned and persecuted. Many of the heroes and heroines were of humble origins. *Ancient Russia (Drevniaia Rus', 1867)* depicted Russian history prior to Peter the Great as a brutal usurpation of the liberties of the *narod* by tsars, princes, and boyars. Stenka Razin is unequivocally the hero of this essay in popular history, which almost certainly owes something to Shchapov's view of the triumphs of Muscovy. Finally, Khudiakov published a number of scholarly articles on folkloric problems, in which his unstable blend of mythological theory and folklore as the people's own history is clearly evident.[11] Despite its subversive intent and skill in execution, a surprisingly large percentage of his propagandistic work got through the censor (though not always unscathed) and became part of the increasing body of such materials upon which rural agitators and radical schoolteachers could draw.

Khudiakov took care that a hostile world would never know the details of how his anticlericalism, popular sympathies, and intellectual radicalism finally moved him into the position of an active revolutionary. His friendship with Eliseev, whom he met early in 1863, and his contacts with several Polish revolutionaries probably helped; he was certainly sympathetic to Poland's cause during the rebellion that began in 1863, and he lived during 1864 and 1865 in a radical bohemia in which a number of Polish revolutionaries also moved.

It is a measure of how quickly Khudiakov became involved with Ishutin, and how deeply, that he and his wife left on a trip to Western Europe on August 6, 1865. The expedition was Ishutin's idea, and it had been financed by Ermolov, the purpose being to find out what was going on in the radical emigration. It seems that Ishutin had heard of some kind of organized revolutionary party abroad, with which he hoped to make contact. Khudiakov was away for more than three months, apparently spending most of his time in Geneva.* We have only the most fragmentary evidence about whom he saw there and of his impressions of various figures in the emigration.†

He returned, however, bearing important tidings. There was, he told Ishutin, a well-organized group in Western Europe devoted to a European revolutionary struggle and particularly to the extirpation of monarchs. The impact of this news on Ishutin and his friends was electric. It seems to have provided the impetus that crystallized their growing impatience and thirst for a revolutionary deed into more tightly knit organizational forms. It led, that is, to the formation of two "organizations" whose names are linked with that of Ishutin: Organization *(Organizatsiia)* and—more directly—Hell *(Ad)*. [12]

Nevertheless, Khudiakov's news of what became known as the European Revolutionary Committee was merely a catalyst. Ishutin was already preoccupied in the fall of 1865 with tighter organization and the possibility of violent measures to precipitate the revolution, before Khudiakov's return on November 20. He appears to have instructed P. F. Nikolaev, a twenty-one-year-old student whom he trusted, to draw up a charter for a new kind of organization. Although the document has not survived,[13] it set forth a program and structure that combined the group's commitment to Chernyshevsky's cooperative program with a new stress on hierarchical organization and direct action. A network of revolutionary circles was to be created, with the two most important in St. Petersburg and Moscow. Final authority was to rest with the "president" of the Moscow circle, who was to have

*Khudiakov may also have hoped to arrange the publication of some of his works abroad. He left a copy of the *Manual of Self-Instruction* with Herzen in Geneva. For a general account of Khudiakov's trip, see E. S. Vilenskaia, *Khudiakov* (Moscow, 1969), pp. 92–101.

†According to the testimony of a police informer who knew Khudiakov in exile, Khudiakov dismissed Herzen as a " 'forties liberal" and said that Ogarëv was the "principal" figure of the two. See V. G. Bazanov, "I. A. Khudiakov i pokushenie Karakozova," *Russkaia literatura* No. 4 (1962), p. 160. On the low opinion of Herzen prevailing among the *Ishutintsy*, see M. M. Klevensky and K. G. Kotel'nikov, *Pokushenie Karakozova*, Vol. I (Moscow, 1928), p. 303.

"unlimited powers," and the provincial nuclei were to be tightly subordinated to the center. Circle members were to continue to try to establish links with the peasants, specifically with religious schismatics, and to create schools and cooperative organizations. But Ishutin's favorite proposition, that the end justifies the means, was to be enshrined as dogma. Furthermore, the draft insisted that in addition to employing propaganda, the group should have recourse to "the knife," if and when it was necessary. It is not entirely clear whether "the knife" was to be used solely against political enemies or against internal deviants as well. But in another place it was suggested that the latter be threatened with "the dagger and poison." This seems to have been the first time that pressure on the membership had been suggested in anything more than a purely conversational context. Nikolaev's draft was shown only to the inner circle, however, and was never really adopted. Its primary value is that it indicates the direction of Ishutin's thinking in the fall of 1865.

Much of Ishutin's energy that fall was given over to the so-called Mutual Aid Society, which began as an offshoot of the bookbinding artel in which the *Ishutintsy* had been involved. The society disposed of a certain amount of capital, and its alleged function was to support various needy individuals and worthy projects; the Ivanova sisters' cooperative of seamstresses, for instance, was granted one hundred rubles. By 1865, Ishutin and his friends could lay their hands on a fair amount of money—not enough, perhaps, to support major communal projects over the long haul, but enough to attract various needy individuals and groups. Many of the more marginal members of the group later testified that they had been attracted to Ishutin or to one or another of his projects because of their own abject poverty and because Ishutin could supply them with a job—teaching in one of the free schools, for instance—or simply give them money when they needed it. Even such central figures as Osip Motkov, the son of a freed serf and common-law husband of Aleksandra Ivanova, and her brother, Dmitry Ivanov, stressed their financial dependence on Ishutin.[14] They were undoubtedly scrambling to save themselves at that stage, but their testimony points to the attractive power of Ishutin's resources (some money had been collected by organizations like the Mutual Aid Society, and some donated by the richer members of the group, such as Ermolov and Maksimiliian Zagibalov, a former medical student whose family estate was worth between five and ten thousand rubles). And it is certainly true that they were desperately poor; for many of the recruits of 1865–66, Ishutin must have been a powerfully attractive figure, with his radical and intransigent idealism, his resources, and the sense he conveyed, directly and indirectly, of being in touch with a myriad organizations and individuals with big plans and prospects. Here is how one participant remembers Ishutin addressing a meeting, called to organize a communal farm:

[We] sat in a circle; in the center was Ishutin the general (we thought of Ishutin as our general). We were all excited. Ishutin, gesticulating with his right hand, is recounting something with passion and anima-tion. The picture changes: everyone remains in the same position with thoughtful faces. Ishutin, seeing that he has hit home, stands up, and to achieve an even greater effect, walks around the room, breath-ing heavily. I don't remember how many times I saw such tableaux.[15]

In any case, the real purpose of the Mutual Aid Society was recruitment. There were large meetings on Sundays, and smaller meetings on Wednesdays to set the agenda. If a prospect was judged to be "ready," he or she was invited to come to the Wednesday meetings as well. After the founding of Organiza-tion, its meetings took over the Wednesday slot. From then on, the Sunday meetings constituted a kind of gathering of Organiza-tion's applicant pool.

Thus the ground was well prepared for Khudiakov when he arrived in late November, bearing his tidings of the European Revolutionary Committee. (He must have had either the First International or Bakunin's International Brotherhood in mind, but he and Ishutin engaged in so much exaggeration and mystifi-cation in describing their relations—present and future—with the committee that no one has ever discovered for sure upon which Western body the accounts were based.) Khudiakov certainly provided the basic information, but the decision to create both Organization and Hell had to be made by Ishutin. Apparently, there was also a good deal of talk about "fulminate of mercury" and "Orsini-type bombs" as possible weapons.*

A word of caution is necessary at this point. It is almost impossible to avoid discussing Organization and Hell as if they were actually functioning bodies—like the Committee of Public Safety or the First International. But in a situation like this, the line demarcating an organization from the *idea* of an organization is rather blurred. As one reads through the testimony of the accused at their trial, it is hard to say whether either Organization or Hell ever *really* existed. For the members of the tribunal it sufficed that a person had been present at a certain number of meetings where the purposes and tasks of Organization were discussed. This was what "membership" was. Over a period of about three months a number of charters were discussed, but none was ever officially adopted; it is far from clear that Organization ever actually *did* anything as a body except discuss what it should be. It is therefore especially difficult to say when Organization actually came into such existence as it did have. Some members spoke vaguely of the final days of 1865, others of January 1866. The government's investigative body decided with admirable precision that Organization was born on February 7.

Far more important than any question of dates is the moral and political atmosphere that surrounded the group at the time and their view of how and to what ends they should organize themselves. If we compare the draft charters with what we know of the structure of Land and Liberty, a new stress on hierarchy, organization, discipline—and terror—is apparent at once. All of them made the provincial centers subordinate to the "center" in Moscow. (In some drafts, there were *two* centers, one in Moscow and one in St. Petersburg; there was some friction about Moscow's leading role.) And the fundamental aim of Organization was to use "all possible means," including regicide, to over-

---

*Fulminate of mercury was an explosive salt of fulminic acid, often used in the manufacture of explosives; Orsini was an Italian nationalist who attempted to assassinate Louis Napoleon with a bomb in 1858.

throw the existing order and inaugurate the social republic.

Many of the more recent recruits disagreed with the *Ishutintsy* on matters of detail, however, and as the weeks passed, these disagreements grew rather than diminished. By late March, as we shall see, Ishutin's position and his whole attitude toward making the revolution had been called into question. Even at the outset there was some disagreement as to whether final authority should rest with a majority of the Moscow center, or whether some single individual (read: Ishutin) should have that power. Should the group plan on an "armed uprising"? Should each member carry a revolver and learn to shoot? It is difficult to reconstruct the debate from the inevitably self-serving testimony of the participants after they had been arrested, but the answer of the majority was apparently yes. Another question that came in for a great deal of discussion was what Organization's attitude should be toward members who got cold feet and tried to leave or who actually "betrayed" their comrades. Here the majority favored what they euphemistically called "punitive measures," but which must have meant death.

There was an increasingly heightened and feverish quality about these discussions, marked by a blend of childishness, cynicism, and ruthlessness. We have already mentioned the spirit of self-sacrifice that animated the *Ishutintsy.* Early in 1866, this began to take on strange and even grotesque forms. Viktor Fedoseev, whose older brother, Pavel, had been involved in radical politics for several years, became a member of Organization through the Mutual Aid Society. Shortly after Christmas, it occurred to him that he could make a real contribution to the cause by murdering his father and then placing his estate at the disposal of Organization. After brooding over this idea for some time, he went to his hometown in April, but was talked out of the plan by his brother.[16] Other unusual fund-raising activities were also discussed. Mail robbery was one, and it was proposed that a group member become the "lackey" of a rich merchant and then rob him.[17] One may perhaps see in these ideas, none of which ever got beyond the talking stage, the ancestors of the bank robberies that were carried out by the

Bolsheviks forty years later to enrich their party's treasury.

If Organization grew in part out of a previous felt need for greater discipline and control, Hell was the direct outgrowth of what Khudiakov told Ishutin about the European Revolutionary Committee. It was, in fact, to have some kind of connection with the European organization. In Russia, its main functions were two: from its membership was to be selected the man who would assassinate the Emperor (the timetable was very vague); and it was to supervise and control the activities of Organization. Thus Organization was to be directed, in an unspecified fashion, not only by its own hierarchy but by a semisecret body drawn from its own membership.*

The *Ishutintsy* began talking about Hell at approximately the same time as they formed Organization. It is best described as semi-secret because although systematic discussion of it was confined to an inner circle, word soon leaked out, and Ishutin discovered that many of his comrades—especially those who had not been tapped for membership—had doubts about such an organization and their relationship to it. Disentangling the strands of truth, falsehood, half-truth, and omission in the discussions about Hell is exceptionally difficult, since nearly all the information that we possess was delivered either to the government's Commission of Inquiry or in court. It was clear to all the defendants that although membership in Organization was a serious matter, membership in, or even knowledge of, Hell was far worse, since Hell was directly linked to regicide. Most of the defendants denied any knowledge of Hell; those who could not tried to maintain—not altogether implausibly—that Hell was merely an "idea" that had been discussed. Ishutin steadfastly denied that there had ever been more than loose talk.

Still, extensive discussions about Hell did take place, and in them the psychological extremism of the *Ishutintsy* is most graphically revealed: their isolation, their adolescent romanticism, their search for a heroic role for themselves in their coun-

*Vilenskaia considers Ishutin, Ermolov, N. P. Stranden, Zagibalov, Iurasov, Karakozov, Motkov, Shaganov, and Nikolaev to have been members of Hell. Note the heavy preponderance of the old Penza nucleus. See *Revoliutsionnoe podpol'e v Rossii (60-e gody XIX v)* (Moscow, 1965), p. 395.

try's history, their longing for "the deed." The member of Hell who was chosen to do the actual job was to prepare himself well in advance.

The potential assassins were to draw lots to determine who should make the attempt, and the man chosen was to cut himself off from his colleagues and adopt a way of life quite at variance with that of a revolutionary. He was to get drunk, find friends in the most doubtful circles, and even denounce people to the police. On the day of the assassination he was to use chemicals for disfiguring his face, so as to avoid being recognized, and to have in his pocket a manifesto explaining his reasons for what he was doing. As soon as he had carried out his attempt, he was to poison himself, and in his place another member of *Hell* would be chosen to continue the work which he had begun.[18]

Unquestionably, this program stirred up considerable opposition. At the trial, Osip Motkov and Dmitry Ivanov came forward as the leaders of those who had opposed Hell and had argued instead that the group as a whole should confine itself to attempting to implement the program of *What Is To Be Done?* Motkov in particular painted a striking picture of the development of opposition to Hell, to Ishutin's leadership, and subsequently to Karakozov's attempt. Motkov tried to persuade the court that it was the hard core of veterans (on occasion referred to as the *Ipatovtsy*, because their landlord was named Ipatov) who developed Hell, while a second group, whom he ingeniously called the "novices" and who were drawn into Ishutin's orbit rather later, fought against the *Ipatovtsy*.[19] But no such clear-cut division in fact existed. Still, Ishutin's self-dramatization and obsession with secrecy, as well as Karakozov's obvious mental instability, were disturbing, quite apart from the discussions about Hell, which reached the majority of the membership in the form of vague rumors. Aleksandr Ivanov presented the most dramatic tableau of the developing opposition to Ishutin and his inner circle of some ten or a dozen. He related that he and several others planned to threaten Ishutin with death in order to get the real facts about Hell; they also planned to threaten the *Ipatovtsy* with denunciation to the police if they did not have Karakozov committed and agree to leave Moscow.[20]

All of which brings us to Dimitry Karakozov and his decision to assassinate Tsar Alexander. Professor Shestakov of the University of Kazan' remembered Karakozov's "pale and tired face, hair flowing onto his shoulders; he was noticeable for the carelessness of his clothes."[21] He was just under twenty-six when he made his attempt, and he was a veteran of five years of personal hardship and vaguely "political" activity. His family were poor, provincial gentry, and the family fortunes had been declining for several generations; prior to the Emancipation, the family apparently owned fewer than fifty peasants. Karakozov's father had served in various posts in the Penza bureaucracy, most of them having to do with the courts. At one time he was a district police officer. About Karakozov's mother we know very little, save that she was Ishutin's aunt. By 1866, both of his parents were dead.

Karakozov finished the Penza gymnasium in 1860 and enrolled in the juridical faculty at the University of Kazan'. He had attended for only a few weeks when he was expelled, along with a number of other students, for "harassing" a professor; such episodes were common enough at the time, as we have seen. He remained out of the university for two years, during which time he lived primarily at home. He worked for a month and a half as a clerk for a local arbiter of the peace, helping to work out details of peasant emancipation. But the arrogance of his boss, together with the general indifference to, and incomprehension of, the needs of the peasantry that he found to be characteristic of the arbiters as a group, considerably deepened his hostility toward the existing order; according to Ishutin, he never spoke of this experience save with indignation and even fury.[22]

Karakozov returned to the University of Kazan' in the fall of 1863, spent a year there, and then transferred to the juridical faculty of the University of Moscow. By this time, he had almost no financial resources, and like many another poor student, he attempted to eke out a living by giving lessons. But he was unable to make ends meet, and in the fall of 1865, he was dismissed from the university for failure to pay tuition. Taken all in all, his was an experience calculated to radicalize a far more sanguine and stable person than Karakozov appears to have been.

Many of his comrades testified that Karakozov was prone to depression and hypochondria. Although he was normally an extremely quiet, solitary person who said little or nothing in meetings, he spoke often to his friends of a desire to commit suicide. On occasion in larger groups, he would burst out with something. One fringe member of the group once heard him say—of regicide—"Don't talk about it—do it. Those who talk about it won't do it." He was suddenly angry.[23] He would spend days at a time by himself, walking around the city or lying on his bed in his room.[24]

On November 11, 1865, Karakozov was admitted to the clinic at the University of Moscow, where he remained for more than a month. He complained to the doctors of a "wracking pain in his stomach, frequent constipation, of an unpleasant sensation of heat in the area of his spinal vertebrae, difficulty with intellectual activities and a poor psychological condition."[25] This last would appear to have been the key factor. The doctors, however, pronounced him to be suffering from intestinal catarrh, compounded by "moderate" exhaustion. Intestinal catarrh was the least of Karakozov's problems; the doctors' report was hasty and superficial. At his trial, Karakozov's initial line of defense was that his disordered state of mind was the "first cause" of his attempt.

Neither Ishutin personally nor the members of Hell collectively were *directly* involved in Karakozov's decision to assassinate the Emperor. He arrived at the idea in an agonized, inward, personal way. His psychological condition clearly worsened after his release from the university clinic. His preoccupation with suicide appears to have grown. It is plausible to suggest, as Venturi does, that he "ceaselessly tormented himself with the thought of having to die before doing anything for the people."[26] In February 1866, he left word in Moscow that he had decided to drown himself and then undertook a pilgrimage of some kind to the Trinity–St. Sergius Monastery in Zagorsk, several kilometers north of Moscow.

Nevertheless, Karakozov's decision to assassinate Alexander

was taken under the influence of the ideas being discussed in connection with the European Revolutionary Committee and the founding of Hell. That Ishutin was the prime mover in those discussions must have impressed his cousin deeply. Perhaps even more important than the "ideas" was the intellectual and moral atmosphere. One contemporary claimed, as well, that ideas of regicide were by no means confined to Ishutin's circle, that other student radicals were preoccupied with them as well.[27] The combination of regicide and suicide became deeply attractive to Karakozov; indeed, he must have come to view it as an ideal solution to his problems. He no longer wished to live, and he wanted to make some kind of supreme sacrifice for the people.

The events that followed bear out this hypothesis. What is difficult to determine is the precise attitude that his comrades in Moscow and Khudiakov in St. Petersburg took toward his maturing intentions.[28] Certainly Karakozov set about the assassination according to the prescriptions that had been discussed in the meetings where Hell and regicide had been the prime topics. Having procured a revolver and several kinds of poison, Karakozov went to live in St. Petersburg in early March 1866. He saw Khudiakov a number of times and told him what he intended to do. The version of events that the *Ipatovtsy* gave at the trial ran roughly as follows. Having learned of Karakozov's intentions from Khudiakov, Ishutin sent Ermolov and Stranden, two of his most trusted disciples, to St. Petersburg to persuade him not to do it and to bring him back to Moscow. The two ran into Karakozov "by chance," and although they did not succeed in bringing him back with them, they did exact from him a promise that he would not make the attempt. Meanwhile, Ishutin sent a letter, which reached Karakozov on March 21, and he then did return to Moscow on the twenty-fifth. By this time, Karakozov had written a manifesto, from which all mention of regicide had been deleted, and distributed it, rather inefficiently. It may well be, as Vilenskaia suggests, that Karakozov originally intended to make the attempt on March 19 or 20.

What Ishutin and his friends said to Karakozov in Moscow is quite unclear. We do know that a few days later Karakozov went back to St. Petersburg. Ishutin and his friends claimed that he did so without either their approval or their knowledge, but we have only their word for that. Khudiakov, almost certainly, was in doubt only about when Karakozov would actually make the attempt; he had given Karakozov the money to buy the pistol, and he was under no illusions as to how it would be spent. A young doctor with radical connections, Dr. Aleksandr Kobylin,[29] had given him several different kinds of poison, which he intended to take after shooting the Emperor, as had been earlier agreed upon by the *Ishutintsy* in such a case.

On April 4, Karakozov entered the Summer Gardens and fired on Alexander as the Emperor was about to enter his carriage. He was dressed in peasant costume, and in his pocket, along with the strychnine, morphine, and prussic acid that Kobylin had given him, were two copies of the manifesto that he had earlier written and addressed to his "worker friends":

Brothers, for a long time I have been tormented by the thought which has given me no rest: why does my beloved, simple Russian *narod,* by which all Russia is supported, live in such poverty? Why does it not benefit by its unremitting hard work, its sweat and blood . . . ? Why, together with our eternal toilers, the simple people —peasants, factory hands and other workmen—do others who do nothing live in luxurious houses and palaces—gentry parasites, a horde of officials and other rich people, and they live at the expense of the simple people . . . they suck the blood of the peasant. . . . I wanted to find out what clever people thought about this, I began to read various books, I devoted myself to reading many books about how people lived in former, olden times. And brothers, I learned that it's the tsars who are the real culprits in all our misfortunes. The tsars gathered to themselves officials to make it easier for them to fleece the people, to make every kind of requisition on them, and so that the people would not think of opposing these collectors, they created for themselves, most opportunely, a permanent army. So that the officials would sincerely serve the tsarist belly and not feel sorry for the peasant's pocket, the tsars began to reward this scum in all sorts of ways. They called them gentry, landowners, and began to hand out land to them right and left. The peasants who until then had been owners of this same land, were delivered into slavery at the hands of their landlord-officials. . . . Thus serfdom came to us in Rus'. Tsars, officials and landlords began to live at the expense of peasant labor. Think about this, brothers, consider it, and you will see that the tsar is chief among the landlords; he has never stretched out his hand to the peasant because—he is the greatest enemy of the simple people.[30]

Thus did Karakozov launch his paper thunderbolt against the rock of peasant monarchism. He then went on to expose the Emancipation and excoriate its imperial author. He described his travels around the country and the popular misery that he everywhere encountered. And so he concluded "sadly,"

I decided to annihilate the tsar evildoer and to die myself for my beloved people. If I succeed, I die with the thought that my death will be useful to my dear friend, the Russian peasant. And if I should not succeed, I believe all the same that people will be found who will follow my path. If I do not succeed—they will succeed. My death will be an example to them and will inspire them. Let the Russian people recognize its chief and mightiest enemy—whether it be Alexander II or Alexander III—and nothing else matters.[31]

Then, without mentioning the word "revolution," Karakozov spoke of his great hope: that the death of the Tsar would mean the automatic destruction or disappearance of the host of petty tyrants whom he had called into existence. With these creatures gone, Karakozov said, there would be liberty *(volia)* indeed. He spoke of the communal future in generally Populist language, but in such a way as to remind us of the particular focus that *What Is To Be Done?* had provided the *Ishutintsy:*

The land will not belong to idle parasites but to artels, societies of the workers themselves. And capital will not be squandered by the tsar, the landlords and the tsarist magnates, but will belong to the workers' artels themselves. The artels will produce a profitable return on this capital and the income will be divided equally among all the workers in the artels. And if the Russian people has these means, it will be able to administer itself even without the tsar . . . everyone will be equal and Russian working people will live happily and honestly, working only for themselves and not for the benefit of the insatiable greed of the Russian tsars, the tsarist magnates, the tsar's family, the landlords and the other parasites. . . . This is my last word to my worker friends. Let each of you, into whose hands this leaflet falls, copy it and give it to your acquaintances to read, and let them put it into other hands.[32]

At the end, Karakozov came back to his own hopes and the message that he wanted to convey to the working people of Russia, whose attention he had despaired of attracting in any other way:

> May the workers recognize that the person writing these lines was thinking of their happiness and that they must look after themselves, rely upon nobody but themselves, conquer their own happiness and deliver all Russia from the plunderers and scoundrels.[33]

Karakozov's shot went wild—either because he was too nervous, or because he had not learned to shoot, or because his cheap pistol misfired. He ran across the garden but was quickly apprehended by two guards.

Alexander came over to him; perhaps under the impression that he was a disappointed office seeker, he asked, "What do you want?"

"I don't want anything," Karakozov replied. When the Emperor asked him who he was, he was able to recover slightly. "A Russian," he said.

Then Alexander told the guards to take him to the Third Section, and a number of bystanders were taken off as well, in case they had anything to do with the criminal.

Despite the hopes of Karakozov (and Khudiakov as well), popular disillusion with the Emperor, with "Little Father Tsar," was still far in the future. The pathos of Karakozov was comprehensible only within the most restricted *obshchestvo* circles. Elsewhere in the country, the initial shock turned to patriotic and pious thanksgiving; the hand of God was generally seen in Alexander's deliverance. Although the most reactionary political forces were quick to exploit this mood, it was genuine enough; ironically, for a time *obshchestvo* and the *narod* did find themselves at one—in relief at the Emperor's survival!

In keeping with his deepest feelings (and his costume), Karakozov maintained for several days that he was a peasant. But it proved impossible to conceal his identity for long. He had on his person a long letter to Ishutin (whose last name, however, did not appear) and a scrap of paper with the name of an accomplice on it. His landlord for the past several days soon missed him, guessed who he was, had his room searched. Characteristically, he had been careless about crucial details. He had left some papers behind; Ishutin's address was written on an envelope. Most of the Moscow group were quickly rounded up, together with Khudiakov—twenty-some persons. General Murav'ëv, fresh from the "pacification" of Poland, was chosen to head up the Commission of Inquiry that was quickly established.

After a lengthy preliminary investigation, thirty-five people were brought to trial. No one presented a model of revolutionary fortitude, although Khudiakov did not disgrace himself by breaking down. Karakozov spent long hours on his knees in his prison cell. He wrote several times to Alexander. His first letter was resolute, composed, unrepentant; it repeated some of what he had written to the workers. He predicted the outbreak of the revolution in the near future and concluded: "As for me, Sire, I can only say that if I had not one but a hundred lives, and if the people demanded that I should sacrifice all the hundred lives to promote their welfare, I swear that I would not hesitate a moment to make that sacrifice."[34] But at his trial he implicated Khudiakov and tried to plead what amounted to insanity, plausibly enough. Upon receiving the verdict that he was to be hanged, Karakozov wrote several more notes to the Emperor, conceding the "monstrous" nature of his offense and again claiming that his abnormal condition of mind was to blame for what he had done. Although he had apparently not been a believer,* he now appealed to Alexander, as Christian to Christian, to forgive him.

*If we look at Karakozov's behavior, beginning with his trip to the Trinity–St. Sergius Monastery in February and ending with his long hours of prayer in prison, it is possible to conclude that he underwent a genuine religious conversion. From a psychological point of view, this would seem quite plausible.

The Emperor resolved this dilemma by replying that as a Christian he freely forgave him, but as the Tsar he could not. On September 3, 1866, Karakozov was hanged in St. Petersburg.

Nearly everyone whose involvement with Ishutin had been more than fleeting received a sentence of some severity. Like Karakozov, Ishutin was to be hanged, but at the very last instant the sentence was commuted to penal servitude for life. After several years of confinement in the Schlüsselburg Fortress, Ishutin was sent to Siberia, where in 1879 he died of tuberculosis in a prison hospital.*

Khudiakov needed a good lawyer, and fortunately he got one. He was attacked with special violence in the right-wing press, largely because the influential journalist Mikhail Katkov took a particular dislike to him. Perhaps the xenophobic Katkov associated him with some kind of subversive Petersburg cosmopolitanism; certainly he was enraged by Khudiakov's manner: defiant but slightly cringing; the high voice and the flickering, nervous half-smile. But Khudiakov was convicted only of failing to denounce Ishutin and the Moscow conspiracy, for which he was to be sent to "the most remote part" of Siberia, which meant the tiny village of Verkhoiansk, in the extreme northeast of the Asian continent, which currently boasts the lowest recorded temperature of any city in the world. His young child was dead of smallpox by this time, and he did not allow his wife to accompany him. His mother, that mysterious figure whom he never mentioned in his memoirs, sold her house and joined him in exile.

For a time, Khudiakov lived in Verkhoiansk with two local cossacks in a tent (this must have been prior to his mother's arrival). He was consumed with the desire to do useful work, as were so many Russian political exiles, and he worked hard for a while on the language of the local Iakut people, producing a grammar and the beginnings of a dictionary. Neither, appar-

---

*For an interview with Ishutin shortly before his death, see S. Bogdanov, "Ishutin," *Katorga i ssylka*, No. 17 (1925), pp. 248–50. Ishutin denied to his interlocutor, another political prisoner, that the group had ever seriously contemplated regicide. He spoke instead of the postrevolutionary world that would come into existence someday, of the building of artels and communes, of how the political authority of the future would somehow emerge from an "alliance" of the communes, which would own all the land in Russia. The language throughout is vaguely Populist; there is no residue of Jacobin extremism.

ently, survived, but his quite ambitious "description" of the region (from the standpoint of climate, geology, botany, and so on) turned up recently and has appeared in a Soviet edition.[35]

Despite these ambitious efforts to stave off despair, the accumulated disappointments of his life (including the realization that Russia was far from a revolution of any sort) took their toll, and in the early 1870s, signs of incipient madness began to appear. There was less and less that, in view of moral considerations, he felt able to eat: vegetables, too, were living things. He finally decided that eating was not a necessity, merely a habit. He began to suffer from what Vilenskaia refers to as "hallucinations with a religious content"; from another point of view, they might be called visions. After he began to have trouble with his memory as well, the local authorities tried to get permission to move him to where he could be institutionalized, but were unsuccessful. He died on September 19, 1876, shortly after the death of his mother, who had remained with him throughout his exile.[36]

Karakozov's assassination attempt had, of course, an enormous impact in Russia, and some abroad. Most working people misunderstood Ishutin and Karakozov in precisely the same way that they had misunderstood the student rebels of the early 1860s— or so it would appear. Any open expression of support for Karakozov would have been both pointless and dangerous, of course. Far better to choose to believe—and this belief was encouraged by various local authorities—that Karakozov's act had been a protest *against* the Emancipation by an agent of disgruntled serf owners. At first glance, however, it is somewhat more surprising to find the United States Congress adopting this position; a joint resolution congratulated the Emperor and the nation on Alexander's escape from the machinations of an "enemy of the emancipation."[37] But it is understandable that American politicians should have imposed their own interpretation on events. In Moscow, students were attacked on the streets, as they had been four years earlier, sometimes by suspiciously well-organized groups; on occasion, they needed protection by soldiers. In the countryside, rumors spread of an aristocratic plot against the Tsar Liberator.[38]

The government had a popular hero of its own to promote: he was a "peasant" named Osip Komissarov, who, it was alleged, had jolted the hand of the assassin and saved Alexander's life. Thus the government countered the revolutionary myth of the peasantry with a myth of its own: a true representative of the *narod* had saved the Little Father. Komissarov became the man of the hour. His portrait was displayed, together with that of the Emperor, all over St. Petersburg; he was eulogized in the press and treated to a seemingly endless round of banquets; he was given a large estate by a group of landowners from Kostroma province and a big house in the capital by someone else; he was ennobled by the Emperor.[39]

But the whole thing was a fake. Komissarov had not jolted Karakozov's hand; he was not a peasant, but a capmaker well along the road to alcoholism. Having been taken to police headquarters in the roundup of bystanders, he had tried to extricate himself by claiming that he had actually *prevented* the villainous aristocrat from carrying out his nefarious plan.

After a while, Komissarov was forgotten, as his drunken and stuttering performances at the banquets were more embarrassing than edifying. I have been unable to discover what happened to his estate, with the "lackeys" and coachmen who had been hired for him, or to the town house. But he did not die until 1892, so the legend that he "soon drank himself to death" appears to be the wishful thinking of the Left.

The government did not limit itself to such public-relations ventures as the banquet campaign for Komissarov ("the Weapon of God"). As they had after the fires, the Right realized that the latest revolutionary outrage presented a golden opportunity. Mikhail Katkov thundered against radicals *and* reformers in the *Moscow Gazette*, demanding that A. V. Golovnin, the moderate and canny minister of education, resign. Golovnin's position quickly became impossible; while Katkov was describing him as a "Herzen in uniform," Dmitry Tolstoy mounted a more considered attack on his policies in the Council of Ministers.[40] Within

ten days, Alexander had thanked him for his services and replaced him with Tolstoy, who moved over from the Holy Synod.
Prince V. A. Dolgorukov, the head of the Third Section, chose to
blame himself for Karakozov's attempt, and within an hour of the
episode had handed in his resignation to his master, confessing
brokenly that he felt too old to deal with such things. Count
A. A. Suvorov, governor-general of St. Petersburg, also resigned
and was replaced by General F. F. Trepov, who had already
distinguished himself as a tough and ruthless chief of police in
Warsaw. Vera Zasulich shot him in 1878 for having a prisoner
brutally flogged; by that time he had become one of the best-
hated men in Russia.

The most important change was probably the replacement of
Dolgorukov by General P. A. Shuvalov, a man who has recently
been described as "terrifyingly able" and "known even to his
intimates as 'power loving' and 'cunning.' "[41] The new head of
Russia's political police wasted no time. He closed down the
Contemporary and the Russian Word—this time permanently.
Measures were threatened against "nihilist women who wear no
crinolines and round hats, blue glasses and short hair."[42] Shuvalov
substantially augmented funds for various security agencies, but
the heart of his program was to increase enormously the power
and scope of the provincial governors, who at the same time were
to be subject to much greater centralized control; this Shuvalov
easily accomplished. He then turned his attention to the newly
created zemstvos, the local administrative organs, which he regarded as even more subversive of public order and morals than
students and Poles. The zemstvos soon found themselves the
object of a concerted campaign of official harassment, and the St.
Petersburg zemstvo was actually shut down for a time.[43]

In the post-Karakozov climate, the decimated ranks of the Left
scrambled to save what they could. Herzen, his influence in
Russia now almost totally gone, denounced Karakozov in the
May 1 number of the Bell as "some fanatic,"[44] and Nekrasov—
radical, poet, and editor of the Contemporary—made a truly
spectacular submission. Apparently hoping to save his journal, he
read two poems at formal dinners in the precincts of the highly

conservative English Club. One was a paean to Komissarov,* and the other—which *must* have stuck in his throat—was a tribute to Count Murav'ëv, head of the Commission of Inquiry that had investigated the Karakozov attempt. Progressive circles had dubbed Murav'ëv "the Hangman of Vilna" for the brutality with which he had suppressed the Polish rebellion, and Nekrasov's reputation for opportunism grew.

Almost nothing now was left of that "liberal" public opinion that had been on the ascendant between 1855 and 1862. Almost all the major figures of the Left were in emigration or in prison —or had lost their following. By contrast, the influence of Mikhail Katkov was increasing dramatically. His constituency had been growing since 1862, but he now became the confidant of high government officials and entered into a kind of collaboration with the new minister of education, Dmitry Tolstoy. A leftish prerevolutionary Russian historian called him the "mouthpiece of the state,"[45] and at certain moments, at any rate, he was probably the most influential man in Russia.

Politically speaking, Tolstoy was a somewhat more complex figure than Katkov. The increase in state control, the classical curriculum, and the general reorganization of Russian higher education that he introduced after 1866 have generally been interpreted as political obscurantism, pure and simple. Recently, however, the American historian Allen Sinel has argued that Tolstoy's aims were less narrow and negative; in addition to stamping out sedition, he was genuinely concerned with the creation of a disciplined and able governing elite for Russia.[46] However that may be, Tolstoy certainly wished in the short run to assert greater state control over the Russian universities, which he correctly observed were the breeding grounds of radicalism and sedition.

To this end stricter rules governing student conduct were issued in 1867. The police were instructed to report student delinquents to

*Nekrasov felt constrained to refer to Komissarov as "the Weapon of God," as did everyone else. For a balanced account of the episode, which takes full account of the panic on the Left, see Kornei Chukovsky, "Poet ili palach," *Nekrasov* (Leningrad, 1926), pp. 5–55.

university authorities, and they in turn were to inform the police of any student acts that might raise doubts of political and moral reliability. Tolstoy's new rules forbade the students to organize public entertainments in order to raise funds for their impoverished colleagues. Funds raised by outsiders were not to be given directly to the students, but to university officials for distribution to those in "genuine need" and "worthy of support."[47]

The period following Karakozov's attempt has gone down in Russian history under the name of "the white terror," and although the terror was mild enough by twentieth-century standards, it did appear for a time as if the reactionaries were to have matters their own way. Even within the universities there were patriotic demonstrations of a variety of kinds. In Moscow, a large crowd of students (led by a violinist playing "God Save the Tsar") marched around town, ending at the offices of the *Moscow Gazette,* where they hailed Katkov vociferously.[48]

Populist sentiment and ideas, of course, could not be stamped out, but they were driven even farther underground. Disillusion with the *narod,* though, reached one of its periodic high points. The career of Sergei Nechaev, to which we shall now turn, marked the culmination of the attempt to substitute the lone figure of the dedicated revolutionary for the strength of a mass movement. It also marked the acme of the revolutionary amorality and mystification that were so striking in Organization and Hell.

11

In Pursuit of Nechaev

*"The oath of the Abreks. You don't know it? At mid-
night the Abrek creeps into the mosque and swears:
'By this holy place, that I venerate, I swear that from
today on I will be an outcast. I will shed human
blood and have pity for no one. I will wage war on
everybody. I swear to rob people of everything dear
to their hearts, their conscience and their honor. I
will stab the child on his mother's breast, put fire to
the poorest beggar's hut and bring sorrow to all
places where men rejoice. If I do not fulfill this oath,
if love or pity ever creep into my heart, may I never
see my father's grave again, may water never quench
my thirst nor bread my hunger, may my body be cast
on to the road and a dirty dog relieve himself on
it.' ": The farmer's voice was solemn, his face turned
toward the sun, his eyes were green and deep. "Yes,"
he said, "that is the oath of the Abreks."
"Who swears this oath?"
"Men who have suffered much injustice."*
—Kurban Said, *Ali & Nino*

*Shatov says to Uspensky: "The Kingdom of Heaven
is at hand." Nechaev joins in: "Yes, in June."*
—Fëdor Dostoevsky, *Notebooks for The Possessed*

With the figure of Sergei Nechaev, Russian Jacobinism presents
us with its most extreme manifestation. Nechaev, of course, is of

his time and place. He cannot be understood without reference to the gloomy provincial hole where he grew up, without reference to the growth and mechanization of the textile industry there, which was transforming thousands of serf families like his, and would transform millions more. And we should see him, too, as Stendhal or Balzac would have seen him at the dawn of his lurid career: a bright and ambitious young man, hating the social circumstances that seemed to hold him back from his destiny in the capital. And we must see him in relation to the intellectual and moral world of Pisarev, Ishutin, and Karakozov.

Despite the efforts of some historians to understand him as either just another Russian Jacobin or as a mere gangster, we ought to be skeptical of such deflation. A consideration of Nechaev's career poses clearly for the first time a vital question that the twentieth century has been forced to live out, if not to resolve: the question of revolutionary ethics. What are the sources of value and what are the moral limits, if any, for a secular revolutionary confronting the established order? Nechaev's contribution to the discussion was the first sketch (a small, crude sketch, to be sure) of what it might be like if the revolutionary were emancipated from all traditional ethical restraints.

A consuming involvement in terrorism is sometimes thought of as analogous to a state of war existing between the individual or group and the larger society; for many terrorists the fit is a good one. But this analogy implies that some "ordinary" peacetime moral code has been suspended only for the duration of hostilities. Nechaev didn't really believe that, or did so in some purely theoretical fashion. He believed that *the revolution itself conferred all value.* Neither his revolutionary contemporaries nor his revolutionary successors have been able to accept him. Nor have they really been able to repudiate him. The question posed by his life remains open in a world that must deal with revolutionary terrorism on a considerable scale.

The only account of Nechaev's childhood that we possess at present is that of his sister, F. A. Postnikova; it was recorded by a Soviet historian in 1922, when she was seventy-six years old, and it had presumably long since achieved the status of family legend.

Prior to 1861, Sergei and his family were serfs. So his attitude toward the Emancipation was entirely different from that of the children of *obshchestvo*, whose naive hopes were followed by a disappointment almost as naive. According to Postnikova, Sergei and his two sisters were brought up largely by their grandparents. Their mother, a skilled seamstress (and, it would seem, a beautiful woman), died when they were all quite young; and their father (who was "strict" with the children) then left the town of Ivanovo and took a job elsewhere as a bartender in a tavern. The children subsequently lived with their grandfather, a painter who worked primarily on local churches and also decorated peasant implements (the shafts on carts are mentioned).

After the children's mother had been dead for a time, her parents asked their son-in-law to marry again, presumably for the sake of the children. He did so, again to a woman who was a dressmaker, and returned to Ivanovo, where he helped his first wife's father with the painting. From time to time, he also worked as a waiter, or a "lackey," serving tea, drinks, and hors d'oeuvres in the houses of the Ivanovo rich. Young Sergei, according to his sister, hated this and wished his father wouldn't do it. (Was he called upon to carry trays himself? One can't help wondering.)

When the boy was nine or ten (this would be about 1857), his father put him to work as a messenger boy in one of the local factory offices. When he had been on the job for only a short time, he lost a letter and was severely beaten by his father. From this episode Sergei's sister dated his resolve to educate himself and escape from the life of humiliation and poverty that seemed to stretch before him.[1] Over the next few years, the desire to escape, to "make it," was to be eclipsed by other ideas—of revenge and revolution.

These memories seem almost too apropos, drawn from a primer on psychobiography—the "strict" father, the humiliation of this powerful figure cringing before the local plutocracy (Ivanovo was a developing textile center, which was with consid-

erable exaggeration referred to as "the Russian Manchester"),
then the crucial episode that leads to the turning point in the
boy's life. In view of the fact that the account dates from 1922 and
of the sympathy with which Nechaev's sister regarded his life,
the probability is high that we are getting a kind of well-polished
family myth, one that had been in the making for a long time.
But myths can be useful; this one directs our attention to the
tremendous class hatred that animated Nechaev.

In September 1870, when he was about twenty-two years old,
Nechaev published an eight-page "periodical" entitled *Commune (Obshchina)*, much of which was devoted to telling the
Western European radical public "who he was" and what he (and
his "party") wanted. In it he answered those questions as follows:

We are the children of hungry, deprived fathers and of mothers who
have been driven to stupefaction and imbecility.
We grew up surrounded by filth and ignorance, among insults and
humiliations; from the cradle we were despised and oppressed by
every possible scoundrel who lives happily under the existing order.
We are they for whom family was a foretaste of hard labor, for
whom the best part of their youth was spent in the struggle with
poverty and hunger; the time of love, the time of passion [was consumed in] the grim pursuit of a piece of bread.
We are they whose whole past overflowed with bitterness and
suffering, whose future holds the same humiliations, insults, hungry
days, sleepless nights, and finally trials, jails, prisons, the mines or the
gallows.
We find ourselves in an unbearable position and, somehow or
other, we want to get out of it.
That is why in the *alteration of the existing order of social relations*
consists all our wished for aspirations, all our cherished aims.
We can want only a popular revolution.
We want it and we will make it.[2]

Behind the rhetoric, one feels the misery and visceral hatred. No
child of *obshchestvo* or gentry Russia could have felt this way.
Nechaev's path to the revolution had nothing to do with guilt.

Vera Zasulich, who was subsequently to have a long and remarkable revolutionary career and would die a Menshevik in
Lenin's Russia, wrote of Nechaev as follows:

[He] was not a product of our intelligentsia milieu. He was alien to it. It was not opinions, derived from contact with this milieu, which underlay his revolutionary energy, but burning hatred, and not only against the government, not only against institutions, not only against the exploiters of the people, but against all of *obshchestvo,* all educated strata, all these gentlefolk, rich and poor, conservative, liberal and radical. If he did not actually detest the young people who were attracted to him, he certainly did not feel the least sympathy toward them, nor a shade of pity, but much contempt. Children of detested *obshchestvo,* bound to it by countless ties and thus far more inclined to love than hate—they could be for him an instrument or a weapon, but in no case comrades or even followers.[3]

The first really "hard" source material we have on Nechaev dates from 1863, when he was sixteen years old. At that time, he was working as a sign painter in Ivanovo. He was the third generation, at least, in his family to be a "painter"—a traditional motif in an otherwise quite untraditional biography. In his apparently considerable spare time, he was slogging away at the gymnasium curriculum. We have a series of letters from Nechaev to F. D. Nefëdov, another young man from a servile background who had succeeded in escaping from Ivanovo and getting to Moscow.[4] Nefëdov's life is striking in relation to Nechaev's: how similar and yet how different. They shared the dreary provincial background, the driving ambition, the hatred of the local merchants and factory owners. But Nefëdov became a respectable radical: journalist, editor, and writer of stories—the champion of the people from whom he had escaped, if perhaps their sentimentalizer as well. In 1865, the young Nefëdov got his first break, as editor of the Moscow journal *Bibliophile (Bibliofil');* in 1872, as Nechaev's astonishing career was coming to an end, Nefëdov was publishing, in the *Russian Gazette,* a highly successful series of muckraking articles entitled "Our Mills and Factories."

Their correspondence reveals the strong impression made on both these young men by V. A. Dement'ev, a writer of vaguely radical and democratic sympathies and avuncular temperament who had also recently left Ivanovo for Moscow. He had, a year or two previously, helped introduce Nechaev, Nefëdov, and other Ivanovo young people to a variety of cultural activities, including drama. They built a theater together; Postnikova recalls that old Nechaev did the sets, so he was certainly not systematically hostile to his son's ambitions. She also tells us that her brother exhibited considerable talent as an actor—a theatrical gift that he was soon to reveal in a quite different context.

It is also clear from the correspondence that the departure of both Dement'ev and Nefëdov was a considerable blow to Nechaev; Ivanovo seemed bleaker, and his desire to escape intensified. Virtually every one of Nechaev's letters contains frantic pleas for books and bitter complaints about the slow progress of his studies; German and mathematics, in particular, he found hard going "without teachers." More and more often, as the months went by, he vented his spleen on the filth and tedium of Ivanovo. He also chronicled with heavy irony the doings of the local "big shots"; on occasion the irony would give way to furious words that reveal more immediately the depth of his feelings. But young Nechaev at this stage of the game was far from a hardened or systematic radical; indeed, he appears to have read almost no radical literature. At the end of one letter, he inquired of Nefëdov if he still observed the fast days.

In early 1865, the letters became more despondent, although he wrote hopefully of coming to Moscow and entering the gymnasium in the sixth or seventh class and going on to the university from there. He wanted to be off by summer, as he had come to feel that his family regarded him as a "drone." His father had been to some degree supportive; now, Nechaev believed, *papasha* just wanted him to take off somewhere. By August he was in Moscow.

At this point our information thins out again. We know that Nefëdov was his initial contact in Moscow; presumably through his agency, Nechaev was lodged in the small pension run by Mikhail Pogodin, the elderly historian and publicist. Dement'ev was apparently important here: he had served for a time as Pogodin's secretary, and it appears that Nechaev followed in his footsteps.[5] Pogodin's biographer does not record the presence of Nechaev anywhere in his twenty-two volumes, but Pogodin made such a bad impression on his student and secretary that he was subsequently marked down on a special list of those to be made away with as soon as the revolution broke out, along with such important pillars of the *status quo* as General Shuvalov.

In Moscow, Nechaev changed his plans; instead of trying to get into a gymnasium, he took his examinations for the post of elementary-school teacher. He did not pass, and in April 1866, he moved to St. Petersburg. He arrived around the time of Karakozov's attempt on the life of the Tsar, and the event made a strong impression on him. He wrote, subsequently, that "the foundations of our sacred cause were laid by Karakozov on the morning of 4th April 1866. . . . His action must be regarded as a prologue. Let us act, my friends, in such a way that the play will soon begin." Franco Venturi observes at this point that the prologue of Nechaev's own life was coming to an end and the main drama beginning.[6]

Between the spring of 1866 and the summer of 1868, Nechaev ceased forever to be the raw boy from Ivanovo and became the astonishing revolutionary intriguer whom we encounter for the first time in the student "unrest" of 1868–69. In St. Petersburg he did succeed in passing his teacher's examination and got a job teaching "the word of God"—that is, religion—in the Sergievsky Parish School. And in this period, too, he acquired a set of revolutionary opinions—or perhaps a revolutionary orientation would be a better way of putting it—to express the hatred within him.

We know little enough of Nechaev's life in the capital in this two-year period, but we can be sure of one revolutionary "influence" on him as we work our way toward 1868—that of Pëtr Nikitich Tkachëv. One of the most determined and articulate of the Russian Jacobins, Tkachëv became really well known only as an émigré journalist in the 1870s. But he had been a radical pamphleteer and activist for more than six years when he encountered Nechaev at some now-forgotten political meeting or social gathering in 1866 or 1867. The two were in the way of being close collaborators by the fall of 1868, and the imprint of Tkachëv's thinking is clear in Nechaev's first recorded political pronouncements.

Tkachëv's biography might be taken as prototypical of a " 'sixties person," as men and women of his generation often referred to themselves. He was born in 1844 into a family of minor Pskov gentry; he lost his father early in his life, and his initial education took place under his mother's supervision. He was sent to St. Petersburg, where he attended the gymnasium and in the fall of 1861 went on to the university. Thus his intellectual formation took place in the euphoric atmosphere of the new era and in the capital, where that progressive atmosphere was most powerful and pervasive. He read Herzen, Dobroliubov, and—significantly —Pisarev. He took part in the student demonstrations of the fall of 1861, was arrested, did time in the fortress at Kronstadt, and was released. During the next several years, he wrote for Pisarev's *Russian Word* and (after it was shut down) for the *Cause (Delo)*. He was arrested three more times prior to 1868, the third time for peripheral involvement with Ishutin, but he was soon released.

Even a casual scrutiny of Tkachëv's life during the 1860s testifies to the degree to which institutions of higher education had become the recruiting ground of Russian radicalism. As has since been the case in other cultures, a large semiradical (or potentially radical) community grew up in cities with a substantial student population. Tkachëv testified frequently and enthusiastically to his belief in the energy and social creativity of Russia's youth, and he lived in that student-based community where a prolonged adolescence was possible and where one's radical identity could be formed.

Tkachëv was also typical of the 1860s in his elitism: the masses, he believed, could be counted on only as a destructive force; and their energies would have to be directed by intelligentsia leaders. A few years later, Tkachëv gave public expression to this revolutionary elitism in his Geneva journal, *Tocsin (Nabat)*, where he set forth his influential view of the proper organization for the revolutionary party: small, disciplined, totally centralized. Nechaev found Tkachëv's point of view much to his taste, and the two became part of an informal circle that read Filippo Buonarrotti's *La Conspiration de Babeuf* and other "Jacobin"

classics that fall—until such time as reading was wholly super-
seded by action.

When the students returned for the fall semester in 1868, they
were probably as disposed to take on the authorities as they had
been at any time since the big student protests of 1861.[7] As had
been the case at that time, the institutions of student corporatism
were the big issue; the complex consequences of student dissatisfaction were no more to be confined to the campus than in 1861.
But now educated society in the capital was not involved or
sympathetic to anything like the same degree it had been seven
years before. And lacking the sympathetic resonance provided
by Petersburg society, the unrest of 1868–69 was a smaller and
more restricted affair.

Three institutions in the capital contributed substantially to
the general student population from which the agitation
emerged—the university, the Medical-Surgical Academy, and
the Technological Institute. The student population of all three
had merged into one body, closely connected by common lodgings, friends, and roommates. The financial need of the poorer
students was well known to this entire population, and so were
the graphic inequalities in the way the various institutions dealt
with their students. Under the reform-minded aegis of Dmitry
Miliutin, the Ministry of War had tacitly ignored the university
rules of 1863 and allowed the students of the Medical-Surgical
Academy to move very far in the direction of corporate institutions. Not only did the medical students have a library and a
kassa for those who needed support, they had a substantial cafe-
teria as well. The library was so much a student sanctuary that
the government inspector made a point of staying away "to avoid
unpleasantness."[8] The other two institutions had nothing comparable.

Radical activity in St. Petersburg had been at a low ebb since
the post-Karakozov roundup in the summer of 1866. But student
corporatist sentiment was on the rise, providing a substantial
body of potential recruits. Shortly after the semester began, the
September number of a new émigré radical journal, the *People's
Cause (Narodnoe delo)*, began to circulate among some of the

students. The lead article, written by Mikhail Bakunin, caused considerable stir among the minority with radical sympathies. In characteristically flamboyant fashion, he heaped scorn on the notion of reforming Russian society through the diffusion of "enlightenment" and proclaimed that only total revolution could cure Russia's ills. Perhaps Bakunin's journal found its way into the shelves of the student library at the Medical-Surgical Academy, which often stocked illegal literature and where radical sympathies among the students were most intense. In any case, students were soon discussing the merits of his case. For some, the subject was soon made manageable by being reduced to a slogan, *"nauka ili trud,"* which may be freely translated as "academics or labor." And the extreme interpretation of "labor" meant abandoning one's privileged life altogether, living with the people—becoming an artisan, perhaps—and devoting one's full time to preparing the revolution. In other words, what would soon become known as "going to the people."[9]

The interest aroused by Bakunin's article helped set the intellectual stage that fall for a sizable group of vaguely progressive students who wanted to legalize and develop the corporate institutions of the university and the Technological Institute, and a minority whose radical goals transcended the student world and centered on the seemingly unquenchable hope of peasant revolt and how to direct it.

The onset of these discussions coincided with Nechaev's arrival in the university milieu as a "free auditor." We are in the dark as to how evolved his political views were in September 1868, but it seems likely enough that this was his first exposure to Bakunin's viewpoint. And it is clear that Bakunin's anti-intellectual formulations suited Nechaev perfectly. Again and again in the articles and proclamations Nechaev was to write over the next several years, he would disparage "academics," "literature," and "study," exalting by contrast a supremely dedicated, active, and allegedly practical revolutionary work. And of course it was to Bakunin that he would turn during his trip abroad the following spring.

As the autumn wore on, the students began to meet in larger and larger groups, and the legalization of *skhodki* became one of their principal demands. By late December, when some of these meetings were drawing up to several hundred students,[10] a clear split had developed between the radical and moderate positions. The radicals—with Nechaev egging them on—were demanding large demonstrations and other confrontation tactics that certainly would not have persuaded the minister of education to smile upon student corporate institutions in the capital of the empire.

It is interesting to observe Nechaev's style at the *skhodki*. He seldom spoke in public; no doubt his preference for behind-the-scenes work was connected with his realization that he did not cut a very impressive figure in a public arena whose style was still in part the product of *obshchestvo* Russia. His violent hatred of "salon oratory" suggests as much, although on several occasions he did speak with some effectiveness. In private he was terse and deeply contemptuous of the moderates; frequently, after the open meeting was over, he would gather two or three particularly bold spirits or well-connected newcomers together and shepherd them back to his lodgings at the Sergievsky School for some private talk. His caution was well founded, as one or more police agents were often in attendance at the larger *skhodki*.

In fact, Nechaev and Tkachëv and several others were attempting to set up a revolutionary organization. Among their colleagues in this enterprise were Zemfiry Ralli-Arbore, a medical student of Rumanian extraction who subsequently became an activist in Swiss anarchist politics, the Ametistov brothers, and Vladimir Orlov, a priest's son who had been a teacher in Ivanovo. Their tactics, in the student politics of the fall and winter, aimed not at the success but at the failure of the campaign for a library and legalized *skhodki;* they hoped that a significant number of the more hotheaded of the students could be brought into serious and public confrontation with the authorities. Having thus compromised themselves and been—at the very least—expelled from the university, they would be available as revolutionary

junior officers to help direct the peasant insurrection that Tkachëv and Nechaev expected to break out on or about February
19, 1870.

The fixing of an exact date for a peasant insurrection has been
interpreted as being a particularly striking example of the un-
founded belief in the *narod,* common among Russian radicals, as
well as being absurdly precise—not the eighteenth of February,
but the nineteenth! In fact the line of reasoning followed by
Tkachëv and Nechaev was by no means as simpleminded as it
might at first glance appear. According to the terms of the Emancipation Statute of February 19, 1861, the freed serfs were to enter
into a period of "temporary obligation," according to which they
would continue to occupy their allotments of land, paying their
former masters money or labor dues for its use. Only at the end
of nine years were they to be confronted with a real option: to
leave without the land, or to continue in possession until they had
managed the herculean task of paying off their debt to the state,
which had purchased their "freedom" from their former owners.
A good many people of a decidedly nonrevolutionary outlook
were beginning to wonder with trepidation what the peasants
would do when the day came and they had to make the crucial
decision about their relations with their landlords and their economic future. Tkachëv and Nechaev were banking on the catalytic effect of this moment—after the disappointment of the
Emancipation and nine years' economic deterioration in the position of the mass of the peasants—which they believed would
lead to a series of local disorders. And these disorders would
either themselves develop into a major agrarian insurrection or
could be made to do so if there were enough dedicated revolutionary activists around the country to abet the process. Hence
their desire to exploit the grievances of the students, to create
from their ranks the organization that could turn these outbreaks
into the revolution.

(The disorders did not materialize, and the revolution had to
be postponed. At least one factor that Nechaev and Tkachëv had
not banked on was the stabilizing influence of the peasant commune. For most peasants, financial redemption proceeded by the

community, and most peasants simply continued in their status of temporary obligation after February 19. Their patience again proved—in the eyes of the radicals—simply inexhaustible.)

Nechaev and his associates drafted a *Program of Revolutionary Action,*[11] which set forth their aspirations and a kind of rough timetable. Until May 1869, the focus would be on recruitment among students in the capitals and to a lesser extent in other university cities. After that date, the radicalized students would move out into the provinces, attempting to recruit first from various *raznochintsy* groups and the village poor, and finally moving to propaganda among the peasantry. In the fall of 1869, a revolutionary center was to be created, making use of "specialists" in the social and natural sciences (a curiously modern note)!

Vera Zasulich, in her memoirs,[12] described an illuminating episode in Nechaev's ongoing effort to control and direct the activities of the student radicals. At a *skhodka* in early 1869, when a number of the moderates had already dropped out, Nechaev made one of his rare speeches. He announced that the time had now come to pass from words to deeds (how he loved to say this!); as a pledge to this effect, those who were not "afraid for their skins" should sign their names to a sheet of paper. Before someone had the presence of mind to say how foolish this was, there were close to ninety signatures on the paper—which went into Nechaev's pocket! The document subsequently found its way to the Third Section, by what route we do not know. If Nechaev actually *did* turn the names in, it would have been perfectly consonant with his idea of "radicalizing" them, willy-nilly, in time for the projected February revolution.

Thinking back subsequently on the winter of 1869, Zasulich found it odd that Nechaev was spending so much time studying French. One suspects that he was already planning a dramatic exit to Europe when, in the first days of March, the student movement reached an unexpected climax. An individual confrontation between a professor and a student led to the expulsion of the student, and the episode served as a catalyst: classes were disrupted, petitions were presented, a large number of students were expelled and some were arrested. Ironically enough, it was the despised moderates who took the lead, but a number of the extremist party were arrested, including Tkachëv, Ralli, and A. G. Dement'eva, who had been living with Tkachëv. Ralli was arrested almost immediately upon his return from Moscow, where he had been organizing and recruiting for the revolution.

Just as the first arrests were imminent, Nechaev contrived a dramatic exit—the first of those memorable examples of mystification for which he became known. An unknown person, calling himself a "student," delivered a letter to Vera Zasulich. He had allegedly been on the street when a carriage passed by (in some versions it is described as a "police coach"); a hand emerged and dropped the letter, which stated that Nechaev had been arrested and was being taken to the Fortress of St. Peter and St. Paul. High officials in the Third Section denied that Nechaev had been arrested; it appears, indeed, that the police knew little or nothing of him at the time. His young, illiterate, worshipful sister—who had been informed by her brother that he expected to be arrested—naturally refused to believe these official denials and nearly went out of her mind with worry. His roommate, Evlampiia Ametistov, also reported that Nechaev had been threatened with arrest, so the belief quickly became general in student circles that he *had* been taken off to the fortress.

The timing of Nechaev's initial piece of mystification provides some food for thought. At this point—January 1869—Nechaev may have felt that his first political involvement had not led to very much. He had not been able to control the student movement. Even the "committee" that was to control the students in the interests of the revolution seems to have remained at the talking stage; Ralli and perhaps others had reacted to his plans with some reserve.[13] Was he unpleasantly conscious of how small he still looked to others? Of how little weight his name carried? Both his phony "arrest" and his involvement with the great names of the emigration were calculated to demonstrate how quickly a "name" could be created if one went about it with sufficient energy and purpose—two attributes he had in abundance!

Some two weeks after the flap about his arrest, his sister, acquaintances, and associates began receiving letters from Nechaev. He had been arrested, he claimed, had escaped, had been
caught in Odessa, had escaped again. He enclosed a proclamation
of the First International over the signature of Bakunin, and
demanded student demonstrations, but no one, at that point, felt
able to oblige.

The second arrest was cut from the same cloth as the first.
Nechaev had in fact gone to Moscow, where Vladimir Orlov had
introduced him (under the name of "Pavlov," one of his favorite
aliases) to Pëtr Uspensky, a young radical of an enthusiastic temperament. Uspensky had known Ishutin and more recently been
close to Feliks Volkhovsky, German Lopatin, and other young
radicals Nechaev wanted to meet. From Moscow, Nechaev went
to Kiev and Odessa, and from there, on to Switzerland. Before
leaving Russia, Nechaev sent Ogarëv a copy of the manifesto he
had drafted a short time before: *To the Students of the University, the Academy, and the Petersburg Technological Institute.*
On April 1, Ogarëv passed it on to Herzen, with a brief note of
explanation: a circumstantial beginning to what was to be a very
trying episode in the lives of the Herzen family, Ogarëv, and—
above all—Mikhail Bakunin.[14]

When Nechaev arrived in Switzerland, toward the end of
March 1869, the public careers of Herzen and Ogarëv were really
at an end. The second half of the 1860s had been a period of
personal and political nightmare for Herzen. The *Bell* had declined into the merest wisp of its former self and had finally
expired in 1868. From the standpoint of émigré politics, the period following Karakozov's attempt saw the climax of the estrangement that had been developing between Herzen and the
younger radicals for several years—they looked on him, as he
bleakly remarked to Ogarëv, as at best "an interesting fossilized
bone."[15] Since leaving England forever in March 1865, Herzen
had traveled here and there across the continent of Europe,
increasingly overwhelmed by personal tragedy; shortly before
his departure, the twins—his children by Natal'ia Tuchkova-

Ogarëva—died in a diphtheria epidemic in Paris, a misery from which their mother (who had lived with Herzen since 1857) never really recovered. Nor were Herzen's relations with any of his children really satisfactory.[16]

Ogarëv, increasingly a prey to alcoholism and epilepsy, had lived in Geneva since April 1865, nursed lovingly and jealously by Mary Sutherland, the English prostitute with whom he spent the last nineteen years of his life. His sobriety was uncertain, and after falling in the street in February 1868, he never entirely regained the use of one leg.

Bakunin had remained far more hopeful about the revolutionary capacities of the "younger generation" than Herzen had. He was neither so spiritually spent as Herzen nor so physically exhausted as Ogarëv; indeed, one of the most active periods of his extraordinary life was in progress at the time of Nechaev's arrival. Bakunin was one of the great organizers of paper and semipaper organizations, but by early 1869 he was involved in the politics of a very real grouping—the International Working Men's Association—in which he was attempting to secure a special role for himself and his International Social-Democratic Alliance. Bakunin was as remarkable a figure in the rather bourgeois radical politics of Western Europe as Peter the Great had been in the Dutch dockyards almost two centuries before. To some— Marx and Engels, for instance—he was anathema; to others, like James Guillaume, he became a revered if sometimes inexplicable master.[17]

In attempting to understand Bakunin's political style, it helps to remember that he came from a cultivated and aristocratic Russian family, and that he had been, throughout his childhood and early adolescence, particularly cosseted and admired. To a great many Russian gentry intellectuals, Western European society had always seemed unpleasantly bourgeois, confining, and philistine, and in Bakunin these feelings achieved their most extreme expression. He was, culturally speaking, a pathological aristocrat—nature's nobleman gone mad. Although he could be extremely generous and was courageous to a fault, he never acquired any of the prosaic virtues for which the middle classes have been noted: reliability, restraint, regularity, or the capacity to foresee the results of one's actions. He was an inveterate, lifelong sponger, as much by temperament as through force of circumstances. And he hated what one might call the bourgeois vices—self-interest, egotism, slyness—with a ferocious passion that never abated. Indeed, it is almost true to say that for him the vices of the petty trader were the *only* vices that really existed. This central aspect of Bakunin's character accounts in large part for his remarkable and protracted credulousness about Nechaev. If there ever was someone ill-equipped to reject a colleague on grounds of fanaticism, it was Bakunin.

Since the fall of 1868, Bakunin and his wife, Antonia, had been settled in Geneva, and since the first days of 1869 he had been occupied almost exclusively with the affairs of his Social-Democratic Alliance and its relationship to the First International. Bakunin's marriage was a less important chapter of his life than those of Herzen and Ogarëv, but it was even more bizarre and within a few years was to become almost as painful. Antonia Kwiatkowska was the daughter of a Siberian merchant; Bakunin had met and married her while in exile in 1858. She was twenty-five years younger than her husband and never shared any of his political interests. As she grew older, the life of poverty and insecurity that marriage to Bakunin entailed took its toll on her, and it is fair to say that by the beginning of the 1870s she cared only for her family, which included her parents and sister in Siberia and her three children. The father of those children was not Bakunin, but his close friend, an Italian revolutionary named Carlo Gambuzzi.

The fact that Bakunin's marriage was apparently unconsummated raises the question of his sexuality, one of those awkward issues that cannot be either resolved or ignored. It cannot be ducked in this case, because a powerful element of sexual attraction clearly bound Bakunin to Nechaev. Bakunin often referred to Nechaev as "Boy" (in English, but punning on the Russian *boi*, meaning "fight" or "struggle"). There are other instances of Bakunin's being attracted to masterly men, and the degree to which he adopted a "feminine" role of submission in relation to

Nechaev is suggested by an odd and apparently apocryphal anecdote that made the rounds of Swiss radical circles. As the story
had it, Bakunin had promised, in writing, to submit to Nechaev
in all things, even to the point of forgery; as a token of submission,
he signed the declaration with a woman's name: Matrëna.[18]

How Bakunin and Nechaev actually met we do not know. The
encounter took place, in all probability, in the second week of
April 1869 in Geneva, and it produced a famous passage, which
has been quoted in every account of the relations between the
two men. On April 13, Bakunin wrote to James Guillaume that

At present I am engrossed in Russian affairs. Our youth, theoretically
and in practice the most revolutionary in the world, is in great ferment. . . . I have here with me now one of those young fanatics who
know no doubts, who fear nothing, who realize that many of them
will perish at the hands of the government but who nevertheless
have decided that they will not relent until the people rise. They are
magnificent, these young fanatics. Believers without God and heroes
without phrases![19]

This passage makes another aspect of the situation clear: Nechaev, from the beginning, had a quasi-mythic stature for Bakunin. Bakunin believed in the escape from the Fortress of St. Peter
and St. Paul, and defended Nechaev from those who were more
cautious or openly skeptical. To him, Nechaev embodied the
long-hoped-for *Russian* revolution—and also provided a kind of
continuity by which Bakunin himself could help shape that revolution. This was the student for whom the aging professor of
revolution had been longing. E. H. Carr expresses this side of
things eloquently:

[Bakunin] had long lost touch with Russia itself. . . . The arrival of
Nechaev brought him, for the first time in many years, a breath of his
native land. He would never see it again. But still, in the midst of his
international preoccupations, it often haunted his dreams; and here
was a chance of working for the cause of revolution in the country
which was nearest to his heart. No other land could appeal to him in
this way. The sentimental side of his nature, which seemed to have
died with his memories of home and childhood long years ago,

revived and reopened for this dangerous and seductive Russian "Boy."[20]

Nechaev's decision to go abroad was motivated, as we have seen, by a justified belief that a police crackdown was coming, a circumstance that did not displease him in the least. Indeed, he contributed in his own way to "radicalizing" the Russian students with whom he had been working, as many of the telegrams and letters that he dispatched from Switzerland after his arrival on March 29 fell into the hands of the police and led to the arrest of their intended recipients. Over the summer, Nechaev sent a staggering quantity of pamphlet literature back to Russia as well —with the same dire results for many of the addressees. The Petersburg authorities alone confiscated 560 pieces of mail, addressed to 387 different people![21] But Switzerland was not merely a political resting place for Nechaev; he also wanted to enlist what remained of the prestige of the radical emigration in the service of his revolutionary organizing. More than those of Herzen and Ogarëv, Bakunin's name was something to conjure with in Russia.

The drafting of proclamations and the writing of articles was the major enterprise of the summer, and Bakunin was a wholehearted collaborator, to the confusion of historians, who have spilled considerable ink in the attempt to resolve who wrote what.[22] Without entering into this fascinating if slightly arcane matter of authorship, we can certainly identify the points of view of the principals. Ogarëv's role was minor. He seems to have written only a brief pamphlet entitled *To the Russian Students!* (which Herzen, arriving in Geneva in May, disparaged). He did take a poem he had previously dedicated to a young radical friend and, at Bakunin's urging, rededicate it to Nechaev. Entitled "Student," the poem boasts a heroic protagonist who ends his life "in the snowy prisons of Siberia." Nechaev took many copies back with him to Russia; this scrap of doggerel added to his mantle of glamour but has further confused those concerned with the details of his biography.

The principal themes of the pamphlet *How the Revolutionary*

Question Presents Itself are clearly Bakunin's. Take the passage on brigandage:

Brigandage is one of the most honoured aspects of the people's life in Russia. At the time when the state of Moscow was being founded, brigandage represented the desperate protest of the people against the horrible social order of the times. . . . The brigand is always the hero, the defender, the avenger of the people, the irreconcilable enemy of the entire state regime, both in its civil and its social aspects, the life and death fighter against our statist-aristocratic, official-clerical civilization. An understanding of brigandage is essential for an understanding of the history of the Russian people. . . . The brigand, in Russia, is the true and only revolutionary—the revolutionary without phrase-making and without bookish rhetoric.* Popular revolution is born from the merging of the revolt of the brigand with that of the peasant. . . . Such were the revolts of Stenka Razin and Pugachëv . . . and even today this is still the world of the Russian revolution.[23]

The separation between the "two Russias," the belief in the revolution as the destruction of the alien (or "German") dynasty and court, the supersession of "privilege Russia" by the *narod*—all this had been formulated by Herzen during his most radical period, by Shchapov, and by Bakunin himself. These Slavophile-tinged propositions had already become central to the general vocabulary of Populism. Shchapov in the early 1860s, and Bakunin a few years later, had come to regard the great peasant revolts as prefiguring the Russian revolution. Both men also understood that the principal ingredient the great jacqueries of Razin and Pugachëv had lacked was *consciousness*—which would be supplied, in the forthcoming holocaust, by the radical wing of the intelligentsia.

Bakunin now believed that he saw the "revolutionary proto-type," who would accomplish this mission, incarnate in Nechaev. In a brief pamphlet entitled *The Revolutionary Catechism*, Nechaev attempted to describe "the revolutionary" in more general and abstract terms, with Bakunin improving the

*Note the similarity between the phrases employed here and those Bakunin used to describe Nechaev in the letter cited above.

style and attempting to link the mission of the contemporary intelligentsia revolutionary with the long history of brigandage and revolt that stretched back into the misty times of the Muscovite autocracy. In time, Bakunin would become bitterly aware of how little Nechaev believed in the *narod,* its values and experience—things that Bakunin never ceased to care about, even when he was most obsessed with "revolutionary prototypes" from the intelligentsia.

Despite Bakunin's participation in the final version of the *Catechism,*[24] its direction and force are completely Jacobin: it is the culmination of the tradition that began with Zaichnevsky's *Young Russia* and was continued in the Hell of Ishutin. And Nechaev was further indebted, in his portrait of the revolutionary, to an earlier sketch by his first mentor, Tkachëv.[25] Just when and how the *Catechism* was written remains obscure, but the most plausible assumption is that it was begun in Russia, in conjunction with the scenario foreseen in the *Program of Revolutionary Action.* Then, during the summer of 1869, it must have been rewritten or at least heavily edited by Nechaev and Bakunin. Whatever Bakunin's role in the *Catechism'*s creation, the old man soon came to think of it (accurately enough) as Nechaev's work; he referred to it (in a private letter to Nechaev) as "your catechism" and as "a catechism of abreks"*[26]—decisive confirmation of what is really clear from a careful reading of the text.

The first half of the *Catechism* is largely a chart of a profoundly hierarchical organization, designed in such a way that information can move up and orders down with maximum efficacy. The cells and sections into which the members are organized are linked together by only one person, in such a way as to keep the membership as isolated as possible from one other. If someone is arrested, he or she will be able to implicate only a very few people; on the other hand, all the sense of solidarity that has so often lent cohesion to less centralized organizations has been lost. At the top of the entire organization is "the Committee,"

---

*An *abrek* was a Caucasian outcast. See the epigraph to this chapter.

whose name Nechaev would later invoke so often in support of his policies. When the initial draft of the *Catechism* was made, the Committee presumably was to include Tkachëv, Nechaev, Ralli, and a handful of others. With the arrest of most of its members in the late winter of 1869, however, the Committee clearly existed only on paper—which did not prevent Nechaev from speaking of it as a real body to Bakunin and Ogarëv. Bakunin, in fact, also invented an imaginary organization—the World Revolutionary Alliance—and made Nechaev a member. This mutual mystification, wrote Carr, "was a delicious situation which can have few parallels either in comedy or in history."[27] The comedy became grim and modern, however, when the Committee demanded the murder of a recalcitrant member a few months later in Moscow.

The second half of the *Catechism* is the famous description of the "revolutionary prototype" and his relationship with the world around him. The revolutionary world so grimly and tersely described here is at the opposite extreme from that later envisaged by the leaders and theoreticians of the Second International, where (oversimplifying only a little) we may say that the revolutionary leadership was seen to grow out of its constituency and express its aspirations in the most natural way possible. The bottom line is the same: the revolution means the "liberation and happiness" of the poorest and most exploited segment of the working class. But Nechaev's revolutionary is an outsider even to those for whom the revolution must be made and whose sufferings will fuel it: "our association will promote with all its power and resources the development and intensification of those misfortunes and those evils which must finally exhaust the patience of the people and impel it to a general uprising."[28] Here, then, is an early suggestion of the strategy generally characterized as "the worse the better," a viewpoint inveterately hostile to every kind of reformist effort and therefore never popular with most working people.

In the prerevolutionary world, according to the *Catechism*, the revolutionary is to live in the most extreme alienation and isolation. Death is an ever-present reality, almost obsessively so.[29] "The revolutionary," Nechaev begins, "is a doomed man."

He has no interests of his own, no affairs, no feelings, no attachments, no property, not even a name. Everything in him is absorbed by a single exclusive interest, a single thought, a single passion—the revolution.

2. In the depths of his being, not only in words, but in deed, he has broken every tie with the civil order and with the entire educated world, with all laws, conventions, generally accepted conditions, and with the morality of this world. He is its implacable enemy, and if he continues to live in it, that is only the more certainly to destroy it.

Gone in the *Catechism* is every trace of the intelligentsia's love of culture and the book. Even science is demoted to a tertiary position: "[The revolutionary] knows of only one science, the science of destruction." We remember Nechaev's solitary struggle to master the gymnasium curriculum in Ivanovo; by now, his hostility to books has become extreme and ideological. "He who learns of the revolutionary deed in books," Nechaev wrote in his periodical, the *People's Vengeance (Narodnaia rasprava)*, "will always be a revolutionary do-nothing."[30] Not only is the revolutionary utterly cut off from all "tender and effeminate feelings" of friendship and love, but honor and integrity must also be sacrificed, and even vengeance and hatred. In other words, personality itself must be extinguished. Here is the program of Hell pushed to its logical conclusion.

The most dramatic expression of the revolutionary's position is the complete repudiation of all traditional moral norms in the name of revolutionary utility. "Moral for [the revolutionary]," wrote Nechaev, "is everything that facilitates the triumph of the revolution. Immoral and criminal is everything which hinders it."[31] And in the coming months and years, Nechaev attempted to live out this prescription in a nineteenth-century world that was not yet prepared to understand him.

Nechaev specified in detail his attitude toward the comrades, sympathizers, dupes, and enemies by whom the revolutionary would be surrounded: a kind of demonic Benthamite schema that one wishes the founder of utilitarianism could have lived to read. All the revolutionaries are "revolutionary capital," and one is to try to derive the "greatest possible return" from the capital at one's disposal. The revolutionary has no tie with his comrades other than their usefulness.

With the enemies of the revolution, practical considerations also prevail: all those whose continued existence harms "the cause" should be eliminated, but those whose bestial behavior brings the revolution closer should be temporarily allowed to live. Liberals should be ruthlessly manipulated and compromised, not to be drawn into the revolution as participants but to sow social chaos. (Nechaev's attitude toward them seems to have hardened since the student politics of the previous winter.) Last, but certainly in this case not least, women are divided into three categories: (1) the "frivolous, vapid, and soulless," who—like their male counterparts—are to be blackmailed and enslaved; (2) the gifted and devoted, but as yet uncommitted, who must be driven into making extreme and compromising declarations, resulting in the destruction of most of them and the recruitment of a few; and (3) the women who are "with us completely," who constitute "our most valuable treasure."

Nechaev's other great concern that summer was with the sinew of revolution: money. He tried to raise some back in Russia through the mails, but his principal target was the so-called Bakhmetev Fund. Amounting to some eight hundred pounds, the fund had been left with Herzen and Ogarëv, about eleven years before, by an eccentric landowner named P. A. Bakhmetev, who then proceeded to the Marquesas Islands to found a utopian community and was never heard of again. With his keen sense of the value of money, Herzen had used only the interest to finance his various enterprises, so the capital was still intact. When Herzen arrived in Geneva in May 1869, he found himself the target of a concerted campaign to pry the money loose. Bakunin (whom Herzen regarded as utterly irresponsible) and Nechaev wisely remained in the background; Herzen was unable to resist the importunities of Ogarëv, who after all was as much entitled to the money as he was. The upshot was that the eight hundred pounds was divided, and half of it rapidly came into the possession of Bakunin and Nechaev through Ogarëv's intermediary. Herzen had heard a good deal about Nechaev and disliked all he had heard; the only recorded meeting between the two of them took place when Nechaev came to pick up the check. It was a brief encounter between two people who might well stand for the polarities of the Russian revolutionary movement.

Armed with several hundred pounds, the *Catechism,* the first number of the *People's Vengeance,* and sundry proclamations, Nechaev returned to Russia in late August, via Bucharest, where he acquired a Serbian passport from a Bulgarian revolutionary acquaintance. He did not go to St. Petersburg, where he was sure to have some explaining to do, but to Moscow. The first person he looked up there was Pëtr Uspensky, whom he had visited on his way out of Russia the previous March.

The twenty-two-year-old Uspensky was ripe for Nechaev. Married to the sister of Vera Zasulich, he had drifted on the fringes of Moscow radicalism for at least four years. He had known Ishutin; subsequently he had been associated with German Lopatin and Feliks Volkhovsky in their Ruble Society, a small and informal organization devoted to studying the *narod* and its revolutionary potential soberly and systematically before creating the most sophisticated and finely honed propaganda. Prior to his arrest, Khudiakov had entrusted his manuscripts to Lopatin, and a good deal of his material was used by Ruble Society propagandists. Lopatin was a man of considerable intellectual sobriety while being, at the same time, a great devotee of secret missions and daring risks; he was the crucial figure in the unmasking of Nechaev. Volkhovsky had reacted coldly to Nechaev's plans even before his flight abroad. However, one of the letters that Nechaev had sent off from Switzerland the previous March had led to the arrest of Lopatin, Volkhovsky, and most of their group— including Uspensky's fifteen-year-old sister, but mysteriously leaving Uspensky himself at liberty.

Thus the cooler heads, who might have been able to temper Uspensky's romantic credulousness, were not on the scene when Nechaev arrived. Uspensky had a deep and personal sympathy for the sufferings of the Russian people, as well as an adolescent attraction to the trappings of conspiracy and "the poetry of struggle." He was also half out of his mind with worry about his sister, who had been sitting for several months in the Fortress of St. Peter and St. Paul, accused of being a "dangerous conspirator." There was no indication what disposition the government intended to make of her case, or when.[32]

At the time of Nechaev's arrival, Uspensky was employed in Aleksandr Cherkesov's bookstore, something of a radical hangout. As his visitor knew, Uspensky was well connected, and soon "Pavlov"* (as Nechaev was calling himself) had been introduced to a circle of radical students at the Petrovsky Agricultural Academy, where Ishutin's influence had been considerable. It was in large part from their ranks that Nechaev recruited his first and only real organization, the People's Vengeance.

The leading spirits in the Petrovsky Academy circle seem to have been Nikolai Dolgov and Ivan Ivanov. Aleksei Kuznetsov and Fëdor Ripman were also adherents; they were, it seems, among the more gifted and influential students in the school. Nechaev employed all his wiles and techniques of mystification on these kids; and, like nearly everyone else, they were immensely impressed by his "energy."[33] He spoke in knowledgeable terms about the sufferings of the people, and gave them to understand that he had just returned from tramping all over Russia on foot. He seemed to sleep only two or three hours a night and was frequently (and mysteriously) absent on unspecified errands. To establish his credentials on the inclinations and mood of the *narod*, he told them that he had been a worker until his seventeenth year. This seems also to have been the period when "Pavlov" built up his personal legend: he had been illiterate until he was sixteen; now he could quote Kant in German!

Above all, he was concerned to tell his young adherents what a towering figure Sergei Nechaev was. He gave them copies of the first number of the *People's Vengeance* (which he had brought with him from Switzerland), and he showed them Oga-

---

*Among his other aliases were "the Baron," "Barsov," "Volkov," "Nikolaev," "Liders," "Karazhdanov," and "Neville."

rëv's poem about Nechaev's heartbreaking death in Siberia. Of course it wasn't long before they began to suspect . . . could it be that Pavlov and Nechaev were one and the same? But this was only a guess, and he continued to be known by his aliases.

Soon Nechaev proceeded to the work of organization; February 19, 1870, after all, was now not far away. He showed Uspensky the document, signed by Bakunin, enrolling him in the World Revolutionary Alliance, and also explained that the Committee had sent him to Moscow to overcome the city's traditional conservatism and whip the local chapter of the People's Vengeance into shape. At first the students were putty in his hands. He exploited their guilt and sense of inferiority to "the people," explaining that only those drawn from the people could work among them, but there were important auxiliary tasks for them. He ridiculed the hopes that Dolgov and Ivanov had for cooperatives, pointing out that the government would never allow them to organize and propagandize for any length of time. When they doubted that a rising would inevitably occur, he reminded them that he was "a worker," that he knew the people. For these young men, the *narod* existed only in mythic terms: as wielders of the ax or embodiments of justice and communality. Their objections were all the more quickly abandoned when Nechaev reminded them that after all there were only two sides: you were either for the people or against them. The threat grew in specificity: the People's Vengeance had its eye on them; the Committee was watching the situation in Moscow!

And so the organization grew, no one can now say how large.* Each of the inner circle received a number, according to the plan in the first part of the *Catechism,* and then the circle that he created was given a double-digit number: those who were members of No. 2's circle were numbered 21 through 26. And so on.

Soon after his arrival in Moscow, Nechaev made the acquaintance of one of the oddest, most eccentric and touching figures

*The only estimate by a participant was Kuznetsov's figure of four hundred, which almost all students of Nechaev regard as a highly inflated figure. See Arthur Lehning, ed., *Michel Bakounine et ses relations avec Sergej Nečaev, 1870–72, Écrits et matériaux* (Leiden, 1971), p. xvii.

in the history of Russian radicalism: Ivan Gavrilovich Pryzhov. This remarkable person was financially on his uppers and spent a great deal of his time hanging around Cherkesov's bookstore, where he had come to know Uspensky and through him Nechaev. In considering the life and works of Pryzhov, we confront Russian life at perhaps its most painful. He certainly belongs to those people whom Dostoevsky called "the insulted and the injured."[34]

Pryzhov's lifelong inability to fit in anywhere was rooted in the circumstances of his family, which had been for many generations serfs of the prominent Stolypin family (from whom was to come the last impressive statesman of Imperial Russia, Pëtr Arkad-'evich). But Ivan Pryzhov's father had been manumitted by his owner and served for forty-three years as a medical clerk at the Marinskaia Hospital in Moscow, an institution for the indigent (where Dostoevsky's father was a physician). For his long years of faithful service in this dreary place, Gavriil Pryzhov was given, at his retirement in 1856, the right to be inscribed as a member of the nobility, although he seems not to have availed himself of the opportunity. He was thus one of the very few Russians ever to have moved in a single generation from the enserfed peasantry to what was—technically, at least—noble status.

Thus Ivan Gavrilovich, born in 1827, was a curiosity in this highly structured society, as Iakushkin was in a different way. Where did he belong? He was neither of the people nor a part of *obshchestvo*. One cannot but think that the confusion about his circumstances added passion to his subsequent identification with the *narod*.

The Marinskaia Hospital was a gloomy place—located, for good measure, next to a lunatic asylum. It is hard not to account in part for Pryzhov's character by his early proximity to poverty, illness, and insanity. In any case, the boy grew up solitary, dreadfully shy, and withdrawn; he was, by his own account, a "terrible stutterer." And as is often true with such children, he became a great reader. Pryzhov finished the Moscow gymnasium in 1848; his high academic achievement conferred on him the right to attend the university without taking entrance examinations. But at this point he had a (somehow characteristic) piece of bad luck. He wanted to enroll in the faculty of the humanities at Moscow, but in the panic that followed the outbreak of revolution in Europe, Nicholas I had ordered the number of students cut back and demanded a hard scrutiny of all who were not the sons of gentry or high officials. Pryzhov was rejected. In order to attend the university, he hit upon the expedient of enrolling in the medical faculty, where the social diversity of the student body was much greater, and there he was accepted.

Despite—or perhaps because of—his early association with the Marinskaia Hospital, Pryzhov had no interest in the sciences or medicine, and in 1850 he was expelled, apparently for academic negligence. In a sense, however, he never left the university. Like many another bohemian rebel and radical, there was no other place where he could feel so at home. And so he stayed and continued his education without official sanction, using the library, listening to lectures, and deriving what social life he had from the university community. He knew several members of Rybnikov's circle, but not Rybnikov himself. He heard with appreciation and profit the lectures of F. I. Buslaev, the Russian adept of the Brothers Grimm; he nurtured his interest in the Ukraine with O. M. Bodiansky; but his real hero was Timofei Granovsky, the liberal Hegelian historian, who must have been personally kind to Pryzhov—it is difficult to see much of his intellectual influence on the young man.

Between 1852 and 1866, Pryzhov also worked as a functionary in the Moscow civil court to support himself. In 1866 he lost this post, apparently as a result of the legal reforms, and from that point his financial situation, which had always been precarious, steadily worsened. He had long been a heavy drinker, but now he certainly became an alcoholic. Even in the 1850s he did some drinking on the job, and, as he himself later described it, ended most days in his "favorite tavern in the intimate companionship of Bacchus." Much of the research for his best-known work, *The History of Taverns in Russia*, was undoubtedly done on the spot. Pryzhov spent a great deal of time wandering through the semi-criminal underworld of greater Moscow, participating in its ac-

tivities in a relatively harmless way, but observing what went on
and noting it down. He did not so much "write" his articles and
small books as select material from his growing storehouse, jotted
down on scraps of paper, often greasy and torn, and splice together an article to sell. It was all one book, really: the real life
of the Russian people.

A partial exception to this, perhaps, was the work on taverns
("bars" certainly conveys the flavor better to an American audience), which was really an ambitious study of the rebellious and
criminal world that centered on the *kabak*. He was interested in
just what people drank, in the variety of deaths from alcoholism
and other ailments, and in classifying the kinds of crime that
emanated from the tavern. Toward the end of his life he evolved
the rather contemporary-sounding notion that the tavern in
Russia was in fact a revolutionary milieu; one could make a better
case for the opposite proposition. The published *History of Taverns* was only the first third of his work; no publisher would touch
the subsequent sections, which dealt more with the milieu of the
tavern, although the head of the Moscow University Press was
reported to have been interested. Pryzhov burned the rest of his
material on the eve of his arrest.

Franco Venturi describes Pryzhov as having "drawn his Populism from a Slavophil source."[35] There is no evidence for such a
"source," and it would be more accurate to describe his views as
a demonization of Slavophilism. He was fascinated by the ritual
of the Orthodox Church and used to conduct his drinking bouts
in a kind of parody of sacerdotal ritual. He seems to have hated
the Church with a devouring passion, and to have wished to
reveal the poisonous religiosity at the heart of Russian culture
and Russian life. He was fascinated by Russia's Holy Fools and
connected their visionary seizures with epilepsy, another of his
interests.

He entertained many grand intellectual designs—the history
of serfdom, the history of liberty in Russia—that were never even
partially realized. He was often hungry and penniless and was
sometimes fed by the working people in whom he was so inter-

ested. In 1865 he had typhus, but that was only the most severe of his many illnesses.

Pryzhov's personal relations are also somewhat mysterious. He was married, but his wife is a shadowy and remote figure in his life; her sympathy for his activities and point of view must have been limited. It is similarly difficult to discern much trace of close friendships. Pryzhov's deliberately cultivated eccentricities, his becoming a "character," must (as with Iakushkin, whom he strikingly resembles) have begun as a response to his shyness. This is also suggested by his relationship to dogs, which has occasioned much interest and some amusement among historians who have written about him.³⁶ It is not too much to say that he identified himself pathetically with dogs, particularly with dogs that had been beaten, chained up, and otherwise abused.³⁷ Pryzhov began his deposition to the court (known as his "Confession") by stating that his "whole life had been a dog's life"; at the end he saw Nechaev as having caused him to "die like a dog."

Pryzhov received two hundred fifty rubles for the sale of *The History of Taverns in Russia,* but more than half went to pay debts. Early 1868 found him desperately trying to sell the publishers another of his major projects, *The Dog in the History of Human Belief.* But on this occasion his difficulties were not produced (as they so often had been) by political censorship.

Out of work since 1866, Pryzhov sank further and further into vagrancy and alcoholism. He tried to drown himself in a pond (with his dog, Leporello), but both were dragged out. He worked briefly for a private railroad company (the revolutionary potentialities of the railroad charmed him initially), but he was by now apparently incapable of holding a job. He spent most of his time drinking and talking with railroad workers, who also helped feed him. The sale of his library in 1869, which brought him to Cherkesov's bookstore, was a final desperate expedient.

How rapidly was Pryzhov recruited? The answer appears to be that Nechaev quickly decided that Pryzhov could be useful, and

Pryzhov did not hold out long against him. He was desperate, angrier at the world than he had ever been, ready to take some "action" if he could. Nechaev appears to have convinced Pryzhov that they had a special bond, since they were both men of the people.[38] Nechaev's hatred of the old order must have gratified Pryzhov even as—perhaps—it frightened him. Pryzhov had connections among lower-level officialdom; he could (and did) write proclamations to Ukrainians in their native language; but above all, he had an unequaled knowledge of Moscow low life, and Nechaev intended to exploit the semicriminal underworld if he could.

Soon Pryzhov had his own group of five, several of whom had been expelled in October from the University of Moscow in another of the many faculty-student confrontations that had played such an important part in radicalizing Russia's students over the preceding fifteen years. Fëdor Ripman was assigned to Pryzhov's group, as he didn't know much about the *narod* (he subsequently told the court) and wanted to learn. Pryzhov sent Ripman off to a likely location, the Khitrov Market, a dreadful slum that was also a center of petty crime and criminals. There Ripman struck up an acquaintance with a few pickpockets and prostitutes—with some difficulty, for he made it a matter of principle that the men and women of the people should inaugurate the conversations. After a while, a sympathetic prostitute warned him that some of the men were planning to rob him. On another occasion, one of the thieves asked him if he knew a place where "you could rip something off."

Ripman was supposed to find out the secrets of influential men from the whores they patronized; it doesn't appear that he was the man for the job. Nor did he have much more success in a rural setting. For a time he served as tutor to a peasant named Dmitry Makarov, to whom he sang revolutionary songs and with whom he had conversations based on suggestive biblical themes, such as loving one's neighbor as oneself. In his court testimony, Ripman no doubt minimized these contacts and made them seem as harmless as possible, but his naiveté was not counterfeit. At his trial, he still professed to believe in the Committee, of which he stood in great awe, since "Nechaev could not have done all that by himself."[39]

Despite Nechaev's dislike of theoretical discussion, his groups inevitably spent a good deal of time going over the pamphlet literature and proclamations that comprised the harvest of the previous summer. Recruitment also proceeded apace, in the characteristic Nechaevist atmosphere of mystification, fraud, and intimidation. Ivan Likhutin, a student at the Medical-Surgical Academy in St. Petersburg, made a trip to Moscow, during which he posed as an "agent of the international society," allegedly come to check on how things were going.[40] Nikolai Nikolaev, a very young man from Ivanovo, "slavishly devoted" to Nechaev (Vera Zasulich's phrase), often played the role of an anonymous representative of the Committee. A certain number of students learned, in a confused and distorted fashion, of the existence of the First International, which (Nechaev told them) had enrolled millions of workers and was led by a "more intimate circle" concerned with concrete political tasks—such as the upcoming Russian revolution. Many students succumbed completely to these visions, particularly those who, like Aleksei Kuznetsov, were just at the point of disillusion with the Emperor Alexander's reforms.[41]

Money continued to be a major problem. The members themselves contributed; Kuznetsov, who was a person of some means, donated two hundred seventy-five rubles, but few others were in a position to do likewise. People's Vengeance letterheads and membership cards were printed, partly to impress potential donors, but not very much came of the solicitations.

The search for funds was the occasion for one of the most grotesque episodes of the autumn, generally described as the "affair of the *veksel'* [promissory note]."[42] Andrei Kolachevsky was a well-to-do young man whom Nechaev and several others (including Ivan and Vladimir Likhutin, their sister, Ekaterina, and Prokhor Debogorii-Mokrievich) decided to blackmail. They evolved the following puerile and theatrical scheme (did Nechaev's early success as an actor prompt him to choose this method?). Ivan Likhutin visited Kolachevsky (the kind of liberal fellow traveler Nechaev hated most) and left a copy of Nechaev's *Revolutionary Catechism* in his possession. A short while later, Kolachevsky was picked up in the street by Vladimir Likhutin and a friend, disguised in false beards and wigs and representing themselves as police officers. Together with Debogorii-Mokrievich, who sat in the rented carriage, they then drove Kolachevsky to a nearby hotel where they put the bite on him: either he could pay them six thousand rubles or they would "prosecute." Naturally he chose to pay, and gave his blackmailers a promissory note for the amount they wanted. Subsequently, Kolachevsky discovered what had happened and refused to honor the note. Confused reports of the attempted extortion soon began to circulate, and increased the (not very effective) opposition to Nechaev among some radicals in Moscow and particularly back in St. Petersburg. Had Nechaev's organization lasted longer, the affair of the *veksel'* might have proved seriously embarrassing.

It may also have been money that led to the murder of Ivan Ivanov, the abrupt end of the People's Vengeance, and the flight of Nechaev. The whole story of the developing hostility between Ivanov and Nechaev will never be known, but it is clear that Ivanov became more and more skeptical about Nechaev personally and about the mysterious Committee that always supported Nechaev in the event of controversy. It may be that a specific disagreement over whether to leaflet the Petrovsky Agricultural Academy (which was Ivanov's particular responsibility) was a key event.[43] But German Lopatin subsequently set himself the task of finding out what had really gone on, with an eye to exposing Nechaev and ending his influence on Russian radicals, both at home and in the emigration. This is his reconstruction of what happened:

Ivanov was well off (perhaps even rich), and had supplied Nechaev with money on more than one occasion. Towards the end he began to have doubts that the money was being put to the right use. One day he said to N[echaev]: "this is the last time I'm giving you any money. You know I am ready to give all I have to the 'cause,' but here I must lay down two conditions: (1.) that the person to whom I am to give the money inspires me with more confidence than you do; (2.) that I have some kind of guarantee that the person himself knows where the money is going and is not merely a blind tool in someone else's hands."[44]

Whatever the nature and sequence of events leading to the estrangement of the two, by mid-November Nechaev had decided that Ivanov had to be eliminated. It is possible that the decision was provoked by Ivanov's having threatened to leave the People's Vengeance altogether. It is even possible (though highly unlikely) that Nechaev feared a denunciation to the police.*

On Sunday, November 16, Nechaev called together Uspensky, Pryzhov, Nikolaev, and Kuznetsov, and told them he had decided to kill Ivanov.[45] In Nechaev's compelling presence, they all agreed to participate, although they were all (except the doughty Nikolaev) reluctant. When Pryzhov said that he couldn't see in the dark and had hurt his leg, Nechaev replied that if necessary they would carry him.

On November 21, Ivanov was lured to an out-of-the-way part of the grounds of the Petrovsky Academy on the pretext that a printing press had been discovered there[46] and the group had to decide what should be done with it. The meeting place was a ruined grotto, near a pond. There, in the late afternoon, Ivanov was strangled, then shot through the head (by Nechaev); his body was thrown into the pond, where it was discovered four days later. None of Nechaev's helpers displayed much sangfroid, and

---

*In *The Possessed*, Dostoevsky attributed the murder of Shatov (Ivanov) to Verkhovensky's (Nechaev's) desire to bind the members of his group to him body and soul. There is no suggestion of any such motivation among the principals. But in early March 1870, Georgy Enisherlov, a student at the Technological Institute in St. Petersburg who had been involved in the student disorders, attributed precisely this motive to Nechaev, basing the charge on conversations the two had allegedly had. Enisherlov, however, is anything but a reliable witness. So great was his detestation of Nechaev that he told the police he wanted to go abroad, find Nechaev, and "kill him like a dog"; he guaranteed the government he would return if he was unsuccessful. See B. P. Koz'min, *Nechaev i nechaevtsy* (Moscow-Leningrad, 1931), pp. 142–43. The recent discovery of Enisherlov's student diaries throws some light on the matter. Although he later became a moderate constitutionalist, Enisherlov was a very cynical and pessimistic young man in 1868–69; he claims in the diaries that Nechaev stole his ideas and even some phrases for *The Revolutionary Catechism!* See N. Pirumova, "M. Bakunin ili S. Nechaev," *Prometei*, No. 5 (1968), pp. 177–81.

Pryzhov in particular was in a pitiable condition. He had not been able to confront the dreadful project in a sober state, so he made a long stop in a tavern along the way, which delayed matters considerably. Subsequently, at Kuznetsov's apartment, with water and blood all over the floor, Nechaev suddenly sent a bullet close by Pryzhov's head and jokingly (?) suggested that if the shot had killed him, he could have taken the blame for the whole business. After his arrest, Pryzhov had a nervous breakdown. Nechaev suffered a severe flesh wound on his hand, where Ivanov had bitten him during the melee. He was in high spirits. On the following day, he and Kuznetsov left for St. Petersburg. "You're now a doomed man," said Nechaev to Kuznetsov, quoting from the *Catechism*.[47] (The historian longs for a film of this incident. Was Nechaev smiling?)

The discovery of Ivanov's body quickly brought the political police into the case. On November 26, still not really knowing what was going on, they made a search of Uspensky's apartment, where they turned up a good deal of illegal literature and, extraordinarily, a long list of names. Further searches of Cherkesov's bookstore and other people's apartments turned up more and more; finally, on February 11, the printing press was discovered, hidden in the wall between the bookstore and the building next door. Within hours of the initial discovery of the names in Uspensky's apartment, the dragnet was out. Nikolaev, Pryzhov, and Uspensky were quickly arrested; Kuznetsov was apprehended in St. Petersburg in early December. In all, 152 people were picked up on charges of involvement with Nechaev; of these, 79 were actually tried.[48] The four principals received lengthy sentences (between seven and fifteen years) at hard labor, to be followed by exile for life to Siberia. Uspensky eventually hanged himself in prison, after some of his followers (unjustly) accused him of being a police spy. Of the four, only Kuznetsov continued his radical activity after the expiration of his sentence.

But Nechaev had slipped through the fingers of the police again. He had gone to St. Petersburg, apparently in the hope of continuing to build up the People's Vengeance. But to do so was impossible after the wave of arrests began. It may also be that he encountered determined opposition there from the moment of his arrival. Mikhail Negreskul, the son-in-law of Pëtr Lavrov, and Mark Natanson, who was to become prominent in the revolutionary movement of the 1870s, were only two of the radicals of the capital who were working to counteract his influence.[49] Nechaev apparently returned quickly to Moscow, and from there went south to Tula, whence, in the company of Varvara Aleksandrovskaia, a thirty-six-year-old radical groupie of unstable disposition,* he made his way abroad.

Aleksandrovskaia's subsequent depositions to the police[50] make it quite clear that the romance of her flight abroad with Nechaev was not merely political. But she was disappointed on all counts. Upon their arrival in Geneva, she was shunted from place to place and generally neglected. She met "some old man" (it was Ogarëv) who asked her vaguely how things were in Russia. Within a few days, Nechaev informed her that it was now time to go back. She was given a quantity of new proclamations and told to deliver them to two students at the Petrovsky Agricultural Academy in Moscow. There was also material addressed to Mark Natanson and others of Nechaev's enemies. On January 11, she was arrested at the frontier. It is entirely possible, as the eminent Soviet historian B. P. Koz'min has suggested,[51] that Nechaev connived at her arrest in order to damage Natanson; her depositions to the government are not edifying. She renewed her offer to work against the revolutionary movement, suggesting that she lure Nechaev to Dresden, where he might be picked up by government agents. Her accounts of her relationship with Nechaev contain striking references to her self-abasement before him, and her entrapment scheme has a nasty overtone of sexual revenge.[52]

Confused reports of Ivanov's murder were already current in Geneva when on January 9 Bakunin learned that Nechaev had

---

*Aleksandrovskaia (of gentry background and married to a St. Petersburg customs official) was arrested in 1862 for disseminating radical propaganda. After spending several months in prison, she was exiled to Tula. After Karakozov's attempt, she volunteered her services to the government in the struggle against the revolutionary movement.

escaped. He was awaiting, he wrote to Ogarëv, "our Boy."[53]
Immediately upon his arrival in Switzerland, Nechaev, together
with Bakunin and Ogarëv, plunged into the work of drafting
more proclamations, calling upon all strata of Russian society to
involve themselves in the coming insurrection, now only a few
months away.[54] At the same time, Nechaev, who knew that the
Russian government would attempt to extradite him, set to work
mobilizing the French, German, and—above all—the Swiss Left
to put pressure on the Swiss government to resist the Russian
efforts. A considerable campaign was mounted, and so great was
the abhorrence of the Russian government by all European radicals that even some who had become thoroughly disquieted by
what they were discovering about Nechaev's methods lent their
names to the antiextradition campaign. The crucial issue was
whether the murder of Ivanov was a political crime or not. If, as
the Russian government claimed, it was *not*, then Nechaev could
be extradited as an ordinary criminal. To rally his potential supporters and bolster the political interpretation, Nechaev represented himself in the radical press as the object of assassination
attempts by the Third Section.

The only segment of the radical political spectrum that was
unswervingly hostile to Nechaev was the Marxian one. Ironically
enough, Marx's associates and disciples wanted to get Nechaev
largely because by exposing his dirty tricks they could strike a
blow against Bakunin, whose quarrel with Marx was soon to
destroy the First International.

Unless he had done them an injury, most radicals were reluctant to condemn Nechaev publicly, perhaps because they had an
accurate (but generally unarticulated) sense that what separated
Nechaev from themselves was no matter of principle but determination to go *all the way;* there was a lot of talk about "giving
oneself over utterly to the cause," but Nechaev was revealing
new meanings in this by-now-hackneyed phrase. The Swiss and
in particular the Russian radicals were also understandably reluctant to do anything that might play into the hands of the Russian
government. But the struggle between Marx and Bakunin within
the International freed the Marxists to make the most of the

grotesque and squalid material that lay amply to hand. They concentrated their fire on two issues—both minor, but both revelatory of Nechaev's style.

The first had its origins in the summer of 1869. At that time, Mikhail Negreskul had, like Nechaev, been in Switzerland. There he encountered Charles Perron, a veteran Swiss radical. Perron deplored to him the fact that Bakunin, the great freedom-fighter, was living in penury and asked the young Russian if something could be done. Negreskul was willing to try, and through his agency it was arranged that Bakunin should translate the first volume of Marx's *Das Kapital* into Russian for a Petersburg publishing house.* Grappling with Marx's "economic metaphysics" (Bakunin's term) proved increasingly burdensome, however, and by the time that Nechaev arrived back in Switzerland, Bakunin was heartily sick of the job and eager to abandon it in favor of promoting the Russian revolution and preventing the extradition of "Boy." Nechaev told Bakunin that he would arrange things; without telling Bakunin what he was doing, he wrote a letter to Nikolai Liubavin, who had arranged matters for Negreskul with the publisher, saying that if he didn't stop annoying Bakunin, the People's Vengeance would deal with him. To make the affair even more unsavory, Bakunin had accepted a three-hundred-ruble advance, which he was now quite unable to pay back, even had he been willing to do so. Marx made effective if rather unscrupulous use of this episode at the Hague Congress of the International.[55]

The second case that was employed to discredit Bakunin and his allies was Nechaev's renewed assault on the depleted resources of the Bakhmetev Fund. The opportunity was provided by the death of Herzen on January 21, 1870. While he lived, the fund was inaccessible, but following his death, Tuchkova-Ogarëva and Herzen's son decided to give the remainder of the money to Bakunin and Ogarëv; Nechaev ended up with most of it. Marx subsequently circulated a garbled account of the affair,

*The edition appeared at the end of March 1872, translated in the event by Lopatin and N. F. Daniel'son. With their customary penetration, the Russian censors allowed the volume to appear, apparently because they thought that such a long, dry book could do no great harm!

alleging that Bakunin had gotten hold of various monies belonging to Herzen that he was using for his own disreputable purposes.

Among the works produced by Nechaev during the first frenetic months of 1870 was the second number of the *Editions of the
Society of the People's Vengeance.*[56] After defending the elimination of Ivanov as necessary for "the *cause*," Nechaev went on to
expound his postrevolutionary vision in a short article entitled
"The Principal Foundations of the Future Social Order." Although Nechaev made specific and approving reference to the
Communist Manifesto, the dominant notes he struck were Jacobin: the Committee was to oversee the revolutionary process
from beginning to end. Although the vast majority of the population in the postrevolutionary period would live in rural or industrial co-ops and artels, the regulation of the economy and its new
structure would still be in the hands of the Committee. From his
references to communal kitchens and dormitories, it is clear that
Nechaev envisioned collectivism on a most ambitious scale (however cursory his formulations); and here, too, the Committee
would be both organizer and enforcer.[57]

The principal drama of the spring, however, concerns Nechaev's relations with Alexander Herzen's daughter, Natal'ia
(known as "Tata"), and with Bakunin himself. Nechaev's efforts
to cajole, seduce, and finally threaten Tata into political cooperation—for her name and family connection were valuable—led,
on Bakunin's part, to some unease, which was increased by his
gradual (and unwilling) recognition of the profoundly authoritarian and statist nature of Nechaev's communism. Nechaev's initial
objective was the resurrection of Herzen's *Bell,* six unsatisfactory
issues of which did appear in April and May, financed by the
greater part of the Bakhmetev money. Then, in May and June,
German Lopatin entered the scene once more, armed with evidence that even Bakunin could not ignore about the murder of
Ivanov, the invention of revolutionary organizations, and, above
all, the double-dealing, intimidation, and blackmail—not merely
of liberal dupes but of "comrades," like Bakunin himself. And
what Lopatin related to Bakunin, coldly and correctly, was all the

harder to deny, as the "Yids and Germans" around Marx were making such excellent use of Bakunin's relationship with Nechaev to destroy the old man politically.

Nechaev approached Tata Herzen in the same way that he had worked so successfully on other members of privilege Russia: through mystification, the projection of "energy," but above all by preying on what one must anachronistically call "liberal guilt." Initially, he made considerable headway, the more so as she was, in the aftermath of her father's death, eager to do something for his cause and quite aware that she had never really acted on the family convictions. But she had a strong strain of common sense that enabled her to see through Nechaev more easily than Bakunin had; furthermore, she had no comparable psychological investment in "Young Russia" and an imminent insurrection. She was quite put off by Nechaev's insistence that the end justified the means and horrified by talk of the necessity of blackmail. What really did the trick, however, was probably Nechaev's rather passionless declarations of love; Tata Herzen was uncomfortably conscious of being an heiress and had rejected admirers more convincing in their declarations than Nechaev because she suspected that their motives were financial.[58]

For Bakunin the struggle was far more desperate, not only because the personal bond was so deep (his letters in this period describe Nechaev as being "virginally pure," "filled with love," and other incongruous phrases) but because a break meant the abandonment of his current vision of the Russian revolution and his place in it, which had become profoundly important to him.

In a fashion at once touching and macabre, Bakunin tried, in his letters to Ogarëv and Tata Herzen, to understand—almost to justify—a manipulative authoritarianism that was repugnant to his deepest convictions. Bakunin's anarchism and belief in federations of communes was striking even among Russian Populists; his conception of Russia's future was closer to that of Shchapov than to Nechaev's "barracks communism." Almost a month after his first conversation with Lopatin, he addressed a "collective message" to Ogarëv, Tata, and others in which he cautioned them against "taking too unfavorable a view of our friend the

Baron [Nechaev]." He accepted Nechaev's notion that Russian youth was "a corrupt and inane herd of jabbering doctrinaires,"[59] and in another place amplified this view, not exactly accepting it or its consequences, but suggesting that any serious revolutionary might be tempted by it:

Our youth is too corrupt and flaccid [runs Bakunin's paraphrase of Nechaev's opinion] to be trusted to form an organization by force of persuasion alone—but since an organization is essential, and since these young people are incapable of uniting and unwilling to unite freely, they must be united involuntarily and unawares—and in order that this organization, half-founded on coercion and deceit, should not crumble, they must be confounded and compromised to such an extent that it becomes impossible for them to withdraw.[60]

A few pages later, Bakunin summed up many of the factors that tempted Nechaev (and how many others!) to the Jacobin alternative in the following cogent words:

[Nechaev] saw with despair . . . the historical backwardness, the apathy, the inarticulateness, the infinite patience and the sluggishness of our Orthodox people, who could, if they realized and so desired, sink this entire ship of state with one wave of their mighty hand, but who appear still to be sleeping the sleep of the dead.[61]

And so, as late as mid-June 1870, Bakunin could not face a complete break with Nechaev and instead presented him with a set of "conditions" for continued collaboration. Bakunin still could not believe that Nechaev was in any sense *vicious,* since he tended to see all vices as deriving from the characteristically bourgeois sins of corruption and self-interestedness.

It is quite conceivable that Bakunin might have continued to deluge his friends (and Nechaev) with mammoth letters and programmatic statements for months, but Nechaev, as we know, had a low tolerance for these intelligentsia games. Early in July, he came out of hiding and paid Bakunin and Ogarëv a brief visit in Geneva. Having already decided, perhaps, that there was little to keep him in Switzerland, he then left for London, taking with him a number of letters and other documents he had stolen from

Bakunin and the Herzen family. By so doing, he helped Bakunin
finally to act with some consistency. On July 24, the old revolutionary wrote the following cautionary lines to a Swiss friend, to
whom, a few short months before, he had given Nechaev a fulsome introduction:

If you introduce him to a friend, his first task will be to sow discord,
gossip, intrigue between you—in a word, to set you at loggerheads.
If your friend has a wife, a daughter, he will try to seduce her, to give
her a child to tear her away from the official morality and plunge her
forcibly into revolutionary protest against society. They regard any
personal attachment, any friendship, any *intimacy* as an evil which
it is their duty to destroy, because all of it constitutes a power which,
existing as it does independently of the secret organization, diminishes the unique power of the latter.[62]

The letter had its effect; late in the summer, Nechaev wrote
angrily from London to Bakunin and Ogarëv about the damage
to him that this and similar letters had done; they had given him,
he wrote unexpectedly, "the kiss of Judas."

While in London, Nechaev produced his final publication: a
slim brochure that he called *Commune (Obshchina)*. Despite his
interest in the *Communist Manifesto*, he was contemptuous of
the lack of revolutionary spirit exhibited by the First International; at the same time, he published an "open letter" to Bakunin and Ogarëv, a document that for its shrewdness and generational viewpoint deserves quotation:

I am taking advantage of this opportunity to tell you that despite our
differences about political ends and means—differences which became apparent when we were confronted with practical affairs which
demanded not only theoretical radicalism but also resoluteness in
action—I, while renouncing from now on all political solidarity with
you, nevertheless continue to regard you as the best representatives
of a generation—a generation which is unfortunately departing the
stage of history without leaving a trace. The ideas of your generation,
gentlemen, not having any roots in your life and situation, received
from without and cut off from your material condition—although for
this reason you could never realize these ideas in practice, they have
nevertheless saved you to some extent from that slime and filth into

which your contemporaries and schoolmates have sunk. . . . Your social convictions have prevented you from becoming proponents of the accursed state structure of the present day, but they have been so little felt by the generation which has come from a non-popular milieu that they have not made anyone a real enemy of that state; because the contradiction between the revolutionary thought and an aristocratic life led to a dismal skepticism and a fruitless disappointment even in such strong minds as the mind of A. Herzen.

All that could be of use in this generation has found its expression in the brilliant literary works of the late editor of the *Bell* and in yours.[63]

We know little of Nechaev's movements during his last two years of liberty. He was in Paris during the Prussian siege of the final months of 1870; by the spring of 1871 he had returned to Switzerland. He stayed for a time with M. P. Sazhin (Arman Ross), in those days an associate of Bakunin, in Zurich. They discussed the situation in Paris and politics in general. Although Nechaev tried for a time to convince Sazhin that he was part of a continuing revolutionary network, he soon gave up and admitted his complete isolation.[64] He worked for a time in Zurich as a sign painter —his old trade—toiling from six in the morning until six in the evening.

In the summer of 1871, with the major protagonist still at large, the trial of his dupes, disciples, and victims, sometimes known as the "Trial of the Eighty-seven," took place under the new legal order introduced by Alexander's reforms. Many conservative figures in the police and other government departments were uncertain about the new format: public proceedings, defense attorneys, and so on. In addition, the drama of the Paris Commune and the possible contacts between participants and some of the accused provided a largely specious link between the two events, which further increased the nervousness of conservative circles. The minister of justice and other high government officials hoped that the public revelation of Nechaev's villainy would have a cautionary effect on the country's radical youth. But everything seemed to go wrong at the trial. The large number of defendants (some of whom had merely received proclamations through the mail), the complexity of Nechaev's involvements, and above all the failure of the government lawyers clearly to separate the murder of Ivanov from minor matters like the distribution of leaflets—all this prevented the trial from becoming the counterrevolutionary morality play that the government had hoped to present to public opinion. In addition, the spectators tended to be young "nihilists," sympathetic to the accused; the "liberal" defense lawyers were far more skillful and daring than those who presented the government's case. The four who had participated directly in the murder received sentences ranging between seven and fifteen years at hard labor (to be followed by exile)—remarkably lenient terms that caused many a conservative to long for the old days when trials were administrative and secret.[65]

But the government succeeded in spite of itself. The trial made an extremely good impression on moderate public opinion. Nikolai Mikhailovsky, covering the proceedings for the radical *Annals of the Fatherland,* found the trial a triumphant vindication of the "new justice." And despite the public sympathy for the defendants evident in the courtroom, there was a substantial movement of radical opinion against Nechaev and his methods, a kind of revulsion that developed steadily in the early 1870s.

Interesting evidence of the shift in radical opinion against "Nechaevism" is provided by the case of several former students at the University of Moscow who had been expelled in the fracas of the fall of 1869 that had added to the membership of the People's Vengeance. They showed up in Zurich in the summer of 1871, while the trial was on; according to Sazhin, only one was interested in meeting Nechaev;* the other three wanted nothing to do with him. But Nechaev, hoping to reconstitute some kind of a group, persuaded several of them to meet with him. His plan, according to Sazhin, was to start a periodical, which was to be financed by blackmailing the Herzen family, using the little archive of compromising material with which Nechaev had left

---

*Nechaev persuaded Ivan Ponomarev, a future chemistry professor at the University of Kharkov, to sign an oath of allegiance to the Committee. There is an odor of self-parody about the episode. See Lehning, *Michel Bakounine,* p. 366.

Geneva the year before. The scheme did not commend itself either to Sazhin or to the students. And Bakunin got wind of the fact that Sazhin was in touch with Nechaev and threatened to have nothing further to do with him if he did not end the relationship. Which Sazhin did.

Zemfiry Ralli had been close to Nechaev during the student protests in the fall of 1869; indeed, he was probably to have become a member of the Committee. He had been arrested, exiled, and in the fall of 1871 escaped to Switzerland, where he took up residence in Zurich. In the spring of 1872, Nechaev arrived for a visit. Ralli provides a somewhat less flattering description than is usual in the memoir literature: "it was the same young man, with the burning eyes and the brusque gestures, scrawny, small in stature, nervous, biting his fingernails to the quick."[66] He was reading Robespierre's memoirs and the *Confessions* of Rousseau. Again, Bakunin's intervention led to a quarrel, which ended with Nechaev's departure. During the final weeks before his arrest, he shared quarters with Kaspar Turski, a young Polish revolutionary from a noble family, who had fought for the Paris Commune and was to collaborate closely with Tkachëv on his journal, the *Tocsin*. Turski was as much a believer in revolutionary will as Nechaev, and as much of a Jacobin. The two got on famously.

One day in the late summer of 1872, Nechaev, who had at the time a Serbian passport issued to one Stepan Grazdanov, walked into a small restaurant on the outskirts of Zurich that was frequented by workers and socialists. According to an eyewitness,[67] he spoke briefly and animatedly with a man at a table, then got up and walked out into the little garden behind the restaurant. In a moment, the door was covered by the local police commissioner, and ten or a dozen men appeared. After a brief scuffle, Nechaev was dragged away, shouting, "Tell the Russians that Grazdanov has been arrested." He had been betrayed by Adolf Stępkowski, a Polish double agent whom he had met through Turski. Several amateurish attempts to rescue him ensued, none of which got off the ground.

On October 9, Nechaev admitted who he was, and to help the

renewed political furor about extradition, claimed that the elimination of Ivanov was both necessary and "a purely political act." But the murder of Ivanov had become notorious, and the Swiss Left was not willing to undertake much on his behalf. On October 26, the Grand Council in Zurich voted 4–3 for extradition, on condition that Nechaev be tried under the regular criminal laws. The following day, he was handed over to the Russian authorities at the Bavarian frontier.*

Nechaev's own trial opened on January 8, 1873, in Moscow District Court. From the outset he denied the right of the tribunal to try him, claiming that he was an émigré and that he had been kidnapped.† After the government had presented an elaborate reconstruction of Ivanov's murder, the jury deliberated only twenty minutes before finding him guilty. He was sentenced to twenty years at hard labor. As he was being taken from the hall, he shouted, "Long live the Assembly! Down with despotism!" There was no doubting his courage or his intransigence, but of course "assemblies" played no role in his thinking. And despotism?

After his trial and condemnation, Nechaev simply disappeared. Subsequently it became known that a decision had been made at the highest level to put Nechaev away in the Alekseisky Ravelin, the grimmest and most impregnable dungeon in the Fortress of St. Peter and St. Paul. The reasons for this violation of legality need no elaboration.

For more than seven years, nothing was known of his whereabouts. Then, in January 1881, the directing body of the People's Will (known as the Executive Committee) received a letter— from Nechaev! Although most of the leadership were at the least dubious about him and his methods, the letter made an enormous impression. Vera Figner, who recounted the episode in her memoirs,[68] described the communication as completely busi-

---

*J. J. Pfenninger, the Zurich police chief, received a "substantial reward" from the Russian government for capturing Nechaev and then persuading the Grand Council to extradite him. See Woodford McClellan, "Nechaevshchina: An Unknown Chapter," *Slavic Review* 32:3 (September 1973), p. 547.

†As he was leaving after the first court session, Nechaev shouted, "I have ceased to be a slave of your despot. Long live the National Assembly!" See B. Bazilevsky, *Gosudarstvennyia prestupleniia v Rossii v XIX veke*, Vol. I (Stuttgart, 1903), p. 416.

nesslike and unsentimental. The message: "Free me." Figner's impression was that all his willingness to lie, cheat, and steal, to shed innocent blood, had been purged by his years in the Ravelin. The Executive Committee agreed that he must be freed!

The letter had been brought out of the fortress by a guard whom Nechaev had suborned, and he claimed that more than forty of his jailers and guards were in some way under his influence. No one doubted the figure. Characteristically, Nechaev's plan for his own liberation depended on a complicated mystification: his revolutionary rescuers were to arrive in uniforms, covered with medals, and announce to the guards that a revolution had taken place. Alexander had been replaced on the throne by his son, who had decreed that the prisoner in the Ravelin was to be freed.

Eventually, however, the Executive Committee decided that the rescue would have to wait until Tsar Alexander had been done away with, and Nechaev was so informed.* But after the assassination, the organization of the People's Will was decimated by the police, and the rescue attempt was never made. A precarious contact existed until April 1, when Nechaev's courier was arrested; more than sixty people were eventually tried and punished for involvement with the prisoner. None of the members of the People's Will who ended in the fortress ever saw him, and now there was no one outside to take advantage of his advice: in order to exacerbate the postassassination chaos, an "imperial manifesto" restoring serfdom should be issued and other, similar misinformation spread. Nechaev was now utterly isolated from all other prisoners; the new, strict regime under which he was placed led to his death, apparently from scurvy, on November 21, 1882, thirteen years to the day after the murder of Ivanov.

In later years, a number of the soldiers whose careers Nechaev had ruined encountered various radicals in exile. Their awe, even fear, according to Figner, continued undiminished. At their

*Figner denies the rumor that subsequently gained credence in radical circles that Nechaev himself volunteered to postpone his rescue until after the attempt on the Emperor. The Executive Committee made that decision. The wide acceptance of that story, however, tells us something about the changing attitude toward Nechaev on the Russian Left after 1881.

trial, many had refused to use the name Nechaev, referring to their nemesis only as "he." "Just try and refuse when he orders you to do something!" said one of them.[69]

Of all the responses to Nechaev in general and the murder of Ivanov in particular, Fëdor Dostoevsky's was the most immediate and is probably still the most famous. Dostoevsky was modern (and neurotic) enough to feel Nechaev's power in a deeper and more prophetic fashion than the radicals of the day; his horrified fascination indicates how well he understood, at one level, Nechaev's *appeal*. After his novel *The Possessed* had been published, Dostoevsky confessed in the columns of the right-wing newspaper for which he wrote: "probably I could never have become a Nechaev, but a Nechaevets—for this I couldn't vouch, but maybe I could have become one . . . in the days of my youth."* Dostoevsky was abroad at the time of the murder, and as he followed the unfolding drama of Nechaev's career in the newspapers at the Dresden public library, a new character invaded the pages of his work-in-progress. Known variously as "the student" and "Nechaev," he finally became Pëtr Verkhovensky.

At one level (his "rational egoism"), Verkhovensky owes something to Chernyshevsky, but the combination of Verkhovensky's manic frivolity and genius for sordid intrigue does not really recall any major figure in the revolutionary movement. Dostoevsky himself professed surprise at the "comic" elements in the character. Despite the archetypal quality of Verkhovensky, some real parallels with the historical Nechaev remain: their devotion to "the ax" and their admiring references to the Jesuits; their hatred of theory in itself and their attraction toward conspiratorial action and criminality. Dostoevsky goes so far as to say of his character, Nechaev-in-transition, that he is "not a socialist but a rebel. His ideas are insurrection and destruction, after

*Fëdor Dostoevsky, *The Diary of a Writer*, Vol. I (London and Toronto, 1949), p. 147. Dostoevsky was of course thinking of his radical youth, when he came within a whisker of being executed for his involvement with the Petrashevsky Circle. Was he also thinking of Pryzhov, six years younger than he, whom he had known at least in passing at the Marinskaia Hospital? There is a minor figure in *The Possessed*, a member of Verkhovensky's group, clearly based on Pryzhov.

which 'let happen what will' on the basis of the social principle according to which whatever might come would still be better than the present, and that the time has come to act rather than to preach."[70] The fit is not exact—one cannot say simply that Nechaev is "not a socialist"—and yet it suggests something that we need to know about how Nechaev put action and belief together. Similarly, Dostoevsky was able to realize how little Nechaev cared for ideas and "discussion"; on the other side, the inveterate discussers who encountered Nechaev were prone to stand in awe of someone who had no time for all that, who was so "energetic."

For all of the traces of the historical Nechaev that may be found in Verkhovensky, however, there is absolutely nothing in Nechaev to suggest a final cynicism about revolution itself. Largely for this reason, Nechaev and Verkhovensky *feel* different. Perhaps this is part of what Dostoevsky meant when he wrote: "I do not know Nechaev, or Ivanov, or the circumstances of this murder." In a prosaic sense, he clearly did "know" a good deal about Nechaev. But Dostoevsky was interested in the revolutionary consequences of atheism. To say that "all is permitted" if God does not exist, however, is not the same as to give a concrete historical rendering of what "all is permitted" might mean in your hometown or your own life. This Dostoevsky was clearly concerned to do in *The Possessed*.

Nechaev also recalls the solipsistic egoism of Max Stirner: he identified the revolution with himself, what he called "the cause" with his person, even in the most squalid attempts at blackmail and revenge on "opponents." He was also "Machiavellian": almost every educated person who came in contact with him had recourse to the term sooner or later. It is applicable, of course, only in the most general sense: his revolutionary politics, like the relations between sovereign states, was carried on without regard to traditional moral norms, secular or sacred. To call Nechaev "Machiavellian" is about as illuminating and precise as to apply the same term to Bismarck, which has been done as often.

For Albert Camus, writing around 1950, Nechaev foreshadowed the nihilist revolutions of the twentieth century that devoured their children, a perspective hard to escape even now.[71] Previously, Camus wrote, there had been a "community of the oppressed," by whom and for whom the revolution was to be made. But Nechaev regarded his cohorts as wholly expendable, as cannon fodder. No revolutionary activist had taken this position so clearly and openly before. But while accepting Camus's perspective, we should observe that his rhetoric takes us far from Nechaev's world. "The community of the oppressed" is an elegant phrase, a compassionate phrase, with just a hint of pathos about it. As when Camus decries "the violence done to one's brothers," we are sensible that we are hearing the rhetoric of a humane person of the Left, a secularized Christian with the experience of the French Resistance behind him. The rhetoric is sympathetic, educated, high-minded in a good sense.

But there is no trace, in Camus's words, of class or racial hatred —nor even an allowance for it. Nechaev did not, could not, recognize such phrases as "the community of the oppressed." At some level, he recognized his kinship with the more miserable and exploited portions of the Russian lower classes—but not the children of gentry Russia, the students he tried to recruit in Moscow or St. Petersburg. For they were the cousins—however "radical"—of the people who ran "the Russian Manchester" and in whose houses his father had carried a tray. The moralist may affirm "the community of the oppressed," but the historian must suspect its ability to explain.

Whatever the insufficiencies of Soviet Marxist historiography on Populism, B. P. Koz'min, the most formidable Soviet student of the problem, sniffed out what Camus's analysis leaves out: the pure, intoxicating, enduring hatred stemming from class. Vera Zasulich sensed it, too. He "was not a product of our intelligentsia milieu," she wrote in her memoirs,[72] and he had as profound a scorn and hatred for his young disciples as for any other aspect of "their" society. But although Nechaev was from the *narod*, although he would make the revolution for its sake, although he hated the *narod* less, perhaps, than he did his radical friends, he had nevertheless fled from his origins into revolution. He was at home nowhere.

Nechaev failed, not because of his "immorality" but because he was a solitary, ignorant provincial who came too soon. Direct analogies between Nechaev and the makers of the Russian Revolution, of a kind which flourished for a time after 1917,[73] are intellectually vulgar and absurd. And yet Nechaev left his footprints in Russia's radical political culture. In the early years of the twentieth century, Lenin told Angelica Balabanoff, in answer to her pained question about the employment of dishonest means to seize power: "Everything that is done in the interest of the proletarian cause is honest."[74] Indeed, a great deal of Balabanoff's book *Impressions of Lenin* is about Lenin's belief that whatever advanced "the cause" was not only ethically sound but necessary—and her growing understanding of and disillusion with that belief. She is naive. Lenin and Trotsky thought her so, although they seem to have remained devoted to her to the last; Lloyd George or Franklin Roosevelt would have concurred in their judgment. All politicians *sometimes* act as if the end justifies the means. But in "bourgeois" political cultures most politicians are not able to admit their disposition publicly or practice it consistently. Clothe this kind of "Machiavellianism" in revolutionary costume and it seems to lose some of its shabby and uneasy air of "realism" and become plausible. Especially when its spokesman is not Nechaev but Vladimir Il'ich Lenin.* In the 1860s, Russian political culture began to become tough, Russian radicals unscrupulous, and the wellsprings of radical idealism more obscure. Nechaev's career is a way station on that path.

There is another connection here, one more easily described. Isaac Deutscher once remarked that "there is . . . the conflict of two souls, the Marxist and the Jacobin, in Bolshevism, a conflict never to be resolved either in Lenin or in Bolshevism at large."[75] At bottom, the persistent recurrence and

---

*There are few traces of Nechaev in Lenin's writings, or in the voluminous "encounters with Lenin"–"recollections of Lenin" literature. He did tell Vladimir Bonch-Bruevich in 1905 of his admiration for Nechaev and Tkachëv. "People completely forget," Lenin said, "that Nechaev possessed unique organizational talent, an ability to establish the special techniques of conspiratorial work everywhere, an ability to give his thoughts such startling formulations that they were forever imprinted on one's memory." Quoted in David Shub, *Lenin* (Garden City, N.Y., 1948), pp. 371–72.

development of authoritarian, hierarchical, and manipulative behavior among Russian radicals (which is largely what "Russian Jacobinism" is) springs from the material and cultural gap between the Russian elite and the working classes. From Pestel in the early nineteenth century to Lenin, Russian radicals irregularly but persistently concluded that the Russian masses were capable of enormous and destructive outbursts of rage but not of building a new order. The optimism characteristic of the Populist vision went against the grain of Russian radical experience, but in the end it gave way to the ruthless realism of Tkachëv and Lenin.

In Russia, "civil society," in the Marxist sense of the term, was always weak, as was the bourgeois world from which it sprang. The pursuit of egoistic private interest, the organizational and institutional means for the creation and enjoyment of wealth were until less than a century ago quite undeveloped. An almost medieval merchantry lingered far into the nineteenth century; industrial entrepreneurs of the Western type appeared very late and were more uncertain than elsewhere in Europe, their self-confidence undermined by the lingering power of agrarian and aristocratic attitudes on the Right and socialist egalitarianism on the Left. With some reform-minded aristocrats (as earlier with Herzen), it is difficult to label the hostility to the bourgeoisie as either feudal or socialist; it was both.

In any case, all "liberal," moderate, constitutional political life in Russia suffered from the resulting sense of weakness—often concealed below the surface of social and political life, but never very far below. One consequence, in the words of Leopold Haimson, was a

deficiency, characteristic of moderate and radical constitutionalists alike . . . the ultimate absence, in their confrontation of the redoubtable and omnipresent state power, of the sense—so pervasive among English country gentlemen in the eighteenth century House of Commons and among the deputies of the French Third Estate in 1789—that they constituted in their own right the adequate representatives of country and nation.[76]

They could not, among other things, either shore up or replace the aristocratic *obshchestvo,* irrevocably in decline after 1861.

The purely industrial tasks that Marx had assigned the bourgeoisie were, however, accomplished—by the state. The first great industrialization drive took its impetus from Count Witte and the Ministry of Finance in the late imperial period; the second was accomplished in nightmare fashion by Stalin, after the Revolution. In that limited sense, it turned out the Populists were right: it was possible to "skip" capitalism. But many things that accompanied bourgeois rule in the West—ideas of citizenship, of social initiative and responsibility—were weakly developed or nonexistent in Russia. Whatever the cruelties of industrialization in Western Europe and America, whatever the degradation and oppression of bourgeois society—and we know they were great—the self-actualizing activity of individuals played its part in the birth of these things, and coexisted with them. Thus there remained a living tradition of citizen opposition to bureaucratic rule from above, whether public or private.

Although Russia had no bourgeoisie able to oppose the state and bureaucracy either culturally or politically, the intelligentsia rejected them outright; this moral and political revulsion had from the first an anarchist quality. Slavophilism arose after the autocracy had been expanding its regulatory and coercive authority over the population for more than a century, changing the crude and heavy-handed patriarchal monarchy into a powerful secular absolutism. The Slavophile critique of Peter the Great was the descendant of earlier attacks on both the secularization of the autocracy and on its final political triumph—which came largely over aristocratic and regional forces in Russia. Much of the Slavophile analysis was taken over by early Populists such as Herzen and Shchapov—more or less purged of its boyar point of view. They viewed the *narod* not as the bulwark of Holy Russia but as the shaping force that would create a new, socialist Russia. Both the Slavophiles and the Populists wrote ideological and tendentious histories of Russia, denigrating the autocracy and its sociopolitical rationalism, deifying the *narod,* and branding the state-builders as "aliens": Mongols, Greeks, or Germans.

During the period of the so-called Great Reforms, decentraliz-
ing and antistatist currents appeared in politically moderate
form, helping to inspire and direct the reforming impulse—most
obviously in the provincialist ideologies that underlay the creation of the zemstvos.[77] But moderate antistatism never became
a powerful force in Russia, largely because of the weakness of
civil society; most of their converts during the remainder of the
century were drawn from the "liberals" who gathered around
the zemstvos and their auxiliary organizations.

In the short run, radical Populism was a much more important
force, which could periodically threaten the government with
serious political crises. Certainly the government's fear of the
Populist Left helped sap its episodic efforts at reform after 1866
—although it will not do to "blame" the radicals for the failure
of liberal reform. Populism, however, could only challenge the
state—historically, politically, mythically—in a total fashion. It
could not seriously modify the scope or policies of the state or
create competing structures; the Populists had no program, beyond the pathos of their intelligentsia belief in the *narod*. And
Populist intellectuals were as hostile to the nascent bourgeois-
capitalist order as to the old regime—if not more so. So had some
kind of Populist coup actually "succeeded," it could have survived only by bureaucratic rule of some kind: a "dictatorship of
the peasantry" (as it might have been called), enduring most
likely only until the legitimist monarchies of Europe could organize to crush it.

So in the unequal struggle between state and society that has
in so many ways given content to Russian history, Slavophilism
and Populism (and their more specifically anarchist descendants)
have created only heroic myths and genealogies—which from
time to time can still flare up into movements that tell us that one
day the Russian intelligentsia and the Russian people will rise and
overthrow their "alien," bureaucratic oppressors.

But from within the Populist movement itself emerged the
politically conscious Jacobinism that accepted the state, sought to
seize it and to make the revolution that way. In Bolshevik form,
a Russian Jacobinism came to power in 1917. Even in the early

days of the Revolution, many of the arguments and controversies
of the Nechaev period resurfaced. Idealists like Angelica Balabanoff thought that the Bolsheviks "used" people in a way that was
not permissible. She has described, in terms that recall Nechaev's
Catechism, how foreign Communists who arrived in Moscow
"were classified as superficial, naive, ambitious or venal. Then
they were used according to this classification."[78] Under Stalin
came the violent and terrible revolution from above. "The end
justifies the means" meant one thing when Ishutin said it, another when the émigré Lenin said it, another when Lenin had
come to power, yet another when it was Stalin who was in power.
Yet those diverse meanings are connected. Stalin united the
Machiavellianism of the Left and Right, as well as their solipsism.
He could say, with Louis XIV, *"L'état, c'est moi,"* but he was also
—as Nechaev believed *he* was—the Revolution.

Notes

INTRODUCTION

1. Even so distinguished an intellectual historian as Andrzej Walicki does this on occasion. On pp. 547–48 of his *Slavophile Controversy* (Oxford, 1975), he writes that Tolstoy's Christian anarchism "was a direct reflection of the social *Weltanschauung* and (partially) of the interests of the exploited and ruined masses of the patriarchal peasantry."

CHAPTER ONE: RUSSIAN SOCIETY ON THE EVE OF EMANCIPATION

1. Alexander Herzen, *Du développement des idées révolutionnaires en Russie* (London, 1853), p. 37.
2. Two accounts of nineteenth-century Russia that employ the term *obshchestvo* are Anthony Graham Netting, *Russian Liberalism: The Years of Promise, 1842–1855* (unpublished Ph.D. dissertation, Columbia University, 1967), and Nicholas Riasanovsky, *A Parting of Ways: Government and the Educated Public in Russia, 1801–1855* (Oxford, 1977).
3. Charles Tilly's *The Vendee* (Cambridge, Mass., 1964) is a classic account of how various, complex, and *local* a peasant counterrevolutionary movement may be.
4. Samuel Collins, *The Present State of Russia* (London, 1671), pp. 52–53.
5. On the idea of the "just Tsar," see V. K. Sokolova, *Russkie istoricheskie predaniia* (Moscow, 1970), pp. 50–96.
6. Daniel Field, *Rebels in the Name of the Tsar* (Boston, 1976), pp. 113–207.
7. Both the quotation and the comment are contained in Teodor Shanin,

The Awkward Class: Political Sociology of Peasantry in a Developing Society: Russia, 1910–1925 (Oxford, 1972), p. 215.

8. For the Razin and Pugachëv cycles, see Sokolova, *Russkie istoricheskie predaniia*, pp. 115–42, and K. V. Chistov, *Russkie narodnye sotsial'no-utopicheskie legendy* (Moscow, 1967), *passim*.

9. For two excellent, brief discussions of the gentry and the peculiarities of its development, see Richard Pipes, *Karamzin's Memoir on Ancient and Modern Russia* (Cambridge, Mass., 1959), pp. 8–21; and Daniel Field, *The End of Serfdom: Nobility and Bureaucracy in Russia, 1855–1861* (Cambridge, Mass., 1976), pp. 8–21. Despite the passage of time, the standard work remains A. Romanovich-Slaviatinsky, *Dvorianstvo v Rossii ot nachala XVIII-go veka do otmeny krepostnogo prava* (Kiev, 1912). See also Donald MacKenzie Wallace, *Russia* (New York, 1961), Vintage edition, pp. 99–159, particularly his brilliant portrait of the two "landed proprietors."

10. Estimates vary considerably, depending on how inclusively the "noble estate" is defined. For two considerations of the problem, see Anthony Graham Netting, *Russian Liberalism*, pp. 43–44, and S. Frederick Starr, *Decentralization and Self-Government in Russia, 1830–1870* (Princeton, 1972), p. 8.

11. A. I. Gertsen, "Iur'ev den'! Iur'ev den'! Russkomu dvorianstvu," quoted in Daniel Field, *The End of Serfdom*, p. 12.

12. *My Past and Thoughts: The Memoirs of Alexander Herzen*, Vol. III (New York, 1968), p. 1153.

13. These figures are taken from Jerome Blum, *Lord and Peasant in Russia from the Ninth to the Nineteenth Centuries* (Princeton, 1961), p. 369.

14. A good place to begin one's study of the problem is with the collection of essays entitled *The Russian Intelligentsia*, edited by Richard Pipes (New York, 1961).

15. Benjamin Schwartz, *In Search of Wealth and Power: Yen Fu and the West* (Cambridge, Mass., 1964), p. 243.

16. The literature on "modernization" is very large. A convenient introduction is C. E. Black, *The Dynamics of Modernization* (New York, 1966). My own brief remarks owe a great deal to Barrington Moore, Jr., *Social Origins of Dictatorship and Democracy: Lord and Peasant in the Making of the Modern World* (Boston, 1966). Theodore von Laue, *Why Lenin? Why Stalin? A Reappraisal of the Russian Revolution, 1900–1930* (Philadelphia, 1964), is a provocative application of a modernization model to nineteenth- and twentieth-century Russia. For a valuable critique of the concept of "modernization," see Dean C. Tipps, "Modernization Theory and the Comparative Study of Societies," *Comparative Studies in Society and History* 15:2 (March 1973), pp. 199–226.

17. Schwartz, *In Search of Wealth and Power,* pp. 237–38.

18. On the social underpinnings of German conservatism, see Karl Mannheim, "Conservative Thought," in *Essays on Sociology and Social Psychology* (London, 1953).

19. For an interesting, if now slightly dated, discussion of the concept of community and its history, see Robert Nisbet, *The Quest for Community* (New York, 1953). In *The Sociological Tradition* (New York, 1967), Nisbet deals systematically with how the social insights of nineteenth-century European conservatives were taken over and developed by sociologists (Marx, Weber, Durkheim, Tönnies, and so on).

20. Nisbet, *The Quest for Community,* p. 25.

21. Kenneth Keniston, *The Uncommitted: Alienated Youth in American Society* (New York, 1965), pp. 248–49.

22. Quoted in Martin Malia, "Herzen and the Peasant Commune," in Ernest Simmons, ed., *Continuity and Change in Russian and Soviet Thought* (Cambridge, Mass., 1955), pp. 211–12.

23. Quoted in Abbott Gleason, *European and Muscovite: Ivan Kireevsky and the Origins of Slavophilism* (Cambridge, Mass., 1972), p. 281.

24. Robert Tucker, *Philosophy and Myth in Karl Marx* (Cambridge, England, 1961), p. 197.

25. Quoted in Colin Legum, "The End of Cloud Cuckoo Land," *The New York Times Magazine,* March 28, 1976, p. 63.

26. For a characteristic statement on the relationship between "overeducation" and underemployment, see Harry J. Benda, "Non-Western Intelligentsia as Political Elites," in John Kautsky, ed., *Political Change in Underdeveloped Countries* (New York and London, 1962), pp. 240–41.

27. For one view of the process, see Marc Raeff, *Origins of the Russian Intelligentsia: The Eighteenth-Century Nobility* (New York, 1966).

28. Martin Malia, *Alexander Herzen and the Birth of Russian Socialism* (Cambridge, Mass., 1961), p. 5 and *passim.*

29. On the origins of the term "intelligentsia," see Allen Pollard, "The Russian Intelligentsia: The Mind of Russia," *California Slavic Studies,* Vol. III (Berkeley and Los Angeles, 1964), pp. 1–32.

30. See Martin Malia, *Alexander Herzen,* especially pp. 313–34.

31. See Andrzej Walicki, *The Slavophile Controversy* (Oxford, 1975), especially pp. 168–75. See also Abbott Gleason, *European and Muscovite,* pp. 154–79, 258–94.

CHAPTER TWO: SLAVOPHILES AND POPULISTS

1. Richard Pipes, "Narodnichestvo: A Semantic Inquiry," *Slavic Review* 23:3 (September 1964), pp. 441–58.
2. Pipes, "Narodnichestvo," especially pp. 454–56.
3. See B. P. Koz'min, "Narodnichestvo na burzhuazno-demokraticheskom etape osvoboditel'nogo dvizheniia v Rossii," in his *Iz istorii revoliutsionnoi mysli v Rossii* (Moscow, 1961), pp. 638–727.
4. The best general treatment of the Slavophiles, which also contains excellent pages on their relationship to the Populists, is Andrzej Walicki, *The Slavophile Controversy* (Oxford, 1975).
5. As in my "Solzhenitsyn and the Slavophiles," *The Yale Review* 65:1 (Autumn 1975), pp. 61–70.
6. P. V. Annenkov, *The Extraordinary Decade,* in Arthur Mendel, ed., I. R. Titunik, trans., *Literary Memoirs,* (Ann Arbor, 1968). The passage was written in the 1870s.
7. Iury Samarin, *Sochineniia,* Vol. I (Moscow, 1877), pp. 195–96.
8. This exchange is contained in a fascinating piece by Alexander Gerschenkron, "Franco Venturi on Russian Populism," *American Historical Review* 78:4 (October 1973), especially pp. 972–74.
9. Vissarion Belinsky, "Pis'mo k N. V. Gogoliu, 3 iulia 1847," in *Izbrannye filosofskie sochineniia,* Vol. II (Leningrad, 1948), p. 516.
10. Donald Treadgold, "The Peasant and Religion," in Wayne Vucinich, ed., *The Peasant in Nineteenth-Century Russia* (Stanford, 1968), pp. 78–80.
11. For an introduction to this fascinating subject, see James Billington, *Mikhailovsky and Russian Populism* (Oxford, 1958), pp. 120–28.
12. Mikhail Bakunin, *How the Revolutionary Question Presents Itself,* quoted in Franco Venturi, *Roots of Revolution* (New York, 1960), p. 369.
13. For one such conversion, see Abbott Gleason, "The Emigration and Apostasy of Lev Tikhomirov," *Slavic Review* 26:3 (September 1967), pp. 414–29.
14. See Abbott Gleason, *European and Muscovite: Ivan Kireevsky and the Origins of Slavophilism* (Cambridge, Mass., 1972), pp. 154–79.
15. Quoted in Sam Dolgoff, ed., *Bakunin on Anarchy* (New York, 1972), p. 196. See also Herzen's attack on Babeuf's dictatorial propensities in *My Past and Thoughts: The Memoirs of Alexander Herzen,* Vol. III (New York, 1968), pp. 1236–42.
16. *Statism and Anarchy,* in Dolgoff, *Bakunin on Anarchy,* p. 329.
17. For a good, brief discussion of Vorontsov and his book, see Richard Pipes, *Struve: Liberal on the Left, 1870–1905* (Cambridge, Mass., 1970), pp. 40–44; and Arthur Mendel, *Dilemmas of Progress in Tsarist Russia* (Cambridge, Mass., 1961).

18. Richard Pipes, *Struve*, p. 43.
19. Ivan Kireevsky, *Polnoe sobranie sochinenii*, Vol. I (Moscow, 1911), pp. 115–16.
20. Quoted in Venturi, *Roots of Revolution*, p. 659.
21. *Ibid.*, p. 667.
22. See Samuel Baron, *Plekhanov: The Father of Russian Marxism* (Stanford, 1963), pp. 67–68.
23. The phrase is George Lichtheim's. See his *Marxism: An Historical and Critical Study* (New York, 1961), p. 373.
24. Frederick Engels, *The Origin of the Family, Private Property and the State* (New York, 1942), pp. 155–57.
25. For an introduction to Katkov's development, see M. Katz, *Mikhail N. Katkov: A Political Biography, 1818–1887* (The Hague, 1966).
26. Herzen's early life and intellectual evolution are splendidly set forth in Martin Malia, *Alexander Herzen and the Birth of Russian Socialism* (Cambridge, Mass., 1961).
27. Alexander Herzen, *From the Other Shore and the Russian People and Socialism* (Cleveland and New York, 1963), p. 167.
28. *Ibid.*, p. 175.
29. *Ibid.*
30. *Ibid.*, p. 180.
31. For a study of Russian peasant myths based on precisely this point of view, see V. K. Sokolova's excellent *Russkie istoricheskie predaniia* (Moscow, 1970), especially Chapter 3.
32. Herzen, *From the Other Shore and the Russian People and Socialism*, p. 183.
33. *Ibid.*
34. *Ibid.*, p. 186.
35. *Ibid.*
36. *Ibid.*, p. 187.
37. *Ibid.*, pp. 189–90.
38. *Ibid.*, pp. 198–99.
39. Alexander Herzen, *Sochineniia v deviati tomakh*, Vol. III (Moscow, 1956), p. 585.
40. Alexander Herzen, *Du développement des idées révolutionnaires en Russie* (2d ed.) (London, 1853), p. xi.
41. For some interesting observations on Herzen's attitude toward America, see Marc Vuilleumier, Michel Aucouturier, Sven Stelling-Michaud, and Michel Cabot, *Autour d'Alexandre Herzen* (Geneva, 1973), pp. 309–24, *passim*.
42. Herzen, *Du développement*, pp. xxii–xxiii.
43. See A. S. Khomiakov, "O starom i novom," *Sochineniia*, Vol. III (Moscow, 1900), pp. 11–29.

44. There is no adequate study of Pëtr Kireevsky. Much can be learned from A. D. Soimonov, *P. V. Kireevskii i ego sobranie narodnykh pesen* (Leningrad, 1971). See also my review of Soimonov's book in *Kritika* 9:2 (Winter 1973), pp. 58–69. There are several interesting essays by Soimonov and others in *Literaturnoe nasledstvo*, Vol. 79 (Moscow, 1968), along with a collection of the song texts contributed to Kireevsky's collection by notable Russian writers of the time.

45. Herzen, *Du développement,* p. 92.

46. *Ibid.,* p. 106.

47. *Ibid.,* p. 127.

48. For an acute analysis of Herzen's "Russian socialism," which stresses far less its debt to Slavophilism, see Martin Malia, *Alexander Herzen,* pp. 395–415.

49. See, for example, Philip Pomper's *Russian Revolutionary Intelligentsia* (New York, 1970).

50. "Peasant worship" was an important cause of the famous quarrel between the *Contemporary* (after Chernyshevsky's arrest) and the *Russian Word*. See B. P. Koz'min, "Raskol v nigilistakh," *Iz istorii revoliutsionnoi mysli v Rossii* (Moscow, 1961).

51. One might possibly cite the ideas of the so-called *pochvenniki,* the most notable of whom was Fëdor Dostoevsky. And there was also Pan-Slavism. But neither had either the breadth of influence or the staying power of the Populist vision. The only real rival of Populism in this period was the unabashed chauvinism, the *kvass* patriotism, of Mikhail Katkov, whose ideas were few and hardly constitute an intellectual system.

CHAPTER THREE: THE NEW ERA AND ITS JOURNALISTS: HERZEN AND CHERNYSHEVSKY

1. *My Past and Thoughts: The Memoirs of Alexander Herzen,* Vol. III (New York, 1968), p. 1483.

2. For two quite different accounts of this process, see Anthony Graham Netting, *Russian Liberalism: The Years of Promise, 1842–1855* (unpublished Ph.D. dissertation, Columbia University, 1967); and Nicholas Riasanovsky, *A Parting of Ways: Government and the Educated Public in Russia, 1801–1855* (Oxford, 1977), especially Chapter 5.

3. Riasanovsky, *A Parting of Ways,* pp. 276–83. The figures appear to be drawn from the Ph.D. dissertation of Gary Marker at the University of California at Berkeley.

4. *Ibid.,* p. 281.

5. *Dnevnik Very Sergeevny Aksakovoi* (St. Petersburg, 1913), p. 102.

6. "Vospominaniia N. V. Shelgunova," in N. V. Shelgunov, L. P. Shelgunova, M. L. Mikhailov, *Vospominaniia,* Vol. I (Moscow, 1967), p. 76. For a fairly broad range of opinion and response to the death of Nicholas and the coming of a "new era," see A. A. Kornilov, *Obshchestvennoe dvizhenie pri Aleksandre II* (Moscow, 1909), pp. 5–16. See also B. N. Chicherin, *Vospominaniia,* Vol. II (Moscow, 1929), pp. 158–64.

7. Quoted in A. Gratieux, *A. S. Khomiakov et le mouvement slavophile,* Vol. I (Paris, 1939), p. 153.

8. Terence Emmons, "The Peasant and Emancipation," in Wayne Vucinich, ed., *The Peasant in Nineteenth-Century Russia* (Stanford, 1968), p. 50.

9. See *Zhurnal ministerstva narodnogo proshveshcheniia,* No. 1 (1862) (insert).

10. Z. P. Bazileva, *"Kolokol" Gertsena* (Moscow, 1949), p. 22.

11. *Ibid.*

12. For Herzen's reply to Turgenev, see his "Another Variation on an Old Theme," published in the *Polar Star,* Booklet III (1857), and reprinted in *My Past and Thoughts: The Memoirs of Alexander Herzen,* Vol. IV (New York, 1968), pp. 1560–73.

13. *Ibid.,* Vol. III, pp. 1296–97.

14. Martin Malia, *Alexander Herzen and the Birth of Russian Socialism* (Cambridge, Mass., 1961), p. 426.

15. Bazileva, *"Kolokol" Gertsena,* p. 32.

16. A Soviet facsimile edition in four volumes was published in Moscow (1974–76).

17. Terence Emmons, *The Russian Landed Gentry and the Peasant Emancipation of 1861* (Cambridge, Mass., 1968), p. 45n.

18. *Golosa iz Rossii,* Booklet IV (London, 1857), pp. 112–25, *passim.* See also Emmons, *The Russian Landed Gentry,* p. 46.

19. Bazileva, *"Kolokol" Gertsena,* pp. 55–56.

20. Cited in Ia. El'sberg, *Gertsen* (Moscow, 1963), pp. 421–22.

21. Bazileva, *"Kolokol" Gertsena,* p. 71.

22. *Ibid.,* pp. 68–69.

23. "Emperor Alexander I and Karazin," *My Past and Thoughts,* Vol. IV, pp. 1558–59.

24. Bazileva, *"Kolokol" Gertsena,* p. 139.

25. Quoted in *ibid.,* p. 77.

26. *Ibid.,* pp. 152–53.

27. Daniel Field, *The End of Serfdom: Nobility and Bureaucracy in Russia, 1855–1861* (Cambridge, Mass., 1976), pp. 169, 239.

28. "'Ispoved' V. I. Kel'sieva," *Literaturnoe nasledstvo,* Vol. 41/42 (Moscow, 1941), pp. 273–74.

29. Bazileva, *"Kolokol" Gertsena,* p. 116.

30. William F. Woehrlin, *Chernyshevskii: The Man and the Journalist* (Cambridge, Mass., 1971), p. 90.

31. *Ibid.*, pp. 14–19.

32. *Ibid.*, p. 48.

33. See, for example, E. Lampert, *Sons Against Fathers* (Oxford, 1965), pp. 109–20.

34. Quoted in Franco Venturi, *Roots of Revolution* (New York, 1960), p. 157.

35. Nicolas Berdyaev, *The Origins of Russian Communism* (Ann Arbor, 1960), p. 45.

36. Avrahm Yarmolinsky, *Turgenev: The Man, His Art and His Age* (New York, 1961), p. 179.

37. I. S. Turgenev, *Ottsy i deti* (Moscow, 1959), p. 42.

38. Woehrlin, *Chernyshevskii*, p. 95.

39. Quoted in Thomas Hegarty, *Student Movements in Russian Universities, 1855–1861* (unpublished Ph.D. dissertation, Harvard University, 1965), p. 26.

40. Venturi, *Roots of Revolution*, p. 151.

41. *Ibid.*, p. 152.

42. For a rather speculative assessment of Dobroliubov's changing attitude toward Herzen, see E. G. Bushkanets, "Dobroliubov i Gertsen," in V. P. Volgin *et al.*, *Problemy izucheniia Gertsena* (Moscow, 1963), pp. 280–93.

43. The most recent Soviet account of the meeting is Iu. Korotkov, "Gospodin, kotoryi byl v subbotu v Fuleme," *Prometei*, No. 8 (1971), pp. 166–88. For a concise account in English, see Woehrlin, *Chernyshevskii*, pp. 253–55.

44. Quoted in Venturi, *Roots of Revolution*, p. 158.

45. Quoted in *ibid.*, p. 159.

46. Quoted in Woehrlin, *Chernyshevskii*, pp. 255–56.

47. An excellent Soviet work that stresses the contribution of Herzen and Ogarëv to Land and Liberty is Ia. I. Linkov, *Revoliutsionnaia bor'ba A. I. Gertsena i N. P. Ogarëva i tainoe obshchestvo "Zemlia i volia" 1860-kh godov* (Moscow, 1964). See also E. S. Vilenskaia, *Revoliutsionnoe podpol'e v Rossii (60-e gody XIX v)* (Moscow, 1965), pp. 84–182.

48. On Chernyshevsky's relationship to Land and Liberty, see the careful discussion in Woehrlin, *Chernyshevskii*, pp. 297–311.

CHAPTER FOUR: UNIVERSITY STUDENTS IN THE NEW ERA

1. Donald K. Emmerson, *Students and Politics in Developing Nations* (New York, 1968), pp. 415–16.

2. See Patrick Alston, *Education and the State in Tsarist Russia* (Stanford, 1969), pp. 10–11.

3. *Ibid.*, p. 26.

4. Thomas Hegarty, *Student Movements in Russian Universities, 1855–1861* (unpublished Ph.D. dissertation, Harvard University, 1965), p. 3.

5. Alston, *Education and the State*, p. 36.

6. Hegarty, *Student Movements*, p. 4.

7. Jean Piaget, "The Mental Development of the Child," *Six Psychological Studies* (New York, 1968), pp. 67–68.

8. See the suggestive study of 405 St. Petersburg radicals provided by Daniel Brower in *Training the Nihilists: Education and Radicalism in Tsarist Russia* (Ithaca, 1975), especially pp. 36–39, 118.

9. See, for instance, Kenneth Keniston, *Young Radicals: Notes on Committed Youth* (New York, 1968), especially pp. 44–76.

10. For biographical data, see William Woehrlin, *Chernyshevskii: The Man and the Journalist* (Cambridge, Mass., 1971), especially pp. 13–61.

11. *Ibid.*, p. 16.

12. For a brief account of Dobroliubov's career, see E. Lampert, *Sons Against Fathers* (Oxford, 1965), pp. 226–71.

13. L. F. Panteleev, "Iz vospominanii proshlogo," *Vospominaniia* (Moscow, 1958), pp. 199–200.

14. For an astute analysis of Kavelin's political position, see Daniel Field, "Kavelin and Russian Liberalism," *Slavic Review* 32:1 (March 1973), pp. 59–78.

15. Anthony Graham Netting, *Russian Liberalism: The Years of Promise* (unpublished Ph.D. dissertation, Columbia University, 1967), p. 512.

16. Hegarty, *Student Movements*, pp. 207–209.

17. Quoted in *ibid.*, p. 383.

18. Franco Venturi, *Roots of Revolution* (New York, 1960), p. 222.

19. Cf. B. P. Koz'min, "P. G. Zaichnevskii i 'Molodaia Rossiia,'" *Iz istorii revoliutsionnoi mysli v Rossii* (Moscow, 1961).

20. Venturi, *Roots of Revolution*, p. 285.

21. Hegarty, *Student Movements*, p. 228.

22. *Ibid.*, pp. 256–61.

23. See, for instance, N. G. Sladkevich, "Peterburgskii universitet i obshchestvennoe dvizhenie v Rossii v nachale 60-kh godov XIX v.," *Vestnik Leningradskogo Universiteta*, No. 8 (1947), p. 108.

24. Panteleev, *Vospominaniia* (Moscow, 1958), p. 160.

25. Alexander Serno-Solovёvich, *Nashi domashnie dela* (Geneva, 1867), quoted in E. H. Carr, *The Romantic Exiles* (Harmondsworth, England), pp. 304–306.

26. See in particular Alain Besançon, *Éducation et société en Russie dans le second tiers du XIXe siècle* (Paris and The Hague, 1974); and Daniel R. Brower, *Training the Nihilists.*
27. See the telling criticisms in Hegarty, *Student Movements,* especially pp. 9–11.

CHAPTER FIVE: THE UNIVERSITY OF ST. PETERSBURG

1. B. A. Modzalevsky, "K istorii Peterburgskago universiteta, 1857–1859 g. Iz bumag L. N. Modzalevskago," *Golos Minuvshago,* No. 1 (1917), pp. 136–37.
2. *Ibid.,* p. 139.
3. *Ibid.,* pp. 141–42.
4. A. M. Skabichevsky, *Literaturnye vospominaniia* (Moscow-Leningrad, 1928), p. 93.
5. L. F. Panteleev, "Iz vospominanii proshlogo," *Vospominaniia* (Moscow, 1958), pp. 131–32.
6. Hegarty, *Student Movements in Russian Universities, 1855–1861* (unpublished Ph.D. dissertation, Harvard University, 1965), p. 79.
7. Skabichevsky, *Literaturnye vospominaniia,* p. 97.
8. Hegarty, *Student Movements,* pp. 79–82.
9. On the Sunday School movement in general, see Reginald Zelnik, "The Sunday School Movement in Russia, 1859–62," *Journal of Modern History* 37:2 (June 1965), pp. 151–70.
10. Skabichevsky, *Literaturnye vospominaniia,* pp. 124–25.
11. The best overview of the subject in any language is Richard Stites, *The Women's Liberation Movement in Russia: Feminism, Nihilism and Bolshevism, 1860–1930* (Princeton, 1978).
12. Quoted in *ibid.,* p. 34.
13. See Barbara Heldt Monter, "Rassvet (1859–1862) and the Woman Question," *Slavic Review* 36:1 (March 1977), pp. 76–85.
14. Panteleev, *Vospominaniia,* p. 213.
15. Skabichevsky, *Literaturnye vospominaniia,* p. 142.
16. Hegarty, *Student Movements,* p. 101. For Spasovich's own brief account of the trial, see his *Sochineniia,* Vol. IV (St. Petersburg, 1891), p. 25.
17. Hegarty, *Student Movements,* pp. 84–85.
18. Skabichevsky, *Literaturnye vospominaniia,* pp. 144–46.
19. Hegarty, *Student Movements,* p. 96.
20. A. A. Kornilov, *Obshchestvennoe dvizhenie pri Aleksandre II* (Moscow, 1909), p. 122.
21. N. G. Sladkevich, "Peterburgskii universitet i obshchestvennoe

dvizhenie v Rossii, v nachale 60-kh godov XIX v.," *Vestnik Leningrad-skogo Universiteta*, No. 8 (1947), p. 106.
22. Hegarty, *Student Movements*, p. 47.
23. *Ibid.*, pp. 52–53.
24. On the students' return to the university, see, for instance, Vladimir Sorokin, "Vospominaniia starogo studenta," *Russkaia starina*, No. 11 (November 1906), pp. 450–51.
25. For Spasovich's account of the Kavelin Commission's activities, see his *Sochineniia*, Vol. IV (St. Petersburg, 1891), pp. 26–27.
26. Hegarty, *Student Movements*, p. 108.
27. Sorokin, "Vospominaniia starogo studenta," pp. 454–55.
28. Hegarty, *Student Movements*, pp. 116–18.
29. *Ibid.*, pp. 120–21.
30. Sorokin, "Vospominaniia starogo studenta," pp. 458–59.
31. Quoted in Patrick Alston, *Education and the State in Tsarist Russia* (Stanford, 1969), p. 49.
32. E. A. Shtakenshneider, *Dnevnik i zapiski (1854–56)* (Moscow-Leningrad, 1934), p. 296.
33. Panteleev, *Vospominaniia*, p. 254.
34. *Ibid.*, p. 248. See also Skabichevsky, *Literaturnye vospominaniia*, p. 149.

CHAPTER SIX: A NEW LEFT AND A NEW RIGHT

1. On the manifesto's distribution and content, see Franco Venturi, *Roots of Revolution* (New York, 1960), pp. 247–50.
2. On the *Great Russian*, see *ibid.*, pp. 237–40; and William F. Woehrlin, *Chernyshevskii: The Man and the Journalist* (Cambridge, Mass., 1971), pp. 287–94.
3. L. F. Panteleev, "Iz vospominanii proshlogo," *Vospominaniia* (Moscow, 1958), p. 274.
4. Cited in Charles C. Adler, Jr., "Domestic Russia in 1861: A Contemporary Perspective," *Canadian Slavic Studies* 3:2 (1969), p. 333.
5. Venturi, *Roots of Revolution*, p. 173.
6. Adler, "Domestic Russia in 1861," p. 326.
7. A. V. Nikitenko, *Dnevnik*, Vol. II (Leningrad, 1955), pp. 265–268.
8. Cited in S. Reiser, "Peterburgskie pozhary 1862 goda," *Katorga i ssylka*, No. 10 (1932), pp. 88–89.
9. See *ibid.*, p. 87.
10. P. Kropotkin, *Memoirs of a Revolutionist* (Boston and New York, 1899), pp. 157–61.
11. Nikitenko, *Dnevnik*, p. 274.

12. Panteleev, *Vospominaniia*, p. 277.
13. Reiser, "Peterburgskie pozhary," p. 101.
14. A. M. Skabichevsky, *Literaturnye vospominaniia* (Moscow-Leningrad, 1928), p. 157.
15. Kropotkin, *Memoirs of a Revolutionist*, p. 165.
16. Quoted in Reiser, "Peterburgskie pozhary," p. 83.
17. For some illuminating introductory observations on panic and crowd behavior, see Ralph R. Turner, "Collective Behavior," in Robert Faris, ed., *Handbook of Modern Sociology* (Chicago, 1964), pp. 382–425. See also Joost Meerlo, *Patterns of Panic* (New York, 1950); and Neil Smelser, *Theory of Collective Behavior* (New York and London, 1962).
18. Quoted in Venturi, *Roots of Revolution*, pp. 292–93.
19. On the circulation of *Young Russia* and its timing, see B. P. Koz'min, *Iz istorii revoliutsionnoi mysli v Rossii* (Moscow, 1961), pp. 222–23.
20. Quoted in Nikolai Barsukov, *Zhizn' i trudy M. P. Pogodina*, Vol. XIX (St. Petersburg, 1905), p. 134.
21. Quoted in Reiser, "Peterburgskie pozhary," p. 108.
22. A. A. Kornilov, *Obshchestvennoe dvizhenie pri Aleksandre II* (Moscow, 1909), pp. 134–35.
23. Quoted in Martin Katz, *Michael N. Katkov: A Political Biography* (Paris and The Hague, 1966), p. 121.
24. Kornilov, *Obshchestvennoe dvizhenie*, p. 161.
25. *My Past and Thoughts. The Memoirs of Alexander Herzen* (New York, 1968), pp. 1309–10.

CHAPTER SEVEN: FROM SLAVOPHILISM TO POPULISM:
A. P. SHCHAPOV

1. For biographical information on Rybnikov, see Franco Venturi, *Roots of Revolution* (New York, 1960), pp. 232–33; Gruzinsky, ed., *Pesni sobrannyia P. N. Rybnikovym*, Vol. I (Moscow, 1909); and A. P. Razumova, *Iz istorii russkoi fol'kloristiki: P. N. Rybnikov i P. S. Efimenko* (Moscow-Leningrad, 1954). There is a delightful excerpt of Rybnikov's account of his song collecting in W. R. S. Ralston, *The Songs of the Russian People* (London, 1872), pp. 63–76.
2. Quoted in Gruzinsky, ed., *Pesni sobrannyia Rybnikovym*, Vol. I, p. lx.
3. The only significant English-language account of his career is in Venturi, *Roots of Revolution*, pp. 196–203.
4. The best available account of life in a bursa is contained in N. G. Pomyalovsky, *Seminary Sketches* (Ithaca and London, 1973).
5. Almost all that we know about Shchapov's life prior to 1860 comes

from N. Ia. Aristov, *Afanasii Prokof'evich Shchapov. Zhizn' i so-chineniia* (St. Petersburg, 1883). See pp. 5–6.

6. Josef Wachendorf, *Regionalismus, Raskol und Volk als Hauptprobleme der Russischen Geschichte bei A. P. Ščapov* (doctoral dissertation, University of Cologne, 1964), p. 4.

7. M. V. Nauchitel', *Zhizn' i deiatel'nost' Afanasiia Prokof'evicha Shchapova, 1831–1876 gg.* (Irkutsk, 1958), p. 9.

8. G. A. Luchinsky, "Afanasii Prokof'evich Shchapov: biograficheskii ocherk," *Sochineniia A. P. Shchapova*, Vol. III (St. Petersburg, 1908), pp. xi–xii.

9. For details on Eliseev's career, see James H. Billington, *Mikhailovsky and Russian Populism* (Oxford, 1958), pp. 46–49 and *passim*.

10. On Shchapov's relationship with Eshevsky, see Luchinsky, "Shchapov," *Sochineniia*, Vol. III, p. xxii.

11. Aristov is explicit on the time. See *Shchapov*, pp. 43–44.

12. Much of Aksakov's writing on history is contained in his *Polnoe sobranie sochinenii*, Vol. I (1861). For a sophisticated and thorough analysis of his ideas, see Andrzej Walicki, *The Slavophile Controversy* (Oxford, 1975), especially pp. 238–83.

13. Walicki, *Slavophile Controversy*, p. 265.

14. Nicolas Berdyaev, *The Russian Idea* (New York, 1948), p. 145.

15. Aksakov's strictures on the sixth and seventh volumes of Solov'ëv's *History of Russia* are contained in his *Polnoe sobranie sochinenii*, Vol. I, pp. 125–72, 217–54. He continued to criticize successive volumes until his death in 1860.

16. On Leshkov, see S. Frederick Starr, *Decentralization and Self-Government in Russia, 1830–1870* (Princeton, 1972), pp. 344–46.

17. It is reprinted in his *Sochineniia*, Vol. I (St. Petersburg, 1906), pp. 173–450.

18. These articles have not been reprinted. Their titles are given and their content briefly summarized in Shchapov's *Sochineniia*, Vol. III, p. xxiv.

19. See, for instance, his *Velikorusskiia oblasti i smutnoe vremia (1606–1613)*, which appeared in the *Annals of the Fatherland* in 1861 and is reprinted in his *Sochineniia*, Vol. I, pp. 648–709.

20. See his two articles on the *Zemskii sobor* in *ibid.*, pp. 710–5⅔.

21. Wachendorf, *Regionalismus, Raskol und Volk*, pp. 52–54.

22. *Ibid.*, pp. 58–61.

23. See Thomas Hegarty, *Student Movements in Russian Universities, 1855–1861* (unpublished Ph.D. dissertation, Harvard University, 1965), pp. 199–250; and G. N. Vul'fson and E. G. Bushkanets, *Obshchestvenno-politicheskaia bor'ba v Kazanskom universitete v 1859–1861 godakh* (Kazan', 1955), pp. 15–68.

24. Hegarty, *Student Movements*, pp. 200–201.

25. Quoted in Wachendorf, *Regionalismus, Raskol und Volk*, pp. 106–107.

26. There is a brief discussion of Shchapov's constitution in Nauchitel', *Zhizn' i deiatel'nost' Shchapova*, pp. 47–54.

27. *Ibid.*, p. 39.

28. Aristov's account of Shchapov's scholarly bad conscience is not convincing to me. See *Shchapov*, pp. 61–63, for his curious and confusing account of Shchapov's mood during the winter and spring of 1861.

29. This episode has recently been investigated by Daniel Field with as great a sophistication and thoroughness as the surviving documentation allows. See *Rebels in the Name of the Tsar* (Boston, 1976), especially pp. 31–111.

30. *Ibid.*, p. 33.

31. Quoted in *ibid.*, pp. 101–102. There are various versions of Shchapov's speech. See the discussion in *ibid.*, pp. 95–103.

32. The best account of the government's reaction and Shchapov's arrest is contained in Luchinsky, "Shchapov," *Sochineniia*, Vol. III, pp. xxxvii–lii.

33. "Pis'mo A. P. Shchapova Aleksandru II v 1861 g.," *Krasnyi arkhiv*, Vol. XIX (1926), pp. 150–65.

34. *Ibid.*, p. 151.

35. Aristov, *Shchapov*, p. 69.

36. *Ibid.*, p. 90.

37. The letter was written to the curator at Kazan', whose father, the poet, had written a poem that Shchapov believed was a personal attack on him, although his name was not mentioned. The letter concludes with some bitter words on the drunkenness of Russian writers, which Shchapov ascribed to the privations and sadness of Russian life. M. V. Nechkina, "A. P. Shchapov v gody revoliutsionnoi situatsii. Pis'mo k P. P. Viazemskomu ot 8 oktiabria 1861 g.," *Literaturnoe nasledstvo*, Vol. 67 (1959), pp. 645–68.

38. *Ibid.*, p. 658.

39. On the *Century*, see B. P. Koz'min, "Artelnyi zhurnal 'Vek' (1862)," *Iz istorii revoliutsionnoi mysli v Rossii* (Moscow, 1961), pp. 68–98.

40. See Michael Cherniavsky's important essay, "The Old Believers and the New Religion," *Slavic Review* 25:1 (1966), pp. 1–39, reprinted in Cherniavsky, ed., *The Structure of Russian History* (New York, 1970), pp. 140–88. Despite Cherniavsky's greater historical sophistication, he follows Shchapov in understanding the development of the Schism as reflecting the opposition of Muscovite society to the social rationalism and political mobilization undertaken by Peter the Great and his successors.

41. Shchapov, *Sochineniia*, Vol. I, pp. 498–502.
42. See Aristov, *Shchapov*, pp. 92–94.
43. For Aristov's authoritative account of their courtship, see *ibid.*, pp. 97–101.
44. The whole affair is fully treated in M. K. Lemke, "Delo o litsakh, obviniaemykh v snosheniakh c londonskimi propagandistami," *Byloe*, No. 9 (1906), pp. 158–207; No. 10, pp. 80–120; No. 11, pp. 194–220.
45. Luchinsky, "Shchapov," *Sochineniia*, pp. lvii–lviii.
46. A. P. Shchapov, *Sobranie sochinenii*, Vol. IV (Irkutsk, 1937), pp. 3–19.
47. On Vasil'ev, see Andrew Malozemoff, *Russian Far Eastern Policy 1881–1904* (Berkeley and Los Angeles, 1958), *passim*.
48. *Otechestvennye zapiski*, No. 5 (1876), p. 183, quoted in Nauchitel', *Zhizn' i deiatel'nost' Shchapova*, p. 50.
49. On Shchapov and the so-called Kazan' Conspiracy, see Venturi, *Roots of Revolution*, p. 305. There is considerable material about Shchapov's relations with student radicals at Kazan' (including an interesting "letter home" from the summer of 1861) in Ia. I. Linkov, *Revoliutsionnaia bor'ba A. I. Gertsena i N. P. Ogareva i tainoe obshchestvo "Zemlia i volia" 1860-kh godov* (Moscow, 1964), especially pp. 245–56.
50. See German Lopatin, "A. P. Shchapov," *Avtobiografiia* (Petrograd, 1918), pp. 128–34.
51. See Mikhail Dragomanov's introduction to *Michael Bakunins Sozialpolitischer Briefwechsel mit Alexander Iw. Herzen* (Stuttgart, 1895), p. lxxi.
52. Vera Figner, "Studencheskie gody," *Polnoe sobranie sochinenii*, Vol. V (Moscow, 1929), p. 93.
53. "Afanasii Prokof'evich Shchapov," *Vestnik Narodnoi Voli*, No. 1 (1883), reprinted in Georgy Plekhanov, *Sochineniia*, Vol. II (Moscow-Petrograd, n.d. 1923), pp. 10–20.
54. S. Frederick Starr, *Decentralization and Self-Government in Russia, 1830–1870* (Princeton, 1972), especially pp. 348–54.

CHAPTER EIGHT: THE EMERGENCE OF POPULIST STYLE: PAVEL IVANOVICH IAKUSHKIN

1. My version of the civil execution is based on the several accounts contained in Iu. G. Oksman, ed., *N. G. Chernyshevskii v vospominaniakh sovremennikov* (Vol. II Saratov, 1959), pp. 19–54.
2. For the most authoritative version of how Iakushkin "saved the girl," see A. I. Balandin, *P. I. Iakushkin. Iz istorii russkoi fol'kloristiki* (Moscow, 1969), pp. 215–22.
3. There is a good deal of biographical information on Iakushkin in S. V.

Maksimov's introduction to Iakushkin's *Sochineniia* (St. Petersburg, 1884) and in the recollections contained in the same volume. There are two Soviet biographies: V. G. Bazanov, *Pavel Ivanovich Iakushkin* (Orël, 1950); and A. I. Balandin, *P. I. Iakushkin*. Neither is up to its subject; both are useful.

4. Iakushkin, *Sochineniia*, pp. xlvii–lxiii.

5. Balandin, *Iakushkin*, p. 13.

6. On Pëtr Kireevsky, see (in addition to the standard literature on Slavophilism) his *Pis'ma N. M. Iazykovu* (Moscow-Leningrad, 1935); the essays in Vol. 79 of *Literaturnoe nasledstvo*, which appeared in Moscow in 1968; and the interesting study by A. D. Soimonov, *P. V. Kireevskii i ego sobranie narodnykh pesen* (Leningrad, 1971).

7. See M. O. Gershenzon's perceptive characterization in *Obrazy proshlogo* (Moscow, 1912), pp. 94ff.

8. On the contributions to the collection from Russia's intellectuals and writers, see *Literaturnoe nasledstvo*, Vol. 79, *passim*.

9. See Balandin, *Iakushkin*, pp. 28–38.

10. A good Soviet edition is *Narodnye russkie skazki* (3 vols.) (Moscow, 1957), with an introduction and notes by V. Ia. Propp.

11. His biography must be among the longest ever written. It is invaluable as a primary source on nineteenth-century Russian history. See N. P. Barsukov, *Zhizn' i trudy M. P. Pogodina* (22 vols.) (St. Petersburg, 1888–1910).

12. A number of splendid examples can be found in Nicholas Riasanovsky, *Nicholas I and Official Nationality in Russia* (Berkeley and Los Angeles, 1961), pp. 104–114.

13. Barsukov, *Zhizn' Pogodina*, Vol. X, pp. 23–27, quoted in Balandın, *Iakushkin*, pp. 24–26.

14. "Velik Bog zemli russkoi," *Sochineniia*, pp. 1–42.

15. Iakushkin, *Sochineniia*, p. lxxxiv.

16. The fullest account of Iakushkin's involvement in the Kireevskv collection is in Balandin, *Iakushkin*, pp. 57–95.

17. Iakushkin, *Sochineniia*, p. xlv

18. *Ibid.*, p. xii.

19. *Ibid.*, pp. lxii–lxiii.

20. *Ibid.*, p. lxxxii.

21. *Ibid.*, pp. lxxv–lxxx.

22. *Ibid.*, p. lix.

23. *Ibid.*, pp. lxix–lxxi.

24. For the careers of three Populist writers of a slightly later period whose biographies have something in common with Iakushkin's, see Richard Wortman, *The Crisis of Russian Populism* (Cambridge, England, 1967), *passim*.

25. On the "Pskov Affair," see the various documents collected in Iakushkin's *Sochineniia*, pp. xcvi–civ. See also Balandin, *Iakushkin*, pp. 125–44.

26. Iakushkin, *Sochineniia*, pp. 43–76.

27. "Prezhniaia rekrutchina i soldatskaia zhizn'," *ibid.*, pp. 142–52.

28. On Herzen and Iakushkin, see Balandin, *Iakushkin*, pp. 224–37.

29. Quoted in *ibid.*, p. 240.

30. Ch. Vetrinsky, "P. I. Iakushkin v Nizhnem Novgorode," *Sovremennyi mir*, No. 4 (1908), p. 45, quoted in A. P. Razumova, *Iz istorii russkoi fol'kloristiki. P. N. Rybnikov. P. S. Efimenko* (Moscow-Leningrad, 1954), p. 11.

31. Quoted in Balandin, *Iakushkin*, pp. 247–48.

32. *Ibid.*, pp. 261–68.

33. *Ibid.*, pp. 257–58.

34. *Ibid.*, p. 260.

35. V. G. Bazanov, *Pavel Ivanovich Iakushkin*, p. 66; Balandin, *Iakushkin*, pp. 208–212.

36. Vladimir Sorokin, "Vospominaniia starogo studenta," *Russkaia starina*, No. 11 (November 1906), p. 444.

37. Balandin, *Iakushkin*, p. 269.

38. Iakushkin, *Sochineniia*, pp. 77–89.

39. Balandin, *Iakushkin*, p. 284.

40. *Ibid.*, p. 298.

41. Iakushkin, "Putevyia pis'ma iz Astrakhanskoi gubernii," *Sochineniia*, pp. 395–452.

42. They have been republished by A. N. Lozanova in her *Pesni i skazaniia o Razine i Pugachëva* (Moscow-Leningrad, 1935), pp. 110–24.

43. Iakushkin, *Sochineniia*, p. 407.

44. *Ibid.*

45. Balandin, *Iakushkin*, pp. 302–303.

46. Iakushkin, *Sochineniia*, p. 452.

47. *Ibid.*, p. xciii.

48. *Ibid.*, p. xcv.

CHAPTER NINE: RUSSIAN JACOBINS

1. Alexander Herzen, *From the Other Shore and the Russian People and Socialism* (Cleveland and New York, 1963). See the Introduction by Isaiah Berlin, p. xx.

2. For a good general account of this "schism among the nihilists," as it was called, see B. P. Koz'min, *Iz istorii revoliutsionnoi mysli v Rossii* (Moscow, 1961), pp. 20–67.

3. N. G. Chernyshevsky, *Chto delat'?* (Leningrad, 1948), p. 14.

4. Quoted in Adam B. Ulam, *The Bolsheviks* (New York, 1965), pp. 65–66.

5. P. Kropotkin, *Ideals and Realities in Russian Literature* (New York, 1919), p. 281.

6. Quoted in N. I. Prutskov, *Russkaia literatura XIX veka i revoliutsionnaia Rossiia* (Leningrad, 1971), p. 106.

7. Vladimir Nabokov, *The Gift* (New York, 1963), p. 289.

8. Nikolay Valentinov, *Encounters with Lenin* (London, 1968), pp. 67–68.

9. Kropotkin found Bazarov "too harsh" and apparently neglectful of his "duties as a citizen." Among Russian radicals of the day, only Dmitry Pisarev and a few like-minded people "accepted" Bazarov as a representative portrait. Most members of the radical intelligentsia, under the sway of Populist ideas, found his attitude toward the *narod* too elitist and tinged with contempt. *Memoirs of a Revolutionist* (Boston and New York, 1899), pp. 300–301.

10. There is some information in M. M. Klevensky and K. G. Kotel'nikov, *Pokushenie Karakozova,* Vol. I (Moscow, 1928), p. 304. There is a bit of additional information in M. M. Klevensky, *Ishutinskii kruzhok i pokushenie Karakozova* (Moscow, 1927), pp. 10–11. See also E. S. Vilenskaia, *Revoliutsionnoe podpol'e v Rossii (60-e gody XIX v)* (Moscow, 1965), especially pp. 189–96.

11. Vilenskaia, *Revoliutsionnoe podpol'e,* pp. 195–96.

12. *Ibid.,* pp. 189–92.

13. *Ibid.,* p. 192.

14. Quoted in *ibid.,* pp. 192–93. For a similar picture of the new spirit in a provincial gymnasium (Viatka, 1862), see N. A. Charushin, *O dalekom proshlom* (2d ed.) (Moscow, 1973), p. 34.

15. Franco Venturi, *Roots of Revolution* (New York, 1960), p. 332.

16. Klevensky, *Pokushenie,* Vol. I, p. 306.

17. Vilenskaia, *Revoliutsionnoe podpol'e,* p. 213.

18. On the Spiridov group, see *ibid.,* pp. 216–28.

19. Quoted in *ibid.,* p. 264.

20. *Ibid.,* p. 270.

21. The charter is discussed in *ibid.,* pp. 272–74.

22. Klevensky, *Pokushenie,* Vol. II, pp. 116–17.

23. See M. M. Klevensky, ed., "Pobeg Iaroslava Dombrovskogo," *Krasnyi arkhiv,* Vol. III (xxii) (1927), pp. 236–41.

24. Klevensky, *Pokushenie,* Vol. I, p. 196.

25. Venturi, *Roots of Revolution,* p. 335.

CHAPTER TEN: THE FIRST SHOT

1. Lopatin's description is from his obituary of Khudiakov (1876), written for Lavrov's journal *Forward (Vperëd)* and reprinted at the conclusion of the French translation of Khudiakov's memoirs. See *Mémoires d'un révolutionnaire* (Paris, 1889).

2. See the descriptions collected by E. S. Vilenskaia in her *Khudiakov* (Moscow, 1969), pp. 22–23.

3. Republished in the Soviet Union as *Zapiski karakozovtsa* (Moscow-Leningrad, 1930). I quote throughout from this edition.

4. *Ibid.*, pp. 83–94, *passim.*

5. The remark was deleted from the published version of his memoirs, but is reproduced by V. G. Bazanov in his "I. A. Khudiakov i pokushenie Karakozova," *Russkaia literatura*, No. 4 (1962), p. 163.

6. See Stith Thompson, *The Folktale* (New York, 1946), p. 370.

7. On Khudiakov's mythological views, see E. Bobrov, "Nauchno-literaturnaia deiatel'nost' I. A. Khudiakova," *Zhurnal Ministerstva narodnogo prosveshcheniia*, No. 8 (August 1908), pp. 193–240. Khudiakov discusses the mythological origins of folklore in "Osnovoi element narodnykh skazok," *Biblioteka dlia chteniia*, No. 12 (1863), pp. 38–45. See also his "Narodnye istoricheskie skazki," *Zhurnal Ministerstva narodnogo prosveshcheniia*, No. 3 (March 1864), especially pp. 43–45.

8. Khudiakov, *Zapiski karakozovtsa*, pp. 54, 77.

9. L. F. Panteleev, *Iz vospominanii proshlogo* (St. Petersburg, 1905), pp. 312–13.

10. See the Soviet reissue of all three volumes: *Velikorusskie skazki* (Moscow-Leningrad, 1964), with an informative if somewhat doctrinaire Introduction by V. G. Bazanov.

11. On Khudiakov's view of folktales, see in particular his "Osnovnoi element narodnykh skazok," pp. 38–45; and his "Narodnye istoricheskie skazki," *Zhurnal Ministerstva narodnogo prosveshcheniia*, No. 3 (1864), pp. 43–69. For an excellent bibliography on both Khudiakov's own works and secondary literature, see the Soviet edition of *Velikorusskie skazki*, pp. 294–97.

12. See " 'Evropeiskii revoliutsionnyi komitet' v dele Karakozova," in B. I. Gorev and B. P. Koz'min, eds., *Revoliutsionnoe dvizhenie 1860-kh godov* (Moscow, 1931), pp. 147–67.

13. E. S. Vilenskaia, *Revoliutsionnoe podpol'e v Rossii (60-e gody XIX v)* (Moscow, 1965), p. 389, for a reconstruction of the draft.

14. Cf. M. M. Klevensky and K. G. Kotel'nikov, *Pokushenie Karakozova*, Vol. II (Moscow, 1928), pp. 125, 325–30.

15. Quoted in Vilenskaia, *Revoliutsionnoe podpol'e*, p. 233.

16. For Fedoseev's testimony and that of several other members of the group, see Klevensky, *Pokushenie,* Vol. II, pp. 206–208.

17. *Ibid.,* pp. 72–73.

18. Franco Venturi, *Roots of Revolution* (New York, 1960), p. 336.

19. For Motkov's account, see Klevensky, *Pokushenie,* Vol. II, pp. 26–29, 94, 144, 325–33.

20. *Ibid.,* pp. 43–44.

21. Quoted in Venturi, *Roots of Revolution,* p. 344.

22. Klevensky, *Pokushenie,* Vol. I, p. 291.

23. See M. M. Klevensky, "Iz vospominanii Z. K. Ralli," in B. I. Gorev and B. P. Koz'min, *Revoliutsionnoe dvizhenie 1860-kh godov* (Moscow, 1931), p. 138.

24. For two sketches of Karakozov, see Khudiakov, *Mémoires d'un révolutionnaire,* pp. 170–75; and D. V. Stasov, "Karakozovskii protsess," *Byloe,* No. 4 (1906), pp. 271–72. Khudiakov stresses Karakozov's lack of vanity, his solitariness—and his lack of competence in worldly matters. Stasov, Ishutin's lawyer, regarded Karakozov as mentally unbalanced and stressed Ishutin's influence over him.

25. See the report of the doctors, quoted in Klevensky, *Pokushenie,* Vol. I, p. 298.

26. Venturi, *Roots of Revolution,* p. 345.

27. Klevensky, "Iz vospominanii Z. K. Ralli," pp. 138–39. One must use this source with caution, however. Ralli clearly exaggerated this regicidal impulse; "all Moscow," he claimed, "knew the phrase of Lincoln's assassin: sic semper tiranis [*sic!*]."

28. For the traditional view—that they were opposed—see Venturi, *Roots of Revolution,* pp. 345–47. For the view that both Ishutin and Khudiakov were much more deeply involved, see Vilenskaia, *Revoliutsionnoe podpol'e,* pp. 417–29; and Adam Ulam, *In the Name of the People* (New York, 1977), pp. 157–68.

29. On Kobylin, the "enigmatic" Dr. Kobylin, see Ulam, *In the Name of the People,* pp. 160–68, *passim.*

30. I quote from the variant found on the person of Karakozov after the assassination attempt; it is printed in Klevensky, *Pokushenie,* Vol. I, pp. 293–94. The versions distributed earlier were more simply written and made no mention of regicide. For a discussion of the varying texts, and the likelihood that Khudiakov had a hand in drafting, or at least editing, the manifesto, see Vilenskaia, *Revoliutsionnoe podpol'e,* pp. 421–25.

31. Klevensky, *Pokushenie,* Vol. I, p. 294.

32. *Ibid.*

33. *Ibid.*

34. Quoted in Avrahm Yarmolinsky, *Road to Revolution* (New York, 1962), p. 141.

35. I. A. Khudiakov, *Kratkoe opisanie Verkhoianskogo okruga* (Leningrad, 1969).

36. My brief account of Khudiakov's final years is based largely on Vilenskaia, *Khudiakov*, pp. 129–42.

37. Yarmolinsky, *Road to Revolution*, p. 140. For the American context, see Albert Woldman, *Lincoln and the Russians* (Cleveland and New York, 1952), pp. 262–63.

38. For one contemporary's slightly confused impression of "reactionary" working-class attitudes, see Klevensky, "Iz vospominanii Z. K. Ralli," pp. 140–42, 144.

39. The best account of Komissarov's activities is contained in Kornei Chukovsky's brilliant "Poet ili palach," in his *Nekrasov* (Leningrad, 1926). See especially p. 26. For an amusing account of Komissarov's social whirl, see Pëtr Veinberg, "4-e aprelia 1866 g.," *Byloe*, No. 4 (1906), pp. 291–95. Veinberg also gives an interesting account of the patriotic fervor in the capital during the twenty-four hours that followed Karakozov's attempt.

40. See Patrick Alston, *Education and the State in Tsarist Russia* (Stanford, 1969), p. 79.

41. S. Frederick Starr, *Decentralization and Self-Government in Russia, 1830–1870* (Princeton, 1972), p. 327.

42. Quoted in *ibid.*, p. 329.

43. *Ibid.*, pp. 329–36, for a discussion of Shuvalov's campaign against the zemstvos.

44. Quoted in A. A. Kornilov, *Obshchestvennoe dvizhenie pri Aleksandre II* (Moscow, 1909), p. 175.

45. Mikhail Lemke, quoted in Alston, *Education and the State*, p. 79.

46. Allen Sinel, *The Classroom and the Chancellery* (Cambridge, Mass., 1973). See especially his balanced assessment of Tolstoy, pp. 253–64.

47. Alston, *Education and the State*, p. 84.

48. S. G. Sviatikov, "Studencheskoe dvizhenie 1869 goda," *Istoricheskii sbornik, Nasha strana* (St. Petersburg, 1907), p. 180.

CHAPTER ELEVEN: IN PURSUIT OF NECHAEV

1. Postnikova's memoirs are contained in N. Bel'chikov, "S. G. Nechaev v s. Ivanove v 60-e gody," *Katorga i ssylka*, No. 14 (1925), pp. 152–56.

2. A facsimile of *Obshchina* is contained in Arthur Lehning, ed., *Michel Bakounine et ses relations avec Sergej Nečaev, 1870–72, Écrits et matériaux* (Leiden, 1971), pp. 435–42. The quoted material is on p. 3 of *Obshchina*, p. 437 of Lehning's text.

3. Quoted in B. P. Koz'min, "S. G. Nechaev i ego protivniki v 60-kh gg.,"

in B. I. Gorev and B. P. Koz'min, eds., *Revoliutsionnoe dvizhenie 1860-kh godov* (Moscow, 1931), p. 223.

4. The letters are published in *Katorga i ssylka*, No. 14, pp. 139–51.

5. B. P. Koz'min, "Novoe o Nechaeve," *Krasnyi arkhiv*, Vol. I (xiv) (1926), p. 151.

6. Franco Venturi, *Roots of Revolution* (New York, 1960), p. 361.

7. For a good, brief introduction to the university situation in the fall of 1868, see Daniel Brower, *Training the Nihilists: Education and Radicalism in Tsarist Russia* (Ithaca, 1975), pp. 130–34. For a lengthier account, from a radical point of view, see S. G. Sviatikov, "Studencheskoe dvizhenie 1869 goda," *Istoricheskii sbornik, Nasha strana* (St. Petersburg, 1907).

8. Quoted in Brower, *Training the Nihilists*, p. 131.

9. For the impact of Bakunin's article, see Sviatikov, "Studencheskoe dvizhenie," especially pp. 184–86.

10. As reported by Vera Zasulich. See her *Vospominaniia* (Moscow, 1931), pp. 20–23.

11. For a good, brief discussion of the *Program of Revolutionary Action,* see B. P. Koz'min, *Iz istorii revoliutsionnoi mysli v Rossii* (Moscow, 1961), pp. 357–59.

12. Zasulich, *Vospominaniia*, p. 24.

13. Sviatikov, "Studencheskoe dvizhenie," p. 194.

14. Lehning, *Michel Bakounine et ses relations avec Sergej Nečaev*, p. xvi.

15. Quoted in Michael Confino, ed., *Daughter of a Revolutionary* (London, 1974), p. 11.

16. The pathos of Herzen's last years is unforgettably captured in E. H. Carr's brilliant *Romantic Exiles* (London, 1933), which has been reprinted numerous times. See also Confino's more accurate and circumstantial *Daughter of a Revolutionary;* and Ia. I. Linkov's *Revoliutsionnaia bor'ba A. I. Gertsena i N. P. Ogarёva i tainoe obshchestvo "Zemlia i volia" 1860-kh godov* (Moscow, 1964), especially Part IV.

17. E. H. Carr, *Michael Bakunin* (New York, 1961, Vintage edition), pp. 368–73.

18. Carr refers to the "story" in *ibid.*, p. 392.

19. Quoted in Confino, *Daughter of a Revolutionary*, p. 20.

20. Carr, *Michael Bakunin*, pp. 392–93.

21. Koz'min, "Novoe o Nechaeve," pp. 148–49.

22. The best attempt to analyze all the documents in question is by Michael Confino. See "Bakunin et Nečaev," *Cahiers du monde Russe et Soviétique*, Vol. VII, Book 4 (1966), pp. 606–622.

23. This pamphlet is reprinted in M. P. Dragomanov, ed., *Pis'ma M. A.*

Bakunina k A. I. Gertsenu i N. P. Ogarëvu (Geneva, 1896). I quote from Venturi's translation; see *Roots of Revolution*, pp. 368–69.

24. For a careful consideration of the degree to which Bakunin may have participated in drafting the *Catechism*, see Philip Pomper, "Bakunin, Nechaev, the 'Catechism of a Revolutionary,'" *Canadian-American Slavic Studies* 10:4 (Winter 1976), pp. 535–46. I quote throughout from the Russian version of the *Catechism* in B. Bazilevsky, ed., *Gosudarstvennyia prestupleniia v Rossii v XIX veke*, Vol. I (Stuttgart, 1903), pp. 331–37.

25. Both Koz'min and Confino have noted the connection between the *Catechism* and an earlier article of Tkachëv, "The People of the Future and the Heroes of the Bourgeoisie." See B. P. Koz'min, *P. N. Tkachëv i revoliutsionnoe dvizhenie 1860-kh godov* (Moscow, 1922), pp. 90–98. And the "people of the future" owe a good deal to the "new people" of Chernyshevsky's *What Is To Be Done?*

26. Confino, *Daughter of a Revolutionary*, p. 243.

27. Carr, *Michael Bakunin*, p. 393.

28. Bazilevsky, *Gosudarstvennyia prestupleniia*, Vol. I, p. 337.

29. During their period of most self-destructive militancy some Black Panthers were much drawn to the *Catechism*. See Paul Avrich's introduction to Sam Dolgoff, ed., *Bakunin on Anarchy* (New York, 1972), especially p. xv. The constitution of the Serbian secret society Union or Death (known to its enemies as the Black Hand) shows the influence of Nechaev's *Catechism*. See Vladimir Dedijer, *The Road to Sarajevo* (New York, 1966), p. 376.

30. Excerpt published in V. Burtsev, *Za sto let* (London, 1897), p. 91.

31. Bazilevsky, *Gosudarstvennyia prestupleniia*, Vol. I, p. 334.

32. On Uspensky, see Zasulich, *Vospominaniia*, pp. 30–34; and Koz'min, "Nechaev i ego protivniki," pp. 196–97.

33. Much of the material on Nechaev's sway over the students is drawn from Zasulich, *Vospominaniia*, pp. 29–48.

34. On Pryzhov, see M. Al'tman's lively but extremely tendentious monograph, *Ivan Gavrilovich Pryzhov* (Moscow, 1932). Al'tman has also put together an excellent collection of Pryzhov's writings: I. G. Pryzhov, *Ocherki, stat'i, pis'ma* (Moscow-Leningrad, 1934).

35. Venturi, *Roots of Revolution*, p. 375.

36. See, for example, Adam B. Ulam, *In the Name of the People* (New York, 1977), p. 189.

37. For a convenient summary of Pryzhov's identification with dogs, see *Ocherki, stat'i, pis'ma*, p. 424, note 23.

38. Vera Zasulich describes Pryzhov as being "in ecstasy" that this work-

ing-class boy could quote from Kant's *Critique of Pure Reason.* See her *Vospominaniia* (Moscow, 1931), p. 41.

39. For Ripman's testimony, see B. P. Koz'min, *Nechaev i nechaevtsy* (Moscow-Leningrad, 1931), pp. 112–15.

40. *Ibid.,* p. 119.

41. Kuznetsov's testimony in *ibid.,* pp. 107–108.

42. See Likhutin's account of the affair in Bazilevsky, *Gosudarstvennyia prestupleniia,* pp. 385–86; and in Koz'min, *Nechaev i nechaevtsy,* pp. 130–32.

43. Vera Zasulich mentions this episode *(Vospominaniia,* p. 50). It is discussed by Ulam (*In the Name of the People,* p. 192).

44. Confino, *Daughter of a Revolutionary,* p. 314. Pryzhov gave various reasons for Nechaev's decision to murder Ivanov, but during his testimony of February 26, 1870, he also suggested that the murder was occasioned by Ivanov's refusal to turn over funds to Nechaev. See Koz'min, *Nechaev i nechaevtsy,* p. 103.

45. The fullest and most consecutive account of the murder is contained in the transcript of Nechaev's trial. See Bazilevsky, *Gosudarstvennyia prestupleniia,* pp. 415–52. See also Ulam, *In the Name of the People,* pp. 192–94.

46. It appears that Ivanov was told that the printing press had been buried at the time of Karakozov's trial. See Koz'min, *Nechaev i nechaevtsy,* p. 15.

47. Vera Zasulich, *Vospominaniia,* p. 54.

48. For these figures and a circumstantial account of the development of the investigation, see the initial report of the minister of justice, delivered at the trial of Nechaev's associates. Koz'min, *Nechaev i nechaevtsy,* pp. 10–14.

49. The none-too-substantial evidence about radical opposition to Nechaev has been assembled by Koz'min. See "Nechaev i ego protivniki."

50. Koz'min, *Nechaev i nechaevtsy,* pp. 137–40.

51. Koz'min, "Nechaev i ego protivniki," pp. 187–88.

52. Koz'min, *Nechaev i nechaevtsy,* p. 140.

53. Letter quoted in Lehning, *Michel Bakounine,* p. xxiv.

54. On the proclamations of this period, see Lehning, *Michel Bakounine,* pp. xxix–xxviii and *passim.*

55. The attacks of the Marxists provoked angry rejoinders not only from Bakunin and his adherents but also from Kaspar Turski and other Jacobin supporters of Nechaev, who were soon to group themselves around Tkachëv's *Tocsin.* See Rolf Theen, "The Russian Blanquists and the Hague Congress," *Canadian Slavic Studies* 3:2 (Summer 1969), pp. 347–76.

56. There is a facsimile edition in Lehning, *Michel Bakounine,* pp. 415–32.

57. Marx called the piece "an excellent example of barracks communism." Quoted in Avrahm Yarmolinsky, *Road to Revolution* (New York, 1962), p. 162.

58. Confino, *Daughter of a Revolutionary,* pp. 19–20.

59. *Ibid.,* p. 297.

60. *Ibid.,* p. 295.

61. *Ibid.,* p. 297.

62. *Ibid.,* p. 307.

63. Lehning, *Michel Bakounine,* p. 442.

64. *Ibid.,* p. 365.

65. For an interesting compendium of government documents, including Third Section reports, reflecting some official reaction to the trial, see Part IV of Koz'min's *Nechaev i nechaevtsy,* especially pp. 158–88.

66. See Ralli's memoirs, reproduced in Lehning, *Michel Bakounine.* The quotation is on p. 377.

67. Dmitrij Richter, "L'arrestation de S. G. Nečaev à Zurich," in Lehning, *Michel Bakounine,* pp. 386–88. See also Woodford McClellan, "Nechaevshchina: An Unknown Chapter," *Slavic Review* 32:3 (September 1973), pp. 546–53.

68. Vera Figner, *Vospominaniia,* Vol. I (Moscow, 1964), pp. 250–58.

69. *Ibid.,* p. 258.

70. Fyodor Dostoevsky, *The Notebooks for The Possessed* (Chicago and London, 1968), p. 349.

71. Albert Camus, *The Rebel* (New York, 1956), especially pp. 160–64.

72. See her *Vospominaniia,* p. 57.

73. As, for instance, A. Gambarov, *V sporakh o Nechaeve* (Moscow-Leningrad, 1926).

74. Angelica Balabanoff, *Impressions of Lenin* (Ann Arbor, 1968), p. 7. See also her penetrating remarks on Trotsky, as well as his too-little-known *Their Morals and Ours* (New York, 1939).

75. Isaac Deutscher, *The Prophet Armed* (Oxford, 1954), p. 95.

76. Leopold Haimson, "The Parties and the State: The Evolution of Political Attitudes," in Michael Cherniavsky, ed., *The Structure of Russian History* (New York, 1970), p. 317.

77. S. Frederick Starr, *Decentralization and Self-Government in Russia, 1830–1870* (Princeton, 1972), *passim.*

78. Balabanoff, *Impressions of Lenin,* p. 105.

Index